A Sociolinguistic History of Parisian French

Paris mushroomed in the thirteenth century to become the largest city in the Western world, largely through in-migration from rural areas. The resulting dialect-mixture led to the formation of new, specifically urban modes of speech. From the time of the Renaissance social stratification became sharper, as the elites distanced themselves from the Parisian 'Cockney' of the masses. Nineteenth-century urbanisation transformed the situation yet again, with the arrival of huge numbers of immigrants from far-flung corners of France, levelling dialect-differences and exposing ever larger sections of the population to standardising influences. At the same time, a working-class vernacular emerged which was distinguished from the upper-class standard not only in grammar and pronunciation, but most markedly in vocabulary (slang). This book examines the interlinked history of Parisian speech and the Parisian population through these various phases of in-migration, dialect-mixing and social stratification from medieval times to the present day.

R. ANTHONY LODGE is Professor of French Language and Linguistics at the University of St Andrews. He is the author of *Le Livre des Manières d'Etienne de Fougères* (1979), *Le Plus Ancien Registre de comptes des Consuls de Montferrand* (1985), *French: From Dialect to Standard* (1993), *Exploring the French Language* (with N. Armstrong, Y. Ellis and J. Shelton, 1997) and *The Earliest Branches of the Roman de Renart* (with K. Varty, 2001).

A Sociolinguistic History of Parisian French

R. Anthony Lodge

CAMBRIDGE
UNIVERSITY PRESS

PUBLISHED BY THE PRESS SYNDICATE OF THE UNIVERSITY OF CAMBRIDGE
The Pitt Building, Trumpington Street, Cambridge, United Kingdom

CAMBRIDGE UNIVERSITY PRESS
The Edinburgh Building, Cambridge, CB2 2RU, UK
40 West 20th Street, New York, NY 10011–4211, USA
477 Williamstown Road, Port Melbourne, VIC 3207, Australia
Ruiz de Alarcón 13, 28014 Madrid, Spain
Dock House, The Waterfront, Cape Town 8001, South Africa

http://www.cambridge.org

First published 2004

Printed in the United Kingdom at the University Press, Cambridge

Typeface Times 10/12 pt.   *System* LATEX 2$_\varepsilon$ [TB]

A catalogue record for this book is available from the British Library

Library of Congress Cataloguing in Publication data
Lodge, R. Anthony.
A sociolinguistic history of Parisian French / R. Anthony Lodge.
    p.   cm.
Includes bibliographical references and index.
ISBN 0 521 82179 7
1. French language – Social aspects – France – Paris.   2. French language –
Dialects – France – Paris.   3. French language – Variation – France – Paris.
4. Speech and social status – France – Paris.   5. Paris (France) – Social life and
customs.   I. Title.
PC2923.L63   2003
306.44′0944′361 – dc21   2003046184

ISBN 0 521 82179 7 hardback

Contents

12   Lexical variation   228

     Conclusion   249

     Appendix   Literary imitations of low-class speech   251
     Bibliography   267
     Index   285

Maps

Tables

Figures

Acknowledgments

This book could not have been written without the help of numerous others, and to them I extend my grateful thanks here. A generous grant from the Leverhulme Trust enabled me to employ an able assistant – Dr. K. Anipa of St Andrews University – for the computerisation of a corpus of medieval and early modern Parisian texts, upon which I have drawn extensively. These data are publicly available in electronic form at the Oxford Text Archive (http://www.ota.ahds.ac.uk/). James Laidlaw and Piet van Reenen gave me access to their medieval corpora, for which I am most grateful. A 'top-up' grant from the Arts and Humanities Research Board greatly accelerated the completion of the project. Numerous colleagues – Jim Milroy, Françoise Gadet, Marie-Rose Simoni-Aurembou, Glanville Price in particular – have at various times offered invaluable advice, and to them must be added the anonymous readers employed by Cambridge University Press, without whose critical eye and constructive suggestions the quality of the work would have been much inferior. Finally, a sincere word of thanks to my wife, Janet, for her patience and support throughout.

The author gratefully acknowledges the following for permission to reproduce copyright material: Bibliothèque nationale de France, Editions Arthaud, Editions de Boeck, Hachette, Editions Picard, Editions du Seuil.

Phonetic symbols

a	patte	b	bal
ɑ	pâte	d	dans
e	fée	f	femme
ɛ	fait	g	gros
ɪ	si	k	craie
ɔ	col	l	lui
o	pôle	m	maman
u	vous	n	notre
ʏ	ty	ɲ	agneau
œ	leur	p	Paul
ə	petit	r	rat (English)
ɑ̃	an	ʀ	rat (French)
ɛ̃	vin	s	son
œ̃	un	t	ton
ĩ	fim (Port.)	v	vous
w	oui	ʃ	charme
j	voyais	ʒ	jadis
ɥ	huit	z	baser

Part 1

Preliminaries

Introduction

Writing a sociolinguistic history of a city as large and complex as Paris is a risky, even foolhardy undertaking. Although not a major centre of population in Antiquity, Paris became, in the medieval period, an urban giant, dwarfing the other towns of France and outstripping even the great conurbations of the Low Countries and northern Italy:

As Fernand Braudel observed, 'Paris is a city on its own', compared not just with the other French cities that it has always completely overshadowed, but, at least up to the second third of the seventeenth century, with the other cities of early modern Europe. What strikes us first of all is the longstanding character of this situation. Whereas Madrid and London did not experience spectacular growth until 1630 or even 1650, and Amsterdam did not become a metropolis until after 1600, the population of Paris had certainly reached or exceeded 200,000 by the beginning of the fourteenth century, prior to the Black Death, the economic depression of the late Middle Ages and the Hundred Years War. . . . With this uniquely large population, Paris, around 1320, was far ahead of the great economic centres of the day: Ghent, Bruges, Genoa and Venice. (Jacquart 1996: 105)

It has remained near the top of the European urban hierarchy ever since. Great metropolises are not only large, they are demographically complex, comprising rich polyphonies of nested and inter-related communities. Handling the historical material available on only a proportion of these should daunt the most determined researcher, for Paris is one of the most written-about and mythologised cities in the world.

We cannot generalise about the speech of a city without taking social differences into account. There may not exist in today's Paris a strongly differentiated vernacular to compare with, say, London's 'Cockney' (see Sivertsen 1960) or with Berlin's 'Berlinisch' (see Schildt and Schildt 1986), but it is impossible to claim for the city a high level of linguistic homogeneity, at any stage of its history. The earliest Parisian manuscripts written in French may already show traces of variation in the spoken language. Fifteenth-century literary texts clearly reflect social differentiation in language, and shortly afterwards linguistic commentators indicate quite routinely that the elites were developing modes of speech which differed markedly from those of the bulk of the

3

population. What makes the linguistic histories of certain capital cities (like Paris and Copenhagen) more complex still is that they have each given rise not just to their local vernacular, but also to their country's standard language. For centuries, standard and vernacular developed in symbiosis within the confines of the city, reflecting the conflicts enacted there and symbolising speakers' desires not just for integration but also for segregation.

The size and complexity of Paris raise problems enough for the linguistic historian, but they are manageable in comparison with the most intractable one of all – that posed by shortage of relevant data. Sociolinguists find it difficult analysing linguistic variability in the cities of the modern world, where data are abundant. As they move back in time, usable sources dry up to almost nothing. Documentation on the written and high-status forms of Parisian French in the past may be plentiful enough, but all save the faintest traces of non-standard, spoken forms of the language have been irretrievably lost.

Perhaps then a sociolinguistic history of Paris, for all its interest and importance, is best left alone. Indeed, no such a history has been attempted before, and steering clear provides the safest solution. However, this will not stop historians of French speculating about the subject. The emergence of Paris in the Middle Ages as a 'primate' city (that is, one which has grown disproportionately large when measured against the rest of its urban system) reshaped not just the economics and demography of a great tract of European territory between the Mediterranean and the Channel, but also its linguistic geography. The role of Paris is so central to the history of French that we are obliged to hypothesise about its sociolinguistic development, whether we wish to or not. As it happens, a usable amount of historical data has survived. These are fragmentary and pitifully defective, but they are there. Conventional histories have prioritised certain types of data above others. Perhaps the time has come for a different perspective on the material. Can we develop a new hypothesis which will account a little better for such data as we have? Would recent developments in urban dialectology help us to make more sense of them than has been made in the past?

The aims of this book must be modest. The data will not allow us to reconstruct with any certainty the history of Parisian French in all its diversity. They will not allow us to plot micro-level changes in the speech of the city. The most we can aim to do will be to identify macro-level tendencies across a broad time-span – from medieval times to the twentieth century. In this preliminary section, let us look first at the treatment of Parisian French in conventional histories of the language, and then outline the principles which might inform a sociolinguistic approach to the topic. In Chapter 2 we will tackle the intractable problem of data, and set up an analytical frame which may help us understand them better.

1 'The French of Paris'

1.1 Traditional approaches

The speech of the capital looms large in all histories of French, but the approach historians have adopted to it has, as a rule, been unidimensional. The expression *le français de Paris* is normally just a synonym for the standard language (= *la langue littéraire, la langue nationale, la langue officielle* and *le français (tout court)*), marginalising if not excluding the non-standard speech of the bulk of the city's inhabitants. Even historians known to adopt a distinctly 'social' approach to the French language look at Parisian French in this restricted way:

quand on dit langage de Paris, on ne dit pas le patois propre des habitants ignorants de la ville bornés à son seul horizon. (Cohen 1987: 185)

This is not to say that historians of French have been blind to the diversity of Parisian speech (see below, §2.1). For instance, Ferdinand Brunot's monumental *Histoire de la langue française* (the *HLF*) examines a sizeable quantity of material on 'popular' speech in Paris (see in particular *HLF* III, 75ff.; VI.1, 1213–16; VI.2, 1860 and X.1, 259–70), but it treats it as a minor side-show beside the development of the standard. If eminent linguistic historians have hitherto taken a largely unidimensional view of 'the French of Paris', there must have been powerful reasons for it. We can group these under three headings: problems of data, the influence of prescriptivism and traditional models of linguistic variation and change.

1.1.1 The data problem

Historical linguists all have to face the uncomfortable fact that 'historical data are inherently bad' (Labov 1994: 74). Most of the information required to reconstruct the speech of the past in a multidimensional way simply cannot be recovered, and that which has survived is fragmentary and not necessarily what they would have chosen. James Milroy articulated this central difficulty when he pointed out that 'historical data have been accidentally preserved and are therefore not equally representative of all aspects of the language of past states'

(Milroy 1992: 45). Evidence about educated written usage in Paris exists in abundance from the thirteenth century on, but access to the vernacular, difficult enough in the contemporary world, is exceptionally hard with speakers long since dead. All the problems raised by the 'observer's paradox' in describing the speech of modern cities (see Labov 1973: 209–10) are multiplied beyond control in cities of the past. *Direct* evidence about speech is of course non-existent, and even the surviving *indirect* evidence (in the form, for instance, of literary exploitation of vernacular forms and contemporary metalinguistic comment) is treacherous. The traces left by the vernacular in the historical record resemble the shadows of Forms on the walls of Plato's cave. In the light of this, we should sympathise with linguistic historians who, *en bonne méthode*, decide that the evidential base for a multidimensional study of Parisian French in the past is not sufficiently robust.

That said, caution about the surviving evidence need not slide into complete pessimism. Various clues about past linguistic variation in Paris have survived in the written record. Thanks to the presence within the city from an early date of a major university and a large ecclesiastical and judicial bureaucracy, to say nothing of a merchant class possessing literacy skills, it would be surprising if the great amount of writing conducted in Paris from the thirteenth century onwards did not contain clues about the state of the spoken language. The coexistence within the population of diverse social groups competing for the resources of the city evidently engendered strong linguistic awareness and eventually metalinguistic comment. Impoverished as it is, the historical record bearing upon non-standard varieties in Paris, when compared with other cities, is in fact relatively rich and relatively long. The fact that these data have not so far been integrated systematically with histories of standard French makes one suspect that other difficulties (ideological and methodological) have deterred historians from doing so.

1.1.2   The influence of prescriptivism

The 'ideology of standardisation' which lay at the heart of the great campaigns of literacy in the nineteenth century (see Milroy and Milroy 1999) has had an enduring influence on the way histories of the French language have been written. In this way of thinking, the standard variety represents the quintessential form of the language. Since the standard language *is* the language, it is only when an innovation has succeeded in modifying the norms of the standard that a significant language change is deemed to have occurred. Colloquial developments which fail to gain acceptance into the standard are not matters of serious concern. Since the standard language is inherently superior to others (through its logic and clarity), there is no compelling need to explain its emergence in social terms.

The standard form of most languages coincides as a rule with the usage of the dominant class. This often makes the usage of 'ordinary speakers' peripheral to the linguist's concerns. Writing about Parisian pronunciation in the middle of the twentieth century, Georges Straka (1952: 33) let slip that: 'Seul le parler populaire continue à palataliser outre mesure', implying that the everyday speech of a sizeable proportion of the city's inhabitants was somehow extravagant and extraneous to his description. Moreover, in the prescriptive view of language, everyday speech is inferior to writing, and attitudes to it are often patronising, even contemptuous (see Blanche-Benveniste 1997). Not all vernaculars are placed on the same low level: the informal style of the educated classes (labelled in French *le français familier*) retains a degree of respectability; provincial rustics' failure to manipulate the standard language correctly is lamentable, but pardonable on the grounds that such people are denied easy access to the standard. The mouthings of the Parisian populace, with its *français populaire*, are, however, doubly reprehensible: these people have the standard language on their doorstep and choose wilfully to disregard its norms.

The idea that urban vernaculars are of little importance, representing corrupt versions of the standard language, is not restricted to France, but it is deeply entrenched there. For centuries Paris has been by far the largest urban community in the country, and, as the undisputed capital, has presented itself to the outside world as a model of all that is excellent and progressive. The symbolic and exemplary role of the capital has led writers to cultivate an impression of the seamless unity of Parisian speech, and to play down the deviations from the norm perpetrated by its uneducated citizens (see Blanche-Benveniste and Jeanjean 1987: 13). In the formation of these prescriptive attitudes we should not underestimate the lasting effects of the social antagonisms which wracked the French capital in the nineteenth century, in particular the Commune of 1871.

In view of all of this, it may be that the reluctance of historians of French to embark upon a more broadly based description of the language of Paris, giving more weight to the development of non-standard speech-forms, springs not solely from the shortage of data, problematic as this is, but also from the heavy incubus of a normative tradition. A third set of factors is no doubt also at work, and these concern the theoretical models of language variation and change underlying conventional histories of the language.

1.1.3   *Traditional models of linguistic variation and change*

The model of language variation implicit in many histories of French involves deep-seated hostility to variation and a hierarchisation of language varieties into 'pure' and 'impure'. Whereas 'pure' varieties are internally homogeneous and externally discrete, 'impure' varieties are the reverse. The category of 'pure varieties' is filled principally with codified literary languages (in French *langues de culture*), and it is felt that vigorous intervention needs to be undertaken to protect them from internal diversification and from external contamination. Certain medieval *dialectes*, thought to have been internally homogeneous and largely untouched by linguistic forms from other areas, were admitted to this 'pure' category too. Possessing the essential characteristic of historical authenticity, they had a particularly important role to play in comparative philology. Unlike *langues de culture*, which are pure by design, these naïve varieties were pure by their very nature.

Dialecte, however, is closely associated with *patois*, localised spoken varieties which are believed to have developed among the peasantry in the post-medieval period and which lack historical authenticity and homogeneity ('purity'). Writing about the *patois* of Saint Ouen and Montmorency in the seventeenth century, Rosset (1911: 364) declares:

> Il serait naturel que les paysans, placés entre le français correct parlé à Paris et le dialecte picard parlé à côté d'eux, ne parlent ni l'un ni l'autre et fassent de l'un et de l'autre un langage mixte, véritable jargon et non plus langue populaire.

Other varieties failed the purity test too. Among them we find, firstly, the various *francais régionaux* (regionally based varieties intermediary between *langue* and *dialecte*), and secondly, of course, working-class Parisian speech (*le français populaire*). As a less conservative variety resulting from ignorance and in-migration, low-class speech in Paris failed on more or less all counts: not only was it not a 'pure' form of *dialecte*, but it even failed to qualify as a *patois*:

> Ce langage que j'appelle patois, pour être bref, ne mérite guère ce nom, pris surtout dans le sens de dialecte; il n'en a ni l'unité, ni l'originalité, ni les règles. (Nisard 1872: 128)

If prescriptive ideas on language variation have kept scholars from a multidimensional approach to Parisian speech, these have been reinforced by traditional ideas about language change. The preference for language purity leads to a preference for endogenous over exogenous explanations of change: after an initial phase of exogenous interference from substrate and superstrate languages (Gaulish and Germanic), the main changes in the medieval and modern phases of French were believed to be endogenous in origin. Likewise, the role of ordinary speakers in the development of language change is traditionally reduced to a minimum. Prescriptive linguistic historians often assume that the driving force in language change is an educated elite, grammarians and creative writers, and that the bulk of the population is linguistically inert. Writing about a 'simplification' of the French language which he believed came about in the seventeenth century, von Wartburg declares:

Un pareil développement ne peut pas partir des classes inférieures du peuple. Celui-ci n'a pas l'habitude de l'effort intellectuel. A une époque comme le 17e s. les forces directrices de la nation se concentrent dans les cercles des 'honnêtes gens'. (von Wartburg 1962: 176)

A more venerable tradition in historical linguistics assumes that language enjoys an existence independent, in fact, of all the speakers who use it, and that it changes primarily in response to system-internal pressures. For many nineteenth-century linguists, a language had a life of its own, and could be likened to a tree growing in a certain terrain, essentially on the basis of its own internal physical composition. For structuralists, the preferred metaphor is one of a mechanical system, with each part moving of its own accord to maintain a delicate internal balance of oppositions and contrasts.

These approaches are often combined in histories of French. For a long period from the end of the Roman Empire to the Renaissance, linguistic evolution was governed by its own internal laws. Following Ferdinand Brunot, Fouché (1934: 218) writes:

Avant la Renaissance, on peut dire de l'évolution phonétique du français qu'elle était entièrement libre. Rien, dans l'ordre social, ne venant contrarier les forces de transformation.

In the modern period, however, once society had come of age, the destiny of 'the language' was taken under the control of the educated members of society (grammarians, literary authors, even the state). Different as these approaches are, they share the view that the interactions of ordinary speakers are of little relevance to the process of language change.

1.2   A sociolinguistic approach

Sociolinguistics calls for a more holistic view of the speech of Paris than the one we have just considered. The assumption that in a big urban community language variation and social structure are irrelevant to its linguistic history can only lead to distortion, particularly when the city in question is a large capital with very special status. 'Historical sociolinguistics' applies the concepts and techniques of sociolinguistics to past states of the language, with the idea that the observed properties of contemporary speech communities, such as variation, the social significance of variants, and social stratification, must also have been typical of earlier speech communities. A sociolinguistic history of Parisian French will then focus on its variability in former times. It will embed language change firmly within the community of speakers, correlating as far as possible linguistic variation and change in the city with historical changes in social and demographic structure. Instead of prioritising the high-prestige standard at the expense of 'ordinary speech', it will emphasise the centrality of the vernacular. The data problem will, of course, remain, but such data as have survived will be evaluated differently. Data previously neglected might now assume greater importance. Let us briefly consider each of these ideas.

1.2.1   Language variation

The variability of urban speech may be plotted along the two parameters of 'dialect' and 'register' (the 'social' and 'stylistic' axes of the Labovian paradigm). 'Dialect' diversity (inter-speaker variation) increases proportionately to the degree of communicative isolation between groups. 'Registers' (intra-speaker variation) arise from the different uses to which one and the same speaker may put their language: for instance, s/he will use it differently according to the level of formality in the situation ('tenor'), according to whether the medium is speech or writing ('mode'), and according to the topic being discussed ('field'). For Halliday (1978: 3) dialect-variation reflects the diversity of social structures, while register variation reflects the diversity of social processes.

The distinction between 'dialect' and 'register' is purely methodological, since the registers a person has access to are a function of his place in the social structure, and a switch of register may entail a switch of dialect. Variants favoured by the higher social classes may also be the variants favoured in careful styles, and *vice versa*, but upper-class speakers are quite capable of using in their informal style linguistic forms conventionally attributed to lower-class speakers, and *vice versa*. In different situations all social groups may use all the variants recognised, but they do so in different proportions. The whole thrust of the Labovian enterprise is to see variation in probabilistic, quantificational terms, rather than in terms of discontinuities, abrupt distinctions and direct correlations with non-linguistic factors.

Although dialect and register cannot ultimately be disentangled, our history of the speech of Paris will prioritise the dialectal perspective – it will be an exercise in historical urban dialectology. The study of urban dialects developed in the 1950s, when it was realised that focusing on rural dialects had led to an almost total neglect of the speech forms used by the majority of the population, namely those who lived in towns. The earliest works in this field, for instance Sivertsen's *Cockney Phonology* (1960), followed very closely the methodology of traditional rural dialect-study. It was the work of Labov during the following decade that led to the full integration of urban dialectology into sociolinguistics (see Chambers and Trudgill 1998: 45–53). The principles elaborated here will provide a central part of the analytical framework we will use to handle our Parisian material.

1.2.2   Language change

A sociolinguistic approach to language change embeds it firmly in the community of speakers: it can only be fully understood with reference to the structure of the society in which the language is used. Weinreich, Labov and Herzog (1968) indicated that an adequate theory of language change (the 'WLH model') must successfully address three central problems: (1) the 'constraints' problem (what are the general constraints on change which determine possible and impossible directions of change in a particular language?), (2) the 'implementation' problem (how is a linguistic innovation transmitted from speaker to speaker within the community and across a geographical area?), and (3) the actuation problem (why does an innovation occur in the speech of one area and not necessarily in others?). The second of these is of particular importance, and, indeed, Weinreich *et al.* decomposed it into more specific issues: (a) the 'transition' problem (what are the routes by which a language changes?), (b) the 'embedding' problem (how does a linguistic innovation become embedded in the surrounding system of linguistic and social relations?), (c) the 'evaluation' problem (how do speakers evaluate a given change and what is the effect of their evaluation on that change?).

When an innovation occurs in one part of the speech community, in order to constitute a change, it needs to be adopted (or 'implemented') by the remainder. For a while, the old and new variants will exist alongside each other, until such time as one is preferred to the other. Certain sociolinguistic variables appear to be remarkably stable and to persist in the language for centuries. Others represent 'changes in progress', as an innovation gradually diffuses through the society and through the language at the expense of an existing form. The reasons for society's ultimate preference may be system-internal – one of the variants may be more economical than the other, for example – but very often such preferences are purely social in origin, reflecting the chance adoption of a particular variant as a symbol of group identity. The importance of subjective attitudes to language is largely neglected in conventional histories of language change. The speed with which an innovation is adopted is likewise determined by social factors. Milroy (1992) draws attention to the importance of social network structures in this connection: the presence of dense, multiplex social networks will tend to inhibit the spread of an innovation from one group to another, whereas loose social networks have the opposite effect, facilitating rapid linguistic change.

While it would be an error to minimise the importance of internally generated language change, it is equally mistaken to assume that language changes
can be understood without reference to society. Milroy (1992: 280) indicates
that:

Both kinds of approach are needed – and one should contribute to the other – because
although linguistic change must be initiated by speakers (and is therefore a social
phenomenon) it is manifested as internal to language.

The spread of changes, moreover, takes place essentially in the day-to-day
encounters of ordinary speakers, obliging the historical linguist to see the locus
of change not in the standard language but in the vernacular.

1.2.3   The vernacular

Urban dialects are invariably vernacular in form and cannot be regarded as derived from standard varieties. But what do we mean by 'vernacular' (see Milroy
1987: 57–60)? Most definitions see it as a relational entity contrasting with the
'standard language', which it normally precedes historically. In contrast with
standard languages, vernaculars are 'undeveloped': they are variable, they are
associated with orality, and, in their discourse and conversational patterns, they
communicate involvement and expressive meanings, pragmatically rather than
through explicit linguistic forms.

A 'diglossic' community is one in which two distinct varieties are current,
with each performing its own set of sociolinguistic functions (see Fasold (1984:
34–60)). In multilingual and diglossic communities, where High (or H) and
Low (or L) varieties represent clearly distinct dialects or languages, the iden-
tification of 'vernacular' is straightforward enough. However, in monolingual
communities where H and L are located at opposing ends of a stylistic spectrum
within the 'same language', the definition is not so simple. Here, discussions
of the term 'vernacular', as of the labels given to particular vernaculars – such
as Vulgar Latin and *le français populaire* – usually run into the sand because
of the multifaceted nature of the reality they are called upon to designate (see
for instance Lloyd 1979 on Vulgar Latin and Valdman 1982 on *le français
populaire*). Difficulties arise over two issues: firstly, whether the vernacular is
primarily a socially defined variety (a dialect) or a situationally defined variety
(a register/style), and secondly, whether 'vernacular' denotes 'a real variety'
or 'an abstract set of norms'.

Is the vernacular to be seen more basically as a dialect or as a register
(see §1.2.1)? The early uses of 'vernacular' as a metalinguistic term imply
that it bore primarily upon the dialectal (inter-speaker) axis of variation. In
Classical Latin *vernaculum* referred to a category of slaves who were local
or 'home-grown' as opposed to those who were brought from outside. When

first used in English in the seventeenth century, 'vernacular' distinguished indigenous dialects from an imported, superimposed dominant language (in medieval times Latin). Petyt (1980: 25) defines it as 'the speech of a particular country or region' (see also Lyons 1981: 276). The term was easily extended to low-status social-class dialects, such as those typically found in cities.

On the other side, 'vernacular' commonly denotes a register or speech-style. The etymological association of the term with home and family means that it has always had the potential for designating a situationally defined variety. Petyt (1980: 25) sees the vernacular as 'a form of speech transmitted from parent to child as the primary medium of communication', that is, the informal, familiar mode of speech adopted in the home, as distinct from the formal, more guarded style adopted in conversational encounters with strangers in the world outside. Labov has defined it as 'the variety adopted by a speaker when he is monitoring his speech style least closely' (see Labov 1972: 208). This definition has been criticised (notably by Bell 1984), but it illustrates a strong tradition where vernacular stands opposed to standard along the stylistic axis.

In reality, of course, the vernacular functions simultaneously as dialect and as register. Depending on the purpose at hand, the analyst may be concerned primarily with the vernacular as sociolect, or primarily as register, but s/he may not lose sight of the simultaneous operation of both sets of variables.

A second difficulty with the term concerns the empirical reality of the variety in question. Does the 'vernacular' (and indeed its counterpart the 'standard language') exist as a 'real variety', or do both of these labels relate to abstractions? It is popularly believed that oral vernaculars (e.g. *le français populaire*) and standard languages (e.g. *le français*) have clearly defined bodies of speakers. In the case of French this usually entails reference to the *peuple de Paris* and to 'the educated Paris bourgeoisie' respectively. However, both of these groups are sociologically too ill-defined and sociolinguistically too diverse to provide a secure empirical anchor-point (see Bourdieu 1983). Moreover, as we have seen, all the social groups may use all the variants recognised, albeit in different proportions. It is preferable, therefore, to follow Valdman (1982) and Milroy and Milroy (1999: 19) in regarding both the standard language and the vernacular not as real varieties at all, but as idealisations or abstract sets of norms to which the usage of particular speakers approximates to a greater or lesser extent, according to a multiplicity of factors related to such things as speech-situation and educational background.

The notion of linguistic norm is traditionally associated only with standard languages, but there exist other sorts of linguistic norm, referred to as 'community norms' or 'vernacular norms', which grow up as a result of consensus within particular communities in order to distinguish between one group and another and to carry a sense of community identity. Highly focused or tightly networked groups seem to foster powerful community norms. The difference between vernacular norms and those of the standard language is that, whereas the latter are uniform, the former are variable, the degree of variability being related to the structure of the groups concerned (Milroy 1992: 81–3).

In this book we will use the label 'vernacular' in the context of Parisian French to refer to the non-standard language varieties spoken within the city of Paris and its immediate *banlieue*. It will embrace at one and the same time linguistic forms favoured by groups located socially some distance away from the elite (though not in most cases exclusive to them) and linguistic forms characteristic of informal speech-styles (as distinct from the forms specific to writing and to the writing-like speech used in formal situations). When there develops a strong public awareness of a vernacular endowed with a clearly differentiated set of norms, it may acquire a name (e.g. '*le chtimi*' for the dialect of Lille-Roubaix, studied by Pooley 1996). This has happened in many British cities ('Cockney', 'Geordie', 'Scouse'). However, no consensus has ever arisen concerning the name for Paris vernacular speech. In the seventeenth century certain observers use the label *le badaudois* (see below, §8.2.1). In the eighteenth century the label which emerged most prominently was perhaps *le poissard* (see §8.2.1). At the end of the nineteenth century (1886) *parigot* appears, and is still quite widely used more than a century later (see below, §11.3). During the twentieth century the expression most commonly used to refer to the Paris vernacular has probably been *le français populaire*, which Guiraud (1965: 9) defines as 'la parlure vulgaire, langue du peuple de Paris dans sa vie quotidienne'. However, this term emerged not among vernacular speakers but among observers of non-standard speech, and the currency it has gained comes largely through an education system dedicated to eliminating the variety it designates. Its use even as a short-hand label is risky.

1.3   The 'French of Paris'

What then do we understand by the 'French of Paris'? The term will be inclusive rather than exclusive and its definition will be geared to the assumptions we make about the nature of speech communities (see Patrick 2002). Gumperz (1971: 101) defines a linguistic community as:

A social group which may be either monolingual or multilingual, held together by frequency of interaction patterns and set off from the surrounding areas by weaknesses in the lines of communication. Linguistic communities may be small groups bound together by face-to-face contact or may cover large regions, depending on the level of interaction we wish to achieve.

Dialects (urban ones as well as geographical) seem to be the product of density of communication among speakers and, in the case of isolated groups, lack of dialect contact. Within dialects so demarcated, however, we do not find homogeneity. A huge and complex city like Paris comprises not one but a large number of nested communities. How can we reconcile the notions of community and heterogeneity?

Labov maintains that heterogeneity within the speech community is not random, but is ordered and patterned, with all its members sharing a 'uniform structural base':

> This orderly heterogeneity normally rests on a uniform structural base: the underlying phrase structure, the grammatical categories, the inventory of phonemes, and the distribution of that inventory in the lexicon. (Labov 1987: 2)

Heterogeneity arises from the fact that each sub-group expresses these shared linguistic resources in its own distinctive way (see Kroch 1996: 42–3). Thus, a speech community the size of Paris comprises a multiplicity of sub-communities all sharing the same 'uniform structural base' and a set of shared norms for the evaluation and social distribution of variants. Following Labov (1973: 120), Halliday (1978: 155) considers that in an urban context, the classical speech community model breaks down, and that the inhabitants of a metropolis are united much less by their speech habits, which are remarkably variable, than by their linguistic attitudes and prejudices, which are remarkably consistent. The community is to be defined not in terms of any marked agreement in the use of language elements but in terms of participation in a set of shared evaluative norms. It should be noted that this consensus model of the community is not one to which all sociolinguists subscribe (see Chapter 8 below).

The speech of Paris looks to have always been heterogeneous, with multilingualism, dialect-mixing, code-switching and style-shifting taking place there as matters of routine. Our concern in this book will be to recover as much as we can of this heterogeneity across the centuries, and to explore the inter-relationship between standard and vernacular in the city. Our approach will necessarily give greater prominence to the vernacular than it receives in standard-oriented histories, but it will not be attempting an 'alternative history of the language', in the manner of Wyld's remarkable *History of Modern Colloquial English* (1921). As an exercise in 'historical urban dialectology', we will be concerned with the overall patterns of variation across the community at macro-level, embedding developments in speech in the demographic, social and economic history of the city.

The fact that we are coming to the subject primarily from the perspective of dialect, rather than register, will have repercussions for the sort of linguistic variable which we will be considering. Hudson (1996: 45) maintains that '*syntax* is the marker of cohesion in society, with individuals trying to eliminate alternatives in syntax from their individual language. In contrast, *vocabulary* is a marker of divisions in society, and individuals may actively cultivate alternatives in order to make more subtle social distinctions. *Pronunciation* reflects the permanent social group with which the speaker identifies.' We will be looking above all at phonological, morphological and, up to a point, lexical variation, and rather less at syntax.

Of course, our 'sociolinguistic approach' is all very sound in theory, but sociolinguistic history requires data, and, even in Paris, these are in very short supply. We will devote much of the next chapter to this central problem.

2   The analytical frame

The desirability of a multidimensional approach to linguistic history is easy enough to argue nowadays. What is nothing like so easy is to find the data which would make such a study possible. This chapter must begin with the central and most intractable problem in the book: that of evidence. We will set out the main types of data available in the different periods of Parisian French, with for ever at the back of our mind the basic uncertainty over whether historical sociolinguistics is possible at all (§2.1). In the second and third parts we will look at general factors in urban history and dialect development which will help us limit the range of constructions we can place upon our very imperfect data-base. Since language and society are inextricably entwined, any patterns we detect in urban dialect development must be compatible with the patterns identified by urban historians in the development of European cities over the relevant period (§2.2). Furthermore, whatever patterns we see in the past must be broadly in line with the insights derived by modern dialectologists from analogous, and infinitely better documented, linguistic situations in the contemporary world. The 'uniformitarian principle' is no panacea, but it may be possible to project backwards to obtain a better understanding of earlier stages of the French language (§2.3). All of this will be incorporated into the general analytical frame which we will set out in the concluding paragraph and which will structure the rest of the book.

2.1   The data problem

The presence of an abundance of written data since the thirteenth century makes writing the history of Parisian *writing* systems a straightforward matter, from the data point of view at least. However, once we try to look behind the written word for the *spoken* language, our problems become very great, if not insuperable (see Schneider 2002). Recovering the formal, message-oriented speech of the educated classes in times past is feasible enough, but reconstructing the everyday, listener-oriented speech of 'ordinary speakers' is highly problematic. Usable historical evidence about precisely those aspects of language which are at the centre of sociolinguistic inquiry (see §1.3) is very difficult to come by.

Does this mean that a sociolinguistic history is impossible? In many cities the honest answer has to be 'yes, for the data simply are not there'. In Paris, we need to be very cautious, but not quite so categorical. The Parisian situation is special because of the sheer quantity of writing that has gone on there over the centuries, among which are valuable clues about the spoken language. It is the extent to which such data are available in Paris that will determine the feasibility of a book like this.

Gerhardt Ernst (1980) categorised the sources for the history of spoken French as follows:
(1) Historical transcriptions of the spoken language
(2) Model dialogues of fictitious speech in didactic texts
(3) Fictitious direct speech in plays
(4) Fictitious direct speech in narrative texts
(5) Metalinguistic texts
(6) Developments of spoken French in geographical areas outside France
Under these headings Ernst provides rich bibliographical information which we will draw upon quite extensively in what follows. However, Ernst was concerned primarily with register variation – with the history of spoken as opposed to written French – so the variables which interested him particularly were those related to syntax and discourse patterning. Our approach is primarily dialectal (social and geographical), and this leads us to be more interested in phonetic, morphological and lexical variables. The sources of information on Parisian speech change over time, so let us review the data, not typologically, but chronologically.

2.1.1   The medieval period

The beginnings of new languages are invariably the least documented. From the medieval period we have only a tiny amount of metalinguistic comment, so we are left with only what we can glean (a) from literary texts, (b) from variation present in manuscripts written before language standardisation, and (c) from back-projecting data drawn from surveys of modern dialects.

Literary texts composed in Paris have something to tell us about the spoken language – we should not underestimate the quantity of literary production which went on in medieval Paris – with dramatic texts like the Miracle plays probably reflecting it more closely than the work of poets like Rutebeuf and Geofroi de Paris. Medieval texts, however, are not easy to interpret linguistically: literary conventions and literary play had a powerful say in how particular characters spoke.

The writing systems used in medieval manuscripts are a more valuable source. Here, literary manuscripts are less reliable than administrative ones, for they are almost all the work of numerous scribes writing at different periods and often in different places. Administrative and business documents have a narrower lexical and syntactic range, but they possess the advantage of being precisely dated and located and the product of a single writer. After the work of Wacker (1916) and more particularly that of Gossen (1967) on the spatial variability of medieval French writing systems, it was for a long time believed that the vernacular (i.e. non-Latin) writing systems of medieval France had only the most tenuous link with speech. However, in a remarkable series of studies published in the 1970s and 1980s, A. Dees was able to demonstrate that the relationship between local pronunciation and local spellings in thirteenth-century French texts was less arbitrary than previously thought. By applying Dees's methodology, it may be possible to find traces of localised linguistic features in certain manuscripts known to have been written in Paris. More recently, several Dutch linguists have computerised a sizeable corpus of thirteenth- and fourteenth-century Parisian legal documents (referred to with the short-hand label of 'charters'), upon which we shall draw extensively later (see van Reenen and van Reenen-Stein 1988).

Help may also be available in modern dialect material. Back-projecting from the data present in modern linguistic atlases, notably the *Atlas linguistique de la France* of Gilliéron and Edmont (1901–10), is controversial, methodologically, for we cannot be absolutely certain either about the equivalence of medieval and modern forms or about continuity. Much of the past may still be with us, but we have no sure way of knowing which. However, work on the spatial distribution of written forms in medieval French by Dees and his team, notably in Dees's *Atlas* (1980), provides support as we deal with the continuity problem, so something may be recoverable by this method.

2.1.2 The late medieval and early modern period

Information about the diversity of Parisian speech becomes more plentiful from the fifteenth century onwards. The most easily accessible source is of course literary texts, particularly plays, which from the fifteenth century onwards depict colloquial language quite routinely (see, for example, Lewicka 1960, 1968, 1974). Highly conscious literary representations of low-class Parisian speech are to be found in seventeenth-century burlesque literature (see Lathuillère 1984), in political pamphlets from the seventeenth and eighteenth centuries (see in particular Rosset 1911 and Deloffre 1999), and in novels, plays and poems composed in the *poissard* style in the eighteenth century (see Moore 1935). Such representations of low-class speech are valuable in many ways, but social stereotypes give only a sketchy and unsystematic view of linguistic structure and place excessive emphasis on shibboleths and social markers.

Perhaps the most striking innovation of the early modern period is the production of large quantities of metalinguistic comment, partly in the form of language teaching manuals destined for foreign learners (see especially Stein 1997 on John Palsgrave), but mainly in the form of grammars, dictionaries and *remarques* produced for native speakers between the sixteenth and the eighteenth centuries. Over a century ago an invaluable compilation of orthoepists' comments on pronunciation was assembled by Charles Thurot (1881 and 1883). This grammatical work provides rich sources of prescriptive information about 'bad' as well as 'good' speech forms.

In the early modern period we find the first *relatively direct* attestations of colloquial speech. The *Journal* of Jean Héroard is an extraordinarily rich document from the first decade of the seventeenth century (see Gougenheim 1931; Ernst 1985; Gorog 1989; Foisil 1989): it records in precise detail the everyday speech of the Dauphin (who was at this time a young child and who became King Louis XIII in 1610). However, this text is an exceptional one-off, and it is difficult to know which variety of Parisian French it most faithfully represents. More usually we find ourselves dealing with colloquialisms which come through unintentionally as less well educated people attempt to write for themselves – for example, personal letters from the sixteenth century (see Wood 1923), the *Journal* of a Paris glazier J.-L. Menétra in the eighteenth century (see Seguin 1992), and the minutes of the proceedings of revolutionary tribunals (see Branca-Rosoff and Schneider 1994). It is likely that there exists more of such material still to be published (see Ernst and Wolf 2001).

A final source of information about non-standard speech in the early modern period is to be found in varieties still extant in overseas territories colonised by French-speakers in the seventeenth century, and which have retained linguistic features discarded by metropolitan French. Here we are concerned primarily with French-based creoles (see Stein 1987; Hull 1988; Posner 1997: 91–9), and Canadian French (see in particular Morin 1994; Gauthier and Lavoie 1995; Mougeon and Béniak 1995). Material found here has a valuable function to play not least in validating the authenticity of linguistic features found in metropolitan texts written at that time. However, we cannot often be sure how far features found in such material were specifically Parisian, or how far they were widespread across France at the time of colonisation.

2.1.3   The modern period

Literary texts continue to be a rich source of sociolinguistic information in the nineteenth century. While an academic tradition perpetuated the literary practices of the classical period, Romanticism encouraged the use of vernacular forms in literature. H. Monnier exploited the resources of everyday Parisian speech in his *Scènes populaires* (1835) and he was quickly followed by Victor Hugo. The spectacle of a criminal world in revolt against civilised society, with an alternative sub-culture and alternative vocabulary, held a grim fascination for a middle-class public who felt particularly vulnerable living alongside a turbulent and rapidly expanding Parisian populace. This picture emerges in the *Mystères de Paris* (1842) of Eugène Sue and in numerous works by Emile Zola, notably *L'Assommoir* (1877). The tradition continues in the twentieth century with writers like Barbusse, Céline and Queneau. Appealing as they are, however, literary representations of the vernacular are not ideal linguistic material.

The tradition of prescriptive works condemning the 'errors' rampant in everyday Parisian speech continues vigorously in the nineteenth century. With the spread of education and literacy an increasing number of people were brought face to face with the norms of correct usage. The linguistic shortcomings of the uneducated population in Paris are enumerated in d'Hautel's (1808) *Dictionnaire du bas-langage* and in Desgranges' (1821) *Petit Dictionnaire du peuple*. Throughout the century, dictionaries provide a rich source of information, not just on lexical matters but also on matters of pronunciation. The quality of this information improved dramatically in the second half of the century, with the gradual emergence of linguistics as a scientific discipline.

Scholarly interest in the vernacular developed with the growth of comparative philology and dialectology. It focused initially upon vocabulary, a large number of inventories and etymological studies on the criminal *langue verte* and *argot* being published between the middle years of the century and the outbreak of the First World War (see below, §12.3.3). Interest in other aspects of low-class Parisian speech came with the work of Agnel (1855 and 1870) and the publication in 1872 of Nisard's *Etude sur le langage populaire ou patois de Paris et de sa banlieue*. This work was short on scientific detachment, but it had the merit of bringing into the public domain a large stock of literary and semi-literary source material for a historical study of the dialect (Nisard 1872: 319–436). More reliable observations about the speech of Paris came with the development of phonetics, notably with the great pioneer of the subject, Paul Passy (see especially Passy 1917).

After the First World War, work on the vernacular moved away from the historical, dialectological approach of the previous century towards synchronic description. The tone was set by Henri Bauche, who worked on everyday speech during and just after the First World War. Bauche's *Le Langage populaire* (first published in 1920) broke with tradition in a number of ways. The sub-title of this work is instructive: 'grammaire, syntaxe, et dictionnaire du français tel qu'on le parle dans le peuple de Paris, avec tous les termes d'argot usuel'. Although vocabulary continues to occupy a large place, discussion of pronunciation is reduced in favour of syntax. Moreover, the vernacular ceases to be seen as a corrupt version of the standard language, but as a linguistic system in its own right. Henri Frei's *Grammaire des fautes* (1929) develops a similar two-system rationale on the basis of an analysis of the 'mistakes' present in the letters written by relatively uneducated French conscripts at the Front. What most characterises the data situation in the twentieth century is increased direct access to the vernacular through the development of electronic recording equipment. The early talking films of the 1930s also have material to offer (see Bernet 1995). The work of earlier researchers now makes 'real time' diachronic studies a real possibility (see Martinet 1969: 168–90).

These, then, are the principal data-sources we have to work with, and their limitations are severe. The data have all been accidentally preserved and are by no means representative of all aspects of the language of past states. There is an inevitable arbitrariness in the corpus in relation to factors such as the nature of the text (literary, administrative or otherwise), the level of formality, and the social or regional background of speakers, with the various different periods in the history of the language having an uneven spread of types of text. Important definitions can become blurred at the edges, and dichotomies such as written/spoken, urban/rural, upper class/lower class, formal/informal (a) can become oversimplified binary oppositions and (b) are tantalisingly easy to conflate with each other. These problems were highlighted by Milroy (1992: 45):

Whereas research into present-day states proceeds in a controlled way by collecting and analysing data for the specific purpose of drawing generalizations about language and about specific aspects of language, the researcher into past states must use materials which were not in the first place collected for this purpose. Some styles and varieties may therefore be over-represented in the data, while others are under-represented. For some periods of time there may be a great deal of surviving information: for others there may be little or none at all.

Furthermore, no part of this data-base is made up of anything approaching 'authentic speech'. As soon as we come near the vernacular, it slips away, leaving only the faintest traces of its passage. All our data-sources are at varying degrees of indirectness. The least indirect are perhaps those where writers, for one reason or another, have operated without the constraint of a written standard and have allowed vernacularisms to slip unwittingly into their writing. This is the case, up to a point, with medieval manuscripts written before standardisation. It is also the case with inexperienced writers in the post-standardisation age. Such sources must be used with great circumspection, even so. Next along the direct–indirect gradient we might place the metalinguistic observations of contemporaries. This category includes the works of orthoepists and lexicographers, and also documents like Héroard's *Journal*. Contemporary observers like these were not sociolinguists, they were caught up to varying extents in a tradition of observation and were each pursuing their own social agenda. Literary representations of colloquial speech are even more indirect:

while based on real life, the resulting artefacts are language refracted through the distorting prism of authors with other aims in mind than the objective replication of speech.

A further source for the past lies in projecting back on the basis of data available in the present. Much of the past may still survive in the present, as we have seen, in conservative rural varieties recorded in modern dialect surveys and in 'colonial' varieties of French which for various reasons have not kept up with mainstream changes. Information gleaned here is potentially very valuable, but there persists the problem of continuity: we can never be sure which parts of the modern data are in fact the old parts.

The severity of the data problem causes us to question the feasibility of historical sociolinguistics. It is clear that if historical sociolinguistics exists as a recognisable discipline, it is a very different animal from sociolinguistics proper. Whereas the sociolinguist can to a large extent control his/her data, the historical sociolinguist cannot. S/he can only extrapolate from what happens to have survived. It is a *donnée* of historical linguistics that direct access to authentic speech is denied: the evanescence of speech ensures that only the faintest traces of past states of the spoken language have come down to us. However, there is little point in deploring these facts, they are the ones we have to work with. Like the archaeologist working with the scattered fragments of long destroyed cities, the skill of a historical sociolinguist lies in creating the most plausible reconstruction on the basis of a minimal number of facts. None of the data-sources we have are 100 per cent adequate, but taken together they might add up to something. The challenge lies in correctly estimating their reliability in each case, and in appropriately gauging the inferences which can be drawn from them. We will never succeed in reconstituting the precise picture with certainty, but we can aspire to join up the dots in the most meaningful way – provided we are satisfied there are enough dots in the first place.

But, even if enough dots survive – and this is a critical question – what allows us to judge what is 'the most meaningful way' of 'joining them up'? Alternative ways will always exist, and our hypotheses will always be at the mercy of current theoretical and ideological assumptions. The best we can do, in the present project, is to ensure that any picture of Parisian speech which we reconstitute across time is sociologically credible on the one hand, and sociolinguistically credible on the other, that is that it is compatible with the current state of knowledge in urban history and urban dialectology. We must be able to accommodate our picture within the overall framework of an evolving urban community, and we must avoid postulating states of affairs in old languages which are not known to exist in modern ones. The 'uniformitarian principle' we are invoking here is of course parodoxical:

The task of historical linguistics is to explain the differences between the past and the present; but to the extent that the past was different from the present, there is no way of knowing how different it was. (Labov 1994: 21)

With all this in mind, let us now consider basic ideas drawn from European urbanisation theory and from modern urban dialectology which may help us to interpret the fragmentary sociolinguistic evidence from the Parisian past.

2.2   European urbanisation, 1000–1950

If it is speakers who change languages and not the other way round, macro-level changes in the speech of a city will be conditioned, if not dictated, by changes in the city's demography and social structure. Sociolinguists are quite capable of generating systems which make perfect linguistic sense, but sociological non-sense, so we should listen attentively to what social historians tell us about the development of cities.

We might be tempted to set our history of Parisian speech in the framework of the turbulent political and 'monumental' history of the city. It is widely assumed that linguistic developments in France are explicable primarily with reference to the power of the state, period-divisions being commonly tied to the regnal periods of French kings. This satisfies a desire to see human affairs controlled by men rather than by deeper demographic, social and economic forces (Adam Smith's 'invisible hand', for instance), but it risks ascribing too much effective power to the government machines of pre-modern, and indeed of modern Europe. In a similar way, a great deal of energy has been devoted to correlating dialect boundaries in France with the boundaries of feudal fiefdoms and other administrative divisions. Very often maps of the French dialects merely replicate the map of the pre-Revolutionary provinces. It is the case that certain ecclesiastical and administrative divisions are extremely ancient, having sometimes been designed by the Romans to coincide with the pre-existing boundaries of Gaulish *civitates*. However, calquing the development of dialects and languages on dynastic, political and even administrative history usually produces disappointing results. After examining long-standing administrative divisions in the Paris region, Durand (1936: 45) concluded:

Il semble donc, dans ces conditions, qu'il soit assez vain de chercher dans les divisions administratives des bases de limites dialectologiques.

The presence of rich and powerful people in a community influences the development of norms and the nature of social stratification within the dialect, but the fundamental determinants of dialect formation are to be found in migration and settlement patterns, in the focusing of communities and changing levels of interaction between groups. The linguistic and sociolinguistic development of cities can likewise be understood only in relation to the development of their populations. For a similar approach to the development of London English, see Keene (2000).

In France, we are fortunate to possess extremely well-documented urban histories in the form of Duby's *Histoire de la France urbaine* and the multi-authored *Nouvelle Histoire de Paris* (Babelon 1986; Boussard 1976; Cazelles 1972; Chagniot 1988; Favier 1974; Lavedan 1975). We need to look outside France, however, for more broadly based theoretical analyses. Hohenberg and Lees' (1985) *The Making of Urban Europe 1000–1950* offers a particularly rich account of the development of urban systems in Europe since medieval times, bringing together the demographic evolution of cities, their functional development, and their relationship with their hinterland and with the wider urban network.

Hohenberg and Lees identify two broad patterns of urbanisation, which they refer to as the 'Network System' and the 'Central Place System'. When a city evolves primarily through the Network System, it constitutes a node in a network of cities linked by trade, operating as a gateway for the towns in its regional 'hinterland', and is linked to the larger network via its 'foreland'. The growth of the city is a function of its attractive powers in terms of commerce and exchange. Its key figures will be merchants and bankers. In this model it is not the region which creates the city, but rather the city which creates the region, providing the stimulus to the production of larger surpluses and drawing on underused reserves of land and labour. The shape of a Network System does not have any particular symmetry: networks are not bound to linear distance in the way they are with 'Central Places'. They are tied in with the trade routes upon which they are situated. Since such cities are links in a network, often neither the first source nor the ultimate destination of goods, they are in some measure interchangeable as are the trade routes themselves. Good examples of cities that developed along this path are medieval Venice, seventeenth-century Amsterdam, twentieth-century Hong Kong.

When a city evolves primarily through the Central Place System it is more firmly grounded in its hinterland: 'The Central Place System is rooted in the stability of the land and its tillers. A neat geometric mosaic of graduated centers structures the commercial, administrative, and cultural needs of a region and eventually integrates regions into a unified nation' (Hohenberg and Lees 1985: 69). Individual markets need to be linked to one another in order to broaden the range of goods traded and to equalise local imbalances. As the volume of local trade and the organisation of civil society increases, a large number of market and administrative settlements crystallise as 'central places' for their surrounding areas. Each centre constitutes the centre of gravity of its service area in order to minimise transportation costs. Such places tend not to be random in size and placement but to locate at even distances from one another and to form a hierarchy. The urban hierarchy thus comprises: (I) national capitals, (II) provincial capitals, (III) county towns, (IV) market towns, etc. According to the Central Place model, the size and complexity of a town or city is determined by its proximity to the centre of the System, which acquires thereby a certain symmetry not possessed by the Network System. The two models are complementary and most larger cities participate in both sorts of system. But, as we consider the long-term development of Paris, it is clear that Paris follows more closely the Central Place model than does, for instance, London.

The collapse of the Roman Empire in the fifth century led to the progressive break-up of the urban network of Antiquity and a large-scale shift of population from town to country. Europe had to wait for six centuries for this movement to be reversed with a new type of urbanisation which began in the eleventh century. In the subsequent period Hohenberg and Lees distinguish three phases in urban development: pre-industrial (eleventh to fourteenth centuries), proto-industrial (fifteenth to eighteenth centuries), industrial (nineteenth to twentieth centuries).

The pre-industrial phase (eleventh to fourteenth centuries) was characterised by rapid population growth through in-migration from the rural hinterland, the towns' expansion being principally led by merchant capitalists engaged in the transformation and exchange of goods produced locally and, as time went on, further afield. The wealth of the larger towns increasingly made them centres of consumption and attracted large numbers of sophisticated artisans and service workers. The population of such towns was drawn largely from the third estate – the majority of the population were poor – but the town's resources were controlled by small urban elites.

The proto-industrial age (fifteenth to eighteenth centuries) was one of demographic stagnation, so changes in the composition of the city tended to be more qualitative than quantitative. In-migration from the countryside continued to sustain the urban population, but during this period the balance of economic power gradually shifted from the countryside to the towns. This was accompanied by an increase in the political and administrative function of cities, and cities became centres of cultural progress. Under the pressure of changing patterns of production and marketing, urban communities became more stratified and a widening gap – cultural and political as well as material – divided rich and poor. The elite began to reject what it saw as vulgar or superstitious popular culture.

The industrial age (nineteenth to twentieth centuries) brought in a period of exceptional growth in the size of European cities. The new industrial order began in the countryside and between 1800 and 1910 the urban population of Europe grew about ten-fold. The more urban a place, the more intense its subcultures: despite high rates of geographic mobility, local communities (based on ethnicity and religion) developed even in the largest cities. Urban work-patterns reinforced the nexus of kinship and neighbourhood. However, industrialisation destroyed proto-industrial popular culture, which slowly reshaped itself in the second half of the nineteenth century.

It is sensible to suppose that the formation and development of urban dialects will shadow the development of their urban populations.

2.3   Urban dialect formation

The linguistic data bearing upon Parisian speech in the past may be highly defective, but they exist and need to be accounted for in a satisfactory way. How do we tell what is 'the most satisfactory way'? A test we can apply is the 'uniformitarian' principle: we can look at the way languages function in the modern world (where data are plentiful) and project this back to the more remote past where data are harder to come by, on the assumption that languages function on more or less the same fundamental principles in all societies. We can 'use the present to explain the past' (Labov 1994: 9–27). This incurs obvious risks: it may lead us to miss what is truly different about the past. However, when faced with an historical explanation that squares with what has been observed in parallel situations in the modern world and with one that finds no analogy anywhere, the former is always preferable. This invites us to look at the development of speech in Paris in the light of the findings of modern urban dialectology.

Much of the work on urban dialectology has been conducted in the English-speaking world. Following Labov's research in New York and Pennsylvania, we have important work on British cities: for example, Norwich (Trudgill 1974), Belfast (Milroy 1981) and Reading (Cheshire 1982). A significant collection of British urban-dialect studies is to be found in Foulkes and Docherty (1999). Elsewhere we have valuable sociolinguistic studies of Berlin (Dittmar, Schlobinski and Wachs 1988), Copenhagen (Gregersen and Pedersen 1991), and Brasilia (Bortoni-Ricardo 1985). In France urban dialect studies, so long neglected, are now starting to blossom (see Salmon 1991; Lefebvre 1991; Pooley 1996). Some of the most interesting work concerns French-speaking Canada (see, for example, Levine 1990) and the mushrooming cities of French-speaking Africa (see Manessy 1994; Calvet 1994a; Ploog 2002). When it comes to historical work on urban dialectology, however, there are few precedents. Occasionally, in the case of industrial towns which burgeoned in the nineteenth century (e.g. Belfast, Roubaix), the researcher widens the time-frame to embrace the origins of the dialect (Milroy 1984; Pooley 1996).

2.3.1   Dialect structure and social structure

For structuralists, as for the neogrammarians before them, language change was essentially a language-internal process. It occurred independently of the speakers using the language.

La langue est un système qui ne connaît que son ordre propre. (Saussure 1971: 43)

In this tradition, André Martinet (1955) demonstrated in exemplary fashion the workings of internal, structural factors in the process of sound-change. However, one of the most significant findings of historical sociolinguistics is that (in contradiction to Saussure) *external* social structure can impact heavily upon *internal* linguistic structure. Andersen (1988) examined the way dialects develop in central, focal areas (as in great metropolises) and the way they develop on the periphery. In this context 'centre' and 'periphery' relate less to simple geographical distance than to the density and orientation of communication networks. He sees speech-communities located at the centre as engaging in a large amount of inter-dialectal communication and as typically having 'open dialects'; conversely, communities located on the periphery engage in less inter-dialectal communication and possess 'closed dialects'. A second distinction drawn by Andersen, which may or may not be superimposed on the first, is that between 'exocentric dialect communities' and 'endocentric dialect communities'. Here he is concerned not with language systems but with speaker attitudes, the former communities being receptive to influence from outside norms, the latter adhering vigorously to their own received norms. Andersen sees dialect openness/closedness and exocentricity/ endocentricity as impinging directly on internal linguistic structure: on the whole, open dialects undergo rapid change and embody simpler phonological and morphological systems, while closed dialects are conservative and possess rather complex phonological and morphological systems.

There is an affinity between these ideas and Le Page's notion of dialect-focusing (see Le Page and Tabouret-Keller 1985) and the Milroys' thinking on language and social networks (see Milroy 1992). The success of an innovation is determined not so much by its internal characteristics, as by its capacity to symbolise social distinctions and by the structure of the speech community concerned. For Le Page, 'highly focused communities' are characterised by a strong sense of shared linguistic norms. Autarchic village communities in traditional peasant economies are typically more focused than large and complex urban communities with a large number of external links. The Milroys see a similar correlation between the network structure of the group and linguistic behaviour:

Relationships in tribal societies, villages and traditional working-class communities are typically multiplex and dense, whereas those in geographically and socially mobile industrial societies tend to uniplexity and spareness. (Milroy 1987: 52)

Loose network ties are seen to be conducive to rapid linguistic change, and *vice versa*. Linguistic change is slow to the extent that the relevant populations are well-established and bound by strong ties; whereas it is rapid to the extent that weak ties exist in populations. (Milroy and Milroy 1985: 375)

2.3.2   Dialect-mixing

Traditional dialectology is above all concerned with recovering and recording dialectal speech in its 'pure' rustic form, typified by the type of informant optimally required, the so-called NORMs (= Non-mobile, Older, Rural Males). It concedes that dialect-mixing takes place in border areas, but tends not to find this phenomenon intrinsically interesting. Modern dialectology has shown that the notion of 'pure dialect' is entirely mythical and that the most normal dialect experience is, in fact, one of dialect-mixing. If this is the case with rural dialects, it is even more applicable to the situation found in large cities. Manessy (1994: 22–3) draws attention to the two-speed development which he discovered between town and country in African cities, resulting precisely from language- and dialect-mixing. This can be transposed to Paris and the French provinces in medieval times.

The most spectacular cases of language mixing have been revealed in studies of the history of pidgins and creoles. Ideas developed here (e.g. the creole continuum, basilectal, mesolectal, acrolectal varieties) are proving helpful in understanding the development of non-creolised languages. Many of them were examined by Trudgill (1986) in *Dialects in Contact*. In the first section of this work (pp. 1–82) the author describes the mechanism known as 'accommodation', whereby speakers of mutually intelligible dialects subconsciously reduce or eliminate linguistic variants which impede communication or which breach Grice's 'co-operative principle', that is features which are felt to be too typical of the speaker's place or region of origin. Trudgill regards accommodation as an individual, short-term preamble to collective, longer-term koinéisation. In the second section of the book (pp. 83–126) he examines the processes of 'dialect levelling' (whereby features typical of a particular dialect fall into disuse) and 'simplification' (the reduction of morpho-phonemic irregularities), which can lead to 'koinéisation'. He highlights the fact that residual variants will survive the process of koinéisation and that these are subsequently susceptible to 'reallocation' in the community as social and stylistic markers. Let us explore the three key ideas found here (koinéisation, reallocation and dialect-levelling) in more detail.

Koinéisation

Koinéisation 'involves the mixing of features of . . . different dialects, and leads to a new compromise dialect' (Siegel 1985: 365, 369, quoted in Hinskens 1992: 15). For Trudgill (1986: 107–8), a koiné is 'a historically mixed but synchronically stable dialect which contains elements from the different dialects that went into the mixture, as well as interdialect forms that were present in none', the basic processes involved being mixing, levelling and simplification. The term is now commonly used to handle the development of creoles, and it can very usefully be applied to the development of new urban dialects.

We can envisage the following idealised scenario for the emergence of a new urban dialect. The rural dialect spoken in a small village surrounded at a distance by villages of a similar size will normally merge imperceptibly into the dialect continuum of the area around it. This situation changes as the village grows into a town or city, for population expansion usually entails an influx of speakers whose dialects are not contiguous with that of the original inhabitants. As the population increases in size, we encounter the mixing of a number of dialects from beyond the immediate hinterland and the arrival of new linguistic forms, perhaps from other urban centres with which the town has particularly strong communication ties. Varying with the level of in-migration, dialect-levelling will then take place in the way we have just described.

Increase in the town's population will eventually cause the density of communication between the inhabitants of the town to exceed that with people from outside. This will lead to a certain degree of sociolinguistic focusing and to the emergence of new linguistic norms somewhat different from those of the hinterland dialects: the speech of the town is thereby modified and gradually rises above the regional dialect continuum to form a new dialect of its own.

Reallocation of variants

After the initial stages of new-dialect development, which imply convergence of non-contiguous dialects, Trudgill points to a second phase, which he labels 'reallocation' and which can, under certain circumstances, lead to divergence within the speech of the 'new' urban community:

Even after koinéization, . . . some variants left over from the original mixture may survive. Where this occurs, *reallocation* may occur, such that variants originally from different regional dialects may in the new dialect become *social-class dialect variants, stylistic variants, areal variants,* or, in the case of phonology *allophonic variants.* (Trudgill 1986: 126)

Reallocation is in some respects similar to exaptation (a process whereby linguistic material which has lost its earlier function is not discarded but acquires a new function). Residual dialect variants may be redistributed across the whole community as stylistic variants, but they can also become the prerogative of particular sub-groups within society, either as areal variants or as social-class variants. It is the latter type that is particularly relevant to our concerns here.

Milroy (1984: 214) makes the point that

phonological systems can vary very greatly within a single city, but that a great deal of variation, often associated with rapid change, is tied to the social characteristics of speakers. Those patterns of social differentiation which are represented in lifestyle, residence, income and education are also faithfully, and in great detail, reflected in patterns of linguistic stratification.

Groups within the urban population which, for whatever reason, wish to set themselves apart from the rest will develop their own in-group linguistic norms, appropriating particular variants as markers of their own identity. Such social-class markers are never invented *de toutes pièces*: they can be borrowed from outside, but, in the main, they involve the reassignment of variants already current in the community. Reallocation normally takes place implicitly, even subconsciously, but it is possible to see it at work explicitly and consciously in the process of linguistic codification and class-based standardisation.

Dialect-levelling and 'simplification'

Hinskens (1992: 11) defines dialect-levelling as 'a process which reduces the number of features separating a dialect from other varieties, including the socially more prestigious standard language'. If we adopt this definition, the pressure for dialect-levelling comes from two directions – horizontally, through increased contact between speakers of non-contiguous dialects, giving rise to acts of accommodation at peer-group level (levelling proper), and vertically, through the diffusion downwards of the standard language (where this exists), usually in response to top-down institutional pressures (standardisation). 'Levelling proper' is thus a more general phenomenon than 'standardisation', the latter being relevant only to situations in which a standard language exists.

Levelling involves the 'reduction or attrition of marked variants' (see Trudgill 1986: 98), the term 'marked' referring generally to the least widely used forms. However, the notion of markedness is not helpful in the context of dialect-levelling, for minority variants are not always the ones to be levelled out: occasionally the principle of economy of effort seems to carry the day, allowing shorter forms to triumph over longer ones. A more useful concept is probably that of sociolinguistic 'salience', but, as we shall see, even here the outcome is more or less impossible to predict. Another way in which the number of features separating a dialect from other varieties can be reduced is through mutual 'simplification', that is 'an increase in morphophonemic regularity' (symmetrical paradigms, fewer obligatory categories marked by morphemes of concord) and an increase in the 'regular correspondence between content and expression' (Trudgill 1986: 103).

Demographic patterns and levels of inter-dialectal contact in the city are constantly in flux. When population growth is slow and gradual, the proportion of immigrants to native city-dwellers remains low and immigrants from different regions simply shift intergenerationally to the dialect of the host community. Their original dialect is eventually lost, leaving little trace on the dialect of the city. In contrast, in periods of rapid population growth, fed principally by in-migration, the proportion of immigrants to native city-dwellers rises more dramatically, triggering a process of reciprocal dialect-levelling and rapid change in the urban dialect, leading eventually to 'koinéisation'. In times of demographic stagnation, the proportion of natives rises and speech within the city is likely to stratify along lines reflecting the distribution of power and wealth across the community, bringing about the 'reallocation' of sociolinguistic variants as social or stylistic markers. The history of many urban communities leads Labov (1994: 24) 'to expect massive population changes several times in a century rather than once a millennium'.

2.4   Summary

In the first part of this chapter we considered the linguistic evidence which might help us create a multidimensional history of Parisian French, and we were cautious about where such an imperfect data-base might take us. Information is there, and arguably in greater quantities than in most other European cities, but does it allow us to say anything sensible? Is there enough information, is it of the right type, and is it sufficiently representative? We then looked at general factors in urban history and dialect development which may help us limit the range of constructions we can place upon our very imperfect data. Working on the principle that developments in the speech of cities are governed by social and demographic change in the community of speakers, we considered patterns in European urbanisation since the year 1000. We noted Hohenberg and Lees's characterisation of this 'as a three-stage process of growth, trendless fluctuation and renewed growth, each phase dependent upon the interactions of demography, technology and markets' (1985: 9). These three phases were labelled 'pre-industrial', 'proto-industrial' and 'industrial' respectively. In the last part of the chapter we considered insights developed by urban dialectologists dealing with well-documented situations in the modern world. We looked particularly at the phenomena of dialect contact and dialect-mixing, which are particularly prevalent in large central places. The processes of dialect-levelling, koinéisation and 'reallocation' highlighted by Peter Trudgill seemed potentially very useful for any attempt to understand the long-term development of an urban dialect.

Following the principle that it is speakers who, collectively, change languages, and not the other way round, we will structure this book chronologically around the three phases of urban development identified by Hohenberg and Lees. Within each phase, we will try to reconstruct not micro-level sociolinguistic changes, but the most significant macro-level processes of change. Over the past millennium, the city of Paris has seen alternating phases of rapid and not so rapid demographic growth, which we might expect to have triggered alternating phases of convergence and divergence in the language of the city (see Lodge 1998, 1999a). Periods of rapid demographic growth, fuelled essentially by in-migration, lead typically to dialect-mixing, to levelling and even koinéisation. Periods of slower growth, during which different social groupings within the city have time to stabilise, are likely to induce dialect-divergence, reallocating residual variants as social-dialect and stylistic markers. It looks as though the three phases in the city's development were characterised above all by the three linguistic processes of koinéisation, reallocation and dialect-levelling respectively. Given the data issues we looked at earlier in this chapter, we must be cautious about applying any *a priori* model: historical model-building is always a high-risk strategy. At the same time, all history writing involves hypothesising, so we must ensure that our model is driven by the evidence and not the other way round.

Part 2

The pre-industrial city

3   The demographic take-off

In this chapter let us look at the development of Paris as an urban community in the medieval or, to use Hohenberg and Lees's term, the 'pre-industrial' period, before considering the city's sociolinguistic development in Chapter 4. We must examine particularly the city's changing demography at this time and its relations with the hinterland populations. The chronology of events needs to be considered carefully, for significant dialect development in the city can only have occurred in conjunction with rapid population change.

3.1   The early history

The site of Paris has seen continuous human occupation for a very long time: traces of settlement have been found on the Ile-de-la-Cité, dating back some 4,000 years (Duval 1961: 43). The city appears to owe its earliest existence to the presence of an important overland route which in Neolithic times passed across the plains and plateaux of northern France from the Low Countries to the Loire and Aquitaine, and which found in the Ile-de-la-Cité the most suitable crossing-point on the Seine (see Planhol 1994: 247–8). The city's subsequent development was determined by the exceptional fertility of the plain situated north of the Seine, and by the fact that the city found itself in an area where several rivers converge (notably the Marne and the Oise with the Seine). It is no doubt for this hydrological reason that Paris's hinterland came to be referred to as the 'Ile-de-France' (see Bloch 1913: 9–10).

The Celtic *Parisii* tribe is known to have created a fortified settlement on *Lutetia Parisiorum*, for the Ile-de-la-Cité offered a natural defensive point against territorial competitors like the *Belgae*. In the Roman period, some expansion of the city beyond the island took place on the Left Bank of the Seine (see Braudel 1986: II, 75), but even in its heyday in the second century AD, the Gallo-Roman city was a provincial town of only medium size, with a population estimated at no more than 8,000 (see Duval 1961: 60). The important cities of Roman Gaul were situated along the strategic axes emanating from Arles at the mouth of the Rhône, westwards to Toulouse and Spain, and northwards to Lyon, Autun and the German *limes* at Trier. The poet Ausonius, writing in the fourth century, lists the major cities of Gaul, but *Lutetia Parisiorum* did not merit a mention among them (see Lavedan 1975: 71–82). In the macro-economy of the Roman world, oriented as it was east–west along the Mediter-ranean, Paris and north-western Gaul found themselves somewhat outside the mainstream.

The political importance of Paris became greater after the collapse of Roman power in Gaul in the fifth century: the Merovingian Franks under Clovis made the city the administrative centre of their province of Neustria (the western part of Gaul running from the Channel to the Loire). For a short while in the seventh century Paris was the chief town of a kingdom extending over the whole of Gaul. The town flourished as a commercial centre. Moreover, the association of Paris with Saint Denis (martyred in the third century) and with Saint Geneviève (martyred two and a half centuries later) conferred on the city and surrounding region considerable religious status, inducing the Merovingian kings to establish their necropolis at the Abbey of Saint Denis situated 11km to the north. To judge by the writings of Gregory of Tours, during this time Paris began to acquire special significance in the imagination of the people of Gaul. However, although we have no reliable evidence upon which to base estimates of population size, it would appear that in Merovingian times the town remained small by Roman standards.

The period that followed witnessed the disintegration of the urban network of Antiquity and the widespread desertion of towns in favour of the country-side, with Paris conforming to the general pattern of urban decline. Planhol (1994: 252) believes that after the reign of Dagobert (seventh century), un-der the later Merovingians and Carolingians, 'the town slipped into a dormant state which lasted for close on four centuries'. The political and institutional role of Paris diminished as the seat of government became peripatetic. Of the 195 charters surviving from the Merovingian period, only nine originate in Paris, and of the surviving 700 Carolingian charters, none originates there (see Rauhut 1963: 269). The centre of Charlemagne's empire was, after all, Aachen. Charlemagne's successors in Neustria located the centre of their activities not in Paris but in the Orléanais (see Pernoud 1966: 22–31; Planhol 1994: 252). The old Roman urban network in northern Gaul finally collapsed under the pressure of the Scandinavian invasions of the ninth century, and the city of Paris was apparently reduced to the size of a 'bourg rural' (see Petit-Dutaillis 1950: 220). De Vries (1984: 41) points out that 'around the year 1000 con-centrated non-rural populations were very small. With the probable exception of Italy, no territories in Latin Christendom then possessed cities of 10,000 or more inhabitants.'

The weight of evidence suggests then that Paris was not an exceptional conurbation in Antiquity or in the early Middle Ages and that, although there was continuity from earlier times, and although the town enjoyed a special religious and political status, it did not emerge as a great centre of population before the general movement of urbanisation in western Europe which got under way in the eleventh century. As far as its linguistic development is concerned, it would be safe to assume that before that time the speech of Paris merged into the dialect continuum of north Gallo-Romance, with only a minimum of dialect-focusing in the city itself.

3.2   The demographic take-off

The tenth to the twelfth centuries featured what meteorologists call the 'medieval climatic optimum', which in Europe consisted of temperatures similar to those of today. This favourable climate assisted the colonisation of Iceland and Greenland by the Vikings, as well as the burgeoning of European civilisation between the eleventh and thirteenth centuries. The absorption of the Vikings into the broader fabric of European society in the tenth century and the removal of other external threats to the security of the region led, slowly at first, but at an accelerating rate, to higher agricultural production, population growth, freer travel, greater circulation of money and a general increase in trade. Urbanisation gathered momentum earliest in two regions: in northern Italy (Genoa, Venice, Milan, Florence) and in Flanders (Ghent, Bruges, Ypres), where André Chédeville discerns 'à la fin du XIe siècle . . . les premiers linéaments d'un "esprit urbain" ' (in Duby 1981: II, 140). Within what is now called France, the north–south divide familiar to dialectologists through the *oc–oil* isoglosses, was replicated in patterns of economic activity and social interaction. Whereas southern Gaul continued to engage with the economic circuit of the Mediterranean, focused on the North Italian cities, the population of northern Gaul increasingly looked to the North Sea, to England, to Germany and, more immediately, to Flanders.

Urban historians are unanimous in the view that it was the twelfth century which saw the economic and demographic take-off of Paris (see Boussard 1976: 130). At the end of the eleventh century the city consisted, physically speaking, of no more than the Ile-de-la-Cité, with a number of religious communities on each bank: Saint Germain l'Auxerrois, Saint Martin des Champs and Saint Gervais on the Right, and various clusters of settlements outside the three abbeys on the Left – Saint Germain des Prés, Sainte Geneviève and Saint Marcel. During the twelfth century, however, particularly between 1110 and 1170, urban expansion got under way so strongly that, like in nuclear fission, it gathered its own momentum and become self-sustaining. Population expanded first on the Right Bank and later on the Left too, filling in all the vacant spaces between the scattered settlements of the previous century. The number of parishes jumped from sixteen in 1100 to thirty-three a century later. A graphic image of the extent of the city's physical expansion is to be seen in the area enclosed by the city wall constructed at the end of the twelfth century (see Map 1).

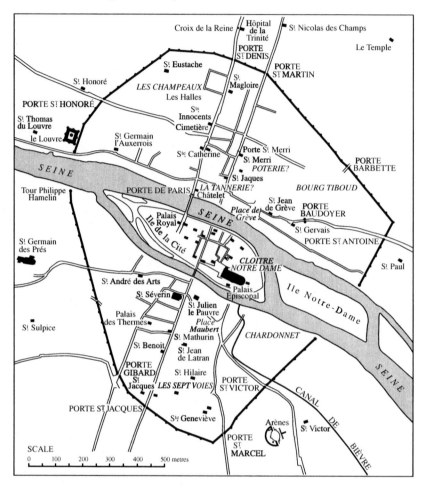

Map 1. The city walls c.1200 (adapted from Boussard 1976: 314)

The population-sizes of medieval towns are impossible to estimate precisely (see Bairoch, Batou and Chèvre 1988: 289–300). Paris offers a case in point, for even when documentary evidence starts to become available in the late thirteenth century – in the form of hearth-tax rolls ('rôles de *Taille*s') – estimates based upon it oscillate wildly from 80,000 to 200,000 (see Cazelles 1972: 131– 47; Lavedan 1975: 133; Le Goff 1980: 190–1, 401–2). That said, if we accept these estimates only as an order of magnitude, there is a consensus among historians that thirteenth-century Paris had become an urban giant, 'by far the largest town in western Europe', surpassing even Florence, Venice and Milan (Planhol 1994: 259; see Table 1).

Table 1. *The largest cities in Europe, 1000–1900 (population in thousands)*

1000		1400		1700		1900	
Constantinople	450	Paris	275	Constantinople	700	London	6,480
Cordoba	450	Milan	125	London	550	Paris	3,330
Seville	90	Bruges	125	Paris	530	Berlin	2,424
Palermo	75	Venice	110	Naples	207	Vienna	1,662
Kiev	45	Granada	100	Lisbon	188	St Petersburg	1,439
Venice	45	Genoa	100	Amsterdam	172	Manchester	1,255
Regensburg	40	Prague	95	Rome	149	Birmingham	1,248
Thessalonika	40	Caffa	85	Venice	144	Moscow	1,120
Amalfi	35	Seville	70	Moscow	130	Glasgow	1,072
Rome	35	Ghent	70	Milan	124	Liverpool	940

Source: Hohenberg and Lees 1985: 11.

Le Goff (1980: 401–2) sees the thirteenth-century urban hierarchy in France and the Low Countries as in the figure.

150,000
Paris
50,000 +
Ghent
20,000 – 50,000
Avignon, Bordeaux, Bruges, Lyon, Rouen,
Saint-Omer, Toulouse, Tournai, Ypres
10,000 – 20,000
Albi, Angers, Arles, Arras, Béziers, Bourges,
Clermont, Douai, Lille, Marseille, Metz, Montpellier,
Orléans, Perpignan, Poitiers, Reims, Strasbourg, Tours

How are we to explain the fact that northern Gaul witnessed the emergence of a major centre of polarisation earlier than the other countries of western Europe? Attempts have been made to account for the development of Paris in terms of the Network System (see above, §2.2). An important factor in the growth of the city was undoubtedly its position in the contemporary trading network. As well as being placed at a major crossing-point on the Seine, Paris is situated at the convergence of three other important waterways: the Marne, the Oise and the Aisne. During the twelfth century patterns of trade began to extend over greater distances, and Paris came to occupy a pivotal position not just in northern Gaul but also in the European urban system as a whole. Taking over the function performed by the fairs of Champagne (it developed a major international fair of its own in the *foire de l'Endit*), Paris became an important point of commercial exchange between the two major poles of

Map 2. Paris and the European trading areas, c. 1200 (adapted from Braudel 1986: II, 133). This map shows the towns linked to the Champagne Fairs (12th-13th centuries). It reveals the existence of two distinct trading areas (north and south), with Paris engaged primarily with the former.

economic activity in Europe: the Low Countries and North Italy (see Map 2). However, the international dimension in Parisian expansion should not be exaggerated. Paris did not become a great centre for financial transactions and capital flows, nor was it among the great port cities open to the outside world and new horizons. Planhol (1994: 256) writes:

The radius of [the city's] regular commercial relations reached as far as Coutances, Dunkirk and Tournai, Liège and Cologne, Châlons and Langres, Beaune and Dijon. But to the south it barely extended beyond the Loire. Visitors from Orléans were to be found in Paris but very few from the Tours, Berri and Anjou districts and virtually none from Poitou and Auvergne. The Seine and its tributaries and the routes to Flanders and Orléans were the essential features in the Parisian sphere of influence at this period.

Paris was essentially a North European city, and its place in the European Network System is probably a less important factor in its growth than the development of the city as a Central Place, firmly grounded in its hinterland.

3.3   The city and its hinterland

The notion of hinterland is not straightforward. It relates to the area on which a city depends for a constant infusion of material supplies (food, fuel and raw materials) and human resources. As such, its extent is subject to change across time. In the early stages the hinterland of Paris comprised no more than a small circle around the city (corresponding roughly to the area referred to in the twelfth to thirteenth centuries as 'France'). However, Paris's demographic preponderance was increasingly to shape its hinterland to suit its expanding needs, and it came eventually to embrace the whole hexagon which duly adopted the name 'France'.

How extensive was the hinterland of Paris in the Middle Ages? To answer this it might be sensible to follow Jacquart (1996: 108–9) when he observes that

from the start of the sixteenth century it was necessary to travel 80–100 kilometres to find urban centres that were autonomous in relation to the capital . . . The Parisian hinterland in the sixteenth and seventeenth centuries was thus a 100km circle, within which occurred the bulk of the exchanges between the city and its surrounding *plat pays* or hinterland.

Outside the circle we find urban centres of a significant size which are autonomous with relation to the metropolis – Rouen, Beauvais, Amiens, Reims, Troyes, Orléans and Chartres (Map 3). Within the circle we find smaller towns like Pontoise, Senlis, Provins, Meaux, Melun and Etampes, whose development was for a long time stunted by the presence in close proximity of the capital. It seems reasonable to restrict our notion of the hinterland in the Middle Ages to this geographical area, for it was certainly no larger in the thirteenth century than in the sixteenth, despite major demographic fluctuation in the period between. Defined in this way, Paris's medieval hinterland is coextensive with what is referred to today as the Ile-de-France (see Bloch 1913; Boussard 1976: 262–79). It comprises the modern *départements* of Seine (in 1964 divided into Hauts-de-Seine, Seine-Saint-Denis and Val-de-Marne), Seine-et-Oise (in 1964 Seine-et-Oise was divided into Essonne, Val d'Oise, Yvelines), Seine-et-Marne, parts of Loiret, Eure-et-Loir, Eure, Oise and Aisne (see Map 6). In medieval times, with its seven districts (Valois, Brie, Gâtinais, Hurepoix, Beauce, Vexin and Beauvaisis) the Paris region was quite heterogeneous. It

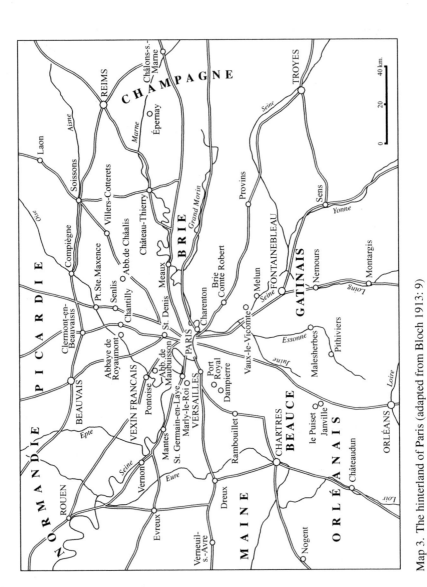

Map 3. The hinterland of Paris (adapted from Bloch 1913: 9)

contained large areas of woodland which encroached much more closely on the city than they do today – to the north-west the forests of Montmorency and Saint Germain, to the south-west the forest of Rambouillet, and to the south-east those of Fontainebleau and Brie. South of the city lay an area of gentle hillsides given over especially to the cultivation of vines. The area immediately north of Paris consisted of a wide fertile plain ('la France') (see Chédeville 1981: 108–9) whose wealth had for centuries been exploited by a cluster of great abbeys – notably Saint Denis, Saint Germain, Sainte Geneviève.

The growth of a large urban population in an overwhelmingly rural France was to produce considerable geographical effects. In particular, a distinctive agricultural region, designed to cater specifically for the needs of Paris, began to stand out against the background of the traditional rural world. The provisioning of the city in food, fuel and raw materials during the medieval period has been analysed in detail (see Cazelles 1972: 383–91), and Map 4 gives a useful summary of the supply-routes. However, this hinterland supplied the city not only with food and fuel, but also with people. Perhaps the single most important factor in the growth of Paris in the twelfth century is the fact that it was situated in an area which was already very densely populated.

The exceptional demographic increase that occurred in the city between 1100 and 1300 cannot be accounted for by natural reproduction: birth-rates were lower and mortality-rates significantly higher in medieval towns than in the countryside. In order to maintain and increase its population the city required a large and constant flow of immigrants. Migratory movement was not unilateral: the Paris population has been likened to a giant accordion, drawing in country-dwellers in times of population growth, and pushing out Parisians in times of dearth. However, in the period which concerns us here, an influx of new Parisians was the more typical. It is well known that twelfth-century Paris attracted groups from all over western Christendom, in particular, students from England and Germany (after it was constituted early in the thirteenth century, the university was divided into four 'nations' – the 'French', the 'Picard', the 'Norman' and the 'English') and merchants and preachers from Italy (the Rue des Lombards still exists in the First *arrondissement*) (see Cazelles 1972: 121–9; Lusignan 1987: 55, 61). That said, statistically speaking, these arrivals from distant parts accounted for little. During periods of even modest demographic increase, simply keeping a metropolitan population steady required the movement into it of considerable numbers of people, most of whom could only be supplied by the rural hinterland.

In periods of accelerated urbanisation, such as occurred in the twelfth and thirteenth centuries, it has been estimated that almost half of the population was born outside the city (see Jacquart 1996: 109). This required the migration of at least 30 per cent of the surplus population in the surrounding countryside (see Hohenberg and Lees 1985: 31–2). Population densities in Paris's medieval

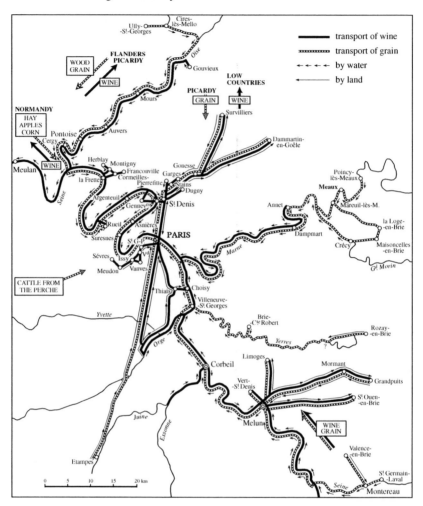

Map 4. Paris's medieval supply routes (adapted from Braudel 1986: I, 231)

hinterland were somewhat uneven, as Map 5 shows. The area north of the city (bounded by the towns of Pontoise, Luzarches and Meaux) supported a population four times denser than the rest of Gaul, and was indeed at that time one of the most densely populated areas in Europe (Fourquin 1964: 88–91). It appears to have been particularly the human flow from this area which fuelled the spectacular growth of the city in the twelfth and thirteenth centuries. Cazelles' (1972: 140–4) analysis of onomastic data contained in Parisian hearth-tax rolls from the late thirteenth century confirms this. Although impressionistic, it

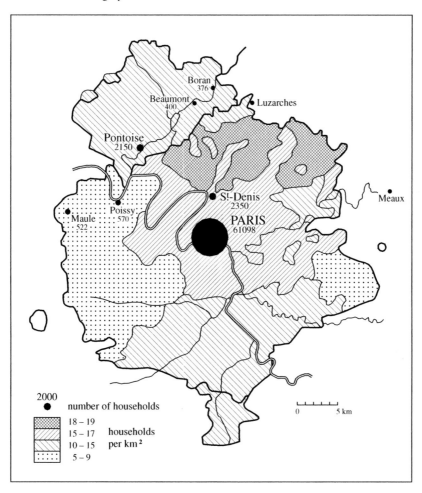

Map 5. Population densities in the Ile-de-France, c.1300 (adapted from Fourquin 1956)

commands respect because the migratory flows into the city which it indicates are strikingly similar to those operating centuries later, in the early modern period.

It appears that the majority of immigrants originated within a 70km radius around the city, though the different segments of that circle were not represented equally. Population surpluses in the area located just north and north-east of Paris provided the main basis of the maintenance and growth of the city's population throughout the medieval and early modern periods. The area immediately to the west and south were more thinly populated and contributed significantly less (see Fourquin 1956: 83). According to Cazelles, in-migration from further afield originated mainly in the north (Picardy with its dense network of rich cloth-making towns) and the west (Normandy, especially the large port city of Rouen), with rather fewer in the east (Champagne) and almost none in the south.

3.4   The functions of the city

The existence of a productive and densely populated hinterland furnished a necessary condition for the exceptional demographic development of Paris in the twelfth century, but of itself it was not sufficient. Any surplus population in the hinterland needed reasons for coming into the city. These reasons were provided in the twelfth century by a dramatic rise in the range and intensity of activities conducted there. The principal functions of cities have been analysed under four headings: mercantile, manufacturing, religio-educative and politico-administrative. Smaller towns participate in only one or two of these functions. Large cities participate in more of them and to a greater extent. What made Paris exceptional in the Middle Ages was that it came to participate in all of them to a very great extent.

An issue which divides western European historians is that of the continuity of urban life between the Roman and medieval worlds (witness the debate between Pirenne (1939) and Lombard (1957)). Jacques Le Goff (in Duby 1980: II, 13) sees continuity in the fact that the most important towns in medieval France (including Paris) were places which had previously been Roman cities, subsequently becoming the seat of bishoprics (*cités*). However, he also points out that the new 'pre-industrial towns' (*villes* or *bourgs*) which developed in Europe between the eleventh and thirteenth centuries, often alongside their ancient forebears, were functionally very different from the towns and cities of Antiquity. Whereas the Roman city had exercised political and institutional control over the province which surrounded it, the nascent town of medieval Europe was dependent for its supply of food and raw materials on a hinterland which it did not control, the land outside the towns being the domain of the feudal aristocracy and the Church (most conspicuously in the form of its monastic foundations). The medieval town was first and foremost a centre for the transformation and exchange of primary agricultural products, a place for merchants, money-changers and artisans, rather than for feudal land-holders.

The functional diversity of Paris was reflected topographically in the development of the three distinct areas of the city: the *Ville*, the *Cité* and the *Université*. Like all other medieval towns of any importance, its prime function, the one that gave rise to all the others, was mercantile. The city's economic take-off in the twelfth century was led by merchant capitalists who plied the Seine, organising trade in the products of the rich and populous hinterland of Paris. These were the 'Marchands de l'Eau' incorporated as a guild in 1121. During the twelfth century their chief competitors were to be found in the merchants of the city of Rouen situated nearer the mouth of the Seine, and it is easy to see why the removal of the Plantagenet presence there at the beginning of the thirteenth century was an economic as well as a dynastic priority. The growth of trade encouraged the development of artisanal activities reprocessing the primary agricultural products into manufactured goods. Increasingly the city attracted skilled artisans and service workers catering not primarily for external trade but for the consumption generated by the city itself. The expansion of these functions in the twelfth and thirteenth centuries took place primarily on the Right Bank, in the part of the city known as the *Ville*. It is here that the bulk of the city's population lived.

The growing wealth of the city induced the Church and the Monarchy to expand their presence there. Among the religio-educative contributions to the growth of the city, most prominent, after the cathedral on the Ile-de la-Cité and the abbeys established centuries earlier, was the accumulation of schools on the Left Bank of the river, consolidated into the University of Paris in 1215. The whole of the city located on the Left Bank, with its transient and heterogeneous population, was referred to as the *Université*. It has been estimated that at that time the number of ecclesiastics in the city, including students, stood at some 20,000. If we consider the number of locals required to 'service' this clerical population, we have to conclude that the demographic contribution of religio-educational establishments was quite considerable.

For economic, strategic and practical reasons the Capetians transferred the main institutions of the state from the Orléanais to the Paris region in the twelfth century. Initially they utilised the bureaucracy available at the abbey of Saint Denis, but as the twelfth century wore on, they set up their own permanent politico-administrative apparatus (the *Curia regis*) on the Ile-de-la-Cité, next to the Sainte Chapelle and in close proximity to the cathedral and its clerks. In due course the *curia in parlamento* became known simply as the Paris *parlement* (comprising four law-courts – the *chambre des plaids*, the *chambre des enquêtes*, the *chambre des requêtes* and the *chambre criminelle*). Control of the resources of the city was for obvious reasons a constant preoccupation, so the Capetians constructed a powerful fortress (Le Louvre) and retained permanent residences there, maintaining law and order through the *Prévôté* housed in the Châtelet. The city wall constructed by Philippe Auguste at the turn of the thirteenth century attests the new-found size and economic importance of the city to the Capetian dynasty. It is certain that the development of the city's administrative function was a major factor in the growth of the city. It is also certain that the growth of Paris was a major factor (perhaps the major factor) in the growth in the power of the French kings.

3.5   The social structure of the city

Medieval towns and cities were characterised by their oligarchic social structure and wide disparities of wealth, but the hierarchies visible there were not the same as those that developed in the early modern period. Post-Renaissance conceptions of capital cities predispose us to see them as dominated by royal palaces and the permanent presence of an aristocratic elite. The medieval kings and their entourage, in fact, resided in Paris relatively rarely, preferring the country life available in the castles and monastic houses of the Ile-de-France and the Orléanais. The royal household was peripatetic for most of the Middle Ages. Solnon (1987: 51) observes:

Si la monarchie a élu Paris capitale du royaume depuis le XIIIe siècle, la cour a longtemps répugné à s'y fixer. Paris est au moyen âge ville plus administrative que royale. Philippe le Bel n'y a guère passé plus d'un trimestre par an, Philippe IV n'y a séjourné que cinq à six mois.

The king and other great feudal barons had their town houses, but these were far from being full-time residences. The dominant culture of the city was bourgeois not aristocratic. Georges Duby (1980: II, 347) succinctly expresses the special social composition of medieval towns as follows:

Des clercs il y en avait partout, les nobles sont surtout hors de la ville, les pauvres sont eux aussi partout . . . des bourgeois il n'y en a que dans les villes. L'originalité de la ville médiévale c'est la bourgeoisie.

Paris was not, of course, a typical medieval town: as well as being a great centre for manufacture and trade, it was the seat of government and administration and a great religious and educational centre as well.

The urban elites were drawn from these three sectors of activity: great merchant and financial dynasties, powerful legal and administrative figures, and major ecclesiastical personages associated with the bishopric, the abbeys and the university. Below these came the bulk of the permanent residents of the city, composed, naturally enough, of townsfolk, engaged in a multiplicity of activities as artisans, traders, workmen, domestic servants (see Cazelles 1972: 95–120). The wide range of trades and professions practised there in the thirteenth century is remarkably documented in Etienne Boileau's *Livre des mestiers* (see Lespinasse and Bonnardot 1879). The different trades frequently congregated together in particular streets – money-changers and goldsmiths on the Grand-Pont, weavers on the Ile-de-la-Cité, butchers close to the Châtelet, tanners close to the little stream of the Bièvre and so on (see Cazelles 1972: 91–2). Residential, commercial and productive activities took place in very close proximity. Pressure of space led to the vertical expansion of housing, with business premises on the ground floor and residential accommodation further up. On the whole 'ordinary Parisians' lived literally 'on top of each other' in a great confusion of social categories.

Des ruelles étroites, des impasses tortueuses, bordées de hautes maisons dont les toits se rapprochent, où le soleil ne pénètre pas, où la population s'entasse, juxtaposent toutes les conditions sociales, toutes les situations de fortune. (Ariès 1971: 121)

Geremek (1976: 79–110) describes the social topography of Paris on the basis of the 1297 *Taille*-roll. Though the rich were more likely to be found on a major thoroughfare, with the poor being more heavily concentrated in smaller back streets, there is no evidence of residential zoning by wealth.

Boussard (1976: 312–13) considers that by the end of the twelfth century the permanent central core of the population of Paris had been established:

On peut donc dire que pendant les dernières années du XIIe siècle et les cinquante premières du XIIIe siècle, la collectivité des habitants de Paris a commencé à prendre conscience d'elle-même.

However, the establishment of a core of permanent inhabitants did not act as a brake on further immigration, for the city's population appears to have doubled in size during the thirteenth century. At the bottom of society, there was an unknowable number of indigents and marginals, a floating population which had not yet established a permanent residence in the urban community. Indeed, Geremek (1976: 286) makes the point that 'la mobilité géographique de la population était . . . plus intense à Paris que dans les autres villes du Moyen Age'. To judge by what happened in the early modern period, immigrants would set up first of all 'in the *faubourgs* where rents were lower and the semi-rural conditions came as less of a shock' (see Jacquart 1996: 109). Often in-comers from different regions grouped themselves together in particular parts of the city (see Braudel 1986: I, 228–9). Prefiguring the urban geography of the sixteenth century, we find the preferred haunts of paupers and marginals to be close by the church of Saint Eustache on the Right Bank and around the Place Maubert on the Left. Eventually the more successful of them became integrated into the various trade-based groupings in the city. However, access to the trade-guilds was restricted severely by father–son transmission of the requisite skills, tools and premises, just as control of the city's economy remained in the hands of an oligarchy of burgesses centred on the corporation of the 'Marchands de l'Eau'.

Hohenberg and Lees (1985: 96) observe that

European cities had almost a dual structure: a permanent cadre of inhabitants and a floating group of immigrants, temporary residents and transients. Although native and permanent residents could be poor and newcomers wealthy, the former dominated the latter in every way: socially, economically, politically. And their control ensured the stability, sometimes the immobility of the city.

The social structure of this population was hierarchical and oligarchic, but the distinction between rich and poor in medieval Paris was probably a less meaningful one than that between long-standing and transient members of the population.

3.6   Summary

After centuries of stagnation where the population of Paris (like that of most western European towns) remained small, the twelfth century saw the city's development become both very rapid and very considerable. Population growth and urbanisation were general across western Europe at this time, but the extent to which they were carried through in medieval Paris was quite exceptional, with Paris emerging as a major centre of polarisation earlier than any of the other modern European metropolises. If the population estimates we have looked at can be relied upon, Paris assumed the size of twenty large towns of the period rolled into one. Demographic growth occurred principally as a result of in-migration of people from its densely populated hinterland, with some influx from further afield, and was accompanied by a dramatic increase in the functional complexity of the city. The resulting economic activity evidently raised the level of social interaction within the city beyond that between the city and its hinterland. These social and demographic developments were on such a scale that we may assume that they had significant consequences for the city's linguistic development.

4   The beginnings of Parisian French

The earliest phases of new languages are always the least well documented and Parisian French in the medieval period is no exception. Given the dearth of contemporary evidence, our attempts at historical reconstruction are fated to remain speculation. However, not all avenues of approach are blocked off. In this chapter, let us examine the set of language varieties present in Paris and the Paris region in modern times – standard French, colloquial Parisian speech and the hinterland dialects – with a view to discovering, by back-projection, how this particular configuration might have arisen historically. In Chapter 5 we will confront our findings with such evidence as is to be found in texts written in medieval Paris.

Urban dialects are commonly seen as modified versions of the standard language, and the uneducated speech of Paris is traditionally thought of as just such a corruption of standard French. Recent work by Milroy (1981) and Harris (1985), on the other hand, has revealed that, as a rule, urban dialects are not failed attempts to approximate to some high-prestige standard, but are modified forms of the dialects spoken in the surrounding countryside. Moreover, human concentrations undergoing rapid growth in the modern world have been shown to provide a prime locus for dialect-mixing and koinéisation. Perhaps something like this occurred in medieval Paris. Back-projection cannot explain the past with certainty, but it limits the range of plausible hypotheses we might wish to set up.

In this chapter let us see what we might infer about the early history of the speech of Paris by looking first at the rural dialects surviving in the Paris region into the twentieth century, and then at hypotheses developed to explain their relationship with the standard language and the urban vernacular which crystallised in the city.

4.1   The hinterland dialect

We have defined the medieval hinterland of Paris as the area located within a 70km radius of the city. Map 6 shows the relevant *départements*, the numbers indicating the various *points d'enquête* visited by the investigator, Edmond

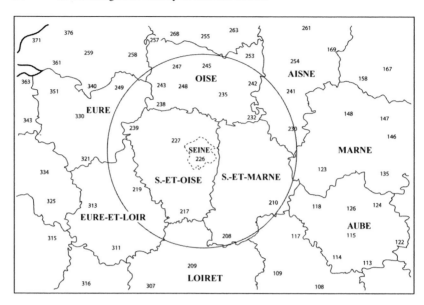

Map 6. Paris's hinterland and the *ALF*

Edmont, Jules Gilliéron's collaborator on the *Atlas linguistique de la France* project (1901–10). Among all the French dialects, the *patois* of this area are the most difficult to say anything about. They were almost completely obliterated during the course of the nineteenth and twentieth centuries and in the eyes of many historians of the language, their status is suspect. The name to be given to the Ile-de-France dialect, and indeed the dialect's very existence, are controversial. The issues go a good way beyond theories of dialect development and impinge upon deeply held beliefs concerning the nature and origins of the French standard language and the founding myths of the nation itself (the 'genèse d'une nation', as Fondet (1995: 189) puts it). Let us look briefly at the controversy surrounding the name, before considering the dialect itself.

4.1.1   The 'francien' question

During the twelfth and thirteenth centuries it was taken for granted that, like everywhere else, the Ile-de-France (i.e. *France*) had its own distinctive form of speech. Roger Bacon distinguished four dialectal zones within northern Gallo-Romance:

Nam et idiomata ejusdem linguae variantur apud diversos, sicut patet de lingua galli-cana, quae apud Gallicos et Picardos et Normannos et Burgundos et caeteros multiplici idiomate variatur. Et quod proprie et intelligentiliter dicitur in idiomate Picardorum horrescit apud Burgundos, immo apud Gallicos viciniores quanto magis igitur accidet hoc apud linguas diversas?[1] (*Opus Majus*, II, 80–1)

Alongside Bacon's Latin term *Gallicum*, the medieval French name used to refer to the speech of the Ile-de-France was *le françois* (see Bader 1969: 72–87, Walter 1988: 83 and Fondet 1980), but quite quickly this label was applied synecdochically to the French language as a whole (see Joseph 1987: 2). During the nineteenth century, Romance philologists called for a more precise labelling of language varieties, and in particular they strove to eliminate confusion between the name of the dialect of Ile-de-France (*le françois*) and that of the future standard language (*le français*). In Germany Suchier (1888: 586) proposed a distinction between *Francisch* and *Französisch*, and a little later in France Gaston Paris (1889: 475) produced a new term, *francien*, to replace the medieval *françois*. The formulation of sound-laws required an unbroken succession of 'pure' dialectal states between Latin and Modern French, and we can suppose that, in creating this term, G. Paris was seeking not only to achieve terminological clarity, but also to provide the nascent standard language with the 'proper' historical credentials, that is, with a 'pure' source-dialect (free from Germanic contamination) suitably located in the region of the capital. We note that Ferdinand Brunot was at pains to emphasise the 'purity' of this dialect when he declared that 'le francien ne doit pas être considéré comme un amalgame' (Brunot 1905: I, 325).

For much of the twentieth century the term *francien*, although shunned by dialectologists, was widely used in the standard manuals of the history of French (e.g. Pope 1952: 33; François 1959: 92; von Wartburg 1962: 90; Bec 1971: 6; Cohen 1987: 86; Rickard 1989: 41). Following Haugen's 1966 typology of the processes involved in standardisation, the dialect of the Ile-de-France (*le francien*) was 'selected' in the twelfth century, 'elaborated' in the late Middle Ages, 'codified' in the early modern period, and 'accepted' by the population of the nation at large in the nineteenth and twentieth centuries. In the 1980s, however, the term came in for severe criticism. Chaurand (1983: 91) considered the meaning of *francien* to be circular, pointing out that there exist no written texts attesting the nature of the dialect prior to the emergence of an embryonic standard language in the thirteenth century, for which *francien* is the supposed antecedent. He dismissed the medieval dialect of the Ile-de-France as a 'variété hybride et peu distincte, dont nous ne savons rien de sûr avant le XIIIe siècle'. Bergounioux (1989) went further, maintaining that a rural dialect requiring the label *francien* never existed in the Paris region, it having been

---

[1] 'For dialects of the same language vary between different speakers, as can be seen in the French language which varies in numerous dialects among the French, the Picards, the Normans, the Burgundians and others. What is correctly and intelligibly expressed in the Picard dialect is unpleasant to Burgundians and indeed to their closer neighbours in the Ile-de-France. How much more likely is this to happen between people speaking different languages?'

annihilated at birth by the linguistic influence of the city (though he declines to indicate how the speech of the city itself originated). As well as denying the existence of any traces of the dialect in medieval texts, Bergounioux rubbished the numerous references to rural speech in this area in the seventeenth and eighteenth centuries, and even denied the validity of modern attestations of the dialect. *Francien* is for him a referring expression with no referent, a politically motivated term designed by Gaston Paris solely to give historical legitimacy to the standard language then being vigorously promoted by the Third Republic.

Cerquiglini (1991: 118) develops this argument to bolster his thesis of written-based standardisation in French: for him the concept of *francien* is entirely dispensable, because the standard language, traditionally believed to derive from *francien*, is in fact descended from a composite written variety engineered consensually by a *coterie* of chancery scribes and literary authors who brought together features from several different dialects in the tenth or eleventh century. Having no need for a spoken base-dialect originating in the Paris region, he is led, like Bergounioux, to assert that Paris and the Ile-de-France did not have a dialect at all:

L'Ile-de-France ne se distinguait par aucun dialecte. Jusqu'aux portes, et sans doute dans les rues de la modeste bourgade parisienne, on devait parler picard, normand ou orléanais.

To describe the largest town in Christendom as a 'modeste bourgade' is odd, and, at the same time, undermines Bergounioux' claim that the rural dialect of the Ile-de-France had long been overwhelmed by the linguistic influence of the city. Even more awkward is Cerquiglini's suggestion that whereas other regions possess their own dialect, the Ile-de-France does not: to claim that any part of a speech community could be dialect-free is to give the word 'dialect' a sense which few dialectologists nowadays can recognise. This approach is suspiciously close to the one dictated by standard ideology which invariably portrays the standard language as a non-localised norm, unattached to a particular region without being a hybrid, and urbane without being urban (see Mugglestone 1995: 26–34).

What all of these writers have in mind when they use the term 'dialect' is the 'pure dialect' of traditional dialectology: rustic, homogeneous, spatially discrete. Only those language varieties possessing these characteristics are to be considered true 'dialects'. Since the speech of the Ile-de-France cannot be shown to have possessed them, it was not a dialect. *Ergo, francien* did not exist. Applying this notion of 'dialect' would, of course, have raised similar difficulties in Picardy, Normandy and Northumberland to those encountered in the Ile-de-France. If the Paris region had a population in the twelfth century – and we have seen that it was one of the most densely populated areas of

France – it necessarily had a dialect. In all probability this dialect was not homogeneous and merged imperceptibly into the dialects of the surrounding regions, but so did all the other dialects of north Gallo-Romance. Whether or not we call it *francien* is a minor issue. To avoid provocation we will refer to it as 'the hinterland dialect of Paris', abbreviated to 'HDP'.

The claims made by opponents of the *francien* hypothesis raise as many problems as they solve, but, at the same time, we need to acknowledge that they contribute important elements to the debate. They highlight in particular: (a) that the empirical basis on which the *francien* dialect is portrayed in the standard manuals is not solid; and (b) that the French standard language is something of a composite, containing a significant number of phonological and morphological elements which are not indigenous to the Ile-de-France. These two issues are hard to disentangle, and raise the question of the extent to which we can reconstruct the dialectal state of northern France in the Middle Ages (see Dees 1988, 1989).

4.1.2   Reconstructing francien

As Chaurand has shown, reconstructing HDP in the medieval period in a way that avoids circularity is exceptionally difficult. In the manuals of Old French, HDP is rarely described empirically. It is simply assumed to have existed as the forerunner (albeit hypothetical) of the standard language, the unmarked dialect against which all the others are defined, the dialect whose essential property was to possess none of the regional characteristics possessed by the other Old French dialects. Apart from toponymic evidence, we have no written documents which unambiguously attest local speech-forms before the thirteenth century. Moreover, the *patois*, which in other parts of France still stand as the modern versions of the medieval dialects, have been effectively eradicated in the Paris region during the industrial period (nineteenth to twentieth centuries). The symbiotic relationship between the city and its hinterland has ensured that, since medieval times, HDP has been much more exposed to the influence of the city and the standard language than dialects situated in areas more remote from the metropolis (see Dauzat 1922: 53 and 139, map VI). However, the data-situation with regard to HDP is not quite as hopeless as all this might suggest (see Simoni-Aurembou 1999).

In terms of medieval sources the Ile-de-France is no less well supplied with vernacular (i.e. non-Latin) archival documents than other parts of north Gallo-Romance. Many of these were admirably described well over a century ago (see Matzke 1880, 1881). Furthermore, documents from the early modern period are a good deal more plentiful here than they are elsewhere (see Simoni-Aurembou 1973b). Besides, there is another approach to the historical reconstruction of languages which can be taken. William Labov (1994: 27) points out that:

'The close examination of the present shows that much of the past is still with us. The study of history benefits from the continuity of the past as well as from analogies with the present.' This principle has to be applied judiciously, given the problem of continuity and the fact that we have no sure way of distinguishing features in the modern world which have been there for a long time from those which have come about only recently. However, traces of areal configurations of earlier periods may still be visible in the linguistic atlases which French dialectologists have put together with such expertise in the twentieth century. By careful use of modern cartographic evidence and the information available in medieval and early modern sources, like Dees's *Atlas des formes et constructions des chartes françaises du 13ᵉ siècle* (1980), it may be possible for us to know something about the evolution of the speech of the Ile-de-France and about its historical relationship with the standard language (see Picoche and Marchello-Nizia 1994: 22).

If we look at the distribution of spatial variables in the traditional *patois* of north Gallo-Romance recorded in Gilliéron and Edmont's monumental *Atlas Linguistique de la France* (1901–10) (abbreviated to *ALF*), we can learn a good deal about past states of the language. The difficulties raised by the concept of isogloss in a situation of dialect continuum are well known (see Chambers and Trudgill 1998: 89–103), but, provided we regard isoglosses solely as abstractions, they provide necessary descriptive tools. The drawing of dialect-boundaries, on the other hand, is more problematic, for there is no scientific way of deciding which isoglosses are more basic than others. In what follows we will not attempt to define the HDP on linguistic grounds. We will simply make broad observations about the distribution of certain isoglosses in the *ALF* in a linguistic zone radiating approximately 100km from Paris. The selection of these particular isoglosses is based ultimately on the work of Fondet (1995), who seems to have made her selection principally on the basis of the number of words affected by them.

What do we find? Firstly, there exist certain features, affecting a large number of words, which are common to the whole area, and which distinguish the speech of this area from that of dialects located to the north, south, east or west respectively; secondly, there exist certain other features which intrude into the area from outside, and which break up the apparent homogeneity of HDP.

To begin with, let us examine the isoglosses visible in the *ALF* which, taken together, form a sort of box around the Paris region. Here we will consider the distribution of four important features which are shared by all the varieties within the box and which distinguish these varieties from those outside.

(A) Along the **northern** edge of the region we find the northern limit of palatalisation of [ka] (see Map 7, *ALF* 250, *chat*). Other examples: *champ* (*ALF* 225), *charrue* (*ALF* 246), *charrier* (*ALF* 245), *fourche* (*ALF* 603), *mouche* (*ALF* 876).

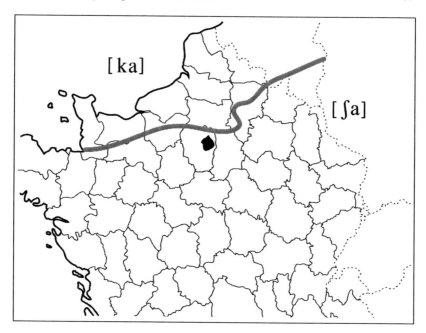

Map 7. *ALF* 250, *chat*

In Picardy and in the northern part of Normandy Latin [ka] remains un-palatalised, whereas in the rest of the *langue d'oil* it palatalises > [ʃa /ʃe /tʃə]. The palatalisation of Latin [ga] > [ʒa] follows a parallel trajectory (see *ALF javelle, gerbe, jardin*), as does that of the non-palatalisation of the group [ke- / ki-]: see *ALF* 704, *ici*. Other examples are to be found in: *ciboule* (*ALF* 284), *cendre* (*ALF* 210), *racine* (*ALF* 1126), *ronce* (*ALF* 1163). In Picardy and in the northern part of Normandy Latin [ke/i] evolves to the alveo-palatal [ʃi /ʃe], whereas in the rest of the *langue d'oil* it evolves to the alveolar [si/se]. See Loriot 1984.

(B) Along the **western** edge of the region we can see the western limit of differentiation of [o] > [ow] > [ew] > [œ] (see Map 8, *ALF* 151, *bouche*). For other examples, see *noeud* (*ALF* 915) and Gauthier 1995: 31. By the twelfth century Latin [o] in stressed open syllables had diphthongised > [ow] across the whole of the *langue d'oil*. Whereas in the west the diphthong subsequently levelled > [u], further east it differentiated to [ew], subsequently levelling > [œ]. From the sixteenth century onwards the [œ] pronunciation spread from Paris into the western part of France (see Wüest 1979b: 204–7; Pfister 1993: 30–1).

(C) Along the **eastern** edge we find the eastern limit of epenthetic consonants in the group [n'r] (see Map 9, *ALF* 1359, *vendredi*). Other examples are to be

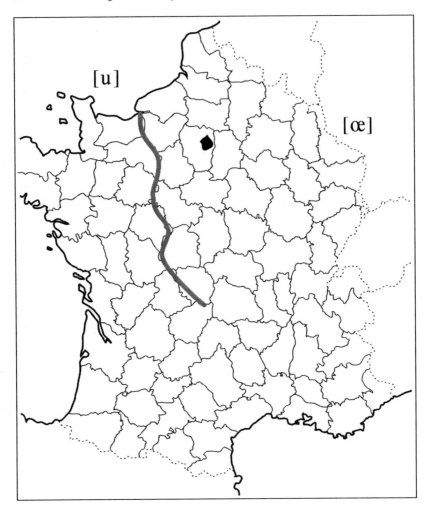

Map 8. *ALF* 151, *bouche*

found in: *ensemble* (*ALF* 464), *gendre* (*ALF* 634), *moudre* (*ALF* 879), *poudre* (*ALF* 1069), *ressemble* (*ALF* 1153), *viendraient* (*ALF* 1366). See also Monjour 1989: 137, 138, 140, 142 and Wüest 1979b: 319. Whereas in the west and centre a glide-consonant is inserted into the groups [-nr-], [-ml-], and [-lr-], none is inserted in the north and east (see Wüest 1979b: 315–20; Wüest 1985: 245–6; Dees 1980: 266; Pfister 1993: 24–6; Fondet 1995: 193).

(**D**) Along the **southern** edge we have to travel a long way south to find the Occitan isoglossses like the raising of Latin [a] in stressed open syllables

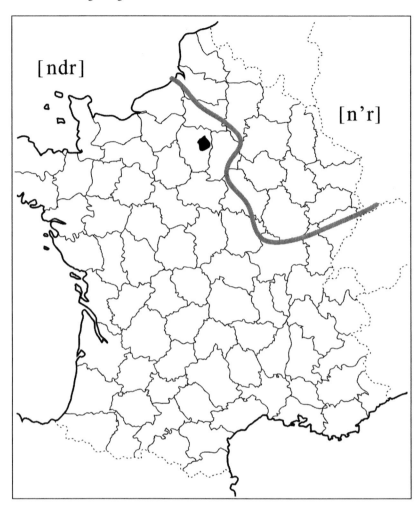

Map 9. *ALF* 1359, *vendredi*

to [e] (see Map 10, *ALF* 992, *pelle*). Other examples are to be found in: *aile* (*ALF* 18), *échelle* (*ALF* 436), *noel* (*ALF* 914), *poteau* (*ALF* 1066), *sel* (*ALF* 1213). The raising of stressed [a] > [e] differentiates the north Gallo-Romance dialects from those of the south (see Wüest 1979b: 170). However, in the east of the *langue d'oil* [a] in this environment diphthongises to [aj] (see Pfister 1993: 35–6), and in the west [a] survives before [l].

If we superimpose these four isoglosses, we produce a box around the Paris region which is of similar shape to Bec's zone IV shown on Map 11. It is not

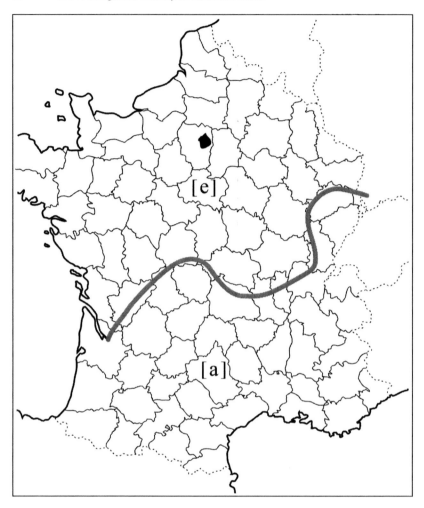

Map 10. *ALF* 992, *pelle*

intended that these four isoglosses be seen as solid dialect boundaries – it is not possible to find significant bundles of other isoglosses which coincide with the ones visible on these maps. This is not odd – it is entirely what we would expect in the dialect continuum that is north Gallo-Romance. The northern part of the box shades into Picard, the western into Norman, the eastern into Champenois. Moreover, we must recognise that the present locations of the sides of the box are almost certainly not coextensive with their locations in earlier centuries. It is most probable that the demographic weight of Paris over the centuries has

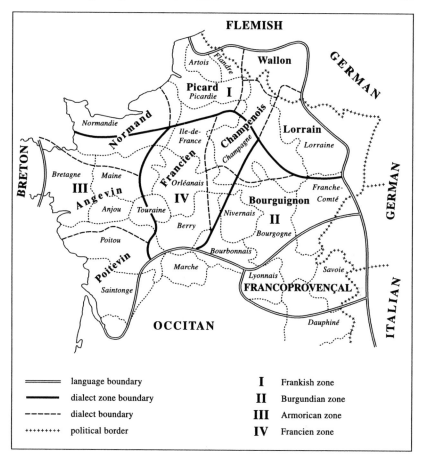

Map 11. The dialect areas of medieval French (adapted from Bec 1971: I Carte no. 1, p. 645)

been such as to have pushed these isoglosses outwards towards the periphery. However, what we can say is, firstly, that the dialects inside the box normally possess these particular features in common, and more importantly, that these features are also present in what has become the standard language.

Despite the presence of these important common features, the dialect space within the box is not homogeneous: with a number of other spatial variables we find a configuration in which an external form intrudes into the middle (the Paris region), to form a sort of bulge. We will note that these bulge features too are also present in the standard language. What is particularly interesting here is the direction of movement implicit in the isogloss configurations. We will consider five key variables:

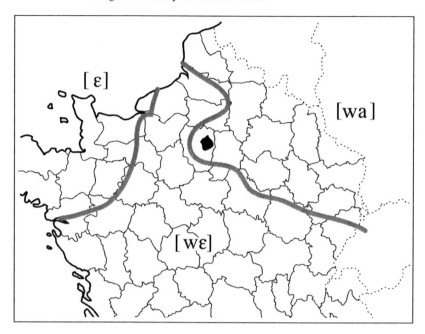

Map 12. *ALF* 1047, *poire*

(i) **[wa]** ∼ **[wɛ]** (Map 12, *ALF* 1047, *poire*). Other examples: *soir* (*ALF* 1238), *droit* (*ALF* 428), *endroit* (*ALF* 460), *froid* (*ALF* 612). See also Wüest 1979b: 203; Monjour 1989. Here we see a concentration of [wa]-forms in the east and a westward-moving bulge in the Paris area. This is one of the *langue d'oil* phonological variables which have been most subject to variation and change. By the twelfth century Vulgar Latin [e] in stressed open syllables had diphthongised to [ej] across the whole of north Gallo-Romance, merging with the diphthong resulting from stressed [e] + palatal. Whereas in the west the diphthong subsequently levelled to [e] (in some areas to [a]), in the centre and east it differentiated to [oi] and [we] (see Haudricourt 1948: 212) and in some places to [wa] (see Wüest 1979b: 198–204, 379; Pfister 1993: 29–30).

(ii) **[jo]** ∼ **[o]** (Map 13, *ALF* 812, *manteau*). Other examples are to be found in: *seau* (*ALF* 1208), *eau* (*ALF* 432). Here we see a strong concentration of [o]-forms in the east and a westward-moving bulge in the Paris area. In Old French, vocalisation of [l] before final [s] in the group -*els* (< Latin -*ellos*) led to the insertion of a glide [a] and the formation of a triphthong [eaw]. The *ALF* data show that this triphthong evolved differently in different dialects. Most of the north Gallo-Romance dialects display the differentiated form [jo],

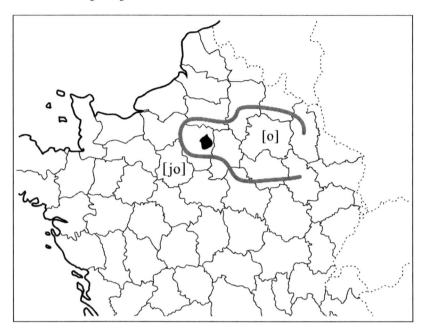

Map 13. *ALF* 812, *manteau*

resulting from a consonantalisation of the first element [e] > [j] and a levelling of the second two elements > [o]. In the Paris region and in a small area in the east of the country we find a simple monophthong [o], believed to have developed without differentiation from Old French [eaw] > [əo] > [o] (see Pope 1952: 200–1). The historical relationship between the two variants in Parisian speech has not been fully elucidated. Dauzat (1927: 40) considers the undifferentiated [o] < [əo] in Parisian speech to have been the form inherited from Latin, regarding the undifferentiated [jo] variant as a rustic form which never penetrated the capital to any significant extent. Fouché (1952: 336) sees [o] < [əo] as a variant created by upper-class Parisians in order to differentiate themselves from lower-class speakers. Wüest (1985: 243) endorses this view, pointing to the widespread use of the spelling 'iau' in thirteenth-century Parisian texts and concluding that 'la différence entre *eau* et *iau* ne pouvait donc être dialectale; elle devait être sociolectale'. The origin of the undifferentiated variant ([o] < [əo] < [eaw]) is uncertain. It is possible that it was an endogenous innovation in upper-class Parisian speech. However, the concentration of monophthongal forms in dialects spoken to the east of Paris (and their presence in western dialects too) makes one suspect that an exogenous origin is in fact more plausible.

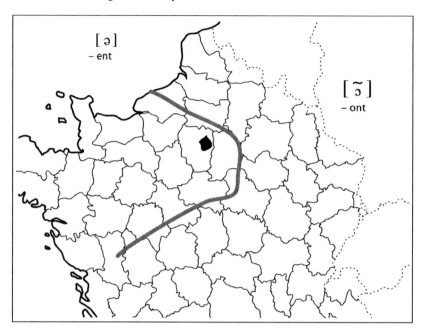

Map 14. *ALF* 1064, endings of the 6th person, present tense

(iii) *-ent ∼ -ont/-ant* (6th person present indicative) (see Map 14, *ALF* 1064). Other examples are to be found in *ALF* maps 311, 574, 679. Here we see a strong concentration of *-ent* forms in the west and an eastward-moving bulge in the Paris area. The traditional dialects in north Gallo-Romance are divided in their treatment of the ending of the 6th person: we find variants where stress falls on the ending (those in *-ont, -ant*) and others, notably in the west, where the ending is unstressed (those in *-ent*) (see Wüest 1985: 234–5). Fouché (1967: 194–5) has nothing to say about the history of 6th person endings in *-ent/-ont*. The *-ent* ending seems to have diffused rapidly across the written language. Pope (1952: 385), on the other hand, finds occasional examples of *-ont, -ant* and a third variant *-ient* in medieval manuscripts from outside the western and central areas. Fondet (1980: 70–2) notes the presence of *-ont* in Ile-de-France speech in the sixteenth century, observing: 'au XVIᵉ siècle la finale dialectale *-ont* est bien attestée; mais l'extension considérable de ce trait interdit d'y voir un phénomène récent'.

(iv) *-ions ∼ -iens* (4th person present subjunctive, imperfect indicative) (see Map 15, *ALF* 512, *étions*). Other examples are to be found in *ALF* maps 100, 515. Here we see a strong concentration of *-ions* forms in the west and an eastward-moving bulge in the Paris area. Fouché (1967: 239, 242–3) sees the *-iens/-eins* ending as having been general across the northern Gallo-Romance zone at the time of 'le français le plus ancien'. He finds the earliest attestations

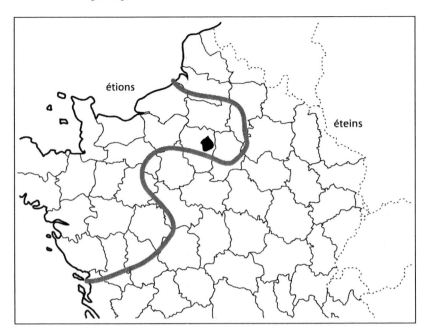

Map 15. *ALF* 512, endings of the 4th person, imperfect tense

of endings containing a back-rounded vowel (*-ium*) in the *Song of Roland*. Pope (1952: 347) observes: 'In the western region *-iiens* was replaced by *-iuns* (*-ium* etc.) in the twelfth century . . . and in the thirteenth century these forms become general in the central region.' See also Fondet 1995: 195.

(v) *-aient* ~ *-aint* (6th person imperfect indicative) (Map 16, *ALF* 10). Other examples are to be found in *ALF* maps 401, 513, 1366. Fondet (1995: 195) writes of 'une vaste partie du domaine d'oil' wherein 'un imparfait de type *-ebam*, etc., est resté au stade [ei], avec nasalisation à la troisième personne du pluriel'. Fouché (1967: 241) attributes the forms in *-aint* specifically to the Orléanais and considers them to be 'très anciennes, antérieures à la nasalisation de la diphtongue *ei* et refaites sur la 3e pers. sing. *-eit*'. Pope (1952: 496) attributes these forms to the eastern region. Wüest (1985: 234) is struck by the 'répartition assez bizarre de ces formes'. Despite the evident disarray of our predecessors, Map 16 shows a strong concentration of *-aient* forms in the west and an eastward-moving bulge in the Paris area.

The particular bulge-like configuration common to each of these five isoglosses in the *ALF* has perhaps something important to say about the linguistic history of the region. It suggests that in each case one of the variants originated outside the HDP box, and that at some point it took root in Paris, from where it subsequently diffused out into a city's immediate hinterland, to form a bulge visible on the modern dialect maps. The outward diffusion of these 'bulge'

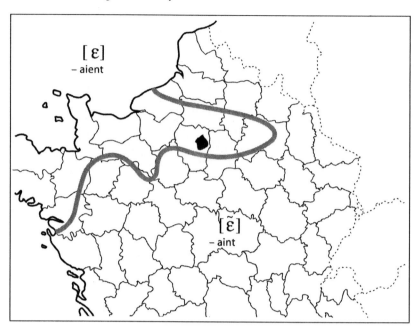

Map 16. *ALF* 10, endings of the 6th person, imperfect tense

forms from Paris into the dialects of the immediate hinterland, from which the traditional features have now been almost completely eliminated, took a long time to be completed. If we look at the more fine-grained regional linguistic atlases published from the 1960s (*ALIFO*, see Simoni-Aurembou 1973a; *ALN*, see Brasseur 1980; and *ALCB*, see Bourcelot 1966), we frequently come across isolated relic forms within the area which clearly pre-date the outward diffusion of urban speech-forms. Moreover, we have a number of written documents from the seventeenth to nineteenth centuries which preserve evidence about the speech of the immediate hinterland of Paris before the obliteration of traditional rural speech in this area in the twentieth century:

> Passy (1891): 'Les villages de la vallée du ru de Gally, petit affluent de la Maudre, ont conservé jusqu'à ce jour un parler assez différent du parisien et du français d'école' (Sainte Jamme, Yvelines, west of Saint Germain en Laye)
>
> Agnel (1855): 'J'étais frappé de ces différences entre la prononciation de notre langue du XIXe siècle, exactement parlée, et la prononciation du langage rustique' ('Département de Seine-et-Oise')
>
> *Lettres de Montmartre* (1750): Montmartre (Seine-Saint-Denis)
>
> *Sarcelades* (1730): Sarcelles (Val d'Oise)

Agréables Conférences (1649): Saint Ouen and Montmorency (Val d'Oise)

What do they have to say about the features forming the 'Paris bulge'?

(i) [wa] ∼ [wɛ], e.g. *poire, droit, froid*

Passy (1891: 16): 'Ordinairement on a *wé* ou *wè*: *mwé* ou *mw*e "moi", *bwét* "boîte", *swéf* "soif", *frwésé* "froisser". . .'

Agnel (1855: 15–16): 'Dans la prononciation rustique la syllabe *oi* se change en *oué*. Par exemple, on dit *la loué, la souéf, le pouél* . . .'

Lettres de Montmartre (1750): contains numerous variants like *dret, dait, voar*

Sarcelades (1730): no examples

Agréables Conférences (1649): contains numerous forms like *touay, foa, bourgeas*

(ii) [jo] ∼ [o], e.g. *manteau, seau, eau*

Passy (1891: 16): 'Le groupe graphique *-eau* est ordinairement représenté par *ó* et non pas par *yó* comme on aurait pu l'attendre. Cependant on dit toujours *é syó* "un seau".'

Agnel (1855: 13): 'Dans le langage rustique, la syllabe finale *eau* se prononce *iau*. Tel est le principe général. Toutefois cette prononciation tombe de jour en jour en désuétude dans les environs de Paris et n'est conservée que dans quelques mots comme *çiau, musiau, biau* pour *seau, museau, beau*. Mais lorsque l'on atteint les arrondissements d'Etampes, de Pontoise et de Mantes ou les départements de l'Oise et de Seine-et-Marne, cette prononciation de la syllabe *iau*, dans les mots finissant en *eau*, reparaît en entier et s'emploie généralement.'

Lettres de Montmartre (1750): contains numerous forms like *biaux, chapiaux*

Sarcelades (1730): contains numerous forms like *troupiau, chapiau*

Agréables Conférences (1649): contains numerous forms like *gastiau, drappiau*

(iii) *-ent* ∼ *-ont* 6th person present indicative stressed on the ending

Passy (1891): no examples

Agnel (1855): no examples

Lettres de Montmartre (1750): contains numerous variants like *changiant, voyaint*

Sarcelades (1730): contains numerous forms like *appellont, chantont*

Agréables Conférences (1649): contains numerous variants like *bouton, scavan*

(iv) *-ions* ∼ *-iens* 4th person imperfect indicative, present subjunctive

Passy (1891): no examples

Agnel (1855): *j'avions* or *javiens* 54, *j'étions* or *j'étiens* 60

Lettres de Montmartre (1750): no examples

Sarcelades (1730): no examples

Agréables Conférences (1649): contains numerous forms like *j'alien, je fezien*

(v) -*aient* ∼ -*aint* 6th person imperfect indicative

Passy (1891: 10): *ín kúprè pá sa* (-*ils ne couperaient pas ça*)

Agnel (1855): *ils avaient* or *ils avient* 54, *il étiont* or *il étient* 61

Lettres de Montmartre (1750): contains numerous forms like *aviaint, etaint*

Sarcelades (1730): no examples

Agréables Conférences (1649): contains numerous forms like *laissient, attendien*

We have plenty of evidence then of relic-forms in the rural speech of the area around Paris which pre-date the outward expansion of standard language features.

In the light of this, the extreme scepticism expressed by certain writers concerning what can be known about HDP is perhaps exaggerated. We cannot reconstruct the medieval form of this dialect in any substantial way, but the modern cartographic evidence and the witness provided by early observers of dialectal speech in the Paris region make it possible to discern the outlines of some parts of its phonology and morphology, at least in the early modern period. How much further back we are entitled to project this picture is of course debatable. However, numerous dialectological studies (see, for instance, Lepelley 2001) and studies seeking to localise forms found in medieval French texts (see, for example, Chauveau 1989) attest the conservative nature of the traditional rural dialects, and the slow-moving nature of isoglosses of the type being discussed here. This situation is clearly manifested in many of the isoglosses visible in Dees's *Atlas* (1980).\

As well as telling us something about the broad outlines of HDP, the body of evidence which we have just considered has important implications for the development of the speech of Paris. It tells us two things:

(1) that the speech of the city is grounded in HDP (variants (A) – (D)). These occur both in the urban dialect and in HDP.

(2) that it contains significant elements introduced from outside (variants (i) – (v)). Important bits of verb-morphology have been imported from the west, and important bits of phonology from the east.

In other words, the city has been the locus of dialect-mixing, making its speech a 'koiné' of some sort.

We must now ask how and when this mixture came about. This will be a delicate task, for the particular combination of features we have just attributed to the speech of Paris is also present nowadays in the French standard language (see Fondet 1995). Does the speech of Paris represent a modified ('corrupt') form of a standard koiné generated elsewhere, or did the standard language itself emerge out of a spoken koiné which developed spontaneously in the speech of Paris?

4.2   Koinéisation, the standard language and Parisian speech

If Parisian French is a sort of koiné, as defined in §2.3.2 above, how could this mixture have come about? Two possibilities present themselves. The standard language could have emerged first, as a written koiné engineered elsewhere and subsequently adopted by Parisian speech, or it could represent an elaborated version of a spoken koiné which developed spontaneously in the speech of Paris. We can label these alternatives the Written Koiné Hypothesis and the Spoken Koiné Hypothesis respectively. Choice between them will not be easy, for it depends on the way we interpret the evidence of medieval writing systems.

4.2.1   The Written Koiné Hypothesis

This hypothesis supposes that the source of the French standard language is to be found in a written koiné elaborated at a very early date. It has its roots in the 'Skriptatheorie' elaborated by C.-T. Gossen in the 1960s to account for the grapheme/phoneme relationship in the Old French writing system (see Gossen 1962, 1967), a problem which has been a central concern of French philologists and linguists throughout the twentieth century (see Wacker 1916; Robson 1955). Although suppression of variation is a good deal easier in writing than in speech, consistency of spelling in the thirteenth century came nowhere near that of Modern French: any one text normally contained a proportion of features 'belonging' to regions different from the one in which it was composed. This is particularly the case with literary texts where poets commonly 'borrowed' forms from other dialects for purposes of rhyme and metre or other literary effect, and where later scribes modernised, usually unsystematically, the spelling of earlier manuscripts to comply with contemporary fashions. Moreover, literary texts, unlike most administrative documents, were perambulatory (see Poerck 1963: 2), so, in the course of their 'life', they commonly acquired layers of linguistic features from regions other than their place of composition. However, even static texts (charters and administrative documents which start to proliferate in the middle of the thirteenth century) contain a considerable mixture of forms (see Monfrin 1968). How is this variability to be explained?

Answers have gravitated between two extreme positions: on the one side Old French spelling has been seen as a basically graphemic/phonemic system, where the primary units are letters representing individual sound segments in a quite direct way, and on the other side it has been seen as a basically logographic system, where the primary units are sets of characters representing whole words and having only tenuous links with pronunciation. A century ago attitudes towards Old French spelling were dominated by a rather Romantic view of the Middle Ages which saw the period as one of naïvety and spontaneity: as a new vernacular (i.e. non-Latin) writing system emerged in the tenth and eleventh centuries, scribes were thought to have been naturally drawn towards the simplest and most transparent one (the graphemic/ phonemic system). Medieval writing systems were believed to mirror individual sound segments in a simple, direct way. Variation within the same manuscript was caused by interference from a neighbouring dialect, the author or scribe being presumed to have lived near some dialect-boundary, or to have moved between dialectal areas. As time went on, so the Romantic thesis had it, medieval civilisation gradually lost its freshness, and, in consequence, towards the end of the Middle Ages, vernacular (i.e. non-Latin) spelling, like medieval art in general, became ever more conventionalised and logographic.

The first quarter of the twentieth century saw a sea-change in attitudes towards medieval culture: the Middle Ages ceased to be viewed as 'natural' and 'spontaneous' and were considered instead to be governed by a complex set of implicit norms and conventions. The nineteenth-century model persisted for many decades, but eventually, no doubt under the influence of Saussure's view that 'langue et écriture sont deux systèmes de signes distincts' (1971: 45), Old French spelling came to be seen as a closed system operating according to its own internal, visual laws, operating more or less independently of speech. While some space was left for the graphemic/phonemic model in the writing systems of the earliest French texts (pre-eleventh century), spellings used in later texts were seen as increasingly arbitrary and opaque, governed not by local pronunciation but by tacit visual conventions developed by and for a small scribal fraternity in a restricted number of scriptoria. In the process, medieval spelling appeared much less variable than had previously been thought. In the *langue d'oil* area at least, all texts were believed to conform implicitly to a supra-regional norm, which admitted only a restricted set of regionalisms. This norm was not based on any real-life spoken dialect, but existed purely as a 'scripta', for the eye only. Nineteenth-century positivism was replaced by a 'post-modern' scepticism of the referential value of written data. The logic of this position leads the linguistic historian to more or less abandon the use of spellings in reconstructing the medieval spoken language, severely limiting the contribution he can make to the problem of sound change.

This line of approach was opened up by Wacker (1916), developed by Remacle (1948) and hardened by Gossen (1967) into the 'Skriptatheorie'. It still retains wide support (see for example Eloy 1997: 53–8). It has come to be widely believed that a mixed, written standard emerged in northern France independently of local variations in speech, at some time before the twelfth century. Delbouille (1970) suggested that such a variety developed as early as the ninth century, prior, in the author's eyes, to the diversification of the *langue d'oil* dialects. Hilty (1973) attached this supra-regional norm to the speech of Paris in the eighth century. Cerquiglini (1991) maintains that a conventional written koiné was elaborated by an 'enlightened' group of scribes and literary authors (see above, §1.1.2) without reference to any spoken dialectal base as early as the Strasbourg Oaths (AD 842):

C'est grâce à l'existence d'une société cléricale, guidée par une 'lumière de raison', animée par les *litterati* désirant illustrer un bel usage littéraire de l'idiome roman, que dès les premiers textes est fondé et pratiqué un 'illustre françois'. (Cerquiglini 1991: 120)

Following in the steps of Balibar (1985), he sees at work here a long-term project devised in Carolingian times to bring about the linguistic and political unity of the country:

Une langue française transcendant la diversité des parlures, inscrite dans le projet d'une forme commune échappant pour des raisons politiques ou esthétiques, à l'échange local et quotidien. (Cerquiglini 1991: 124)

In the Written Koiné Hypothesis selected spelling and morphological variants were brought together from different *langue d'oil* dialects, to form a mixed written standard specially designed during the ninth and tenth centuries for the inter-regional diffusion of literary texts and even official documents. This written koiné was allegedly adopted as a norm by the royal chancery and used, with a certain degree of latitude, across northern France in twelfth-century literature. The embryonic standard, having been established in writing at an early date, subsequently provided the basis for standardisation in the spoken language too. Although it began life purely as a norm for writing, it was eventually handed on to the royal court as the norm for speech, to be passed down subsequently to those parts of the unlettered populace who were anxious to better themselves socially and culturally:

Ce fut, en France, la langue littéraire de la *scripta*, qui, sans être artificielle, s'élabora dans des conditions sociologiques différentes de celle des idiomes populaires. A partir du XIIIᵉ siècle, le parler urbain, stratifié, certes, mais proche de celui de la classe aisée, n'a cessé de s'opposer au parler rural jusqu'à la Révolution. (Fondet 1995: 201)

According to this view, the koiné found in Old French texts did not mirror the spoken language, but instead it dictated it (initially for the educated elite), in a way that anticipated the teaching of standard French via the *dictée* at the end of the nineteenth century. When it subsequently came into the hands (or mouths) of the ignorant Parisian populace, this cultivated variety was corrupted to give rise to an urban vernacular referred to prescriptively as *le français populaire*. The Hypothesis can be summed up as in the diagram.

Written koiné

↓

Written standard

↓

Spoken standard

↓

Paris vernacular speech

How tenable is this model? The process of graphisation is an indispensable part of standardisation (see Joseph 1987: 32–42), and indeed, standardisation of other languages (for instance German and Italian) appears to have been based initially on a written variety. When applied to medieval French, however, the Written Koiné Hypothesis runs up against serious difficulties: firstly the 'data and chronology problem', secondly the 'implementation problem'. Let us take them in that order.

The dialect-mixing visible in early French texts has led many scholars to suppose that the conventions of a supra-dialectal writing system had become established by the beginning of the twelfth century. However, much of this mixing can be attributed to the perambulatory nature of literary manuscripts, and while it may have occurred on an individual, *ad hoc* basis, the textual evidence to support the existence of a *stable* written koiné in use across the country is sparse. The number of French texts surviving in manuscripts written before 1200 is extremely small, dropping to zero in the case of administrative documents (see Pfister 1993). The number of French manuscripts surviving from before 1100 is even smaller, and quite insufficient to support the idea that a stabilised supra-regional written koiné was in existence before that time. It is difficult, moreover, to find any institutional framework, like a royal chancery, which might have made this development possible. The royal administration in Paris, for instance, did not start using French until well into the thirteenth century (see Giry 1894: 464–72). Serge Lusignan has recently written: 'le français du roi s'est construit au XIVe siècle à la chancellerie et à la cour de Charles V, dans un rapport d'échange avec le latin' (personal communication).

In modern times 'standard French' denotes a form of language – that is, of its phonology, morphology, syntax and lexis – which is superordinate to geographically variant forms, and which is realised in both spoken and written modes, and in the latter by a consistent orthography. As a pre-standardised language, Old French differs sharply from this, firstly in that standardisation of speech belongs to a much later period (the sixteenth and seventeenth centuries), and secondly in that even in the fourteenth century standardisation of writing was only at an incipient stage, with consistency in orthography nowhere approaching that of modern standard French. For a discussion of a similar situation in Middle English, see Burnley (1989: 23–4). Dees's examination of the variability present in medieval French written documents demonstrates that clear progress towards standardisation of the French writing system was not achieved before the fifteenth century, the emergence of standard norms for the spoken language took a good deal longer. His patient quantitative work, on large numbers of dated and located administrative documents from the thirteenth century, leads to the conclusion that there existed no stable supra-regional norm in the written language before the fourteenth century:

La notion de koiné écrite, ainsi que la notion corrolaire de scripta régionale, n'ont aucune adéquation observationnelle pour la période antérieure à 1300. (Dees 1985: 113)

The diffusion of a standard orthography across the country on the basis of chancery style was in large measure achieved by the end of the fifteenth century, but there is insufficient evidence to allow us to push this date further back.

The second difficulty raised by the Written Koiné Hypothesis is the 'implementation problem' (see above, §1.2.2). Any attribution to tenth and eleventh-century monastic scribes of the long-term uniformising motives characteristic of modern language-planners is wildly anachronistic, and should not detain us further. The idea that a partially standardised written language profoundly modified the speech of a sizeable part of the Paris population during the Middle Ages is only slightly easier to accept. While it is true that writing need not remain a mere record, and can come to embody a code of its own, capable of influencing the community of speech (see Haugen 1966: 163), it is doubtful whether, in the thirteenth century, the prestige of French written forms, or even familiarity with them, was sufficiently high to allow this to happen on a large scale, even among the elites.

The medieval 'scripta' naturally influenced the subsequent development of the norms of the written language, but their influence on spoken norms in a period when levels of literacy were low can only have been very small. It may well be that an acrolectal variety was being cultivated in the entourage of the royal court as early as the twelfth century, setting the *'courtois'* apart from non-noble elements in society (see Delbouille 1962; Muscatine 1981). It is more or less certain that this exerted a powerful influence on the forms used by the literary entertainers of the day. The much-quoted passage from Conon de Béthune, in which the poet apologises for showing traces of a dialect not approved of by the royal circle, is clear testimony to this fairly obvious fact:

> La Roine n'a pas fait ke cortoise
> Ki me reprist. Ele et ses fueis li Rois;
> Encoir ne soit ma parole franchoise,
> Si la puet on bien comprendre en franchois
> Ne chil ne sont bien apris ne cortois
> S'il m'ont repris se j'ai dit mos d'Artois,
> Car je ne fui pas norris a Pontoise.[2]
>
> (see Lodge 1993: 99)

By the same token, it is most doubtful that strong influence was exerted in the opposite direction, that is, that members of the royal court were moved to imitate a set of linguistic forms presented to them by passing *jongleurs*.

The fact remains, nevertheless, that both the standard language and the colloquial speech of Paris have long embodied the specific mixture of dialect forms we considered earlier in this chapter. It is unlikely, on the grounds both of the chronology of the textual evidence and of the mode of implementation, that a written standard came first, to be subsequently extended to speech. On the other hand, the cartographical data we examined in §4.1.2 make it look as though developments could have occurred the other way round: that dialect-mixing may well have happened first in the everyday speech of Paris, and that the 'new' spoken variety resulting from this provided the basis for subsequent elaboration and standardisation.

4.2.2   The Spoken Koiné Hypothesis

The Spoken Koiné Hypothesis shares with Chaurand and others the notion that the norms of the standard language were not derived directly from the *francien* dialect as conceived of by G. Paris, F. Brunot *et al*. However, it diverges from current orthodoxy in suggesting that the mixed variety (which forms the basis of the standard language) crystallised initially in the innumerable everyday interactions of ordinary speakers and did not spring fully armed from the mind of a group of literary authors and early medieval language-planners. The earliest sources of standardisation in French are to be found not in a composite written variety elaborated at a very early date by a *coterie* of scribes, but in a dialect-mixture which developed spontaneously through real-life interactions between speakers. How, when and where could such a koinéisation have occurred?

Historians of French commonly allude to an *ancien français commun*, a lowest common denominator dialect which speakers of Old French allegedly switched into for purposes of inter-dialectal communication, and which some

---

[2] 'The Queen, along with her son the King, acted discourteously when she criticised me: although my speech is not that of Ile-de-France, one can still understand me in French. And those who criticised me for using words from Artois are not courteous or polite, for I was not born in Pontoise.'

regard as the basis of the future spoken standard. While subscribing to the idea of a 'diasystem' and some abstract overarching north Gallo-Romance *langue*, it remains the case that *ancien français commun* is a pure abstraction with no empirical base, constructed by linguists to aid description. The research of Dees and his collaborators has highlighted the inherent variability of Old French and has demonstrated that this variability can best be analysed not in terms of deviations from a central norm, but in terms of the quantitative differences in the distribution of key linguistic variables (see van Reenen 1991). In the centuries following the social and economic fragmentation of Roman Gaul, it is more than likely that speakers of different dialects contrived to understand each other not by having recourse to some pan-dialectal *langue commune* (implying a sort of diglossia), but by making individual acts of accommodation on an *ad hoc* basis using internalised sets of automatic conversion formulae (see Weinreich 1953: 2).

Accommodation between speakers of different dialects is a completely normal part of the everyday use of language. Whenever speakers from non-adjacent sectors of a dialect continuum come into contact, temporary mixed varieties arise. Sometimes it is restricted groups of speakers (or texts) who move around different parts of the country, levelling out their most salient local features to facilitate communication in the different dialect areas to which they travel. Sometimes it is groups of speakers migrating from different dialect areas who converge on a central place, bringing together forms of different provenance and eliminating the most strongly marked regional forms in their day-to-day interactions. Speakers of Gallo-Romance have moved about the area for all time, accommodating their dialectal speech to that of their interlocutors at every encounter. However, these countless individual acts of (short-term) accommodation are unlikely to have resulted in a stable koiné until certain conditions had been met. New koinéised varieties come about only after a period of regular and intense interaction, during which time the individual acts of accommodation all gradually come to point in roughly the same direction (see Kerswill 2002). Koinéisation is particularly favoured when a significant focusing of interactions occurs in some central place.

The prime location of such intensified levels of interaction are towns. In the centuries following the fall of the Empire, the fragmented urban network was quite unconducive to dialect-focusing, rather the reverse. In Chapter 3 we saw that it was only in the eleventh century that things began to change: with a remarkable upsurge of urbanisation across western Europe. The process got underway first in northern Italy and in the Low Countries, but during the twelfth century one city moved ahead of all the others in a most remarkable way – Paris. As we have seen, Paris emerged from nowhere at this time to become an urban giant with a population of 100,000 people in 1200, and double that a century later, dwarfing all the other conurbations of north-west Europe.

Exceptional demographic development on this scale cannot be ignored by historians of the language. Just as twelfth-century Paris radically restructured the geography and agriculture of northern France, in the same way we must suppose that it had a great impact on the dialectal state of the region. An exceptional increase in the level of socio-economic and linguistic interaction within the city involved speakers not only from the city's immediate hinterland (the traditionally labelled *francien* area) but from Normandy, Picardy, Champagne and beyond. One can safely predict that the intensity and regularity of such interaction would lead to the focusing and stabilisation of a new koinéised variety which in time would raise the speech of the city above the dialect continuum not only of north Gallo-Romance in general but also of its hinterland dialect.

If we are looking for a koinéised variety to act as the initial source for language standardisation in French, it would be imprudent not to relate it closely to a real-life koiné which probably developed in the burgeoning primate city in the twelfth century. Penny (2000: 43–4) reports an analogous development in Madrid when that city became the capital of Spain in the sixteenth century. Such a hypothesis falls foul neither of the 'data and chronology problem' (the evidence supporting the existence of some supra-regional norm before the twelfth century is fragile, and Pfister (1973a) demonstrated some time ago that Paris speech emerged as a distinctive, prestigious variety only at that time), nor of the 'implementation problem' (if the koiné originated in the speech of the city, the diffusion of non-indigenous speech-forms through the Parisian social hierarchy become much more explicable). We can set out this set of developments as in the diagram.

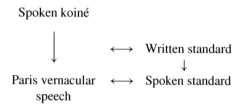

According to this model, there was no initial blueprint created by a group of clerks for the future development of the standard language. The crystallising of the norms of the standard occurred in an empirical, haphazard way, only after centuries of jostling among the competing variants in the everyday speech of the city. Back-projection from surviving hinterland dialects and from the modern standard language many not provide incontrovertible evidence for koinéisation in medieval Paris, but it makes it look very likely.

4.3   Summary

We have attempted here to visualise the beginnings of Parisian French in the twelfth century by projecting back from modern data – from the rural dialects that survived in the Paris area into the twentieth century and from modern Parisian French. We have argued that the French standard language has its origins in a spoken koiné which developed in Paris during a spectacular surge of demographic growth in the twelfth and thirteenth centuries, and that separation between standard and vernacular in the city happened only centuries later (see Dauzat 1935: 200). Instead of seeing colloquial Parisian speech as a corruption of the standard, it is more realistic to suppose an unbroken line of descent between the spoken koiné which developed in medieval times and the colloquial speech of today, and to consider the standard language as a special variety which was elaborated later. Reconstructing the past by back-projecting the present in this way allows us to set up a plausible hypothesis for the beginnings of Parisian French. However, it can only be a hypothesis until it is corroborated by documentary evidence from the relevant period. So, let us now turn to the written documents from the time to see what support they might provide.

5   The medieval written evidence

We tried to show in Chapter 4 how a specific *français de Paris* may have developed initially through a process of koinéisation in the social and linguistic melting-pot of the medieval city. In this chapter we will see what information may be gleaned from contemporary written documents. If we follow the quantitative methodology pioneered by A. Dees, we might be able to discern in the writing system used in medieval Parisian documents distant traces of the dialect-mixing and variation characteristic of medieval Parisian speech. We will conclude the chapter with general remarks on the city's sociolinguistic structure at the end of the thirteenth century.

Although Paris was not a port-city with colonies of speakers drawn from widely scattered areas of the known world, in the thirteenth century it became a dialect melting-pot, and has continued to be one ever since. It attracted relatively large numbers of English-speakers, Flemish-speakers, Italian-speakers, Latin-speakers (see Beaulieux 1927: 112–26), but the most important element in the formation of its patterns of speech was the constant flow, in and out of the city, of speakers of other north Gallo-Romance dialects like Picard, Champenois and Norman, and, of course, HDP. It has been observed that in bourgeoning cities in the modern world, high levels of in-migration and population-mixing induce a corresponding level of dialect-mixing, which may lead eventually to koinéisation (see Manessy 1994: 23). Urban speakers accommodate to each other linguistically, levelling and simplifying their original dialect to eliminate variants which impede communication or which interfere with co-operation in the Grician sense. Monfrin (1972: 762) provides a revealing anecdote about conscious dialect mimicry on the streets of Paris in the fourteenth century:

Ledit de Chastillon cognut au parler que icellui Thomas estoit Picard, et pour ce, par esbatement, se prist a parler le langage de Picardie; et ledit Thomas qui estoit Picard, se prist a contrefaire le langage de France, et parloient ainsi longuement.[1]

---

[1] 'The said Chastillon recognised by his accent that yonder Thomas was a Picard, and for this, as a joke, he began to speak with a Picard accent; the said Thomas, who was a Picard, started imitating the Parisian accent, and they carried on talking like this for quite a while.'

We may infer from this that subconscious inter-dialectal accommodation was as normal at this time is it is today. On this passage, see also Lebsanft (2000).

The integration of the new arrivals in medieval and early modern Paris probably followed patterns similar to those followed in modern cities. This is what has been observed in twentieth-century Brasilia:

> In a first stage of the rural-to-urban physical and psychological transition process the migrants are usually emmeshed in insulated networks in which kinship and pre-migration relations constitute their reference group. In a later stage of the process they are likely to switch from insulated networks in larger and more heterogeneous integrated networks in which they will be more exposed to mainstream urban culture and language and more susceptible to the influence of an exterior reference group. (Bortoni-Ricardo 1985: 240)

In medieval Paris immigrants are known to have set up first of all 'in the faubourgs where rents were lower and the semi-rural conditions came as less of a shock' (see §3.5).

As the population expands, communications within the city come to exceed those with the outside world, bringing about a degree of sociolinguistic focusing which in time detaches urban speech from the rural dialects that surround the city. In Trudgill's typology, dialect-mixing is followed, in the right circumstances, by a process of koinéisation involving a gradual reduction in the variability produced by dialect-mixing and the crystallisation of what may be perceived as a new dialect or language. Although it is reasonable to suppose that the sociolinguistic development of medieval Paris proceeded in this way, parallels with developments in the modern world must not be carried too far. Paris may have been exceptionally large by medieval standards, but it was not particularly large by modern ones. Furthermore, population movements in pre-industrial times were on a smaller scale and took place over shorter distances than nowadays. New-dialect development accomplished in a few decades in twentieth-century Abidjan or Brasilia probably took many more in medieval Paris. Language change is likely to have proceeded at a rather slower pace in the medieval city.

Let us now see if anything can be learnt about the dialect-mixing and variation in medieval Paris from the main contemporary source available to us: the spellings present in thirteenth- and fourteenth-century documents.

5.1   Manuscript evidence

We have no data which provide anything like direct access to everyday speech in Paris in medieval times – no transcriptions of Parisian speech into foreign writing systems (e.g. Arabic, Cyrillic), no writings produced by semi-literate writers, no detailed metalinguistic comments from orthoepists. If we are to gain any idea about variation in the phonology and morphology of the medieval urban dialect, the bulk of the evidence we have to work on is of a very indirect sort, namely the writing system present in surviving French manuscripts.

In the early period (up to and including the twelfth century) the manuscript situation in Paris is bleak: there survive no manuscripts (either administrative or literary) written in French and known to have been produced in Paris before 1200 (see Monfrin 1968: 22). As far as administrative documents are concerned, this should not surprise us: in the whole north Gallo-Romance area (Anglo-Norman England excluded), the use of any language other than Latin in administrative functions was unknown until the very end of the twelfth century. Administrative documents written in French make their appearance in Paris only towards the middle of the thirteenth century. What is more surprising is a similar dearth of twelfth-century literary manuscripts. Although the use of French as a literary language was well established by the middle of the twelfth century, we in fact have no literary material preserved in Parisian manuscripts from that time (see Pfister 1973a: 232).

Too much should not be made of the absence of literary manuscripts from Paris before the thirteenth century. In this regard, Paris fares no worse than most of the other regions of northern France. Pfister lists only eight French literary texts of which a surviving manuscript can be confidently dated to the twelfth century, and five of these were copied in England. In a later article he adds to this list the manuscripts of two literary texts composed in the Plantagenet west of France at the very end of the twelfth century (Pfister 1993: 21). In Paris, as elsewhere, absence of manuscripts does not signify lack of literary production in French – the earliest manuscript of the *Roman de Renart* dates from the second half of the thirteenth century, yet it is quite evident that its earliest 'branches' were composed in the Paris region in the 1170s (see Lodge and Varty 2001). Any texts originally composed in Paris have survived only in copies made much later. Twelfth-century literary manuscripts in French were evidently almost all replaced by more up-to-date copies in the following centuries, save in England where updated copies were perhaps more difficult to produce and where older versions of literary texts may have been more highly valued. It is perhaps to be expected that replacement of the old by the new was more characteristic of Paris than elsewhere, given the vitality of the book-trade in that great university city and the easy availability (relatively speaking) of new copies.

A further difficulty we encounter in Paris is that there are very few literary texts whose composition can be unequivocally attributed, on non-linguistic grounds, to the Paris region before 1200. The great centres of literary production at this time were located in the Plantagenet courts in Normandy and Anjou and in the court of the Counts of Champagne. Epic texts of the *Guillaume* Cycle have been attributed to the Ile-de-France on the basis of internal, ideological evidence, but it is not safe to use such localisations for linguistic purposes. We are perhaps on surer ground with a text like the *Roman de Renart*, of which certain branches have been attributed to a 'Pierre de Saint Cloud', but even this attribution is not solid. Literary material composed in Paris becomes abundant in the thirteenth century. An idea of the size of the corpus of literary manuscripts surviving from Paris in this period is to be gained from the list published in Dees (1987: 527). Of particular relevance are the works of Rutebeuf (see Faral and Bastin 1959), and the *Chronique métrique* of Geofroi de Paris (see Diverres 1956), where the author and subsequent scribes are known to have composed their texts in the city. However, the multi-layered nature of the language found in literary manuscripts (it is difficult to separate the language of the author from that of subsequent generations of copyists) means that the most valuable linguistic data we possess from the period are probably contained in administrative documents.

The practice of using French as an administrative (written) language began in the early years of the thirteenth century in the cloth-towns of northern Picardy. It began to be adopted in Paris only several decades later, first in the *Prévôté* (handling the local government of Paris from the Châtelet) and only later in the royal chancery. The switch from Latin to French in the royal administration did not in fact become general until the fourteenth century, and in the *Parlement* not until the sixteenth (see Giry 1894: 464–72; Beaulieux 1927: 87–112). Administrative documents, of the type produced in increasing quantities in Paris after about 1250, have the advantage over literary texts of being explicitly dated and located and of being the work of only one writer. The majority of these go under the loose title of 'charters', and a valuable list is provided by Dees (1980: 310). In addition there survives an important collection of *Taille*-rolls from the years 1292, 1296–1300 and 1313 (see Géraud 1837; Michaëlsson 1958, 1962), which, although syntactically and morphologically impoverished, are of considerable phonetic value because of the number of place-names they contain, many of which did not as yet have a fixed written form.

Surprisingly, no comprehensive examination of the variation present in thirteenth- and fourteenth-century Parisian manuscripts has so far been undertaken (see de Jong 1992). To rectify this adequately would require a research effort far exceeding the scope of this book. We have restricted ourselves, therefore, to a mere sounding of the data, exploring a set of administrative documents emanating from the *Prévôté de Paris* spanning the period from the mid-thirteenth to the mid-fourteenth centuries. These data, comprising some 150,000 words, were generously made available to us in machine-readable form by P. van Reenen of the Free University of Amsterdam. Here is a sample:

Charter 1260

A touz ceus qui ces letres verront et orront, je Nicolas de Castenoi, chevaliers, et ma dame Agnes, ma feme, saluz. En Jesucrit nous fesons a savoir a touz ceus qui sont et qui a venir sont que, comme contenz fust entre nous d'une partie et religieuse gent le prieur et le couvent de Saint Martin des Chans de Paris de l'autre partie, sur ce que nous et Ferri e le Juene mes freres et sa feme disions et demandions seur une piece de terre, qui siet ou terroir de Chastenoi par devers Puiseus, joignant de cele partie a la terre Renart le Tainturier, jadis bourgois de Paris, et de l'autre partie par desus au jardin Basile de Charni, lequel jardin elle tient de nous a une maalee de cens, et au jardin Aveline la Peletiere, et de une partie d'en costé au pré Ferri le Juene et de l'autre partie a la terre Ernoul Bridoul deux garbes de blé pour raison de champart, l'une par reson de nostre iretache et l'autre par reson d'achat d'Adam Morree, le quel achat nous aviens fait a Adam Morree. Et us aviens nous et nos devantiers d'avoir et de recevoir les devant dites jarbes par reson de champart en icele piece de terre par lonc tens. La quelle chose devant dite li religieus nous nioient nous enquise la verité, par le conseil de bone gent avons renoncié et renoncons du tout et expresseement a la chose et au content desus dit, et quitons et avons quiti du tout les garbes desus dites et queque reson et queque droiture nous aviens ou poienz avoir en icele piece de terre, sans riens retenir ne riens des ore en avant n'i reclamerons ne ferons reclamer par nous ne par autrui. Et en tesmoing de ce nous avons seelees ces letres de noz seaus, ce fu fait en l'an de l'Incarnation mil et ii cens et sessante ou mois de juin.

The documents in this corpus all relate to the property held by the abbeys of Saint Martin des Champs and of Saint Magloire. They form a continuous run beginning in 1249 and ending in 1365, with forty charters from the thirteenth century (1249 to 1299), containing some 22,000 words, and a larger corpus of 139 charters from the fourteenth century (1300 to 1365), containing some 126,000 words. The chronological spread of the documents is set out in Table 2.

The written forms we encounter in these documents cannot be interpreted in a simple referential way. Medieval French spellings could stand for a multiplicity of pronunciations, and could travel independently of speech. Our thirteenth-century Parisian scribes did not invent a writing system *ex nihilo*: they were building on a conventional system matching up sounds and letters which was thoroughly well established before they set to work. The existence of a certain level of conventionality in the Old French writing system when it came into widespread use in the twelfth and thirteenth centuries must be taken for granted. The inherent conservatism of writing systems had almost certainly led, even in the thirteenth century, to a time-lag between the development of innovations in speech and their recording in the written documents, a time-lag that was to increase progressively as the fixation of the writing system proceeded in the succeeding centuries.

However, the fact that we are dealing with speech refracted through the prism of a writing system, and that the relationship between speech and writing was complex, does not mean that there was no relationship between the two codes,

Table 2. *Vernacular documents in the Prévôté de Paris, 1249–1365*

Date	Number	Date	Number	Date	Number
1249	1	1303	4	1334	1
1253	1	1304	2	1335	1
1265	3	1306	2	1337	1
1276	1	1310	5	1338	1
1277	1	1312	4	1339	4
1279	2	1313	1	1340	5
1281	1	1314	2	1341	3
1282	1	1315	6	1343	1
1283	1	1316	1	1344	1
1284	1	1317	1	1345	1
1285	3	1318	2	1348	3
1286	2	1319	2	1350	1
1287	1	1320	1	1351	2
1288	1	1321	3	1352	3
1290	1	1322	2	1353	2
1291	2	1323	7	1354	3
1292	2	1324	5	1355	5
1293	2	1325	3	1356	1
1294	4	1326	2	1357	2
1295	2	1327	5	1358	2
1296	3	1328	7	1359	2
1298	2	1329	3	1360	1
1299	2	1330	2	1361	1
		1331	6	1363	1
		1332	1	1364	4
		1333	1	1365	7

particularly in the early stages of the development of a writing system. When we encounter particular Old French spelling variants rather than alternatives, we must not infer that the writer intended particular pronunciations in each particular case, but, analysed quantitatively, we might expect that variation in the writing system to correlate in some measure with variation in the speech of the community.

5.2 Variation and change in the administrative corpus

In Chapter 4 we claimed that the speech of Paris in the twelfth and thirteenth centuries underwent a process of koinéisation. Let us now examine our corpus of medieval administrative texts to see whether a process of dialect-mixing is reflected there, looking in particular at the phonological and morphological variables we considered earlier (§4.1.2). It will be recalled that we classified these into two categories:

(1) those variants which the speech of Paris shares with the HDP,

(2) those variants which appear to have diffused into Parisian speech from outside the HDP.

In order for comparisons to be made between usage in our texts and the distribution of these variables across north Gallo-Romance, we will refer the reader in each case to the appropriate maps in Dees's 1980 *Atlas*, where these exist (for an example see Map 17).

5.2.1   The central HDP variants

Not surprisingly the Paris charters display, almost invariably, the four central phonological characteristics of HDP which we used earlier to place a 'box' of isoglosses around the Paris region (see above, §4.1.2).

Palatalisation of [ka-] (see Dees 1980: 29 and 1987: 48). Apart from learned words (e.g. *canon*, *cavilations*) and place-names from outside the HDP area (e.g. *Caigni* = *Cagny*), the word-initial group [ka-] invariably palatalises to [ʃa] or [ʃje] (e.g. *charge*, *chief*). Word-internal [ka-] normally produces the voiced affricate [dʒ] (e.g. *jugier*), but sporadically this is de-voiced to [tʃ] (e.g. *granche* = *grange*, *berchier* = *bergier*, *charchiée* = *chargiée*), as in other contemporary texts localised within the HDP area (see Matzke 1881: 82). The groups [ke-] and [ki-] appear to palatalise almost invariably to [tse] (e.g. *ce, cent*), though occasionally in final syllable we find the spelling 'che' as opposed to the more frequent 'se' and 'ce' (e.g. *parroche* (once) – *parroisse* (8 times) and *tierche* (once) – *tierce* (36 times)).

Differentiation of [ow] → [ew] (see Dees 1980: 93). In these documents the variant 'eu' is entirely dominant. Sporadically, in the thirteenth century we find lexically determined occurrences of the 'western' undifferentiated [ow], normally before the consonant [r]. In the fourteenth century this list has been radically reduced (see Table 3). We find variation between these forms in roughly the same proportions in Geofroi de Paris (see Diverres 1956: 29; Matzke 1880: 406–11; Pfister 1993: 31–2).

Insertion of epenthetic [d] (see Dees 1980: 255 and 1987: 429). In words involving the group [n'r] epenthetic [d] is almost invariably present, e.g. *tendra*, *vendra*. The only exception occurs with the word *vendredi* in the later texts (see Table 4). In words involving the group [l'r] epenthetic [d] is invariably inserted (see Dees 1980: 266, 1987: 412, 373; Pfister 1993: 24–6). This coincides with what we find in Geofroi de Paris (see Diverres 1956: 33).

Raising of stressed free [a]. In this position [a] is invariably raised to [e] (e.g. *abbé*, *acordez*).

It is evident then that the four criterial variants for HDP which we examined earlier are all but categorical in our corpus of Parisian charters. This set of HDP variants could no doubt be extended to embrace, for example, the reflexes of open [ɔ] + palatal (e.g. *noctem* → *nuit*), of open [ɛ] + palatal

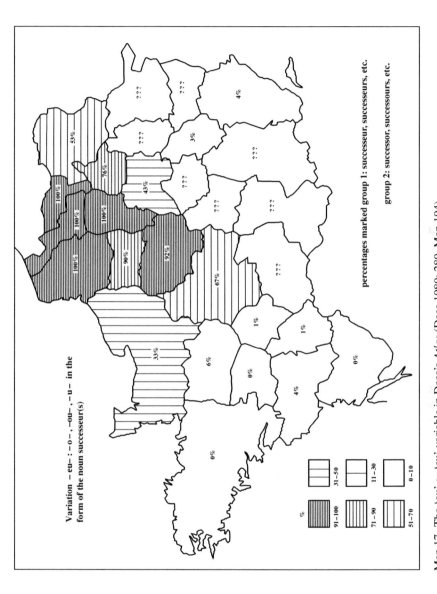

Map 17. The 'ou' ~ 'eu' variable in Dees's *Atlas* (Dees 1980: 280, Map 194)

Table 3. *Spelling variants 'ou' ~ 'eu'*

Thirteenth century		Fourteenth century	
leur (171)	*lour* (14)	*leur* (1,340)	–
meneur (1)	*menour* (1)	*meneur* (8)	–
pluseurs (1)	*plusors* (2)	*plusieurs* (100)	–
prieur (7)	*priour* (2)	*prieur* (91)	–
–	–	*prieure* (16)	*prioure* (2)
religieus (27)	*religious* (7)	*religieus* (967)	–
seigneurie (1)	*seignourie* (5)	*seigneurie* (32)	*seignourie* (39)
successeurs (3)	*successours* (1)	*successeur* (134)	–

Note: The figures quoted in brackets indicate the number of tokens for each variant.

Table 4. *Spelling variants 'n'r' ~ 'ndr'*

Thirteenth century		Fourteenth century	
vendredi (3)	*venredi* (-)	*vendredi* (19)	*venredi* (2)

(e.g. *lectum* → *lit*), of the toponymic suffix *-iacum* (e.g. *Aureliacum* → *Orly*) (see Matzke 1880–1).

5.2.2   *Features introduced from outside the HDP*

We saw earlier that in a number of cases, the present-day speech of Paris has seen the indigenous HDP variants replaced by variants introduced from outside the HDP area (see above, §4.1.2). Following Fondet (1995), the variables we focused upon particularly were:

  (i) [wa] ~ [we], e.g. *poire, droit, froid*
 (ii) [jo] ~ [o], e.g. *manteau, seau, eau*
(iii) *-ent* ~ *-ont*, 6th person present indicative stressed on the ending
(iv) *-ions* ~ *-iens*, 4th person imperfect indicative, present subjunctive
 (v) *-aient* ~ *-aint*, 6th person imperfect indicative

With respect to these variables, we can observe in our charters a higher degree of variation, shadowing approximately the diffusion of these innovations into Parisian speech. We might suppose that the more frequent the variant, the earlier it was absorbed into the speech of the city. We will discuss the variables not in the order given above, but according to the level of variability they contain, beginning with those on the lowest level and moving to those on the highest.

6th person imperfect in -*aient* versus -*aint*. No trace of the HDP ending in -*aint* is to be found in the Parisian charters. It has been completely replaced by -oient/-aient, which appears to have originated in the west. Pope (1952: 496) finds occasional examples of -aint in manuscripts from eastern France in the fourteenth century, but the -oient ending seems to have diffused rapidly, in the written language at least. These were not the only imperfect indicative endings to be found in Old French texts, endings in -event and -oent being common in texts from the north-east and south-west respectively (see Pope 1952: 493, 499).

6th person present in -ent versus -ont, -ant. The unstressed -ent ending, which appears to have originated in the west, evidently diffused early into Parisian usage, for no traces of the HDP endings in -ont, -ant are to be found in the charters, except in the monosyllabic forms ont, sont and font. The only medieval attestations of stressed -ont, -ant are to be found in texts from the south-western region (see Pope 1952: 499).

4th person imperfect in -ions versus -iens. To judge by our corpus of Parisian texts, the non-HDP 'western' variant -ions appears to have become established quite early in Parisian usage, alongside the HDP form -iens. However, competition between forms of the 4th person imperfect persisted for a long time. In the thirteenth-century charters we find considerable variation:

-iens (e.g. aviens, poienz)	44%
-iemes (e.g. aviemes)	22%
-iom (e.g. fesiom)	11%
-ions (e.g. disions, demandions)	22%

In the fourteenth-century documents this variability is greatly reduced, in favour of the 'western' -ions ending:

-iens (e.g. aiens, devians)	15%
-ions (e.g. devions, povions)	85%

We have no example of the present conditional in the thirteenth-century documents in our corpus, though conditionals in -iens are well attested at that time in Parisian texts (see Matzke 1881: 90). However, our fourteenth-century documents reveal a similar pattern of -iens ∼ -ions alternation:

-iens (e.g. receveriens, ariens)	28%
-ions (e.g. ferions, serions)	72%

The imperfect subjunctive shows analogous variation:

Thirteenth century	
-ien (e.g. eussiem)	50%
-om/-ons (e.g. feissom, contrainsissons)	50%
Fourteenth century	
-iens/-ians	26%
-ion/-ission	74%

[e] ~ **[we]** ~ **[wa]** (see Dees 1980: 116). The reflexes of Latin [e] tonic free (e.g. *peram* → *poire*) and of tonic [e/o] + palatal (e.g. *tectum* → *toit*) remained subject to great variation and change in Parisian speech until modern times. As we saw earlier (see above, §4.1.2), three principal variants came into competition with each other in Parisian speech in the medieval period: the indigenous HDP form [we], the 'western' variant [e] and, rather later, an 'eastern' variant [wa].

Medieval and early modern spellings related to this variable are particularly difficult to interpret, given the multiple phonetic values attributable to the digraph 'oi'– [we], [ɛ], perhaps even [wa]. Interchangeability among the spellings 'oi', 'ai' and 'e' was normal in thirteenth-century Parisian texts, as illustrated, for instance, by ms. M of the *Roman de Renart*:

achoison (= *achaison*)	*abai* (= *aboi*)
demoine (= *demaine*)	*vait* (= *voit*)
foible (= *faible*)	*plaié* (= *ploié*)
oirre (= *erre*)	*abaier* (= *aboyer*)
poine (= *peine*)	*naiant* (= *noient*)
voist (= *vait*)	

In the charters analysed here the reflexes of Latin [e] tonic free and of tonic [e/o] + palatal are normally represented by 'oi', but alternatives are to be found:

Occasionally we find spellings in 'oe' or 'oue', implying a pronunciation [we] (see Table 5).

Table 5. *Spelling variants of 'oue'* ~ *'oi'*

Thirteenth century	Fourteenth century
pressoer (1)	*louenz* (1) = *loing* (1)
terroer (1)	
terrouer (3) = *terroir* (2)	*terrouer* (6) = *terroir* (14)
tirouer (1)	

There is a restricted set of words which, variably, display the spellings 'ei', 'e' and 'ai', alongside 'oi'.

Table 6 shows that, in the small set of lexical items which display 'oi' ~ 'ai' variation in these documents, 'oi'-type spellings rise from 60 per cent in the thirteenth century, to 87.5 per cent in the fourteenth. In imperfect and conditional verb-endings, 'oi' is already almost categorical (97.9 per cent) in the thirteenth century, with all competition from 'ai' ceasing in the fourteenth. It is impossible to draw strong inferences from this regarding variation and change in Parisian pronunciation. In the case of the imperfect and conditional endings, we know that, despite the disappearance of 'ai' spellings here, [ɛ] had triumphed over [we] by the sixteenth century. Pope (1952: §522) explains

Table 6. *Spelling variants 'e/ei/ai' ~ 'oi'*

Thirteenth century		Fourteenth century	
Stressed syllables			
acrere (1)	*acroire* (-)	*acrere* (-)	*acroire* (3)
anglais (2)	*anglois* (1)	*anglais* (9)	*anglois* (6)
–	–	*galais* (1)	*galois* (1)
aveine, avaine (2)	–	*avaine* (4)	*avoine* (2)
cres (11)	*crois* (12)	*cres* (60)	*croix* (8)
dreit (3)	*droit* (49)	*dreit* (1)	*droit* (415)
heirs (27)	*hoirs* (18)	*heirs* (32)	*hoirs* (286)
otree (1)	*otroie* (7)	*otree* (-)	*otroie* (30)
		povair (4)	*povoir* (34)
Unstressed syllables			
citeyen (1)	–	*expletter* (2)	*exploitter* (9)
leal (18)	*loial* (6)	*leal* (7)	*loial* (4)
lealment (1)	*loialment* (3)	*lealment* (1)	*loialment* (35)
sexante (5)	*soissante* (9)	*sexante* (5)	*soissante* (48)
Imperfect/conditional endings			
-ait/-aient (7)	*-oit/-oient* (323)	*-ait, -aient* (6)	*-oit, -oient* (2, 423)
[*povet* (2)		[*povet* (2)	
povaient (2)		*povaient* (2)	
porraient (1)		*niait, nyet* (2)]	
estaient (1)			
poursivaient (1)]			

the presence of 'ai'-spellings in Parisian texts primarily as an endogenous reduction of the diphthong [we], which occurred 'in uneducated speech in Paris and adjacent regions to the east and south-east' in the later thirteenth century. Our data, showing as they do a progressive elimination of forms in [ɛ], do not support this. It is more feasible to regard the [ɛ]-forms as being ultimately exogenous in origin ('western' according to Pfister 1993: 29–30), resulting from earlier dialect-mixing.

In the *Taille*-rolls the 'ai' spellings are somewhat in the majority compared with spellings in 'oi' in geographical names like *Englais, Français*, etc. and in place-names derived from Latin *-etum* (e.g. *Chastenai, Fontenai, Tremblai*). In Geofroi de Paris (see Diverres 1956: 27–8, 40) we find the pronunciation [e] present at the rhyme in the imperfect endings, and in the following items: in *loi, Loire, sermantois*, from which it was eliminated relatively early in Parisian speech, and in *connoistre, croire, estroit, froit, voire* where it persisted much longer.

Although sporadic examples of spellings implying a pronunciation in [wa] have been found in the thirteenth-century *Taille*-rolls, e.g. *tirouar* (see

Michaëlsson 1959: 290–2), they do not appear in our texts. This suggests that the widespread diffusion of [wa] into Parisian speech did not occur until later.

'iau' versus 'eau' (see Dees 1987: 129, 156, 160). It is generally accepted that the modern standard pronunciation [o] of words such as *beau, seau, eau* arises historically from the progressive levelling of the Old French triphthong [eaw]. At a very early stage in the development of the language, the Latin group '-ellus'/ '-ellos' typically saw the reduction of the geminate [ll] and elision of the unstressed [o]. Located in Old French in pre-consonantal position, [l] gradually vocalised > [ɫ] > [w], forming a diphthong with the preceding vowel. A glide [a] then developed between the two elements of the diphthong to form a triphthong. Thus: '-ellos' > [-els] > [-eaws].

In forms where final [s] was not present (i.e. the accusative singular and the nominative plural of masculine nouns and adjectives) no such triphthong developed, giving rise in Old French to an alternation between the subject and the oblique forms:

	Singular	**Plural**
Subject	*manteaus*	*mantel*
Oblique	*mantel*	*manteaus*

Alternating forms are still present in certain western dialects (see *ALF* 822). During the Middle Ages the Old French triphthong [eaw] evolved in two ways. In some areas it was gradually levelled: [eaw] > [əo] > [o]. The group [əo] was still diphthongal in sixteenth-century Paris, but by the seventeenth it had been monophthongised completely (see Pope 1952: §539). In other areas (including HDP) the first element was consonantalised: [eaw] > [jaw] > [jo].

Since the monophthongal [o] form (written 'eau') has formed part of the standard language since the sixteenth century, it is normally assumed that this has always been the Parisian form. The [jo] variant is seen as an innovation introduced into 'vulgar Parisian speech' from the northern and north-eastern dialects (see Pope 1952: §539–40). The textual evidence makes this sequencing of events untenable. In all texts written in Paris up to the second half of the fourteenth century, the dominant spelling is not 'eau' but 'iau'. See §4.1.2 and Matzke 1881: 75–7. Wüest (1985: 243) sees the [jo] variant as the indigenous form, and [o] as an endogenous innovation in upper-class speech. Let us consider the evidence provided by our charters.

In the thirteenth-century documents the HDP variant '-iau' is used in 100 per cent of cases. The variant '-eau' is first attested in 1329 (in the word *heaumier*) and was still only a minority form in the middle of the fourteenth century (see Table 7). The incidence of the '-eau' variant rises to a proportion of 13 per cent around the middle of the century. A similar chronology is visible in other thirteenth- and fourteenth-century Parisian texts: no examples of the spelling '-eau' are to be found in Rutebeuf (see Faral and Bastin 1959: 144); Michaëlson

Table 7. *Spelling variants of 'iau' ~ 'eau'*

	'iau'	'eau'
1300–19	*Boifliaue* (1)	
	Jumiaus (6)	
	yaues (1)	
1320–39	*appiaus* (16)	
	biau (1)	
	Guibonniau (1)	
	hiaumer (1)	*heaumier* (1)
	iaue (1)	
	nouviau (3)	
	tonniau (4)	
	trumiaus (1)	
	Ysabiau (1)	
1340–65	*aniaux* (1)	
	appiaus (5)	*appeaulx* (1)
	Biauvez (2)	*Beaufort* (1)
	Blondiau (6)	*Boileau* (1)
	boissiau (1)	*eaues* (1)
	Charonniau (1)	*nouveau* (1)
	Grimardiau (1)	
	quarriaus (1)	
	Roussiau (1)	
	Ysabiau (5)	

(1959: 289) observed its presence in small numbers alongside '-iau' in the 1292 *Taille*-roll, but almost none are to be found in the rolls for 1296 and 1297; no examples are to be found in the early fourteenth-century Chronicle of Geofroi de Paris (see Diverres 1956: 37). However, a quantitative analysis of the works of Christine de Pizan (writing in the first third of the fifteenth century) shows the two variants to be present in the proportions '-eau' 80 per cent: '-iau' 20 per cent, indicating the rapid adoption of this variant at least in cultivated usage in the second half of the fourteenth century. In the works of the poet Villon composed in the middle of the fifteenth, '-iau' spellings are completely absent, despite the strong vernacularising tendencies of his poetic style.

The '-iau' variant does not represent, therefore, some sporadic aberration, but the indigenous form shared initially by HDP and the speech of Paris. The innovation in Parisian speech is in fact the '-eau' variant which subsequently became established as the standard form. We cannot exclude the possibility that the '-eau' variant developed endogenously in the speech of Paris during the thirteenth century, but Dees's maps suggest instead an exogenous, eastern origin for this form (see Dees 1987: 129, 156, 160), which began to be diffused into the speech of the city no earlier than the end of the thirteenth century.

5.2.3   Sporadic 'Parisianisms'

Variation in our documents comes about not only as a result of the gradual importation of 'outside' features. The writing system found in our thirteenth and fourteenth-century charters was susceptible throughout the period to influence from features occurring in a more sporadic, less generalised way in HDP. We will find all of the following vernacular features achieving great salience in later centuries.

Raising of back-rounded vowels [o] ~ [u] (see Dees 1980: 139). The distribution of the back-rounded vowels [o] and [u] was highly variable in Parisian French until the seventeenth century. It became so salient in the sixteenth century that it received the name 'ouisme'. The raising of [o] to [u] seems to have begun in the north and to have spread gradually south to Paris (see Dees 1980: 139 (*coutume*)). In our documents variation between the spellings 'o' and 'ou' is considerable (see also Diverres 1956: 29, 40). Some of the variation is syntagmatically constrained: in monosyllables (e.g. *tout, court, jour*) and in disyllabic words ending in unstressed '-e' (e.g. *toute, bouche, boule*) the 'ou' spelling is categorical from the thirteenth century.

In the initial syllable of other disyllabic and polysyllabic words (e.g. *somme, prochienne*) regular patterns of development are less easy to discern. Normally Old French [o] was raised to [u] (e.g. *costume* ~ *coutume*), but in many words this raising was resisted (e.g. *dommage, nommer*). In our charters we find numerous examples of [o]-raising even in words that eventually resisted the process (Table 8).

Table 8. *Spelling variants 'o' ~ 'ou' ('ouisme')*

Thirteenth century		Fourteenth century	
domage (5)	doumage (1)	domage (56)	doumage (3)
nommer (7)	noumer (1)	nommer (28)	noumer (3)
prochain (2)	prouchain (1)	prochain (29)	prouchain (8)
cordouannier (3)	–	cordouannier (6)	courdouannier (3)
Thomas (4)	–	Thomas (48)	Thoumas (16)
volenté (4)	–	volenté (53)	voulenté (2)
–	fourme (5)	forme (3)	fourme (40)
–	proufit (1)	profit (35)	proufit (38)
–	enfourme (1)	–	enfourme (8)
–	–	comment (30)	coument (5)
–	–	–	Coulombes (4)
–	–	–	coulombier (2)
–	–	–	froumagier (2)
–	–	–	Ourge (1)

Lowering of unrounded nasals. The spellings 'en' and 'an' are generally kept separate in the charters, being reserved for use in words derived from Latin i/e + n (e.g. *Acension, argent*) and from Latin *a* + *n* (e.g. *Alexandre, Andri*) respectively. However, a certain level of interchangeability is evident, implying the gradual merging of the two nasal vowels [ɑ̃] and [ɛ̃]. Pfister (1993: 31–2) sees this as a feature which spread from the north-east of the Gallo-Romance area. In our texts we find 'an' diffusing into words traditionally spelled with 'en' (e.g. *prendre* → *prandre*) more commonly than the reverse (e.g. *estant* → *estent*), with the movement gathering pace as the charters pass from the thirteenth to the fourteenth centuries. In the thirteenth-century documents 'an' spellings affect 9 per cent of potential sites, and in the fourteenth century this proportion rises to 12 per cent. By 'potential site' here we mean the lexical types, not lexical tokens.

We find a higher degree of variability between the spellings 'ien' and 'ian', particularly in word-final position (e.g. *ancien* ∼ *ancian*). In the thirteenth-century charters there are no cases of 'ien' diffusing into words traditionally spelled with 'ien', but in the fourteenth century the proportion reaches 36 per cent of potential sites (e.g. *mairian, moian, physician*). This feature is widely attested in HDP (see *ALF* 618, *fumier*) and in the thirteenth-century *Taille*-rolls (see Michaëlsson 1959: 289, 292–4).

Table 9. *Spelling variants 'er'* ∼ *'ar'*

Thirteenth century	Fourteenth century
jerbes (2) ∼ *jarbes* (2)	*cherra* (–) ∼ *charra* (2)
verront (19) ∼ *varront* (1)	*derrenier* (24) ∼ *darrenier* (25)
	escherront (1) ∼ *escharront* (1)
	Espernon (5) ∼ *Esparnon* (1)
	Cernay (–) ∼ *Sarnay* (12)
	menroit (–) ∼ *marroit* (1)
	percevoir (16) ∼ *parcevoir* (3)
	perpetuelement (60) ∼ *parpetuelement* (1)
	Therouanne (3) ∼ *Tarouenne* (1).
	cf. also *esgous* (8) = *agous* (8)
Examples of hypercorrection	
apartenances (5) ∼ *apertenance* (6)	*barbier* (4) ∼ *berbier* (1)
	Barnabe (3) ∼ *Bernabe* (1)
	Barthelemi (1) ∼ *Berthelemi* (24)
	Darnestal (15) ∼ *Dernestal* (7)
	marcheant (3) ∼ *mercheant* (1)
	parroisse (6) ∼ *perroisse* (2)

Lowering of [er] → **[ar].** The lowering of 'er' → 'ar' (e.g. *gerbe* ∼ *garbe*), although sporadic, increases in frequency as we move from the thirteenth- to the fourteenth-century documents (see Table 9). Occasionally we find examples of a sort of hypercorrection. This feature occurs sporadically across a wide variety of Gallo-Romance dialects. It is commonly found in Anglo-Norman and English, for example *clerc* → English [klark], *persone* → English [parson], *sergeant* → English [sardʒent]. However, it is attested particularly frequently in HDP (see *ALF* 641 *gerbe*, 686 *herbe*, 998 *perchoir*). It commonly appears in Rutebeuf (see Faral and Bastin 1959: 143), in Geofroi de Paris (see Diverres 1956: 26), in *Renart* (ms. M) (e.g. *aparcevoir, charront, partuis*) and in the 1296 and 1297 *Taille*-rolls (e.g. *Parruquet* ~ *Perruquet, Barthaut* ~ *Berthaut, Sarpent* ~ *Serpent*).

The suffix 'aige'. The traditional form '-age' is invariable throughout the thirteenth-century charters, as in the 1296 and 1297 *Taille*-rolls, and does not occur in the early fourteenth-century chronicle of Geofroi de Paris (see Diverres 1956: 36). The variant spelling '-aige' makes its first appearance alongside '-age' in the third decade of the fourteenth century, e.g. *aaige* ~ *aage, mesaige* ~ *mesage* (Table 10). The [ɛʒ] variant is common in HDP, becoming more frequent in the west and south (see Dees 1980: 216; *ALF* 1199 *sauvages*; Wüest 1979a: 220). See Marchello-Nizia 1979: 75.

Table 10. *Spelling variants '-aige' ~ 'age'*

	'-aige'	'-age'
1300–19	(0%)	41
1320–39	28 (25%)	113
1340–65	10 (11%)	94

Others. Very occasionally in the thirteenth-century documents we find examples of the rounding of [e]-sounds, [e] → [ø], and [əm] → [ym], e.g. *Evangiles/Evangeliste* (4) ~ *Euvangiles/Euvangeliste* (17) and *premierement* ~ *prumierement*. On one occasion we find the interchangeability of medial [r] and [z], e.g. *Voisin* ~ *Voirin* (see Fouché 1952: 603–5).

5.2.4   Inferences

What light does this rather laborious analysis of our *Prévôté* corpus shed on the question of koinéisation in medieval French, which we raised in Chapter 4? We must be cautious, naturally, about any claims we make on the basis of this type of data. The conservatism and conventionality of writing systems (even medieval vernacular, i.e. non-Latin, ones) forbid us to read the documents as anything like direct transcriptions of speech. The corpus itself is not large, and, moreover, the range of variables examined is small – we have focused on a restricted set of key variables selected initially by Fondet (1995), whereas Dees's 1980 *Atlas* used some 268. That said, four broad conclusions suggest themselves: (i) the extent of variation and change visible in the corpus indicates that the *Prévôté* scribes, while probably conforming to a local house-style, were not working to a rigid, pre-established template; (ii) the phonetic and morphological features we have examined display a mixture of endogenous and exogenous forms, which, when compared with the geographical data present in Dees's *Atlas*, appears to be specifically Parisian; (iii) this mixture of dialectal elements changed over the century covered by the documents, indicating that the process of koinéisation in Paris was an on-going one; (iv) the endogenous variables were, on the whole, more stable than the exogenous ones, and, of the exogenous ones, the morphological variables were less subject to change than the phonetic ones.

The fact that the in-mixing of exogenous elements in Parisian French affected verb-morphology rather earlier than phonology, substantiates Trudgill's (1986: 25) and Lass's (1997: 157) suggestions that morphosyntactic characters diffuse (relatively) more easily than phonological ones. This is borne out by the changes we see in the endings of the present and imperfect tenses (Table 11).

Table 11. *Endings of the present and imperfect tenses*

Present	Imperfect
chant-Ø	*chant* -oie
chant -es, -s	*chant* -oies
chant -e, -t	*chant* -oie
chant -om, -ons	*chant* (-iens) ≥ **-ions**
chant -ez, -iez	*chant* -iez
chant (-ont) ≥ **-ent**	*chant* (-aint) ≥ **-oient**

Source: adapted from Posner 1997: 303, 316–17.

Here the forms in bold are the ones imported from outside HDP. They served to regularise the paradigms, evidently on the pattern of similarity between the endings of persons 1, 2, 3, and 6, and the specialisation of *-ons* in the 4th person. Dialect-levelling and koinéisation normally entail this sort of morphological 'simplification'.

5.3   Language diversity in medieval Paris

The process of koinéisation that we believe occurred in twelfth and thirteenth-century Paris looks to have given rise to a new set of speech-norms which, as time went on, were to diverge progressively from those of the more conservative dialects spoken in the rural hinterland. The thirteenth century certainly sees Parisian speech enjoying very great prestige throughout western Europe (see Kristol 1989). However, there is as yet little to show a distinction in people's minds between the speech of urban Paris and that of rural 'France' (= Ile-de-France). Jean de Meung refers specifically to the speech of the 'town':

> Ne n'ay nul parler plus habile
> Que celui qui keurt a no vile.[2]
>
> (Jean de Meung, *Boece*,
> quoted in Lodge 1993: 100)

but he is here making no specific contrast with the speech of the countryside. Roger Bacon, an acute outside observer of the French sociolinguistic scene in the mid thirteenth century, normally refers to the speech of the Paris region as *gallicum*, but on one occasion he introduces the term *parisiense* alongside, as if this were a different entity:

ut Picardum et Normanicum, Burgundicum, Parisiense et Gallicum: una enim lingua, est omnia, scilicet Gallicana sed tamen in diversis partibus diversificatur accidentaliter; quae diversitas facit idiomata non linguas diversas.[3] (*Compendium studii philosophiae*, VI, 478–9)

None of this carries much weight, however. It is safest to conclude that, at this stage, the gap between urban and rural speech was too slight to impinge on social awareness.

The gradual coalescence of a new urban dialect is unlikely to have induced a high level of linguistic homogeneity in the city. The needs of trade and the famous university brought various groups of foreign-language speakers into the community. Of these, English-speakers were apparently the most numerous, their familiarity with Anglo-Norman no doubt facilitating their assimilation into Paris society. Other groups constituted important but less well integrated sections of the community: Jews and Italians. Both of these were engaged above all in money-changing and finance and occupied specifically defined quarters of the city. The Rue des Lombards exists to this day. Parodies of Anglo-Norman and Italian speech found in the twelfth-century *Roman de Renart* (the earliest part of which is attributed to a 'Pierre de Saint Cloud') suggest that such foreign speakers were familiar figures in the city (see Lodge 1995a; Lodge and Varty 2001). However, the foreign language which played the most significant role in the life of the city was perhaps not even regarded as a foreign language at all – Latin.

Medieval Paris was a diglossic community. Descriptions of the pivotal role of Latin in medieval European society are numerous and need not be repeated

---

[2] 'I consider no speech more subtle than the one which is current in our town (Paris).'

[3] 'Picard, Norman, Burgundian, Parisian and French: they are all the same language, namely French, but they vary accidentally in different regions; this variability makes for different dialects but not different languages.'

here (see, for instance, Chaytor 1945 and Lusignan 1987). Although the role of Latin lay principally in writing, we should not underestimate its use as a spoken language in the city. All public events in the Church, in the University and in certain parts of the Law were conducted in Latin as a matter of course. In a community comprising such a high concentration of ecclesiastics, lawyers and scholars, levels of literacy (in Latin) were exceptionally high. Insofar as reading normally took place aloud, use of Latin automatically entailed a spoken dimension. In the world of the Church and the University, Latin was the *lingua franca* between speakers from different parts of Europe: the whole of Paris located *intra muros* on the Left Bank, and referred to as the *Université* (as distinct from the *Cité* and the *Ville*), came to be known popularly as the Latin Quarter. The English philosopher Roger Bacon, who lived a large part of his professional life in Paris, claimed to have three mother tongues (English, French and Latin), and was strongly aware of differences in the pronunciation of Latin according to the region of origin of the speaker (see Lusignan 1987: 71–2). University authorities required the use of Latin as a spoken language within their various colleges (see Lusignan 1995), though their recourse to informers known as *signatores vulgarisantium* (see Lehmann 1959: I, 78) attests their lack of success. It is clear that the ability to speak Latin possessed powerful social symbolical value, differentiating clergy from laity and town from gown. Latin clearly enjoyed very special status as the H-language in a diglossic community.

Within Parisian French itself, the prime area for stratification probably lay in the divergence between the speech of established citizens and the motley collection of dialects spoken by the newcomers constantly entering the city. We saw at the beginning of this chapter how the natives mocked the speech of incomers. When it comes to the speech of the city's permanent residents, while there may have been the beginnings of an acrolect in the royal circle, strong evidence of sociolinguistic stratification is not to be found.

Literary texts might have provided clues, given that contemporary manuals of rhetoric prescribed an explicit link between linguistic style and social status (see below, §12.1). However, close examination of thirteenth- and fourteenth-century texts produces nothing substantial. We might have expected to see traces of low-status speech in apparently plebeian literary productions like Guillaume de Villeneuve's *Les Crieries de Paris* and various *Dits de Paris* (see Cazelles 1972: 397–9; Franklin 1977: 748–51; Franklin 1984), but the results are negative. The Parisian poet Rutebeuf looks like a promising literary source for colloquial speech, for many of his comic and satirical poems provide a vivid depiction of everyday life in the city. He in fact uses a considerable number of Parisianisms which we know to have been stigmatised in later centuries (see Faral and Bastin 1959: 143–4). Here is part of a semi-ritualised exchange of insults between two itinerant entertainers:

La desputoison de Challot et du Barbier

. . .

– Barbier, or est li tens venuz
De mal parler et de mesdire,
Et vous serez ainçois chenuz
Que vous lessiez ceste matire;
Més vous morrez povres et nuz,
Quar vous devenez de l'empire.
Se sui por maqueriaus tenuz,
L'en vous retient a 'va li dire'.

– Charlot, Charlot, biaus douz amis,
Tu te fez aus enfanz le roi.
Se tu ies, qui t'i a mis?
Tu l'es autant com a moi.
De sambler fols t'es entremis;
Més par les iex dont je te voi,
Tels t'a argent en paume mis
Qui est assez plus fols de toi.[4]

(see Faral and Bastin 1959: II, 263–4)

This text offers an early French example of the practice of ritualised insults, characterised by Labov as 'sounding' (see Lagorgette 2003: 5–10), but this is contrived literary writing and we find little here that might be construed as low-status variants.

Dramatic texts like the great corpus of *Miracles de Nostre dame par personnages* contain a large amount of spoken style, and frequently put on to the stage representatives of the Parisian poor. In the following extract specific reference is made to parts of the city frequented especially by beggars and paupers:

DEUXIESME POVRE	S'aler y voeil, ou irons nous? Or ne me truffes.
PREMIER POVRE	Nous yrons chiez Robert de Ruffes Assez près du four Saint Martin. A trois tournois y arons vin Et bon et gent.
LE TIERS POVRE	Il y va et vient trop de gent; Tu diz en la fourmagerie Assez près de la guanterie? Mais alon chiez le tavernier

[4] The Slanging Match between Charlot and Barbier

'Barbier, the time has come for hurling insults and abuse, and you will be old and grey before you give this up. But you will die naked and poor, for you are on the slide. If people see me as a go-between, you are considered a pimp.'

'Charlot, Charlot my fine friend, you're making yourself the king of the idiots. If you are, who put you there? You're up to your neck in it just like me. You've set about looking a fool. But by the eyes I see you with, anyone who hands money over to you is a bigger fool than you are.'

Qui soloit estre cervoisier,
C'on nomme Pierre Filion.
J'ay trop bien en regipcion
Qu'i serons miex.
LE QUART POVRE Tu as dit voir, se m'aïst Diex:
Il y a pour nous meilleur place.
C'est a la pointe saint Uitasse
Oultre un petit.[5]

(*Miracle d'un Marchant et un Juif*,
ed. Paris and Robert, VI, ll.226–44)

Here too, however, it is hard to discern significant differences between the
speech of these lower-class characters and that of characters of higher rank
appearing elsewhere. The editors of the text maintain that the form *regipcion*
(= 'memory') belonged to criminal slang, but produce no supporting evidence.
They likewise claim that the form *Uitasse* is a 'popular' deformation of the more
cultivated *Eustache*. The fact that the 1296 and 1297 *Taille*-rolls systematically
use an almost identical spelling – *la pointe Saint-Huitace* – confirms the authenticity of the form but not its low-prestige status (see Michaëlsson 1958: 46).

All in all, in literary representations of everyday speech from thirteenth-
century Paris, social variation (in phonology and morphology at least) is not
prominent. A possible explanation for this might be that variation in pronunciation was added *extempore* by the performer. However, it is more likely that, at
this stage, variation within Parisian French was not yet heavily invested with
social meaning. This squares with what we know about the culture and social
composition of medieval towns: towns were essentially 'bourgeois' creations,
with a popular culture that was *broadly speaking* everyone's culture. Before the
onset of standardisation, dialectal speech tends not to be so heavily stigmatised.
The main linguistic divides look to have been between the Latinate and non-
Latinate members of the community, and between incomers and permanent
residents.

5.4   Summary

In this section we have developed the idea that, during the period of exceptional
growth which Paris experienced in the twelfth and thirteenth centuries, the

---

[5] 'SECOND PAUPER If you want to go there, where shall we go? Don't trick me now.
FIRST PAUPER We'll go to Robert de Ruffes' place, near Saint Martin's bakery. For three-
pence we'll get good, fine wine there.
THIRD PAUPER There are too many comings and goings over there. What about the cheese-
shop near the glove-maker? But let's go to the innkeeper who used to be a beer-seller, by the
name of Pierre Filion. I've a very good inkling (?) we'll be better there.
FOURTH PAUPER You're right, God help us. There is a better place for us, and it's a bit
further on at the end of Saint Eustache church.'

speech of the city followed a pattern of urban-dialect development similar to that observed in the new cities which burgeoned in Europe in the nineteenth and twentieth centuries. Increased levels of interaction led to the focusing of a new urban koiné. The dialect of the city, while based on the speech of its hinterland, was modified in significant ways by contact with other dialects. To demonstrate this we used a sort of back-projection, considering the historical links between the hinterland dialects, the speech of Paris and the standard language. We rejected the idea that the koiné upon which the standard is based originated in writing, and that it was subsequently diffused top–down as the norm for speech. We preferred the hypothesis that this koiné arose spontaneously in everyday Parisian speech through normal processes of dialect-contact, and that the standard language was derived from that, at a later date.

We went on to examine a corpus of administrative texts to see if they might support this hypothesis in any traces they may contain of language variation and change in the medieval city. We saw that the Parisian writing system embodied a specifically Parisian mixture of dialect forms, and, while resisting the temptation to see these spellings naïvely as direct representations of speech, we followed Dees's thinking that variability in the writing system, analysed quantitatively, correlated up to a point with variation in speech. No valid reconstruction of the spoken language is possible, of course, but it would appear that koinéisation in Paris occurred progressively, with different exogenous elements being absorbed into the Parisian system at different times. Anecdotal evidence suggests that, as early as the late twelfth century, the city's permanent inhabitants were aware of local speech-norms and that they regarded the dialectal speech of unintegrated incomers (Englishmen, Italians and Picards) with amusement. However, while there may have been the beginnings of an acrolect in aristocratic circles, we have no clear evidence of social differentiation in the French of the established residents. The most socially significant linguistic divide in the thirteenth-century city was probably still that separating the H-language (Latin) from the L (the various vernaculars).

Part 3

The proto-industrial city

6   Social and sociolinguistic change, 1350–1750

Koinéisation in medieval times may have involved the emergence in Paris of a new, relatively stable mixture of dialect features, but it did not entail homogeneity, as we have seen. Persistent and often violent demographic fluctuation in the 'proto-industrial period' favoured more variation in language, not less. The first explicit moves to suppress such variation and establish a standard language come with the Renaissance, and it is the process of disentangling standard and vernacular in the speech of the early modern city which will provide the focus for Part 3.

In the fourteenth century, according to Hohenberg and Lees (1985), European cities entered a new stage of development, which lasted until the onset of industrialisation four hundred years later. The feature of proto-industrial development that impacts most on the sociolinguistic situation in Paris is an increase in hierarchical thought, which widens the gulf between the culture and lifestyle of the elites and those of the population at large. This is compounded in Renaissance Europe by the spread of literacy, which accentuates the divergence between the written culture of the elites and the traditional oral culture of the masses. A new polarity crystallises in the social psychology of the city, setting 'urbanity' against 'rusticity'. In this new cultural setting, Latin is progressively restricted to its religious functions, and variation within the vernacular takes on a social importance that it appears not to have had previously.

The period covered in this Part (fifteenth to eighteenth centuries) is a long one, during which profound transformation took place in the internal structure of the French language. This chronological division is quite unusual in histories of French, for they traditionally subdivide it into 'Middle French', 'Renaissance French' and 'Classical French'. Indeed, we ourselves will devote separate chapters to the fifteenth to sixteenth centuries and to the seventeenth to eighteenth centuries. However, the periodisation we are proposing underscores the parallelism between the city's socio-demographic development in the proto-industrial period and the city's sociolinguistic evolution. For Hohenberg and Lees (1985), the 'proto-industrial period' represents a distinct phase in urban development, as it does for other social and economic historians (see Braudel

1981). We will see that on the sociolinguistic level too, key processes can be observed which begin in the fifteenth century and continue through until the eighteenth.

Following the pattern set in Part 2, we will devote Chapter 6 to an overview of the demographic and social development of the city in the proto-industrial period, before examining the sociolinguistic process which characterises it most strongly, that of 'reallocation' (see above, §2.3.2). In Chapter 7 we will first look at the outlines of the city's sociolinguistic profile in the fifteenth and sixteenth centuries and then at the most salient sociolinguistic variables visible in sixteenth-century data. Chapter 8 will follow a similar pattern for the seventeenth and eighteenth centuries. Chapter 9 will bring together some of the linguistic details of reallocation from the sixteenth to the eighteenth centuries.

6.1   Demography and society in the proto-industrial city

6.1.1   Demographic change

The period of sustained demographic growth in Europe which began in the late tenth century came to a rather abrupt end in the fourteenth. Various human factors were involved, including the over-rapid population growth of the earlier period, and the extension of agriculture into less fertile land, but the effects of climatic change need to be brought into the equation too. The years 1314 and 1315 issued in a long series of cold, wet summers which appear to have triggered population decline across Europe even before the Black Death of 1347–9. For three centuries after 1450 Europe experienced what meteorologists have labelled 'the little ice age'. Whatever the causes, population growth in European towns, between the fourteenth and eighteenth centuries, was in some cases stagnant and in others fluctuating.

In the period up to the seventeenth century, the population of Paris underwent wild fluctuations (see Fig. 1). The effects of famine, plague (which raged sporadically before and for three centuries after the catastrophic epidemic of 1348), and prolonged warfare (the Hundred Years War), reduced the population in the second half of the fourteenth century from its previous 200,000 to about 80,000. Recovery took several generations. By the mid sixteenth century the city had acquired some 300,000 inhabitants, only to see almost a third of them disappear in the second half of the century during the Wars of Religion (1562–94). In the first half of the seventeenth century the city not only made up the gaps left by war and famine, but actually doubled its size from 220,000 to 430,000. In the second half of the century and thereafter till the onset of industrialisation in the late eighteenth century, the city's population continued to grow, though not at the rates achieved by Amsterdam and London.

thousands

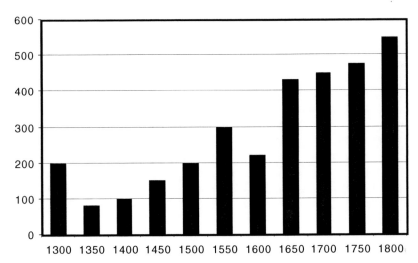

Fig. 1. The population of Paris, 1300–1800
Source: Compiled from data published in Dupâquier 1988 and the various
volumes of the *Nouvelle Histoire de Paris* (see p. 25)

Demographic fluctuation on this scale may surprise modern observers. However, as Benedict (1989: 13) points out,

a fundamental characteristic of medieval and early modern cities was the considerable turnover of their population from year to year and generation to generation. A sixteenth-century town could be likened to an accordion, expanding when harvest failures or warfare led inhabitants from the surrounding countryside to seek refuge or charity behind city walls, shrinking when plagues sent the rich fleeing to the safety of their country estates or prolonged economic difficulties provoked the emigration of skilled artisans. Beyond these short-term fluctuations, a constant stream of migration steadily replenished the ranks of the permanently resident population.

The high proportion of immigrants in towns stemmed in part from the basic inability of proto-industrial cities to reproduce themselves. Rates of mortality were particularly high among infants, as a result both of the notorious insalubrity of town life, and of the widespread habit, prevalent among town-dwellers of all classes, of placing infants in the care of rural wet nurses. At the same time, some of the immigration into cities served to replace city-dwellers who had left for other communities, for migration from city to city or back and forth between city and countryside was widespread. Up to the middle of the seventeenth century the proportion of non-natives in the city was particularly high. Thereafter, it gradually fell.

6.1.2   Functional change

It is not possible to detect major evolution in the religio-educative function in Paris during the proto-industrial period. The city remained a prime centre for the Catholic Church, and, outside intellectual circles, French Protestantism was a largely provincial affair. In the sixteenth century, Paris was the scene of perhaps the most chilling event in the Reformation conflict, the Massacre of Saint Bartholemew (1572), and in the following century it was the spearhead of the Counter-Reformation movement in France, with the establishment of some eighty new religious houses within its walls. At the same time, between the sixteenth and the eighteenth century, the medieval University with its collegiate structure languished in seemingly irreversible decline, being finally abolished by the Revolution in 1792. However, as a centre of learning and intellectual innovation Paris was unrivalled in Europe (see Martin 1999). The city remained one of the greatest centres of the European book-trade and levels of literacy were much higher there than elsewhere in France.

Few dramatic changes took place in the sphere of manufacturing. Although the fourteenth and fifteenth centuries saw significant technological developments (for example in the invention of gunpowder and of printing; see Friedrichs 1995: 93–100), the modes of production remained essentially artisanal, and the technology and size of individual units of production underwent little change. In seventeenth-century Paris the state, through the agency of Colbert, became actively involved in the development of certain industries producing luxury goods like tapestry and porcelain. We are dealing, however, with the 'proto-industrial' developments rather than with 'industrial' ones.

The volume of European trade expanded greatly in the period from 1450 to 1750, not only at local and regional level, but also over long distances, including to other continents. This required expansion in the facilities for banking and credit which could only develop in towns. In the long run, Paris did not participate in the development of an imperial mercantile system as successfully as Amsterdam or London, but it benefited greatly from it even so. The prosperity of Paris depended above all on its location at the top of the French Central Place System, whereby goods and services flowed up and down the hierarchy of towns and villages linked politically and economically to it. During the proto-industrial period the relationship between city and hinterland gradually changed. The medieval town had been heavily dependent on its rural hinterland, developing as a centre of exchange and transformation of primary agricultural products. The land was controlled by the great feudal land-holders: the Church and the nobility. Now the balance of land-ownership shifted as the wealthy urban merchants bought into land themselves, controlling the growth of rural industry and reversing the traditional order of dependence. At the same time, nobles began identifying more and more with the city and spending more time there.

With the shift in power from the feudal land-holders towards the urban merchants, we find a significant shift in the nature of the French state. During the fifteenth century, the feudal monarchy began to be replaced by a bureaucratic one, and from this time we can see a progressive expansion of the administrative elite based in Paris. The main institutions of the kingdom remained in the capital: the old *parlement* of Paris, the *Chambre des Comptes*, the *Grand Conseil*, whose role grew in the sixteenth century, plus some of the services of the *Chancellerie*. This institutional presence in Paris implied a concentration not only of office-holders but also of an extensive auxiliary personnel of court clerks, officers, procurators and lawyers. The administrative framework is estimated to have required 5,000 royal officers in 1515 (see Jacquart 1996: 107). This movement culminated in 1528 with the declaration by François I of his intention to establish his permanent residence within the city of Paris.

Tres chers et bien amez, pour ce que nostre intention est doresnavant faire la plus part de nostre demeure et sejour en nostre bonne ville et cité de Paris et alentour plus qu'en aultre lieu du royaume: cognoissant nostre chastel du Louvre estre le lieu le plus commode et a propos pour nos loger; a ceste cause, avons delibere faire reparer et mettre en ordre ledict chastel . . .[1] (quoted from Babelon 1986: 45)

Although this was part of a wider European trend, it is important to emphasise the novelty of François I's move in the French context (see Hautecoeur 1961: 105 and Jacquart 1996: 107). The medieval kings had always needed to control the wealth of Paris, but rarely resided there in person on a long-term basis. After the failure in 1527 of his Imperial ambitions in a series of extravagant Italian adventures, François I determined to consolidate his power at home, seeking to establish himself in the eyes of Europe as the perfect Renaissance prince, with Paris as the ideal city. This attracted into the city large numbers of the aristocracy who had previously resided principally on their country estates. As the city moved from being simply the administrative and economic centre of the kingdom to being a capital in the modern understanding of the word, the monarchy began to redesign the city to make it a symbol of its power. The architecture of absolutism, inspired by that of ancient Rome, was designed for glory and spectacle rather than profit and comfort, and is plainly visible in the redesign of the Louvre, the Tuileries and what was eventually to become the Place de la Concorde and the Champs Elysées. The most extraordinary

---

[1] 'Dearly beloved friends, because our intention henceforth is to make the greatest part of residence and stay in our goodly city of Paris and its surrounding area, rather than any other place in our kingdom, recognising that our castle of the Louvre is the most suitable for our accommodation, for this reason we have determined to repair and put in good order the said castle.'

expression of this urge to overawe the spectator with the sight of a huge planned townscape was of course Versailles, to which the royal court retreated in the second half of the seventeenth century.

6.1.3   Social stratification

Under the pressure of changing patterns of production and marketing, and with the increasing movement into the towns of members of the aristocracy in the early sixteenth century, urban communities became more stratified and a widening gap – cultural and political as well as material – divided rich and poor.

Proto-industrial development accentuated the divisions between men of property and proletarians lacking both economic and political privileges, as well as the disparities of wealth and power among burghers. (Hohenberg and Lees 1985: 131)

Urban elites throughout western Europe, in the late fifteenth century, began distancing themselves from the masses, culturally, and eventually spatially.

We derive a useful insight into how Parisians saw their own urban community at the beginning of the seventeenth century from Loiseaux' *Traité des Ordres* (1614). Here, social stratification is perceived not in the terms of wealth more familiar to modern observers, still less in terms of social class, but in the medieval terms of 'orders' and 'estates'. This was a highly conservative vision, with members of each estate jealously guarding their status vis-à-vis upward-moving members of lower estates – estate-membership implying modes of living, dressing and, presumably, speaking which were appropriate to each rung on the social ladder.

A different social analysis is to be found in the pattern of wealth-distribution across the city. Information from the early period is sparse, but François Furet (1961) examined fiscal material from the eighteenth century in the form of the poor-law tax of 1743, and was able to distinguish five social categories according to official estimates of their weath (see Table 12). Below these five groups of permanent residents there existed a large tranche of population who, by definition, were excluded from the poor-law tax, the Paris poor themselves. By all accounts, the number of paupers and marginals in Paris continued to be very large, even in the eighteenth century.

If we allow for demographic fluctuation, the social structure of the city evolved only slowly across the proto-industrial period. Roche (1981a: 57–8) visualises it in three tiers. At the top he sees an extremely rich elite striving to distance itself culturally from the bulk of the population. Medieval cities had seen the emergence of a small network of bourgeois families who dominated urban affairs. These families were not only extremely wealthy in comparison with the rest of the population, but they were often successful in transmitting their privileged status from one generation to the next. Patrician power was

Table 12. *Distribution of wealth in eighteenth-century Paris*

		Proportion of the population	Per capita units of wealth
I	Haute noblesse, aristocratie	1.5%	29.0
II	Grands officiers civils	3.8%	9.0
III	Avocats, professions libérales	8.1%	4.5
IV	Maîtres artisanaux, marchands	33.2%	2.3
V	Gens de métier	53.4%	1.0

increased by the development of the bureaucratic state in the fifteenth century, though it was challenged shortly afterwards by the arrival in the city of important sections of the landed aristocracy.

In the middle Roche sees the bulk of the population, for whom the focus of communal life remained as it had always been, the *quartier*, and their principal means of support the ties of family and trade. Economic life for the majority of inhabitants was organised around the numerous trade-guilds and corporations. Particular trades continued to be exercised in particular streets and in particular *quartiers*, fostering the maintenance within the various neighbourhood communities, of dense and multiplex social networks (see Garrioch 1986).

Perhaps what distinguishes most conspicuously the social structure of medieval and proto-industrial cities in Europe from that of modern cities was the presence at the bottom of society of a large but unknowable number of paupers, marginals and transients (see §§3.5 and 6.1.1). For Roche this group is impossible to pin down, not just because their lives have left little trace in the historical record, but also because of the permeability of such social categories as the workless, the drifter, the hawker, the prostitute, the beggar, the thief. The frontier between vagrants and criminals, on the one hand, and less threatening groups of temporary or recent migrants, on the other, was fluid. The authorities were constantly in search of devices for distinguishing the 'false' or criminal poor from the 'true' or deserving poor.

Migrants from the countryside who eventually found work and settled in the city on a permanent basis were to be found in the greatest concentrations in the eastern part of the city and, *extra muros*, in the *faubourgs* Saint Antoine and Saint Marcel. A sixteenth-century description of the life of such people is to be found in N. du Fail's *Propos rustiques* (1547) (quoted in Sainéan 1912: 295–9). Those who failed to settle and remained as transients were referred to by the resident population as *gueux* and viewed with deep fear and suspicion (see Roch 1992). Contemporary police records indicate the high proportion of rootless provincials among the city's wrong-doers (see Chagniot 1988: 127–50, 223–5). Such people congregated in large numbers in open spaces within the

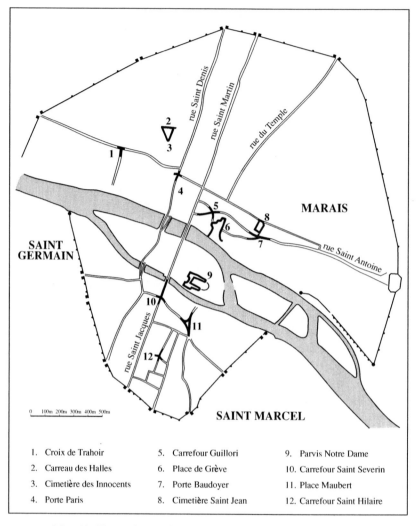

Map 18. The main meeting-points in proto-industrial Paris (adapted from Favier 1974: 49)

1. Croix de Trahoir
2. Carreau des Halles
3. Cimetière des Innocents
4. Porte Paris
5. Carrefour Guillori
6. Place de Grève
7. Porte Baudoyer
8. Cimetière Saint Jean
9. Parvis Notre Dame
10. Carrefour Saint Severin
11. Place Maubert
12. Carrefour Saint Hilaire

city walls (for example, in the cemeteries of the Innocents and of Saint Jean, in the Place de Grève and on the Parvis Notre Dame) and at the city's main cross-roads (for example, in the 'carreau des Halles' and at the Place Maubert). The Halles and the Place de Grève became the emblematic meeting-points between town and country (see Map 18).

In medieval times, vertical stratification in Paris society was not accompanied by residential zoning. During the proto-industrial period, spatial segregation of the classes begins to appear. Descimon (1989: 99) notes that as early as the sixteenth century the rich were forsaking the high densities of the Ile-de-la-Cité and the areas of the Left and Right Banks immediately facing it. He observes that

> two cities had begun to coexist within the confines of the capital, as they would continue to do for centuries to come: the antiquated Paris of the central parts of town, where artisans and merchants squeezed tightly amid one another; and a newer Paris just inside and outside the walls, where the fashionable residential neighbourhoods of the rentier classes alternated with the working quarters and *faubourgs* dominated by an artisan and labouring population. Both of these cities, however, appear to have been marked by similar patterns of social behaviour, for in both the members of different corporate groups chose to live in locations nearer other members of their group, thereby reinforcing the associative links of the group.

The dense, petrified world of central Paris was no longer the most attractive part of town for the wealthiest inhabitants of a city increasingly dedicated to the theatrical display of power. Typical of this was the construction of expensive residences on reclaimed land in the Marais, on the Ile-Saint-Louis and in the *faubourg* Saint Germain in the first quarter of the seventeenth century. This movement was accentuated in the eighteenth century with the large-scale development of the land situated to the west of the city wall as residential accommodation for the well-to-do. The poorest *quartiers* were situated east of the Rue Saint Denis on the Right Bank, and east of the Rue Saint Jacques (focusing on the Place Maubert) on the Left. Writing about the *faubourg* Saint Marcel at the end of the eighteenth century, L.-S. Mercier declares:

> C'est le quartier où habite la populace de Paris, la plus pauvre, la plus remuante & la plus indisciplinable. Il y a plus d'argent dans une seule maison du fauxbourg Saint-Honoré, que dans tout le fauxbourg Saint-Marcel, ou Saint-Marceau, pris collectivement. (Mercier 1782:I, 268)

6.1.4   Social conflict

The proto-industrial city was the arena of permanent competition for resources between the established population and the human mass which moved in and out of the city following the rhythm of the economic cycle. Public order was difficult to maintain, and food-riots were a regular occurrence whenever the harvest failed (as it did once every eight years, according to one estimate). The Valois saw fit to make their residence permanently in Paris, but their Bourbon successors had strong personal reasons for distancing themselves from the city's huge and turbulent population. Henri IV was assassinated in the Rue de la Ferronnerie in 1610 and the ten-year-old Louis XIV was forced by the mob to flee the city in the dead of night in 1649. It is not surprising, therefore, that after the troubles of the Fronde (1648–52) we find the monarchy residing increasingly rarely in Paris itself, and preferring the safer and more congenial environments of Saint-Germain en Laye, Fontainebleau and, finally, Versailles.

A second, less visible, arena of conflict is that between the Paris merchant and administrative class, whose power was based in the law, finance and trade, and the landed aristocracy which moved in large numbers into the city at the beginning of the sixteenth century. The issue must not be over-simplified, for the two groups were not distinct. Many urban capitalists bought into land and sought (and gained) ennoblement, just as many nobles engaged heavily in the financial and commercial markets. The sale of offices brought ennoblement to numerous members of the administrative and judicial class. However, the underlying conflict of interest existed, and contemporary observers were very aware of it, encapsulating the opposing sides in the short-hand terms *la Cour* and *la Ville*.

Throughout the seventeenth century the Crown deployed strenuous efforts to bring into line non-compliant members of secular society, the most notable of whom were to be found among the great feudal barons on the one side and in the Paris merchant class on the other. In the long term it found it easier to accommodate the barons than the merchants. A moment of crisis came during the minority of Louis XIV with the troubles of the Fronde (1648–52). This uprising brought together disaffected members of the aristocracy, members of the judicial and mercantile elite of Paris, and the bulk of the townsfolk in an unlikely alliance against the first minister Mazarin. The rebellion was eventually suppressed, and absolute royal power was fully reasserted at the beginning of the 1660s.

However, tension between the the aristocratic and merchant classes remained a constant of Ancien Régime society until the Revolution. The definitive move of the Court and government services to Versailles in 1682 no doubt facilitated both the exercise of royal power and the indulgence of the monarch's appetite for spectacular display. These advantages were evidently bought at the price of the Crown's links with the vital economic and cultural forces at work in the metropolis, whose elites became increasingly frustrated by the spectacle of the political and economic advantages denied to them being enjoyed by their counterparts and commercial rivals across the Channel, and who, in consequence, were increasingly attracted by the rationalist, libertarian ideas of the 'Enlightenment'. The eighteenth century saw a progressive tilting of the balance of power between *la Cour* and *la Ville* in favour of the latter.

For much of the period this conflict was overlaid, up to a point, with a religious one. With the triumph of Catholicism at the end of the Wars of Religion Paris became an important centre for the Counter-Reformation, notably through the activities of the Jesuits. Religious dissent in the capital did not disappear, however. It was driven underground and in time Jansenism replaced Calvinism as its main vehicle. The original focus of this movement was the Abbey of Port-Royal, better known to linguists through the so-called *Grammaire de Port-Royal*, published in 1661 by Lancelot and Arnault. It would appear that Jansenist ideas took root very extensively in the Paris population, first among the elites and later among a wider section of the community. Royal attempts to suppress these ideas through the Bull *Unigenitus* (1713) led to decades of conflict, adding a further dimension to the hostility between the dissenting, if not outright humanist *Ville* and the more orthodox *Cour*. The former eventually triumphed with the expulsion of the Jesuits in 1762.

6.1.5   Cultural change

Changes in the function and demography of cities in the early modern period were accompanied by significant cultural change. The model was provided by the cities of northern and central Italy – Venice, Milan and, especially, Florence – whose wealth and technological advancement incited the towns of northern Europe to emulate their achievements from the fifteenth century until well into the seventeenth.

Although in 1500 the elite may already have had a loyalty to the ideas and customs of the high tradition, we can say . . . that at that time popular culture was everyone's culture. Then, as the intellectual currents we group under the labels humanism, Counterreformation, and Enlightenment diffused, the elite began to reject what it saw as vulgar or superstitious popular culture. The affirmation of civilized values over folk culture was not a simple matter of city versus country. While urban elites decried local folkways, they partially adopted those of the rural gentry. Horse races and indoor balls for the rich joined the theater as substitutes for civic pageants. Although increasingly urban in taste as well as residence, the aristocracy retained its commitment to virile pursuits, above all hunting. Within the city, the upper classes first contracted out of popular celebrations and then moved to suppress rowdy and licentious spontaneity. The people were offered instead sanitized and passive festivities, generally for the greater glory of the sovereign. (Hohenberg and Lees 1985: 150)

The Renaissance gave birth to what we now regard as the classical notions of 'culture' and 'civilisation' (see Williams 1976). Implicit in them is a set of oppositions segregating high culture (associated with *urbanitas*) from the low, popular culture (associated with *rusticitas*). Elites had of course existed throughout the Middle Ages, but in the earlier period they had been located in seigneurial castles (*cortois* versus *vilain*) and in cathedral chapters (*clerc* versus *lai*). Now they were increasingly located in towns.

Popular culture and the home-grown were rejected in favour of the cosmopolitan. Traditional wisdom and folk medicine were downgraded. The heritage of the elders was no longer a model but a gauge of ridicule. The stylised art-forms of opera and ballet came to be preferred by the elites to popular song and dance, which they regarded as brutish and artless. Ancestral traditions were renounced and new codes of politeness were developed, regulating the behaviour of the *Cortegiano* (in Italy), the Gentleman (in England) and

Table 13. *Levels of literacy in seventeenth-century Paris*

	%
Notables	100
Marchands	80
Maîtres	60
Domestiques	50
Tisserands	30
Compagnons	25
Ruraux	10

Source: Chartier 1981

the *Honnête Homme* (in France). Such codes covered matters of dress, social etiquette and, most particularly, language. The development of printing and the spread of literacy downgraded the culture of orality and attributed high value to the written word (see Lohisse 1981). Rates of literacy are always higher in towns than in the countryside, but when we find fairly reliable evidence about them in seventeenth-century Paris, they are surprisingly high, though of course they did not reach universality until the twentieth century. With the usual caveat concerning variation by sex, Chartier (1981) provides figures for levels of literacy in Paris (see Table 13). Linguistic hierarchies developed in towns which mirrored social hierarchies, giving rise to the whole set of beliefs referred to as 'the ideology of the standard' (see above, §1.1.2). This was to be central to the codification of the new standard languages and to the 'reallocation' of linguistic variants.

6.2   Reallocation

The processes of dialect-mixing and koinéisation that look to have occurred in medieval Paris produced a mixture of dialect-forms which was stable and structured but at the same time subject to variation and change. At the end of the Middle Ages, predictably enough, there persisted in Parisian speech a large number of variants left over from any original mixture. Trudgill (1986: 126) observes that in situations of dialect contact the phase of koinéisation is commonly followed by another, which he labels 'reallocation'. Variants left over from koinéisation are recycled as *social-class dialect variants, stylistic variants, areal variants,* or, in the case of phonology, *allophonic variants* (see above, §2.3.2). Consciously or not, speakers seek to maximise the communicative value of residual variants, instead of leaving them floating in free variation. Reallocation is akin to 'exaptation' (see Lass 1990: 316–24), that is, recycling old linguistic material into new uses. We will argue in this section that it is a process such as this which characterises the sociolinguistic development of Parisian speech in the proto-industrial period.

Over the medieval centuries the Parisian speech community might be said to have acquired a 'uniform structural base', but in the subsequent period, sub-groups within the community sought to distinguish themselves by finding new ways of expressing these shared linguistic resources. How were these resources to be shared out or 'reallocated'? In the dialect situations examined by Trudgill (in twentieth-century Norwich and Belfast), reallocation takes place uncon-sciously, and we may assume that this is how it normally happens. However, in early modern Paris we can see it at work consciously and explicitly, in the movement of linguistic codification which was such a feature of social life in the capital at this time (sixteenth to eighteenth centuries):

All communities properly so called have a social structure. This implies a hierarchy of persons, and it is a short step thence to a hierarchy of behavior, with certain persons regarded as admirable, then as preferable, and ultimately as right. Any alternative pat-terns are excluded; in our society this is achieved by labeling them substandard. The projection of hierarchical evaluations on to dialects thus has strong roots in general behavior, but it comes into full form upon the increase of hierarchical thought and in awareness of language engendered by writing and the onset of standardisation. (Joseph 1987: 58)

Codification involves, among other things, the explicit reallocation of variable parts of the community's linguistic resources to different functions or to dif-ferent styles, normally on the basis of the usage of its most powerful and most prestigious members.

6.2.1   Sources of data

In medieval Paris finding data to inform us about social variation in the lan-guage, and indeed about attitudes to it, is exceptionally difficult. In the proto-industrial period, the data remain 'inherently bad', but the situation becomes easier, thanks to the development of printing and the survival of a greater num-ber of written records. Predictably enough there survives only a tiny amount of relatively *direct* evidence about variation in the city's speech. The bulk of our evidence comes from *indirect* sources, metalinguistic works and literary representations of everyday speech. Although these sources provide reliable information about the variants in circulation, they automatically channel it through the prism of the observers' subjective evaluations. In some respects this reduces the contribution such indirect material can make, but it does not destroy it completely, for subjective evaluations are what drive the whole re-allocation process forward. We saw earlier (§1.3) that the community is to be defined not in terms of any marked agreement in the use of language elements but in terms of participation in a set of shared evaluative norms. In a forthcoming paper Katia Ploog observes:

Les situations de contact génèrent des représentations – souvent conflictuelles, toujours différenciées – chez les locuteurs, représentations qui se répercuteront dans les pratiques linguistiques, avant d'affecter le système lui-même.

A quantity of vernacular data have survived from this period which are of a relatively direct type. We find them, for instance, in the direct notation of the everyday speech of the young Dauphin made by Jean Héroard in the early seventeenth century (see Ernst 1985). This is an extraordinary one-off. A more normal source is provided by the writings of inexperienced writers (e.g. personal correspondence (see Ernst 1996), and the *Journal* of Menétra (see Seguin 1992)). Precious as such material is, it is preserved in the most accidental and fragmentary way and provides only momentary glimpses of the real-life sociolinguistic situation.

Most of the surviving material on everyday speech is of the indirect type, that is, data which come down to us through the writings of contemporary observers. Into this category we must place, first of all, the large corpus of metalinguistic works produced in Paris during this period. The works in question include not only systematic grammars and dictionaries, but also the recommendations of orthoepists, polemical pieces about the state of the language, and the whole genre of *remarques* (unstructured collections of linguistic comments) which came into vogue after the publication of Vaugelas' *Remarques sur la langue françoise* (1647). The richness of this material may be gauged by inspecting the two volumes of comments from orthoepists and lexicographers on French pronunciation compiled by Charles Thurot (1881, 1883). Into this category we could also place the corpus of pedagogic grammars produced for foreign learners of French analysed by Radtke (1994). This metalinguistic material provides useful evidence not only about high-status forms which prescriptive authors recommend, but also on the low-status colloquialisms they reject.

It is easy to over-estimate the influence of prescriptive grammarians and lexicographers at this time, and to see them dictating the whole process of codification and reallocation (see §1.1.3). Glatigny (1992) and Trudeau (1992) have provided us with a clear account of the evolving discourse of metalinguistic commentary in France in the sixteenth and seventeenth centuries. They show how the language attitudes of linguistic commentators were a faithful reflection of more general social concerns. The grammarians did not stand outside society: they participated in the community's evaluative norms like everyone else. The importance of their work for linguistic historians is less its direct social impact than the explicit evidence it provides about the language variants in competition and about their social value at a particular time. Reallocation involves the development of a new consensus in which the whole community is involved, consciously or not.

Another type of indirect evidence is to be found in literary and semi-literary representations of everyday Parisian speech. The proto-industrial city brought into existence a tradition of burlesque writing which used low-class speech as a vehicle for satire and humour. Texts written in this tradition frequently embody modifications to conventional spelling, which makes them valuable sources for non-standard phonetics as well as grammar and phraseology. A corpus of seven specimen texts is published in the Appendix. Texts like these cannot be read as transcriptions of naturally occurring speech. They are pieces of written language posing as speech, and they are written by people whose personal language was much higher up on the standardisation scale than the literary characters in the piece. These texts do not give equal treatment to all parts of the linguistic system: they focus particularly on variants located at the bottom of the socio-stylistic spectrum. Writers of this time rarely manipulated sociolinguistic variation for the sake of greater 'realism', they were most often concerned with the social symbolism of the varieties involved. They concern themselves almost exclusively with those variants that impinged most strongly on the consciousness of contemporary speakers.

What these texts offer us is a 'folk' view of the world based on what was perceivable and available to everyone. In the past, this has led linguistic historians to ignore them more or less completely. We will argue that they were wrong to do so. Not only do texts like this provide reliable evidence on the forms circulating in colloquial Parisian speech, but, like the grammarians, they offer valuable insights into the community's shared evaluative norms and precise details about the changing social values ascribed to particular variants.

6.2.2   Reallocation and salience

The working of reallocation depends less on the objective characteristics of linguistic variants than on social evaluations placed upon them by speakers and on subjective factors like relative 'salience' (the level of awareness associated with particular variants). Trudgill (1986: 11) attributes salience to a number of factors – overt stigmatisation, linguistic change, phonetic distance and phonological contrast – which we can exemplify here with data found in sixteenth-century Parisian French.

As an example of a high-salience variant which attracted overt stigmatisation in the sixteenth century we could quote the variable [o] ~ [jo]:

Vitanda est autem vitiosissima vulgi Parisiensis pronunciatione in hac triphthongo, nempe *l'iaue*, et *siau* pro *seau, beau, ruisseau* et similia.[2] (Bèze 1584: 53)

---

[2] 'To be avoided, however, is the highly defective pronunciation of this triphthong found in the Parisian populace, namely *l'iaue*, and *siau* for *seau, beau, ruisseau* and so on.'

The indigenous variant [jo] found itself increasingly in competition, from the fourteenth century onwards, with a diphthongal variant [əo] > [o] (see above, §5.2.2). The form [əo] > [o], lacking the consonantalised first element, seems to have been adopted early by upper-class speakers, leading to strong stigmatisation in the sixteenth century of [jo].

As an example of a highly salient variant undergoing a process of linguistic change during the sixteenth century we can quote the complex shifting between [we], [e] and [wa] in the speech of Paris:

Pour *voirre* ou, comme d'autres l'escrivent, *verre*, on prononce vulgairement a Paris et on escrit tres mal *voarre*.[3] (Bèze 1584: 52)

Certain variables were salient because the variants involved were phonetically radically different. This was the case with the [er] ~ [ar] variable. In the sixteenth century the [ar] variant came to be construed in Paris as a rural form, and very early on this led speakers to hypercorrect, with women apparently leading the way:

Les dames de Paris, en lieu de A prononcent E bien souvent, quant elles disent *Mon mery est a la porte de Peris ou il se faict peier.* En lieu de dire *Mon mary est a la porte de Paris ou il se faict paier.*[4] (Tory 1529: f.33v)

An example of a high-salience variable where loss of phonological contrast was involved is Parisian nasal-lowering:

Phase I	Phase II
[ĩ]	[ɛ̃]
[ɛ̃]	[ɑ̃]

Speakers were evidently very aware of this:

Le Parisien prononce tous les mots terminez en *in* en *ain* . . . Autres y a qui prononcent à la parisienne *in* comme *ain*. Exemple, *J'ay beu de bon vain a la pomme de pain*, pour dire *j'ay beu de bon vin a la pomme de pin*.[5] (Tabourot 1588: 92v)

Kerswill and Williams (2002) highlight potential circularity in Trudgill's notion of salience, and point out that it is ultimately difficult to know why some variants come to be avoided and others favoured. However, they conclude that Trudgill's idea of salience remains a useful one: in contact with speakers of other varieties, speakers tend to modify those features of their own varieties of which they are most aware, that is, the most 'salient' ones. Labov (1994: 300–1) views the

---

[3] 'For *voirre* or, as others write *verre*, people in Paris pronounce (and write) in a very vulgar way *voarre*.'

[4] 'The ladies of Paris very often pronounce E instead of A when they say *Mon mery est a la porte de Peris ou il se faict peier.* Instead of *Mon mary est a la porte de Paris ou il se faict paier.*'

[5] 'The Parisians pronounce all the words ending in *in* as *ain* . . . There are others who pronounce *in* for *ain* in the Parisian manner.'

trajectory of a sound change across the community in the following way. At an early stage in the process an opposition of two linguistic forms may come to symbolise an overt opposition of social values. This association of linguistic and social values may remain below the level of social consciousness and result in an unconscious 'indicator', or, alternatively, it may rise above that level and result in a 'marker' or even a 'stereotype'. At a later stage, one of the two forms of the marker wins out and there follows a long period when the disappearing form is heard as archaic, a symbol of a vanished prestige or stigma, and is used as a source of stereotyped humour until it is extinguished entirely.

The level of salience associated with a particular variable is then an important factor determining its fate: a very high level of salience normally leads to its elimination, lower levels of salience will lead to reallocation of the variants either lexically, or as socio-stylistic markers, or as mere indicators. At all events, the process of linguistic change is not a straightforward mechanical one dictated by internal factors alone. Speakers' subjective perceptions about the social value of particular variants have a crucial role to play. The difficulty for the historian, at this distance in time, is to find reliable information not just about the socio-stylistic distribution of particular variants in real-life usage, but also about social evaluations of them. On the latter question, the literature of the proto-industrial period which we specified in §6.2.1 offers considerable help.

6.2.3   Shared norms and prototype theory

City speech is characterised on the surface by extreme heterogeneity, but beneath it there exists a fundamental orderliness (see §1.3). The inhabitants of a metropolis are not united in their speech habits, which are remarkably diverse, but they are by their linguistic attitudes and prejudices, which are remarkably consistent. The speech of individual speakers may be idiosyncratic, but this idiosyncracy is constrained by evaluative norms shared with everyone else. Speakers' attitudes to language variation are known to be more regular and uniform than actual usage within the community, and to be slow to change. In the France of our own day Gueunier, Genouvrier and Khomsi (1983) have shown that less-educated speakers generally share the negative judgements made on their speech by speakers located higher up the social scale.

Is it possible to discern any consistent patterns in language attitudes in proto-industrial Paris? Is it possible, at this distance in time, to gain access to the community's shared evaluative norms, for it is these that are likely to have determined the various selections and de-selections involved in reallocation? We saw earlier (§6.1.5) how, at the time of the Renaissance, a new polarity began to crystallise in the social psychology of the city, setting the concept of 'urbanity' against its negative counterpart, 'rusticity'. In their drive for identity and status, the urban elites used all aspects of cultural life (such as dress, domestic furnishing, art, entertainment and, of course, language) to distinguish themselves from people below them. Their desire to draw lines around accept-able speech prompted the emergence of an army of prescriptive grammarians. The representations of metropolitan speech which we find in the metalinguistic writings and in the literature of this period are dominated by a polarity between Good and Bad. We frequently find, alongside idealised images of the Gentle-man (*Honnête Homme*), equally idealised images of the Peasant (*Paysan*). In the one, high, socially approved variants regularly co-occur with one an-other and are associated with genteel, upper-class speakers, and in the other low, stigmatised variants regularly co-occur in a sort of implicational scale (see Rickford 2002), and are associated with peasants and low-life Parisians.

The authenticity of linguistic portraits of the Gentleman produced at this time is rarely questioned. The images of the Peasant, on the other hand, are generally dismissed as 'literary stereotypes' and caricatures with no linguistic value, the authors who produced them being slaves to convention and literary tradition. This underestimates their significance. Social typing is not just a literary phenomenon but a general feature of cognitive information processing. It is probably a necessary part of our procedures for coping with the outside world (see Saville-Troike 1989: 195). We have no means of knowing for certain, of course, but the pervasiveness and long-standing nature of the stereotype of the Urban Peasant (and of the Gentleman) in proto-industrial Paris suggests that the authors who activated it were not engaged in a simple *salon* exercise in intertextuality, but were articulating subjective views of language variation which were widely, if not universally, held across the city over a long period. The fact that speakers generally agree on the evaluation of the very linguistic norms that symbolise divisions between them suggests that these authors were not articulating a limited upper-class view of the sociolinguistic scene, but were responding to a broader set of sociolinguistic pressures moving like tectonic plates below the surface of society.

Perhaps the recurrent groupings of sociolinguistic variants such as those we find in those images are best considered not so much as 'stereotypes', which are fairly superficial, but as 'prototypes', which are more deep-rooted:

Prototype theory . . . offers us a possible way of looking not only at how concepts may be formed . . . but also at how we achieve our social competence in the use of language. We judge circumstances as being typically this or typically that, and we place people in the same way. (Wardhaugh 2002: 236)

In a period of sociolinguistic uncertainty prototype-based concepts are es-sential: when speakers hear a new linguistic item, they associate it with those who typically seem to use it and what, apparently, is the typical occasion of its use. What we find emerging in proto-industrial Paris is a pair of antithetical sociolinguistic 'prototypes' of the good and the bad speaker, encapsulated in the figures of the Gentleman (*l'Honnête Homme*) and the Peasant (*le Paysan*). It is the presence of these contrasting prototypes, embedded in the social psychology of the city and embodying the most salient sociolinguistic variables of their day, which reflected the social evaluation of particular variants and largely dictated the process of reallocation.

6.3   Summary

In this chapter we looked first at changes in the socio-demographic structure of Paris which we suspect conditioned sociolinguistic developments over the proto-industrial period. We then examined what may have been the dominant sociolinguistic process at work ('reallocation of variants'), paying particular attention to the notion of 'salience'. Reallocation can be seen to underpin much of the codification of French that took place at this time. Codification was not, however, a matter simply for the grammarians: it involved the development of a new consensus in which the whole community participated, knowingly or not (see Keller 1992). We have only tiny fragments of contemporary evidence that give us glimpses into reallocation in real-life Parisian usage. However, we have plenty of information in literature and in metalinguistic comment which indicates what the most salient variables were. Social information of this kind is essential if we are to chart the reallocation of variants between standard and vernacular. There is always a danger of interpreting contemporary representations of the spoken language as direct embodiments of real-life speech. Extreme caution needs to be exercised with material of this sort, for the relationship between 'representation' and 'reality' was far from simple and direct. On the other hand, it is too simple to believe that there was no relationship between them at all. The prototypes we are postulating here are abstractions to which the behaviour of individual speakers approximated more or less, according to his or her social characteristics and the situation of utterance.

7   Variation in the Renaissance city

Proto-industrial changes in European cities had interesting and far-reaching sociolinguistic effects: in general, they induced heightened awareness of stratification in urban speech, and led eventually, in the great capitals, to language standardisation. In Paris, there was a good deal of continuity from the medieval past: permanent city-dwellers evidently continued to speak the urban variety which had been developing over the preceding centuries, and a swathe of population at the bottom of society, fed by consistently high levels of inmigration, ensured the continued presence in the city of rustic speech-forms. At the top, however, things changed more dramatically: a significant fraction of the nobility now competed for pre-eminence with the established urban elites, and increased pressure for the differentiation of an acrolectal variety. During this period, information enabling us to inject a degree of multidimensionality into our history is more plentiful than in the pre-industrial period. However, it allows us to penetrate deeper into social attitudes to language variation in the city than into socio-stylistic variation itself. We will devote this chapter to the growing awareness among Parisians of social differentiation in language, which first appears in the fifteenth century, and which becomes quite explicit in the sixteenth. We will conclude with an examination of a short text that may provide glimpses of 'actual usage' at this time to set against the representations of usage we consider elsewhere.

7.1   Growing awareness of social differentiation

Renaissance ideas about civilisation and urbanity, which spread north from Italy in the fifteenth century, modified the whole conception of the city and urban life inherited from the Middle Ages. The gap between the culture and life-style of the elites gradually grew apart from those of ordinary townspeople, bringing with it a sharper social differentiation in speech. At the beginning of this process relatively *direct* evidence on vernacular speech is lacking. Letters written by such figures as Alain Chartier and Christine de Pizan provide insights into the speech-forms of the cultivated elites. Practical texts like *Le Ménagier de Paris* (ed. Brereton and Ferrier 1981) and the *Journal d'un Bourgeois de*

Paris 1405–49 (ed. Tuetey 1881) deal with matters of everyday life and emanate from personages located a little further down the social scale, but they too contain no specifically low-class features. Specimens of writing produced by inexperienced writers from lower social milieux are, to the best of our knowledge, completely absent. Consequently, the only evidence pointing to social differentiation in language at this time is provided by literary texts, which invariably give a particular skew to the data.

In the fifteenth century the most informative texts are the mystery plays and farces which were produced in considerable quantities. In the thirteenth-century Miracle plays we discussed earlier, few linguistic differences could be detected between upper- and lower-class characters (see above, §5.3). The situation is quite different two centuries later. Brunot (1905: I, 526–8) observed long ago that the authors of mystery plays routinely used language variation to signal social differences between their characters. Many of these differences are to be seen at discoursal level, with lower-class characters engaged in conversations where positive politeness strategies predominate, and with upper-class characters showing greater propensity to negative politeness. Very commonly, social differences are expressed lexically. For example, in the *Mistère du Viel Testament* the words of God and of the religious personages who address Him directly contain a great deal of latinism (see I, ll. 547–66), and the speech of criminals and executioners shows a high incidence of *argot* (see, for example, VI, ll. 46,056–48,219). More recently, H. Lewicka (1974: 61) has made similar observations with regard to farces, and E. Caron (1996) with regard to Passion plays. We cannot rely on literary authors to provide a direct reflection of variation in the spoken language, but we can infer from their work that social variation now mattered more than in the past.

The most celebrated literary source for Parisian French in the fifteenth century is François Villon (1435–65), whose poetry expresses his vision of 'low life' in Paris in the middle years of the century, and makes ample use of the speech of this milieu. The low-class features that figure most frequently in Villon's work are lexical ones – words drawn from the *argot* of the criminal fraternity (see Guiraud 1968). We will deal with these more systematically later (see §12.3.1). We also find the poet using at the rhyme a significant number of apparently stigmatised phonetic variants:

> [er] ~ [ar], e.g. *Barre: terre, Lais* ll. 178–81, *Robert: Lombart, Testament* ll. 750–2, *ardre: aherdre, Testament* ll. 817–19, *Barre: erre, Testament* ll. 937–8, *Marne: yverne, Testament* ll. 1655–6
>
> [we] ~ [wa], e.g. *Barre: poirre, Testament* ll. 1095–1100
>
> [jɛ̃] ~ [jɑ̃], e.g. *ancïen: an, Testament* ll. 1356–60, *ancïen: Valerien: an: crestien, Testament* ll. 1552–7
>
> [e] ~ [œ], e.g. *seuf* (= *soif*): *esteuf, Testament* ll. 929–31
>
> [aw] ~ [o], e.g. *hospitaulx: maulx: os, Testament* ll. 1645–8

Villon has been described as a sort of 'Cockney' poet, the voice of the common man, but his poetry has a literary sophistication beyond that of popular song. The fact that his works were printed in the very early (and expensive) days of printing – the first printed edition appears in 1489 – attests to his appeal to the educated classes, and by the same token to general familiarity with the vernacular forms he uses.

In the following century consciousness of social stratification within Parisian French becomes explicit (see Kibbee 1990; Morin 2000). It is probably no coincidence that the decision to establish the royal Court permanently in Paris in 1528 was immediately followed by a rush of publications – notably Tory (1529), Dubois (1531) and Bovelles (1533) – drawing attention to the shortcomings of the French language in comparison with Italian, perceived to be more ordered and polished. The following decades saw the publication of the earliest grammars of French (R. Estienne), the earliest dictionaries (R. Estienne), treatises on spelling and pronunciation (Meigret, Peletier), and general discussions on aspects of the French language (Tory, Bovelles, Bèze, H. Estienne).

The sixteenth-century elites sought to make Paris a Renaissance city, to rival the great Italian cities, with a language to match. Paris and its language became objects of intense pride. Henri Estienne, a Protestant who was no lover of Rome, compares the position of Paris in France with that of Athens in Ancient Greece:

A moins que, comme Athènes fut appelée la Grèce de la Grèce, on ne préfère appeler Paris, pour ce qui concerne la langue, la France de la France.[1] (H. Estienne 1582: Preface; see Demaizière 1988)

Many observers evoke the dialectal diversity of France, and insist on the special status of Parisian French. Acknowledgment of the superiority of Parisian French made them all the more intolerant of what they considered blemishes within it, H. Estienne (1582: 3) denouncing low-class Parisianisms as *des verrues dans une jolie figure*. How do contemporary observers picture the linguistic (and social) hierarchy in Paris? They refer to the bulk of the Paris population with such expressions as *vulgus (parisinus)* and *(Parisiis) plebs*, but their attitudes to the speech-forms of this large social group are curiously ambivalent. Most condemn them unreservedly, but some are more cautious, pointing out that they were the property of everyone, and that upper-class speakers were thoroughly conversant with them. Abel Matthieu (1559), for instance, refers to colloquial Parisian as the *commun populaire* and stresses its central importance

---

[1] 'Unless one prefers to call Paris, in linguistic matters, the France of France, just as Athens was called the Greece of Greece.'

in the everyday exchanges of all classes of Parisians. He recommends that provincials wishing to acquire a good overall mastery of metropolitan speech should frequent members of the Paris legal fraternity, for, at the same time as being well versed in the more highly valued varieties of the language (the speech of the Court and the legal chambers), they provide an excellent model for the local vernacular (*le commun populaire*), which they use most of the time:

Car aveuques ce qu'ilz ont le parler exquis, propre & familier se faisans accessibles au commun populaire (qui est le principal en eulx), le courtisan ou le plus friand parler du Roy & de sa court leurs est notoire.[2] (Matthieu 1559: 29v)

Pierre de la Ramée insists that people right at the top of society habitually used low-class forms in their everyday speech:

Le vulgaire, voire les Princes & grands seigneurs ont ordinairement en la bouche, *le dirons, le ferons*. Ce qui est condampné par aucuns Grammairiens disans, que le Francoys ne seuffre jamais nom ou pronom supposé au verbe soit de nombre different: mais je pense bien que l'usaige sen dispensera, & qu'il renversera le jugement de ces censeurs.[3] (Ramée 1572: 164–5)

It is reported that the Italian Queen Mother, Catherine de Médicis (1519–89), herself had mastered colloquial Parisian speech very effectively:

La royne-mère parloit aussi bien son goffe parisien qu'une revendeuse de la Place Maubert, et l'on n'eust point dit qu'elle estoit Italienne. (*Scaligeriana*, 1667, p. 46, quoted in Jacob 1859: 230)

On the expression *goffe* ('uncultivated talk'), see H. Estienne (1578: 68). Certain Parisian speech-forms were beyond the pale, however. H. Estienne (1582: 3) explicitly excludes from legitimate Parisian usage that of the *faex plebis* ('the dregs of the populace') which he elsewhere refers to as *le peuple grossier (qu'on appelle aujourd'hui la populasse)*. He associates this group with rurals temporarily resident in the city (*les gros rustaus et les piquebeufs*) and with marginals and criminals (*les gueux*). The speech-forms of the *gueux* elicit particular anxiety. Three places in the city where they congregated become emblematic : the Halles, the Place de Grève and the Place Maubert. The

---

[2] 'For as well as having exquisite speech, both formal and familiar, having access to the ordinary speech of everyone (which is their main usage), they are also familiar with the courtier or the most delectable speech of the King and his court . . .'

[3] 'The common people, and even princes and great lords commonly come out with *le dirons, le ferons*. The which is condemned by certain grammarians who say that French never permits a noun or pronoun preceding a verb to be of a different number: but I think that usage will dispense with this rule and will overturn the judgment of these censors.'

proximity between low-status speech and the dialects spoken in the city's rural hinterland had earlier been pointed to by Dubois:

Etiam si in agro Parrhisiensi et Parrhisiis quoque *vée, ése, Pontése*, etc., pronuntiari quotidie audiuntur.[4] (Dubois 1531: 25)

oi autem pro *o* & quandoque pro *i* omnes Galli recipiunt. Pro *e* autem Normani & agri Parrhisiensis homines, atque adeo Parrhisiensium non pauci respuerunt.[5] (Dubois 1531: 31)

H. Estienne nevertheless prefers this variety to that of the current italianising 'Court Set':

> Si en ce langage rural
> Les mots sont prononcez fort mal,
> Mots sont pourtant de bonne race,
> Suyvans des vieux françois la trace.[6]
> (H. Estienne 1578: 49)

Of more vital interest to the orthoepists was linguistic usage at the top of society, at the acrolectal level, where the great social conflicts in which they themselves were engaged were being played out. One of their prime concerns was to identify the 'best' form of French which would provide the basis for 'fixing' the language. Early grammarians like Dubois (1531) sought to base the norm on a supposed historical archetype which existed in Gaul after the demise of Latin but before the dialectal fragmentation of French. Later authors saw the need to base their concept of the norm on some empirical reality, and this usually meant identifying the persons of highest status and with greatest potential for exercising power. In the sixteenth century and for much of the seventeenth this was not self-evident. Latent throughout the period there was conflict between the traditional urban elite (made up of administrators, merchants and financiers) and the relative newcomers on the Parisian scene, the Court and the king's aristocratic entourage.

As early as 1529 Geoffroy Tory attacks the affected lexical innovations of courtiers. Indeed, given their own social origins, hostility to the 'Court Set' was endemic among the grammarians (see Smith 1966). However, under François I (1515–47) the prestige of the crown was such that Marot (1533), Peletier du Mans (1549) and Pillot (1550) all felt able to locate the high-prestige norm in the entourage of the king. The presence of women in this group further contributed to the '*douceur*' of its speech. Meigret (1550) and

---

[4] 'Even if in the countryside around Paris and in Paris itself people can be heard everyday pro-nouncing *vée, ése, Pontése*, etc . . . '

[5] 'Every Frenchman accepts *oi* as *o* and sometimes as *i*. The Normans and people in the countryside around Paris and even quite a few Parisians spew this out as *e*.'

[6] 'Even though in this rustic French words are pronounced very badly, their words are nevertheless of good stock, following in the way of older forms of French.'

R. Estienne (1557), Protestants writing at the time of Henri II (1547–59), were more ambivalent. The former distinguished between 'good' and 'bad' courtiers (which he sees as '*mignons efféminés*'). The latter expressed nostalgia for the language used in the entourage of the king ten years earlier, a veiled criticism of court usage under Henri II, at the time when his *Traicté* was published. He accepts that certain of the *plus savants en nostre langue* are to be found at the royal court, but he also gives weight to members of the legal and administrative class.

Writing as a Protestant after the outbreak of the Wars of Religion, Robert Estienne's son Henri was virulent in his criticism of the speech of the Court, peopled as it was with Catholics and the Italian followers of Catherine de Médicis. He attacks courtiers not only for their use of italianisms but also for inverted snobbery in their recourse to stigmatised features of colloquial Parisian speech:

N'ont-ils point peur que les suppots de la place Maubart (car ceux qui disent *frere Piarre* disent ainsi *la place Maubart*) ne les facent adjourner, comme estans troublez par eux en la possession & saisine de leur langage?[7] (H. Estienne 1578: 163–4)

It looks as though courtiers were ostentatiously using these forms to mark themselves off from their closest rivals for power and influence, the patricians of the Parisian merchant and administrative class. We are reminded constantly of the all-pervasive nature of low-class forms within Parisian society in the sixteenth century, and of the fact that reallocation of a number of variables was still in progress and not yet completed. Acrolectal forms in sixteenth-century Paris represent what Labov calls 'changes from above': these do not normally affect the vernacular patterns of the dominant class or other social classes, but appear primarily in careful speech, reflecting a superposed dialect learned after the vernacular is acquired.

Before closing this contemporary overview of language in sixteenth-century Paris, a remark has to be made about differences between male and female speech evoked by various commentators. Tory (1529: f.57r) attributes to female speakers the deletion of final consonants. Erasmus, followed by Dubois (1531) and Pillot (1550), highlights the tendency among females towards the assibilation of medial [r]:

Idem faciunt hodie mulierculae Parisinae, pro *Maria,* dicens *Masia,* pro *ma mere, ma mese.*[8] (Erasmus 1528: 45)

---

[7] 'Are they not afraid that those rogues in the Place Maubart (for those who say *frere Piarre* say *la place Maubart* in this way) may not take them to court on the grounds that they are disturbed by these people appropriating their language?'

[8] 'Certain women in Paris do the same thing nowadays, saying *Masia,* instead of *Maria, ma mese* instead of *ma mere.*'

Tory sees females as being particularly prone to hypercorrection, his prime example being the stigmatised lowering of [er] → [ar]:

Les dames de Paris, en lieu de A prononcent E bien souvent, quant elles disent *Mon mery est a la porte de Peris ou il se faict peier.* En lieu de dire *Mon mary est a la porte de Paris ou il se faict paier.*[9] (Tory 1529: f.33v)

The use of the term *dames* rather than *femmes* may simply be the product of politeness, but it could also be interpreted as referring to mesolectal, even acrolectal speakers. The tendency among middle-class women to hypercorrection is well attested in Western societies, though it should not be exaggerated (see Wardhaugh 2002: 328).

Let us now look more systematically at the phonetic and morphological variables which emerge at this time as being the most salient (on this term, see §6.2.2) and hence the most susceptible to reallocation.

7.2   The most salient variables

Thanks to Thurot's compilation of the comments on pronunciation made by all the main orthoepists working in the early modern period (Thurot 1881, 1883), it is a fairly easy matter to gauge the attention given to particular variables at particular times. This offers us a rudimentary barometer of their salience.

(i) Deletion of word-final consonants (see Thurot 1881: II, 4–17; Pope 1952: §§617, 623). The long-term drift in French towards a CV.CV syllable structure led to the effacement of consonants in word-final position during the late medieval and early modern period. However, certain consonants (e.g. [r]) and certain contexts (e.g. liaison forms, word-final position) resisted change more successfully than others. Indeed, the presence of liaison in modern French indicates that the change has still not been completed. As a general rule we can say that the chronology of final-consonant deletion is the following:
(1) before a word-initial consonant (e.g. *amende(s̲) douces*)
(2) before a pause (e.g. *amendes douce(s̲)*)
(3) before a word-initial vowel (e.g. *amendes douce(s̲) et ameres*)

The comments of contemporary orthoepists bore primarily on stage (1), to a lesser extent on stage (2) and hardly at all on stage (3). As we have just seen, Tory (1529: f.57r) draws attention to Parisian women leading the way in the deletion of word-final consonants, before words beginning with a consonant and in pre-pausal position. H. Estienne (1582: 99) highlights final-consonant deletion before following consonant in colloquial speech.

---

[9] 'The ladies of Paris very often pronounce E instead of A when they say *Mon mery est a la porte de Peris ou il se faict peier.* Instead of *Mon mary est a la porte de Paris ou il se faict paier.*'

(ii) Assibilation [r] → [z] (see Thurot 1883: II, 271–4; Pope 1952: §§397, 399; Joseph 1987: 155–6). This feature was first noted by Erasmus, who attributed it specifically to female speakers. He was followed by Palsgrave (1530: 13v), Dubois (1531: 52) and Pillot (1550: 10). At the same time Tory (1529: f.55r) drew attention to uncertainty in speakers' minds over the distribution of medial [r] and [s], denouncing it as an *abus*. Bovelles discusses this feature several times (1533: 36, 71, 89). He saw it as being so widespread in Paris that it was used by educated people as well as by the ignorant masses. It even found its way on to inn-signs:

id etiam publica domorum signa Parrhisiis in vicis profitentur *au gril cousonné*.[10]
(Bovelles 1533: 37)

It seems likely that this variable reached its high point in public awareness in the middle of the sixteenth century, though it continues to receive grammatical attention after that (see, for example, Tabourot 1588: 9v). However, by the 1620s the variable had lost much of its salience, a fixed lexical distribution having been established within the standard language (where the [z] variant was generalised in *chaise, nasiller* and *besicles*), the [z]-variant being reallocated as a stigmatised low-class feature.

(iii) [e] ~ [we] ~ [wa] (see Thurot 1881: I, 352–414; Pope 1952: §523–5; Joseph 1987: 136–7, 150). In the fifteenth and sixteenth centuries the three main reflexes of the old [OI] diphthong had for long been in competition in Parisian speech (see §5.2.2). Their particular distribution in modern French is relatively recent: [wa] is the default case, [e] is reserved for certain morphological and lexical sets (e.g. the endings of the imperfect and conditional, certain adjectives denoting geographical origin like *anglais, français*, and certain nouns like *craie, tonnerre* and *verre*, etc.), and [we] survives in a tiny number of lexical items like *couenne*). The use of [wa] was geographically restricted in Old French, so the essential development across time since then has been the diffusion of this variant through the lexicon and through society at the expense of the other two. Throughout the proto-industrial period the variable was highly salient, with the different variants assuming different social values at different times. Chronologically, the [e] ~ [we] variable achieved salience before [we] ~ [wa], though the second change was in progress long before the first was completed.

[e] ~ [we]. In sixteenth-century Paris the default variant appears to have been [we], but in numerous words there was variation. The most salient of these were: *connaitre/ paraitre, croire, croistre, dois, droit, estroit, foi, francois/anglois,*

---

[10] 'Also inn signs in the streets of Paris proclaim *au gril cousonné*' (instead of *couronné* = 'crowned').

froid, Oise, Pontoise, reine, vais, voie, voire, together with the endings of the imperfect/conditional. In the first half of the century the [e] variant was still seen as a 'Normanism' (see Dubois 1531: 21).

Later on in the century, when it is used by members of the Court, observers condemned it either as a vulgar affectation or as an italianism (see Des Autels 1551: 20). The [e] variant is condemned several times by H. Estienne (1578) in *français* (pp. 36, 64, 404), and *droit* (p. 64), but is approved of as 'virile' in *harnais* (p. 406).

In the endings of the imperfect/conditional, the [e] variant seems to have been dominant (see Thurot 1881: I, 378). Dubois (1531: 122) and Bèze consider it to be the normal colloquial form. Peletier (1548: 85), Des Autels (1551: 20) and H. Estienne (1578: 82, 405) all point out that it was widely used in Court circles as well as lower down in society. The [we] variant is not attributed to a particular sociolect, but several orthoepists express their preference for it over [e] (Des Autels 1551; Pasquier 1572; H. Estienne 1578).

[we] ∼ [wa]. The [wa] variant is first attested in Parisian speech in the thirteenth century (see above, §5.2.2), and seems to have become thoroughly well established in colloquial usage by the end of the fifteenth century. Palsgrave (1530: 13) considers it to be the normal pronunciation in monosyllables (e.g. *bois, fois*) and in the stressed syllable of di-syllabic words ending in orthographic *s, t* or *x* (e.g. *aincois, francois*).

Sixteenth-century grammarians attest the variant in low-class usage particularly before [l] and [r]: it was early generalised in the word *poêle* (pronounced [pwal]), and R. Estienne's dictionary contains the spellings *foarre* (= *foire*), *voarre* (= *verre*), *voarrier* (= *verrier*) and *voarriere* (= *verrière*). His son sees the variant spreading in colloquial speech (see Estienne 1582: 48), and he is particularly incensed to find it in common use among members of the Court (H. Estienne 1578: 46, 147, 163). Bèze (1584: 54) follows suit:

Corruptissime vero Parisiensium vulgus . . . pro *voirre, foirre,* scribunt et pronuntiant *voarre* et *foarre,* itidemque pro *trois, troas* et *tras.*[11]

Here we see a further variant [a] appearing, stripped of the initial semi-vowel (see below §7.3).

(iv) [o] ∼ [jo] (see Thurot 1881: I, 434–40; Pope 1952: §538–40). The [jo] variant remained widespread in colloquial Parisian speech throughout the proto-industrial period and beyond. It is mentioned by Palsgrave (1530) and by Dubois (1531) without stigmatisation. Peletier observes that:

Les Parisiens . . . au lieu d'*un séau d'éau* diset *un sio d'io.*[12] (Peletier 1550: 21)

---

[11] 'In the most incorrect way the common people of Paris write and pronounce instead of *voirre, foirre, voarre* and *foarre,* and in the same way, instead of *trois, troas* and *tras.*'

[12] 'Parisians say *un sio dio* instead of *un seau dèau.*'

Later in the century prescriptive hostility towards the form grows (see Bèze 1584: 53).

(v) **[er]** ~ **[ar]** (see Thurot 1881: I, 3–20, Pope 1952: §§ 496–8, Joseph 1987: 135, 148–9). The raising of [a] to [e] especially before [r] was widespread in HDP as it was in Picard, and is commonly attested in Parisian manuscripts from the thirteenth century onwards (see §5.2.3). Fifteenth-century poets from the top end of society, like Alain Chartier and Christine de Pizan, make occasional use of it at the rhyme (e.g. *lermes: armes*), as does Villon, who, we might suppose, reflects lower-class usage (see Marchello-Nizia 1979: 73–4). In the first half of the sixteenth century the spelling 'ar' for 'er' is still commonly used by the aristocracy and even in royal correspondence. However, [e]-raising before [r] becomes progressively stigmatised in Paris. J. Dubois (1531: 87) castigates the pronunciation *jarbe* for *gerbe*, and thereafter, the theme becomes a constant in French grammatical literature. Half a century later H. Estienne returns to this feature several times (H. Estienne 1582: 10–11). He criticises members of the Court for using this 'low' pronunciation, presumably as a form of inverted snobbery.

(vi) **Ouisme** (see Thurot 1881: I, 240–66; Pope 1952: §581–2, Joseph 1987: 135–6, 149). The distribution of O-sounds, particularly in countertonic syllables, had been subject to much variation in Parisian speech since medieval times (see §5.2.3 and Brunot 1906:II, 251–4). The question of whether words like *chose* should be pronounced [o] or [u] achieved such a high level of public awareness in the sixteenth century that participants in the debate were referred to as either 'ouystes' or 'non-ouystes' (see Tabourot 1587: 32). The orthoepists ascribe the raised [u] variant to members of the Court. H. Estienne asks them:

> Si tant vous aimez le son doux,
> N'estes vous pas bien de grands fous,
> De dire *chouse* au lieu de *chose*?
> De dire *jouse*, au lieu de *jose*?[13]
>   (H. Estienne 1578: 46)

(vii) **Merger of [ĩ] and [ɛ̃]** (see Thurot 1883: II, 481; Pope 1952: §452–4). The nasal vowels [ĩ] and [ɛ̃] in such forms as *vin* and *pain* remained distinct as late as the fifteenth century: the two sounds do not rhyme in Villon's poetry. However, they appear to have merged in colloquial Parisian speech during the sixteenth century, attracting the attention of the orthoepists (see Bovelles 1533: 90; Tabourot 1588: 92v).

(viii) **Elision of post-consonantal [l]/[r] before final schwa** (see Thurot 1883: II, 268, 281–2). The elision of post-consonantal [r] and [l] + [ə] was to

---

[13] 'If you are so much in love with the sweet sound, are you not then great idiots for saying *chouse* instead of *chose* and *jouse* instead of *jose*?'

become a widespread feature of colloquial Parisian French (e.g. *autre* → *aut'*). No grammarian picks this up in the sixteenth century, but Estienne condemns a related, perhaps hypercorrect, form involving the insertion of [l] in this position in the words *boutique, musique, demoniaque*. This gives rise to such forms as *bouticle, musicle* and *demoniacle* which he classes among:

des mots ou la faute est aisee a cognoistre & ou elle n'est pas volontiers commise que par le peuple grossier (qu'on appelle aujourd'hui la populasse) ou pour le moins que par ceux qui n'ont aucunes lettres: du nombre desquels nous scavons estre la plus grand' part des courtisans.[14] (H. Estienne 1578: 157)

(ix) Past historics in –*i* (see Fouché 1967: 262; Pope 1952: §1008). Remodelling of the endings of the simple past of *-er* verbs in *-i-* rather than *-a-* (e.g. *donismes* ∼ *donasmes*) had long been occurring in Parisian speech. It is widely attested in Christine de Pizan and Alain Chartier, though it may well have had a Picard origin (see Pope 1952: §1321.xxxi). This variable is discussed by most of the grammarians of the sixteenth century, who normally express preference for the *-a-* variant (see Palsgrave 1530: f.126v; Dubois 1531: 126; Meigret 1550: 86; R. Estienne 1557: 41; Ramus 1572: 84; Cauchie 1570: 126; H. Estienne 1578: 162). These perfects continued in colloquial use in Paris into the nineteenth century.

(x) Endings of the imperfect indicative/ present conditional (see Fouché 1967: 240, 242; Pope 1952: §917–20). During the sixteenth century almost the entire paradigm of the imperfect indicative/present conditional was in the process of reorganisation. Firstly, there was hesitation about the vowel used in the endings of the 1st, 2nd, 3rd and 6th persons, the variants being [e] and [we] which we discussed in (iii) above.

Secondly, in late medieval Paris the endings of the singular underwent change from an older pattern ending in schwa: *-oie, -oies, -oit*, to a new one where the final schwa was effaced. By the sixteenth century, this change seems to have been generalised, though memory of the earlier form had not been completely eradicated (see Thurot 1881: I, 180). The change gave rise to a new pattern in the written language: *-ois, -ois, -oit*. However, since word-final consonants were now silent, the question as to whether the new forms with *s* were for the eye only became a matter of prolonged debate among the orthoepists (see Thurot 1883: II, 41–58).

Thirdly, the ending of the 1st person plural had for centuries been subject to variation in Parisian speech, the variants being an older form *-iens* and a

---

[14] 'Words where the mistake is easy to spot and where it is committed not just by the rough common people (nowadays known as the populace) or by illiterates, but by people in whom we must include most of the courtiers . . .'

newer form *-ions* (see §5.2.2). The older form was still common in colloquial Parisian, particularly in the verb *estre*, giving the form *estiens*.

Finally, there was variation in the 6th person between forms retaining schwa in the final syllable (e.g. *estoient*) and forms without (e.g. *estoint* and *estiont*) which were widespread in HDP (see §4.1.2). Fouché (1967: 241) is at pains to distinguish this variable from the schwa-less endings in the singular that we have just looked at. This variable achieved high salience in the sixteenth century, to judge by the attention it received from the grammarians (see Dubois 1531: 125; Meigret 1550: 10–11; Cauchie 1570: 148, 150; H. Estienne 1578: I, 11, 172).

(xi) *je* + *-ons* (see Pope 1952: §§74, 81; Joseph 1987: 138–9; Brunot 1906: II, 335–6). A feature widely attested in the HDP (see *ALF* 27) and in Parisian speech in the early modern period is the use of the 1st person singular pronoun *je* + *-ons*, normally with 1st person plural reference. Attention to it is first drawn by Palsgrave:

In comune speche they use to saye: *ie allon bien, ie ferons bien.* (Palsgrave 1530: f.100r)

Very often it is not clear whether we are dealing with a verb in the royal plural or a 4th person *nous* form (see Hull 1988). If we follow Cotgrave (1611), the basic reference is to the 4th person:

Ie (a pronowne) 1: Sometimes used by the vulgar Parisians in stead of *nous*; as *ie sommes*; we are.

However, cases of its use as a royal plural are frequent. It is condemned by Meigret (1550: 53; see Trudeau 1992: 79), and by Ramus (1572: 164–5, see Trudeau 1992: 102), who find it to be widespread across society. Its use by members of the Court is condemned several times by Estienne (1578: I, 11, 172–3, 284, II, 241).

This list of sociolinguistic variables could be extended, but we have limited it to the most salient, the ones that look to have been rising in social awareness to the level of markers, even of stereotypes (in the Labovian sense).

7.3   The 'Urban Peasant'

As public awareness of variation within Parisian speech became stronger and pressures to differentiate between good and bad speech became greater, habitual groupings of stereotypical features began to coalesce in the collective mind as sociolinguistic 'prototypes' (see §6.2.3). The characteristics of ideally good speech gradually crystallised in the notion of *bon usage* and the prototype of the *Honnête Homme* ('the Gentleman'). This has attracted a great deal of scholarly attention (see, for instance, Trudeau 1992). At the same time the characteristics of ideally bad speech crystallised in the anti-thetical notion of *mauvais usage* and the prototype we have labelled the *Paysan de Ville* ('the Urban Peasant'). Rather less attention has been devoted to this.

In common with many European cities at the time there developed in late fifteenth-century Paris a heightened sense of the contrast between urbanity and rusticity. In all areas of social life, including language, the urbane man of culture stood in contrast to the rustic and boorish peasant. Elevation of the manners of one social group brought about the automatic disparagement of those of the rest, and in Paris, as a little later in London, this began with the speech of the peasantry residing in the immediate vicinity of the City. What stood outside the civilised realm of the City was increasingly perceived as rustic and bar-barous. However, sharp cultural contrasts were also evident within the City itself. What was urban was not necessarily urbane. The interpenetration be-tween the city and its rural hinterland meant that 'peasants' (in the sense of 'uncultivated people') could be found *intra muros* as well as *extra muros*. Prescriptive observers in all probability wilfully blurred the urban/rural dis-tinction, but the interpenetration of town and country at the bottom of society meant that the speech of rustics and the 'urban peasantry' were very similar.

7.3.1   Down-grading suburban speech

The earliest manifestations of the 'Urban Peasant' prototype are to be found in two fifteenth-century farces poking fun at the speech of rustics from villages situated in those days just outside the city. The first is entitled *Monologue du franc archier de Baignollet* (ed. Picot and Nyrop 1968: 47–70). Bagnollet is situated about three miles to the north-east of the city centre, and is now of course engulfed in the general conurbation. The amount of linguistic informa-tion contained in this text is limited, but it points clearly to a developing sense (among Parisians) of the urbanity (and superiority) of city life compared with the rusticity and boorishness to be found outside its walls. Awareness of the differences between urban and suburban speech is expressed more explicitly in the *Farce des Enfants de Borgneux* (ed. Cohen 1949: 211–17, and discussed by Lewicka 1974: 64–6). 'Borgneux' (= Bagneux) is situated three or four miles to the south-west of the city centre. Here is a short extract:

TIBAULT: Mais j'ay un point qui me destruit.
GUILLOT: Et quel point?
TIBAULT: Je suis trop franc,
           Aga! Se je n'avoye qu'un blanc   *Regarde*
           Et tu voulois les deux deniers,
           La vertu goy! Tu les auroies.   *Dieu*

GUILLOT: Autel te dis, il ne pert mie
            Aussi à nostre <u>filomie</u>   *physionomie*
            Que <u>je n'avons</u> gentil couraige.[15]   *nous avons.*
                    (*Farce des Enfants de Borgneux*, ll.193–200)

In this farce we find a good proportion of the rustic linguistic variants which were to be the hallmarks of low-class Parisians in the centuries to come:

Phonetic features

– variants in the evolution of the [OI] diphthong (e.g. *tect* (= *toit*) 62, *tournas* (= *tournois*) 247)
– ouisme (e.g. (*moucques* (= *moques*) 23)
– confusion of [er] and [ar] (e.g. *cheriant* (= *charriant*) 300)
– velarisation of [dj] (e.g. *par la vertu goy* (= *Dieu*) 25, 197, 215)
– rounding of [e] (e.g. *fumellez* (= *femelles*) 296).

Morphological features

– 4th person in *je* + *-ons* (e.g. *je n'avons* 200, 266, *je fringuerons* 258, *je ferons* 259, *je sommes* 265)
– past historics in *-i* (e.g. *j'entry* 77, *je bailly* 166)
– imperfects in *-ié* (e.g. *je meniés* 210, *tu saultiés* 49, *c'estiés* 208, 211, *il estient* 178).

Lexical features

– frequent use of swear-words (e.g. *Ventre Saint Canet* 2, *Michié* 5, *Sanc de moy* 14)
– common exclamations (e.g. *c'est mon* 6, 73, *aga* 195, 302)
– deformation of learned words (e.g. *filomie* 199).

A more elaborate manifestation of this prototype appears in the middle of the sixteenth century, in the guise of the *biau fys de Pazy*, the difference being that the figure is not a rustic from outside, but a middle-class resident of the city itself.

7.3.2   *The Epistre du biau fys de Pazy (c. 1550)*

The *Epistre* takes the form of an exchange of love-letters (in octosyllabic couplets) between a young Parisian bourgeois and a married woman of the same class. The social origins of the protagonists are not in doubt: we are told that the deceived husband has a shop (l. 34), and an apprentice (l. 104), and that

---

[15] 'T. But there is one thing which lets me down.
  G. And what's that?
  T. I am too generous. Blimey, if I had a silver sixpence and you wanted twopence of them, Streuth, you would have them.
  G. I tell you this, it does not appear on our faces that we have a noble heart . . .'

the lover makes business trips to Niort (l. 49) and to Lyon (l. 168). The author mocks not only the speech-habits of the couple, but also their clumsy handling of courtship ritual, their outmoded tastes in literature, dance, dress and so on.

The piece is an extended joke constructed essentially around the contemporary Parisian vogue for the assibilation of [r] → [z], but numerous other stigmatised features are introduced too. Here are the opening lines of the poem (the complete text is to be found in the Appendix, Text 1):

	Madame, je <u>vous raime</u> tan,	*vous aime*
	Mais ne le dite pas pourtan;	
	Les <u>musaille</u> on <u>derozeille</u>.	*murailles; des oreilles*
4	Celui qui fit les gran merveille	
	Nous doin bien to couché ensemble,	
	Car je <u>vous rayme</u>, ce me semble,	*vous aime*
	Si fort que ne vous <u>lore dize</u>,	*l'ose dire*
8	Et vous l'ay bien voulu <u>escrize</u>	*escrire*
	Affin de <u>paslé</u> de plus loing.	*parler*
	Pensé que j'avoy bien <u>beroing</u>	*besoin*
	De deveni si <u>amouzeu</u>!	*amoureux*
12	O que je <u>sesoy</u> bien <u>heuzeu</u>,	*serais, heureux*
	Ha! Madame la <u>renchesie</u>,	*rencherie*
	Se n'est que vostre <u>fachesie</u>,	*facherie*
	Non <u>pa pou vou le reprochez</u>,	*pas pour vous le reprocher*
16	May si to que je veu <u>touchez</u>	*toucher*
	Vostre joly tetin molet,	
	Vou m'appellé peti folet,	
	En me <u>diran</u>: 'Laissé cela:	*disant*
20	Vou n'avé rien caché yla;	
	Dieu, vous deviné <u>mou</u> privé!	*mon*
	Ou pensé vou estre arrivé?'[16]	

Although this text attributes extra-strong salience to one particular variable, the assibilation of medial [r], other phonological, morphological and indeed lexical variants are featured too. This enables us to identify not only what variables were salient at this time, but also, if we consider the frequency with which each of them occurs, their *relative* salience. For instance, in the *Epistre* tokens of the [r] ∼ [z] variable occur seventy-four times, those of the [o] ∼ [jo] variable (e.g. *beau* ∼ *biau*) ten times and those of the [er] ∼ [ar] variable (e.g. *Pierre* ∼ *Piarre*) four times. These frequencies are to a great extent determined

---

[16] 'Madam, I love you so much, but do not say it out loud; walls have ears. May He who performed great marvels grant us to lie together soon, for I love you, so it seems to me, so strongly that I dare not declare it to you, so I have opted to write it down, in order to speak to you from further off. It's not that I needed to fall so much in love! Oh how happy I would be, Madam-hard-to-get, if it were not for your contrariness. Not that I hold this against you, but as soon as I wish to touch your pretty soft breast, you call me a crazy fellow, saying "Stop that, you've not hidden anything there. God, you are becoming intimate with me! How far do you think you have got?"'

by the number of phonetic contexts in which the variables may potentially occur, and by the general frequency of the words involved. However, insofar as the author had total control over the words he chooses, it is more than likely that his lexical choices were influenced by their potential for carrying a particular stigmatised form. It seems reasonable to assume, therefore, that the relative frequency of particular variables in the text is correlated in a loose way with their relative salience at the time when the text was composed. Let us then consider the variable features in this text, beginning with lexis.

Recognising the high-salience lexical items making up a parody is easy enough when the target group engaged in a high level of lexical innovation. This was the case with Rabelais' parody of the *escolier limousin* (see below, §12.2.1), with H. Estienne's parody of italianisms in the Court Set, and with Molière's parody of the speech of doctors, lawyers and the *Précieux*. However, with social groups in the past which were felt to be behind the times and to be clinging to an archaic vocabulary, identifying the salient items is more difficult. In the present text it is possible to identify certain archaisms denoting realia which had themselves gone out of fashion or had lost social status. This is the case with the dances that the couple refer to: *Basse danse* 64, *branle* 66, *haye de Bretaigne* 62, *passepié d'Allemaigne* 63, *recoupe* 66. Other archaisms are less easy to recognise, however, and are difficult to distinguish from low-value words in general. The figures quoted here are line-numbers.

The principles governing the reallocation of lexical items between styles and sociolects were normally geared to the social connotations of the words involved, and to the developing sense of etiquette (with built-in negative politeness). Words evoking in a direct, concrete way notions belonging primarily to home and family, to the world of intimacy and privacy, tend to be reserved for vernacular use. This looks to be the case with the following: *marmiteu* 27, *parmanda voize* 95, *quinau* 27, *marcher sur le pie* 87. This applies to phrases and fixed locutions (termed at the time *proverbes*) as well as to individual lexemes: *plu dur qu'un potizon* 37, *menu comme chair a pasté* 68, *aussi claize que l'iau de puy* 82, *vestu comme un oignon* 138.

Social groups whose lexical range did not extend far outside the vernacular were felt to be incapable of appropriately handling words of a higher register. This perhaps accounts for the metathesis present in *Norman de la Rore* (= *Roman de la Rose*) 30. In other cases it is difficult to detect any obvious sociolinguistic rationale: *ort* (=*sale*) 48, *sen* (= *ce*) 39, *yla* (= *là*) 20.

Let us now turn to the non-lexical variants present in this text, dealing first with phonetics and then with morphology.

(i) Deletion of final consonants. This is the most frequent non-standard variable to figure in the text, producing over 200 tokens. The consonants concerned are: [s] (84 deletions, to which may be added 19 deletions of 'x', and 18 of 'z', which in Middle French were often orthographic alternatives to 's'); [t] (50 deletions); [r] (11 deletions); [d] (6 deletions); [nt], 6th person ending (2 deletions). [r] of the infinitive is commonly replaced by [z]: *allez* 114, *aprochez* 122, *dansez* 62, *frequentez* 115, *touchez* 121, etc. Spellings indicating the effacement of [l] in *il* are attested in Parisian texts from the thirteenth century onwards (see Pope 1952: §841), and they are featured several times here: *qui = que + il* (100, 102, 118, 134) *qui = que + ils* (154). It is even deleted from the feminine *elles*: *qui = que + elles* (113, 182).

It is not easy to quantify the frequency of this variable in a way that permits comparison with others occurring in the text. Should we treat each category of final consonant deletion as an individual variable, or should we conflate as one composite variable? It is occasionally unclear whether we are dealing with the deletion of final consonants from phonetic words or merely from their orthographic form. For example, in *pry (= prix)* 41, it is probable that in the mid sixteenth century, deletion of final [s] was categorical in Parisian speech, not variable, and that deletion here is an orthographic variant for the eye only. However, the least we can say is that by deleting final consonants in such large numbers the author is obviously making a statement about the contemporary salience of this variable, in certain contexts at least.

Table 14. *Assibilation of [r] → [z]*

[r] → [z]	[z] → [r]
Inter-vocalic	
amouzeu (11)	*aburée* (111)
aventuze (79)	*aymer* (107)
claize (82), etc.	*ayre* (129), etc.
Pre-consonantal:	
paslé (9)	*touriour* (110, 138, 146)
voys le (50)	*m'aymer tan* (107)

(ii) **Assibilation [r] → [z].** The assibilation of medial [r] to [z] was widespread in HDP and in other Gallo-Romance dialects (see Bloch 1928: 271–4; Table 14). It was attested in medieval Parisian documents (see above, §5.2.3) and Villon made use of it at the rhyme. A similar hesitation between [s/z] and [r] took place occasionally before voiced consonants (where pre-consonantal [s] had not been effaced): in medieval Picard texts we find Old French *vaslet > varlet* and *desve > derve* (see Pope 1952: §378); Villon produces the rhyme *Marle: mesle* (*Testament* 1266–8); in a fifteenth-century manuscript of the *Quinze Joyes de Mariage* we find the spelling *tourjours (< tousjours)* (see Rickard 1976: 47), which commonly recurs in the first half of the sixteenth century.

(iii) **[e] ∼ [we] ∼ [wa].** In the present text certain forms occur uniformly with the conventional spelling 'oi': *croize (= croire)* 71,109, *ivoize (= ivoire)*

150, *memoire* 149, *moy* 114, *noir* 151, *veoir* 152, *voy* 79. Some occur with both the 'oy' and the 'ay' 'e' spellings (*croy* (= *crois*) 58, *cray* (= *crois*) 117), and the imperfect and conditional 1st-person endings (*avoy* (= *avais*) 10, 80, *sesoy* (= *serais*) 12, *mousoy* (= *mourais*) 36, *contesoy* (= *conterais*) 161, *avetz* (= *avais*) 180, *sesetz* (= *serais*) 130, 179, *vouray* (= *voudrais*) 47, *estetz* (= *étais*) 105). Some occur solely with the 'ay'/'ey'/'e' spelling: *saye* (= *soie*) 170, *set* (= *soit*) 153, *seynt* (= *soient*) 182, imperfect and conditional 3rd-person endings (*regardet* 84, *ardet* 85, *diset* 100, *souspiset* 102, *resjouyset* 131). On two occasions we find spellings representing the stigmatised [wa] pronunciation: *voua* (= *vais*) 43, *foua* (= *fais*) 118. This precise example is commented on by Tabourot (1588: 92v).

(iv) [o] ∼ [jo]. Our bourgeois protagonists make frequent use of the stigmatised [jo] variant: *biau* in the title, 33, 45, 55, 126, 141, 145, 170, *iau* 82, *ruisieau* 154, *Siau* 155.

(v) [er] ∼ [ar]. This variable is featured four times in the text: *pazouquet* (= *peroquet*) 42, *Piar* (= *Pierre*) 83, *sarrant* (= *serrant*) 88, *varriez* (= *verriez*) 151.

(vi) **Ouisme**. No examples.

(vii) **Merger of [ɪ̃] and [ɛ̃]**.

Little prominence is given in this text to the development of nasals, but the spelling *sin* (= *saint*) probably refers to the early merging of [ɪ̃] and [ɛ̃] in colloquial speech.

(viii) **Word-final [k] + schwa**. In colloquial Parisian speech [l] was sporadically inserted between [k] and final schwa: *musicle* (= *musique*) 133, *bouticle* (= *boutique*) 134.

(ix) **Endings of the past historic**. Endings in *-i* occur frequently in the text: *ally* 185, *arrivit* 91, *clochy* 88, *commencite* 76, *entry* 78, *marchiste* 86, *rachevite* 77, *rencontry* 79, *recully* 26, *sembly* 81, *trouvit* 92.

(x) **Endings of the imperfect indicative/present conditional**. We saw earlier that these verb-endings were subject to variation and change in three areas. Firstly, there was hesitation between [e] and [we] in the endings of the 1st, 2nd, 3rd and 6th persons. The spellings of our text show a preference for the [e] variant. Secondly, the ending of the 1st person singular varied between an older form ending in schwa, e.g. *portoie*, and a newer form ending in [s], e.g. *portois*. In our text the use of the new form is generally highlighted, though sometimes final [s] is emphasised (*avetz* (= *avais*) 180, *sesetz* (= *serais*) 130, 179, *estetz* (= (*étais*) 105) and sometimes it is deleted (*avoy* (= *avais*) 10, 80, *sesoy* (= *serais*) 12, *mousoy* (= *mourais*) 36, *contesoy* (= *conterais*) 161, *vouray* (= *voudrais*) 47). Thirdly, the ending of the 1st person plural varied between an older form in *-iens* and a newer form *-ions*. In this text, it is the older form which is highlighted (and mocked): *etien* 75, *estien* 167. Similarly archaic 2nd-person forms are to be found in *tu scaviez* (39) and *tu feriez* (167).

(xi) je + -ons. We find one example of this in the text: *j'estien* 167.

A comic text like this was not composed as a realistic portrayal of middle-class Parisian speech in the middle of the sixteenth century. The author's prime concern was with the social symbolism of the variants presented. For us, its importance lies in the insight it provides into the relative salience of particular sociolinguistic variables in the social psychology of the time. It is worth noting that the poet attributes these negative variants not to the lowest and most despised members of Paris society, but to members of the merchant class. This no doubt reflects the aristocratic disdain for 'trade', but it also reinforces the impression that at this time stigmatised colloquial forms were still on the lips of quite well-placed members of society.

It is tempting to infer from the grossness of the mimicry linguistic that the forms involved were largely a figment of the author's imagination. We are not dealing with the Yahoo language of Lilliput: in texts like this the joke will only work if the reader recognises the imitation. It so happens that we possess tiny specimens of less self-conscious language from the same period (the middle of the sixteenth century), which attest the existence of the principal variants highlighted here, not among low-class speakers, of course, but in the verbal repertoire of the highest in the land.

7.4   Personal correspondence

The type of data which is likely to contain the strongest traces of everyday speech is perhaps the personal letters of people whose normal business was not writing. Less influenced by ingrained habits of a conventionalised spelling system, inexperienced writers might be expected to show a higher level of vernacular influence than people like secretaries or clerks, who spent their whole professional lives writing. This cannot always be relied upon (see Branca-Rosoff and Schneider 1994), but any such data are worth investigating. Not many documents of this kind have survived from the sixteenth century, or if they have, not many of them have been published. Priority in publication has gone, understandably, to the personal correspondence of the most powerful historical figures. We have examined two collections of such letters: the *Lettres de Marguerite d'Angoulême* (see Génin 1841) and the *Foreign Correspondence with Marie de Lorraine, Queen of Scotland, 1537–1548* (see Wood 1923).

In these collections, letters signed by the sender but written under dictation by secretaries show little of interest, but autograph letters, particularly those written by children, are more revealing. Of particular interest is a letter from Mademoiselle de la Tousche to Marie de Lorraine dated probably 1548, which we print *in toto* below (see Wood 1923: 214–16). The writer was a lady-in-waiting who had left the Queen Dowager's service in Scotland to return to Paris to care for her dying husband, and who finds herself short of money.

A la Royne en Escosse

Madame, de puys que je suys partie de voutre conpagnee j'é tant heu d'annuy et de trouble que je n'é seu trouvez le moyan vous faire antandre ma malleureuse fortune, qui est, Madame, que j'é pardu mon marri et mon filx ezne et suis demeuree la
4 plus maleureuse parsonne de tout le monde; quar onques famme ne filx plus grande parte. Madame, sy vous plest savoir en l'ettat ou il a torgous ezte de pui son retoror d'Angleterre la ou il s'est tourgous trouve mal, et a sezte reson, incontinant qu'i feut a Paris, il se mist entre les mens des medessins qui [. . .] du tout, de sorte qu'i
8 me fallit en menez par eau et en une litiere gousque a sa maison ou de puys n'a ezte sans sieurgiens, medessins et appotiqre pour cuder trouver moyan de le garir, mes il n'i eut seu trouvez remedde, quar il dises tous que s'toict poyson. Madame il a torgous heu jousque a son darnier jour, qui feut le septiesme de septanbre, ung grant
12 regret qu'i n'a peu retorner en Ezquosse pour vous faire sarvisse et sy souheztoict a toutes heures tot en l'ettat qu'il ettioct, quar il luy sanblet que sy luy pouvret aller qu'il seroit gari. Madame, il n'est creable a seulx qui l'ont veu la sorte en quoy il eztoit devenu quar il eztoict diminue qui ne pesoit poinct ung anfant de quenze ans.
16 Madame, quant a l'ettat ou je suis demeurree, c'est que ge trouve pour treze sans frans de dettes dont je suis contrente d'en pager la moytie et sy n'e que la moytie de mes meubles par se que ma belle mere vivante je ne peus rien prandre en seulx de la Touche et sy me voulles faire pardre mon [bien] et mon doyre quar elle se dict
20 dame du tout. Madame je vous suplie tres heunblement me voulloyr pardonnez la hardiesse que je prans de vous en [. . .] mes grans et piteuses forteunes. Madame je croy que avez bien antandu commant le feulx Roy a fes baller quatre sans esqueus pour la ranson de feulx mon marri; sepandant qu'il ettoit en Angleterre il avoict
24 enpreunte du quapitene Seri vengt set esqueus et vent d'eung espagnol, qui s'etiens (= *se tient?*) au Louvre a Paris, qui sarvoit de pie en Angleterre, et quenze de ung autre homme de Paris qui estoict segretaire de l'Admiral d'Andleterre, et douse de Monsieur de Vassay et a Gorges Obston et a Monsieur d'Anaucourt mes je ne sse
28 conbien il luy en ballises pour san venir. Madame, je vous suplie tres heunblement me faire tant de bien que de commander au tresorier de me baller les gages de feulx mon marri, qui est ung an et demi, pour m'aider a payer mes dectes quar sans l'aide de Dieu et de vous il m'est inpossible le pouvoir faire, vous supliant tres
32 heunblement, Madame, avoir pitie et souvenance de moy comme de selle qui ne derise en se monde que de vous pouvoir faire servisse et de vivre et mourir en voutre companee sy Noutre Saigneur et vous, Madame, me donnies tant d'eur et de bien. Madame, il vous plut me dire au partir que sy fortune m'arivoict que je me retirasse
36 a Madame voultre merre, se que je ne heuze faire sans savoir sa voullonte quen ez escrit a Monsieur de la Brosse pour luy en parles pour savoyr se qui luy ples que g'en fasse. Madame, je vous suplie tres heunblemant me faire tant d'onneur et de grasse que de me tenir touzgous du nonbre de vous plus que tres heunbles et obeisantes
40 sarvantes. Prie noutre Saigneur, Madame, vous donnez en sante tres bonne vie et longue de Lenge se quatriesme d'avril. Voutre plus que tres heunble et tres obeisante servante.[17]

[17] **A La Reine en Ecosse**
Madame, depuis que je suis partie de votre compagnie, j'ai eu tant d'ennui et de trouble que je n'ai su trouver moyen de vous faire entendre ma malheureuse fortune, qui est, Madame, que j'ai perdu mon mari et mon fils aîné et suis demeurée la plus malheureuse personne de tout

What traces of vernacular usage can be found here? We will see that the features attested show a strong resemblance to those found in the *Epistre* with which this letter is almost exactly contemporary.

(i) Deletion of final consonants. Very few final consonants are deleted, e.g. *ples/plest* 5. However, as in the *Epistre*, the [nt] of the 6th person endings are lost, to be replaced in this text by 's', presumably as a plural marker: *dises* (= *dirent*) 10, *voulles* (= *veulent*) 19, *ballises* (= *baillirent*) 28, *donnies* (= *donnent*) 34. 'r' of the infinitive is normally replaced by 'z' (on one occasion by 's'): *trouvez* 2, 10, *menez* 8, *pardonnez* 20, *parles* 37, *donnez* 40. Spellings indicating the effacement of [l] in *il* are attested several times : *qui* = *que* + *il* 6, 7, 12, 37.

(ii) Assibilation [r] → [z]. This feature is attested in three words: *dises* (= *dirent*) 10, *ballises* (= *baillirent* = *baillerent*) 28, *derise* (= *desire*) 33. The form *touriour* in the *Epistre*, which shows the reverse process, is also found

le monde; car jamais femme ne fit plus grande perte. Madame, s'il vous plaît de savoir l'état où il a toujours été depuis son retour d'Angleterre, là où il s'est toujours trouvé mal, et pour cette raison, dès qu'il fut à Paris, il se mit entre les mains des médecins qui [. . .] du tout, de sorte qu'il me fallut [l'] emmener par eau et dans une litière jusqu'à sa maison, où, depuis [ce temps-là] il n'a jamais été sans chirurgiens, médecins et apothicaires pour imaginer trouver moyen de le guérir, mais il n'a pas su y trouver remède, car ils disent tous que c'était [l'effet d'une] poison. Madame il a toujours eu jusqu'à son dernier jour, qui fut le sept septembre, un grand regret qu'il n'a pas pu retourner en Ecosse pour vous rendre service et il le souhaitait à toutes les heures malgré l'état où il était, car il lui semblait que s'il pourrait aller, il serait guéri. Madame, il n'est pas croyable, à ceux qui l'ont vu, l'état dans lequel il était tombé, car il était diminué [à tel point] qu'il ne pesait pas un enfant de quinze ans. Madame, quant à l'état où je suis demeurée, c'est que je trouve pour treize cents francs de dettes dont je suis contrainte de payer la moitié, et pourtant je n'ai que la moitié de mes meubles parce que, ma belle mère étant toujours en vie, je ne pus rien prendre de ceux de La Touche, et ainsi ils veulent me faire perdre mon bien et mon dot, car elle se dit maîtresse de tout. Madame je vous supplie très humblement de bien vouloir me pardonner la hardiesse que je prends de vous [. . .] ma grande et lamentable infortune. Madame, je crois que vous avez bien entendu comment le feu Roi a fait donner quatre cents écus pour la rançon de feu mon mari; pendant qu'il était en Angleterre, il avait emprunté au capitaine Seri vingt sept écus et vingt d'un Espagnol, qui se tient au Louvre à Paris, qui était secrétaire de l'Amiral d'Andleterre, et douze de Monsieur de Vassay et à Georges Obston et à Monsieur d'Anaucourt, mais je ne sais pas combien ils lui en donnèrent pour s'en venir. Madame, je vous prie très humblement, de me faire tant de bien que de commander au trésorier de me donner le salaire de feu mon mari, remontant, à un an et demi, pour m'aider à payer mes dettes, car sans l'aide de Dieu et de vous il m'est impossible de pouvoir le faire, vous suppliant très humblement, Madame, d'avoir pitié et souvenir de moi comme de celle qui ne désire en ce monde que de pouvoir vous rendre service et de vivre et mourir en votre compagnie, si Notre Seigneur et vous, Madame, me donniez tant de bonheur et de bien. Madame, il vous plut de dire lors de mon départ que, si le hasard faisait que je me retire du service de Madame votre mère, ce que je n'ose faire sans savoir sa volonté, qu'en ai écrit à Monsieur de la Brosse pour lui en parler pour savoir ce qu'il lui plaît que je fasse. Madame, je vous prie très humblement [de] me faire tant d'honneur et de grâce que de me tenir toujours du nombre de vos plus que très humbles et obéissantes servantes. Prie Notre Seigneur, Madame, vous donner en santé très bonne vie et longue, de Lenge (?) ce quatrième d'avril. Votre plus que très humble et obéissante servante.

in this text (*torgous, tourgous* 5, 6, 11), alongside the more orthodox spelling *touzgous* 39. See also the letter from Mademoiselle de Guerinière to the Queen of Scotland (see Wood 1923: 75 (after 1538)).

(iii) [e] ∼ [we] ∼ [wa]. Variation in the reflexes of the Old French [OI] diphthong is not to be found, save in the imperfect endings: *sanblet* 13, *pouvret* 13, alongside the traditional 'oi' spelling (*arivoict* 35, *souheztoict* 12, *seroit* 14, *eztoict* 13, 15, 15),

(iv) [o] ∼ [jo]. The only spelling present is *eau* 8.

(v) [er] ∼ [ar]. This variable appears several times: *pardu* 3, *parsonne* 4, *parte* 5, *garir* 9, *darnier* 11, *sarvisse* 12 (cf. *servisse* 33, *servante* 42), *pardre* 19. This variant was evidently in common use in royal circles: François I himself uses the spelling *tartre* for *tertre* in a letter to Marguerite d'Angoulême (see Genin 1841: 467). The young François d'Orléans uses the spelling *darriere* for *derriere, darnierement* for *dernierement* in letters to his mother Marie de Guise, Queen of Scotland (see Wood 1923: 81 (1542), 87 (1543), 205 (1548)).

(vi) Ouisme. The following examples are to be found: *Voutre* 1, 33, 36, *noutre* 34, 40, *voullonte* 36, *vous* (= *vos*) 39.

(vii) Lowering of nasals. Numerous spellings attest the lowering of nasals: *annuy* 1, *antandre* 2, 22, *famme* 4, *septanbre* 11, *sanblet* 13, *anfant* 15, *sans* 16, *prandre* 18, *prans* 21, *commant* 22, *sepandant* 23, *s'an* 28, *mens* 7, *moyan* 2, *contrente* 17, *quenze* 15.

(viii) Elision of post-consonantal [l]/[r] before final schwa. No examples are attested.

(ix) Past historics in -*i*. The text contains two examples of past historics in -*i*, though an accumulation of non-standard features makes them difficult to recognise: *fallit* (< *fallut*) 8, *ballises* (< *baillerent*) 28. The young François d'Orléans (aged seven) uses the form *souppy* for *soupa* in a letter to his mother (Wood 1923: 82, 207). A further example of a non-standard past historic is to be found in the form *respondut* (Wood 1923: 25).

(x) Endings of the imperfect indicative/present conditional. The normal spelling used here for the endings of the 1st, 2nd, 3rd and 6th persons is 'oi', which leaves open the possibility of pronunciations in both [e] and [we]. However, the spellings *sanblet* and *povret* and analogous spellings elsewhere in the collection (see, for example, Wood 1923: 25) indicate the widespread use of the [e] vowel in this ending. The stigmatised form of the 6th person *estoint* (= *estoient*) is to be found in a letter from M. de la Brosse to the Dowager Queen of Scotland (see Wood 1923: 118).

(xi) *je* + -*ons*. In this text we find no examples of the use of the 1st person singular pronoun *je* + the ending of the 1st person plural, with 1st person plural reference. However, we find numerous examples elsewhere in the collection, particularly in the correspondence of Marie de Lorraine:

... *j'avons* retrouve le menage ou je vous puis asurer avons trouve nostre petit filz aussy joly et en bon point qu'enfant peut estre[18] (see Wood 1923: 19; see also 7, 52, 61, 72, 92, 95, 113).

The young François d'Orléans writes to his mother:

J'en attandons la rezolution dedans viii jours ...[19] (Wood 1923: 207 (1548))

François I uses it in his personal correspondence:

... car *j'avons* esperance qu'y fera demain beau temps, veu ce que disent les estoilles que *j'avons* eu tres bon loysir de veoir ...[20] (see Genin 1841: 467–8, l.15)

The points we have just listed do not exhaust the vernacular phonetic features present in this curious letter. We find other features not highlighted in the *Epistre du biau fys de Pazy*. The first involves the lowering of [u] and [y] > [oe] (Pope 1952: §458): *heunblement* 20, 28, 32, 38, *forteunes* 21 (cf. *fortune* 2), *esqueus* 22, 24, *enpreunte* 28, *eung* 28. The second involves a rounding of E-sounds → [oe], as, for example in *veve* > *veuve* and *bevrage* > *breuvage* (see Pope 1952: §486). This change seems to have taken place unobtrusively except in the case of the word *chez* > *cheux*, which we find in the letter of M. de la Brosse to the Dowager Queen of Scotland (see Wood 1923: 148 (1546)).

This evidence from personal correspondence points to two conclusions: (a) contemporary literary representations of the vernacular were not quite as grotesque and unrealistic as we might be tempted to think; (b) the proliferation of vernacular features in personal correspondence emanating from the highest in the land shows how pervasive they were in sixteenth-century Paris, and that at this time reallocation of these variables still had a long way to go.

7.5   Summary

In this chapter we have looked at the main evidence available on language variation in fifteenth- and sixteenth-century Paris. Contemporaries were evidently more sensitive now to the socio-symbolic value of French than they had been in earlier generations: certain variants had achieved very high salience, and were probably being caught up in the process of reallocation. In the social psychology of the city we see the beginnings of a polarisation between the twin prototypes of the *Honnête Homme* and the *Paysan de Ville*. The fact that many of the variants stigmatised at this time are attested in medieval texts and

---

[18] 'We are reunited with the family and I can assure you that we have found our grandson as bright and healthy as any child can be.'

[19] 'We await the outcome in eight days' time.'

[20] ' ... for we have every hope that tomorrow the weather will be fine, given what the stars tell us, and we have had every opportunity to observe them'.

in documents from the seventeenth and eighteenth centuries attests to the conservatism of vernacular speech. Roche (1981a: 41) makes a similar point about urban vernacular culture in general. We do not have sufficient data to make any strong claims about the real-life social distribution of variables. It may be that the gap between upper- and lower-class speech was beginning to widen at this time, but, to judge from the fragments of personal correspondence we considered, a clear separation of upper-class *bon usage* and lower-class *mauvais usage* was still some way away.

8 Variation under the Ancien Régime

The extreme violence with which the Ancien Régime was overthrown in 1789 gives an idea of the depth of social division and conflict which had been developing in Paris society during the preceding century and a half. Hierarchisation of society engendered rigid stratification of language, and over the two centuries that concern us here, reallocation of variants between H and L, which we saw happening in the sixteenth century, became a major social concern. J.-P. Seguin (1999: 280) observes that 'Il y avait toujours eu des prononciations méprisées. On peut dire que les deux grands siècles classiques ont donné à ce mépris une force institutionnelle.'

In standard-oriented histories of French the codification which took place in seventeenth- and eighteenth-century Paris is portrayed as a matter of straightforward rational development:

> Le 17e siècle, qui a cru pouvoir tout plier aux exigences de la raison, a sans doute donné à la logique l'occasion de transformer dans le sens de la raison la langue française. Aujourd'hui encore il est évident qu'elle répond beaucoup plus que toutes les autres aux exigences de la logique pure. (von Wartburg 1962: 170)

It is more likely that codification (and the reallocation of variants this entailed) occurred in a conflictual manner, the allocation of variants to the high-prestige standard being determined not by their inherent quality, but by their capacity to symbolise social distinctions.

We saw earlier (§1.2.3) that some sociolinguists define the speech community on the basis of everyone sharing the same evaluative norms, even when this means disparaging their own speech-habits. Not all sociolinguists take this consensual view. Romaine (1982: 234–8) and J. Milroy (1992: 209) prefer a conflictual model, where any sharing out of linguistic resources occurs as a result of sharp divisions in society and competition for resources. The two contrasting models are not mutually exclusive. It is a common experience to submit to social norms of which one disapproves and which one may bitterly resent. Moreover, beneath the overarching evaluative norms in which the whole community participates, divergent norms exist for internal use among the different sub-groups that make it up.

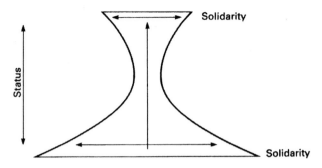

Fig. 2. The anvil-shaped status/solidarity model

Standard norms generally have their origin in the speech of people at the top of society, but lower down the scale there also exist, in all urban societies, sets of non-standard, vernacular or 'community' norms which are more variable, and no less constraining. In the course of their everyday interactions individual speakers are torn between pressures exerted by these competing sets of standard and non-standard norms. J. Milroy (1992: 213) has drawn attention to the role of social networks as norm-enforcement mechanisms: groups characterised by dense and multiplex social networks are also characterised by strong linguistic norms. He further points out that the tightest networking and, by implication, the strongest linguistic norms tend to be found in social groups located at the top and at the bottom of society (Fig. 2). In seventeenth-century Paris we find the elites drawing ever more restrictive lines around themselves as a protection against encroachments from below, while at the bottom there are indications that the poor in the various *quartiers* were doing the same, no doubt as a protection against pressure from above.

What data are available to show what was happening during this period? On this question, see Ayres-Bennett (2000). Most of the evidence of everyday speech is of the indirect type we described above (see §6.2.1), but there survive a few pieces that provide slightly more direct access. We will consider in particular two remarkable documents. The first is Jean Héroard's *Journal* documenting the speech of the young Dauphin (the future Louis XIII) between 1605 and 1610. Here we find *verbatim* reports of the words of the royal child, written in an *ad hoc* phonetic spelling, and providing intriguing information about colloquial grammar, vocabulary and pronunciation. The second is the *Journal de ma vie* of the auto-didact glazier, J.-L. Menétra, writing in the second half of the eighteenth century. As an inexperienced writer he occasionally allows vernacular features to slip through the filter of the writing system.

Attitudes towards language variation in the literary and metalinguistic sources of the time were not uniform. To use terms taken from M. Bakhtin, some observers were of a 'monoglot' disposition, while others were of a 'polyglot' one (see Crowley 1996: 30–53). The convergent, 'monoglot' tendency nurtured the hope of ultimately suppressing variation in the language, it focused primarily on the acrolect and was implacably hostile to the vernacular. The divergent, 'polyglot' tendency, by contrast, celebrated the diversity of Parisian speech, rejecting the formal, acrolectal varieties as sterile and ludicrously restricted, in favour of vernacular usage. The majority of the metalinguistic works of the period belong to the 'monoglot' tendency, but certain lexicographers (for example Oudin 1640, Richelet 1680 and Le Roux 1718, 1735) were fascinated by non-standard forms. The grammarian Chiflet (1668) shows a particular interest in colloquial Parisian (see Brunot, *HLF* XII, 391). Moreover, the positions adopted by grammarians seem to reflect their individual socio-political affiliations. Reighard (1980) interestingly divides the grammarians into 'insiders' (= Parisians) and 'outsiders' (provincials and foreigners) in the seventeenth century, and into 'progressives' (supporters of the *Ville*) and 'reactionaries' (supporters of the *Cour*) in the eighteenth. While writers of burlesque and of parodic/satirical texts all belong very obviously to the carnivalesque 'polyglot' tendency, authors of plays and novels are less easy to categorise, for they oscillate between the two camps (see Lathuillère 1984 and Gondret 1989).

In this chapter we will match the sounding of the sociolinguistic situation we made in 1550 (see above, §7.3.2) with two further soundings, in c.1650 and in c.1750. As we did in Chapter 7, we will consider first the ways in which contemporary observers represented the speech of the city, and then set them against surviving fragments of more direct evidence.

8.1   A mid seventeenth-century sounding, c.1650

In the middle years of the seventeenth century, Paris had lived through five decades of exceptional demographic growth fed principally by migration from the surrounding countryside. This had raised the proportion of non-natives in the population to a high level (see above, §6.1.1). The city was experiencing the acute social tensions engendered by the minority of the king and by the Fronde insurrection (see above, §6.1.4), and this seems to have engendered a widespread sense of linguistic as well as social insecurity and a clamouring for order and 'rules'. It is in this context that images of 'good' and 'bad' in the metalinguistic literature become very sharply delineated.

8.1.1   Contemporary images

It is not a coincidence that the turbulent middle years of the century saw the publication on the one hand of the most influential of prescriptive commentaries of the century, Vaugelas' *Remarques sur la langue françoise* (1647), and on the other a flood of satirical pamphlets (*Mazarinades* 1649–52) flouting social norms in a spectacular way to give public prominence to the most stigmatised forms of Parisian French. The first embodies in a most explicit way the prototype of the *Honnête Homme*, the second that of what we have termed the *Paysan de Ville*.

The Honnête Homme

At the beginning of the seventeenth century, as the threats posed by overt civil and religious war receded, an autocratic social and political régime became established. M. Douglas underlines the relationship between power-structures in society and attitudes to linguistic purity:

A social structure which requires a high degree of conscious control will find its style at a high level of formality, stern application of the purity rule, denigration of organic processes and wariness towards experiences in which the control of the consciousness is lost. (quoted in Anderson and Trudgill 1990: 64)

The power of language as a social symbol and the political implications of language standardisation were not lost on Cardinal Richelieu, who was first minister from 1625 to 1642. He was no doubt aware of the part played by the linguistic debate in the political and religious conflict of the previous century, and unwilling to see positions of influence here fall to political opponents potentially with the calibre of polemicists like Henri Estienne. When he instituted the *Académie française* in 1635, he brought the purist tendency in Paris society into the ascendant (the term *puriste* is first attested in French in a linguistic sense in 1628). Its explicit brief was to

nettoyer la langue des ordures qu'elle avoit contractées ou dans la bouche du peuple ou dans la foule du Palais, ou dans les impuretez de la chicane, ou par le mauvais usage des courtisans ignorants . . . (quoted in Chaurand 1999: 235)

For all its official endorsement, the reinforcing of linguistic norms at the top of society essentially took place in the community of speakers, notably in the tightly networked elite groups which began to constitute *salon* societies for the cultivation of letters and for the development of conversation as a fine art. The most distinguished of these was that of Madame de Rambouillet, attended by all the fashionable *literati* of the day, including the influential poet and grammarian F. de Malherbe. It was in aristocratic gatherings such as these that the concept of the *Honnête Homme* with all its sociolinguistic ramifications was crystallised.

The notion of *honnêteté* was a key one in Ancien Régime Paris and it has been analysed minutely (see Jordan 1989; Bury 1996). We are not dealing here with 'honesty' in the English sense of 'truthfulness'. The French word is more closely associated with the word 'honour': the *Honnête Homme* achieved 'honour' by adhering to an approved ethical code elaborated by the seventeenth-century elite. Within this system the culture of the Town was infinitely to be preferred to that of the Countryside, that of the Capital to that of the Provinces. However, the *Honnête Homme* had to be urbane without being urban. He had to distinguish himself from the common populace in all spheres of activity, in dress, in household furnishings, in residence, in behavioural etiquette, in leisure pursuits and aesthetic taste, and most conspicuously in language. Since the *Honnête Homme* is upper-class, he must avoid the vocabulary of the populace (*mots bas*). Since the *Honnête Homme* does not turn his hand to work, he must avoid using technical vocabulary (*mots techniques*), including legal jargon (*mots du palais*). Since the *Honnête Homme* is a discreet follower of fashion, he must avoid using old-fashioned words (*mots vieux*). Since the *Honnête Homme* is exceptionally courteous to ladies, he scrupulously shuns the use of *mots sales* which might offend their delicate sensibilities.

As a member of the upper class, the *Honnête Homme* always had to appear to be in control, not just of the situations in which he found himself, but most particularly of his own responses. He could not, therefore, give expression to unbridled emotion, either of pleasure or pain. Like his English counterpart, he had to maintain 'a stiff upper lip' in the face of adversity, and express his reaction to events by understatement and irony rather than by forthright openness. What we find here is a rejection of the vernacular in all its manifestations, and the promotion of the strategies of negative rather than positive politeness identified by Brown and Levinson (1987). These authors point out that dominant groups tend to espouse positive politeness cultures while dominated groups in society do the reverse. In his study of the speech of upper-class Philadelphia, Kroch (1996: 40) notes the same sense of 'entitlement' that members of the upper class learn in childhood and maintain throughout their life. It includes a sense of their own importance and an expectation that their views and desires will be treated with respect.

Lack of fear of disagreement leads to a diminished concern for accommodation and a relaxed use of emphasis. Etiquette manuals in the seventeenth century illustrate the application of this principle even to matters of speech volume:

C'est aussi le propre d'une parole éventée en s'approchant de quelque compagnie, de crier à ceux que nous connaissons le plus, comme quelques-uns font à gorge déployée, 'Monsieur', ou 'Madame', 'vostre serviteur'; 'je vous donne le bonjour' etc. . . . , mais il faut s'approcher doucement, et quand on est tout contre, faire son compliment d'un ton de voix modeste . . .

On sçait aussi que lorsqu'on doit répondre non, pour contredire quelque personne de qualité, il ne faut jamais le faire vivement, mais par circonlocutions en disant, par exemple, 'vous me pardonnerez, Monseigneur'. (A. de Courtin 1671, quoted by Milliot 1995: 284–5)

The cultivation of a distinctive upper-class pronunciation took place automatically:

Il faut, quiconque veut estre mignon de court
Gouverner son langage à la mode qui court.
Qui ne prononce pas *il diset, chouse, vandre,*
Parest, contantemans, fût-il un Alexandre,
S'il hante quelquefois avec un courtisan,
Sans doute qu'on dira que c'est un paysan,
Et qui veut se servir du français ordinaire,
Quand il voudra parler, sera contraint se taire.[1]
(*La Satyre de la Cour,* 1624, quoted by
Rosset 1911: 367)

The practical linguistic details of the purist mode of thought were given expression in Vaugelas' *Remarques sur la langue françoise* (1647), which set in train a long tradition of linguistic commentary geared to the maintenance of acrolectal speech-norms, designated in the terminology of the day *le bon usage*:

Voicy donc comme on definit le bon Usage . . . c'est la facon de parler de la plus saine partie de la cour, conformement a la facon d'escrire de la plus saine partie des Autheurs du temps. Quand je dis la Cour, j'y compren les femmes comme les hommes, et plusieurs personnes de la ville ou le Prince reside, qui par la communication qu'elles ont avec les gens de la Cour participent a sa politesse.[2] (Vaugelas 1647: II, 3)

This same climate of ideas led to the mode of linguistic behaviour known as *préciosité*, in which social distinction was to be achieved by distancing oneself as far as possible from 'everyday' modes of expression (see Magendie 1970). The absurd extent to which this principle was applied was famously satirised by Molière in his play *Les Précieuses ridicules* (1665), where 'Voiturez-nous ici les commodités de la conversation' (Scene ix) means 'Bring up the chairs.' The protagonists in this comedy are female and newly arrived members of the bourgeoisie: contemporaries were obviously sensitive to the operation of the 'sociolinguistic gender pattern', and to the 'linguistic insecurity' of aspirant members of the upper class. We note that the readership of manuals of linguistic etiquette like Vaugelas' *Remarques* consisted not of members of the elites but of members of the *professions libérales* who aspired to join them (see Ayres-Bennett 1987: 197–200).

---

[1] 'Whoever wishes to be a favourite at court must rule his language according to the current fashion. Anyone who does not pronounce *il diset, chouse, vandre, parest, contantemans,* be he an Alexander, if he keeps occasional company with a courtier, people will undoubtedly say that he is a peasant, and anyone wanting to use ordinary French when he talks will be obliged to keep quiet.'

[2] 'This is how one defines good usage . . . it is the way of speaking of the most sensible part of the Court, when that accords with the way of writing of the most sensible part of the authors of the day. When I say Court, I include in it women as well as men, and several persons of the town where the Prince resides, who in view of the contacts they have with the Court share in its refinement.'

Thus, while vigorous attempts were being made in the seventeenth century to define the limits of acrolectal speech and to erect this variety into the *social* norm (the kind of norm of which speakers are explicitly aware and which refers to the wider social acceptability of linguistic variants), we are frequently reminded that this was far from being the *empirical* norm (see below, §8.2.2). The grammarians of the time were concerned above all with the public use of language, in literature, in society *salons*, in public oratory (in the law-courts and in the pulpit). What they produced was a *langue de parade* designed to mark the speaker's status on public occasions. We must regard the acrolect in seventeenth-century Paris as being more of a style than a sociolect, as more of an ideal, an abstract set of norms, than a real variety. The *Honnête Homme* is a social prototype not an empirical reality.

The 'Paysan de Ville'

The first half of the seventeenth century saw migration of rustics into the metropolis on an unprecedented scale (see above, §6.1.1), and we find the figure of the urban peasant constantly recurring in the literature of the period. The *Paysan de Ville* incorporates all those features of social behaviour which the *Honnête Homme* rejected. He figures prominently in numerous comic and burlesque works, for example the *Caquets de l'Accouchée* set in the Rue Saint Denis, farces by Tabarin, the popular songs of Gaultier-Garguille, novels like C. Sorel's *Francion* (see Béchade 1981), Furetière's *Le Roman bourgeois*, and the whole set of burlesque writings composed by Scarron and others (see Bar 1960). As the century wore on, burlesque texts become rarer, though their style lived on among the *livres de colportage* designed for a non-elite readership (see Brochon 1954). Various metalinguistic works, notably Beroalde de Verville's *Le Moyen de parvenir* (1610), Adrien de Montluc's *Comédie des proverbes* (1633) and Antoine Oudin's *Curiositez françoises* (1640), celebrate stigmatised colloquial forms. These focus strongly on the lexicon and phraseology – in seventeenth-century French, *proverbe* embraced predictable utterances of all sorts, idioms and clichés as well as 'proverbs' proper. They provide early examples of the use of *verlan* (e.g. Oudin's quotation of *jouer du Luc renversé* in the sense of *faire l'amour*). This period also sees first descriptions of the *jargon* of the unassimilated, criminal elements in the community, notably O. Chéreau's *Le Jargon ou langage de l'argot réformé*, first published in 1628, and reprinted in 1632, 1634 and 1660 (see §12.3.1).

The figure of the Urban Peasant reaches its apogee in the middle of the century, in the satirical texts known as '*Mazarinades*'. These consist of a large number of political pamphlets, directed against the first minister Mazarin, at the time of the Fronde (1648–52). Most of them were written in the standard French of the day, but a proportion sought, for satirical purposes, to replicate the vulgar speech of the Common Man. In these pamphlets, protest against general establishment values entailed a rejection of the high-status linguistic norms being promulgated at precisely this time by Vaugelas and his followers. We will look in more detail at these texts in Chapter 9, but it needs to be said that the low-status speech-forms found here are not themselves being ridiculed but are being used to ridicule the current holders of power.

Celebration of the despised speech of low-class Parisians is to be found in another burlesque text of this period, which sets out to provide a sociolinguistic overview of the city in these troubled times: Le Sieur Berthaud's *La Ville de Paris en vers burlesques* (1650). In this work, the author takes a putative provincial visitor on a day-long tour of the city, eavesdropping on the conversations of individuals living and working in the different *quartiers*. This work can be associated with other tours of Paris composed at this time which include *La Foire Saint Germain* (1643) by Scarron and *Les Tracas de Paris* (1666) by Colletet. Milliot (1995: 232–3) situates texts like this in a broad context of Ancien Régime representations of the *peuple de Paris*, alerting us to the conventional nature of much of the information they provide. However, if we wish to see how seventeenth-century Parisians saw themselves and their language, this text provides an interesting way in.

Berthaud's sociolinguistic picture of Paris belongs firmly in the polyglot tradition we mentioned earlier (see p. 150 above) and is intentionally selective:

Tout le monde envoye dans les Provinces des relations de ce qui se passe de beau dans cette grande et celebre ville . . . Mais c'est une matière trop sérieuse, je veux dans celle que je vous envoye vous parler de quelque chose qui ne soye pas si fort estimé . . . (*Préface*, i–ii)

Conspicuously absent from the portrayal is any mention of the cultivated speech of the upper class.

The visit starts on the Pont Neuf, where the list of dubious trades being practised includes pickpockets and *argotiers*. It continues on the Right Bank of the river, at La Samaritaine, where we listen in on the 'entretiens d'un Gascon' (pp. 6–8), the speech of southerners being a standing joke in Paris throughout the Ancien Régime. We return to the Ile de la Cité to hear the sales patter of various shopkeepers (a bookseller, a haberdasher, a gents' outfitter), before moving into the *Palais* (pp. 18–37) to witness the solemnity of legal ritual and the voices of uneducated and inexperienced litigants (a peasant up from the country to recover his sheep and a Parisian wife seeking a divorce). We are next taken across the river again, this time by the Pont-au-Change, to hear a public scrivener in the cemetery of Saint Innocent (pp. 40–59), shopkeepers in the Rue de la Friperie (pp. 60–71), and fish-wives hurling abuse in the Halles (pp. 74–91). After a brief visit to the Rue de La Huchette on the Left Bank (pp. 91–2), the tour ends in the *quartier des Halles* in the Rue de la Ferronnerie (scene of a street-incident reminiscent of the one in which Henri IV had perished forty years earlier) and the Rue Tirechape (pp. 93–7).

In presenting the voices of the different parts of the city, as a writer of burlesque, Berthaud naturally selects only the most salient, the most stereotypical features of the sociolects he is depicting. Thus, his picture of the speech of the Gascon at La Samaritaine is restricted to examples of *bétacisme* (confusion of [v] and [b]), and his characterisation of the speech of a Parisian housewife goes little further than her use of past historics in -*i*- (e.g. *alis = allai, enfermit, traittit, demeuris*). These tell us nothing new about the speech of immigrants from the south-west, or of Parisian housewives, but their inclusion in the linguistic picture heightens the impression Berthaud wishes to convey of the heterogeneity and richness of metropolitan speech.

Berthaud devotes two important sections of his text to the speech-forms of a peasant at the law-courts (pp. 18–19) and of a fish-wife in the Halles (pp. 82–3). The term *harengère* ('fish-wife') denoted a 'femme de la plus basse condition de Paris' (see Panckoucke 1748: 183–4).

Le Paysan

Ardé, regardé bien <u>Monsieu</u>,
Je <u>sis</u> tout mouillé, car <u>y pleu</u>;
Et si pourtant je vous apporte
Cette poule, le <u>guièbe</u> emporte,
Plaides-moy fort <u>bian</u> & fort <u>biau</u>,
Car je creve dedans ma <u>piau</u>,
Et je <u>sis</u> si fort en <u>colèze</u>,
Que <u>pargué</u> je ne me <u>pis taize</u>,
<u>Voigeant</u> mes brebis en prison.
<u>Morgué</u>, c'est une trahison
D'un des <u>biaux frezes</u> de ma <u>fame</u>.
Vouy j'enrage, dessus mon ame,
Boutez, <u>gaignez</u>-moy mon procez.
Si j'en <u>pouvons</u> avoir le succez
Que j'en <u>ayons</u> les mains levées,
Et que mes brebis soient sauvées,
Je vous <u>fezé</u> un <u>biau</u> present,
Je scay qu'<u>ou</u> estes bien disant,
Allez, plaidez-moi <u>bian</u> ma cause,
C'est sur vous que je me repose.[3]

La Harengère

La commere Anne, <u>Noutre</u> Dame,
La male peste de la femme,
Elle & la soeur à Jean Pignon
Nous port<u>ont</u> toutes deux guignon
A cause <u>qui</u> sont un peu belles.
<u>Tou</u> chacun veut aller <u>sieux</u> elles,
Tous ces <u>guiebles</u> d'hommes y vont,
Je <u>scavons</u> bien ce qu'ils y font.
<u>Marci guieu</u> sont de bonnes bestes
Mais tous les jours ne sont pas festes.
<u>A n'aron</u> pas <u>tourjou</u> bon <u>tans</u>.
Peut estre avant <u>qui set</u> deux ans
<u>I</u> <u>pouraint</u> bien avoir les huitre
<u>Pu</u> salles que de vieilles vitres.
Vraman vouy, & la la j'<u>aurons</u>
Et peut estre que je <u>scaurons</u>
Aussi bien qu'eux faire des <u>mienne</u>.
N'est-il pas vray dame <u>Basquienne</u>
Que je <u>varons</u> bien <u>queuque</u> jour
Que tout chacun <u>ara</u> son tour?[4]

---

[3] **The Peasant**

Attention, regardez bien Monsieur,
Je suis tout mouillé, car il pleut;
Et si, pourtant, je vous apporte
Cette poule, diable m'emporte,
Plaidez pour moi fort bien et fort beau,
Car je crève dans ma peau
Et je suis tellement en colère,
Que, pardi, je ne peux pas me taire,
Voyant mes brebis en captivité.
Morbleu, c'est une trahison

[4] **The Fish-Wife**

La commère Anne, par Notre Dame,
Peste soit de la femme!
Elle et la soeur à Jean Pignon
Nous portent toutes les deux malheur,
Pour la seule raison qu'elles sont un peu belles.
Tout un chacun veut aller chez elles,
Tous ces diables d'hommes y vont,
Et nous savons très bien ce qu'ils y font.
Par la merci de Dieu, ce sont de bonnes bêtes,
Mais tous les jours ne sont pas fériés.

Comparison of the non-standard speech-forms present in these extracts shows that Berthaud saw the speech of people at the bottom of Paris society, epitomised by the *harengères*, as being more or less identical to that of non-resident rustics. Both of the extracts accumulate the maximal amount of stigmatised forms (the main ones are underlined), typified by the use of oaths and swear-words (see *le guièbe emporte, pargué, morgué, vouy j'enrage, dessus mon ame* in the Peasant, *Noutre Dame, la male peste, marci guieu, vraman vouy* in the Fish-wife). At one point the author suggests (ironically) that urban speech could be even less aesthetically pleasing than rural. Referring to the speech of the fish-wives in the Halles, he asks:

> Hé bien! As-tu pris du plaisir
> De les entendre discourir?
> Les servantes de ton village
> Ont-elles un si beau langage?

The author's inability/unwillingness to discriminate between low-status language varieties could mean what we have here is a dustbin of stigmatised features attributed willy-nilly to all speakers of low social status. However, such a judgment made three and a half centuries later may be hasty. 'Folk' views of the sociolinguistic make-up of society, of the sort we find here, although impressionistic and oversimplified, are usually based on some sort of lived experience. Paris lived in close symbiosis with its rural hinterland, and at any one time thousands of country-dwellers were travelling in and out regularly to supply the city's markets with food, fuel and raw materials, or were striving to establish themselves permanently in the city as domestics or as workers. While rustic speech was no doubt 'broader', it was probably not substantially different from that of Parisians of the lowest status. In the seventeenth-century Parisian experience, it is quite likely that the speech of the suburban peasants and that of many urban proletarians were to all intents and purposes the same.

Berthaud offers us here his activation of the prototype of the Urban Peasant, which we find also in comic drama and in satirical literature. What is striking

---

Footnote 3 (*cont.*)
D'un des beaux frères de ma femme.
Voui! J'enrage, sur mon âme,
Allez, gagnez mon procès pour moi.
Si nous pouvons réussir dans cette affaire
De sorte que nous ayons la victoire
Et que mes brebis soient sauvées,
Je vous ferai un beau présent.
Je sais que vous êtes bien éloquent.
Allez, plaidez bien ma cause,
C'est sur vous que je me repose.

Footnote 4 (*cont.*)
Elles n'auront pas toujours beau temps.
Il se peut que avant qu'il soit [passé] deux ans,
Ils pourraient bien avoir les huîtres
Plus sales que de vieilles vitres.
Vraiment, voui, et là là nous [les] aurons,
Et nous saurons peut-être
Aussi bien qu'eux faire des grimaces.
N'est-ce pas vrai, Madame Bastienne,
Que nous verrons bien quelque jour
Que tout un chacun aura son tour?

is that, on the whole, proletarian speech is not here an object of ridicule. On the contrary, the voice of the Common Man usually serves to undermine the verbal contortions and pretentiousness of members of the establishment. In the following extract from Molière's *Les Femmes savantes* (1672) the servant-girl Martine is taken to task by her mistress for her uncultivated speech:

MARTINE   Tout ce que vous prêchez est, je crois, bel et bon;
             Mais je ne saurois, moi, parler votre jargon.
PHILAMINTE   L'impudente! Appeler un jargon le langage
             Fondé sur la raison et sur le bel usage!
MARTINE   Quand on se fait entendre, on parle toujours bien,
             Et tous vos biaux dictons ne servent pas de rien.
PHILAMINTE   Hé bien! Ne voilà pas encore de son style?
             Ne servent pas de rien!
BELISE   O cervelle indocile!
             Faut-il qu'avec les soins qu'on prend incessamment,
             On ne te puisse apprendre à parler congrûment?
             De *pas* mis avec *rien* tu fais la récidive,
             Et c'est, comme on t'a dit, trop d'une négative.
MARTINE   Mon Dieu! je n'avons pas étugué comme vous,
             Et je parlons tout droit comme on parle cheux nous
             . . .
BELISE   Ton esprit, je l'avoue, est bien matériel.
             Je n'est qu'un singulier, *avons* est pluriel.
             Veux-tu toute ta vie offenser la grammaire?
MARTINE   Qui parle d'offenser grand'mère ni grand-père?
                        (Molière, *Les Femmes savantes*, Act II, scene 6)

The stereotypical lower-class forms are underlined, but, throughout the play, the laugh is on Belise, not Martine.

The antithetical prototypes we have considered in this section offer an excessively simplified vision of sociolinguistic reality. However, while linguistic usage in cities is notoriously heterogeneous, social attitudes to language are remarkably regular and slow to change. It is these that, we suspect, governed the way particular variants were reallocated up or down. Are there any empirical data from the time which might momentarily raise the veil on evanescent everyday speech?

8.1.2   Empirical data

Such empirical data as we have on real-life speech in seventeenth-century France are dispiritingly limited. G. Ernst has recently edited the letters written by an industrial worker, 'Chavatte' (Ernst and Wolf 2001). These carry traces of everyday spoken language, but, emanating as they do from Lille, they are not informative on specifically Parisian usage. The most significant piece of empirical colloquial data comes from Jean Héroard's *Journal* documenting the speech of the young Dauphin (the future Louis XIII) between 1605 and 1610.

This lengthy document provides extraordinary insights into everyday speech at the very top of Paris society. Here is an extract.

12 October 1605

.... se joue .... a ung petit cabinet d'Allemagne faict d'ebene .... hausse et abbaisse le couvercle, le ferme a clef, et l'ouvre tousiours *le vela famé*[1] *moucheu le Dauphin ne saré*[2] *enté*[3] *j*[4] *passera pas le jadin*[5]. Ie luy dis, mais Il fault ouvrir a Mr le Dauphin. D. oui, ouvre et abbat, et soudain hausse et ferme a clef disant *ho non j*[6] *fau pa que moucheu Dauphin ente*[7] *là, y a de la verole* .... Tenoit ung sifflet d'jvoire *je vou fairai peu*[8] *de mon sifflet* .... [Au dîner il ne veut pas de panade, mais il en mange] luy ayant dict que c'estoit pour empescher que les crestes ne chantassent dans son ventre. D. *chanteré telle*[9] *coquerico dan mon vente*[10]*?* Poulet bouilly, ung pilon, *moucheu Euoua vela une de vo*[11] *guegue*[12] .... [Il se querelle et se bat avec sa nourrice.] ce fust la grosse querelle // *a ma fouëte*[13], et a Jinjures. *vilaine je vou tuerai.* .... [Il joue aux soldats, tire; on lui demande:] sentinelle pourquoy avés vous tiré? D. *ce que* (façon de parler) *l'ay tire a un enemi qui eté*[14] *venu pé*[15] *du fossé.* Ie luy demande, Mr qui estoit cest ennemi? *C'ete un jlandé*[16]. Va sur la terrasse de la salle pour voir l'Eclypse du soleil dans une chaudiere pleine d'eaue. L'eaue bransloit *he je ne sare rie<n> voi*[17]. Estant rassise, *Ie le voi*[18] *le solé*[19] .... envoie querir ung virebrequin par Me le Coeur femme de chambre, elle l'apporte. D. *l'av'ou*[20] *prins bien doucemen*[21]*?* C. ouy Mr D. *e pui vous avé couru tan que vous avé peu*. Faict luy mesme deux trous a ung ais avec le virebrequin fort dextrement, puis dict a son page *Bompar allé queri une code*[22] *qui sé*[23] *bien rude*[24] *pou mette*[25] *dan ce trou, pou la mete su ma fontaine que m'a doné Ioly.*

1 fermé 2 -oit 3 entrer 4 Il 5 jardin 6 il 7 entre 8 peur 9 chanteroient elles 10 ventre 11 vos 12 gregues 13 elle m'a fouetté 14 -oit 15 près 16 Irlandois 17 scaurois rien voir 18 vois 19 -eil 20 l'avés vous 21 -ent 22 corde 23 soit 24 fort 25 mettre
(see Ernst 1985: 233–4)

The text has to be read intelligently, for certain forms perhaps belong less to the general vernacular than to the language of a young child in whom the process of language acquisition is not yet complete (see Ayres-Bennett 1996: 216–21). However, Ernst's (1985: 35–67) analysis of the phonology of the young prince shows it to contain a large number of vernacularisms. In this short extract we might observe the following:

(1) [ɛr] ~ [ar]: *famé = fermé*
(2) Distribution of [ɛ], [wɛ], [wa]: *vela = voilà, saré = sauroit, se = soit*
(3) Elision of post-consonantal [l]/[r] before final schwa: *vente = ventre, mett = mettre*
(4) Elision of pre-consonantal [r]: *jadin = jardin, code = corde*
(5) Elision of post-vocalic [r]: *peu = peur, Euoua = Eroard, voi = voir, queri = querir*
(6) Elision of final consonants: *j = il*
(7) Reduction of consonantal clusters: *enté = entrer, guegue = grègues, pé = pres*

The form *l'av'ou = l'avez-vous* was heavily stigmatised. Added interest is provided by forms like *moucheu* (= *monsieur*) which occur quite frequently in the text and which are normally associated with Picard dialect. Did the Dauphin's earlier wet-nurses come from the north of the country? Wittmann's 1995 study of the sources of Quebec French points to the presence of various picardisms in seventeenth-century Parisian speech.

Empirical data on real-life seventeenth-century speech are fragmentary and unrepresentative of all states of the language. Héroard's *Journal* indicates that the dichotomy present in the literary and metalinguistic material between 'good' and 'bad' speech is massively over-simplified, and that, right at the top of Parisian society, stigmatised colloquial forms were quite normal in informal situations. What we lack, unsurprisingly, are any empirical data allowing us to make analogous observations about everyday speech at the bottom.

8.2   A mid eighteenth-century sounding, c.1750

When we come to the city's sociolinguistic profile a century later, it is clear that, while there was continuity, much had changed. Under Louis XIV and his successor Paris lived through a century of social and political stability, on the surface at least. Demographic growth had continued, but at a slower rate than in the first half of the seventeenth century, causing the proportion of native Parisians to rise and bringing about an entrenchment of social attitudes and patterns of behaviour. At the same time, the sheer size of the city meant that the traditional mechanisms of municipal government and social control became progressively less effective. For many, 'order' now meant stasis and a mismatch between the established institutional framework and the social and economic requirements of the new age. Historians, such as Furet (1961), Farge (1979) and Roche (1981a), all point to mounting social tension in the century preceding the Revolution. These conflicts were reflected closely in the sociolinguistic discourse of the day.

8.2.1   Contemporary images

La Cour et la Ville

At the top of society, the old antagonism between the traditional landed aristocracy (*la Cour*) and the merchant and administrative class (*la Ville*) became more acute as the eighteenth century wore on. After the traumas of the Fronde, Louis XIV (1643–1715) succeeded in spectacular fashion in shifting the locus of power away from *la Ville* towards *la Cour*. This was graphically symbolised by his moving the court from the Louvre in central Paris to the newly built palace Versailles. It was reflected sociolinguistically in the increased disparagement by courtiers of the speech of the Parisian bourgeoisie. The grammarian Saint Réal declares, with reference to remarks made by another of his kind:

Il fallait se défier encore de la prononciation des Parisiens plus qu'il n'a fait, je n'entends pas du peuple, j'entends des honnêtes gens de Paris. (quoted in Brunot, *HLF* IV, 174)

The title of F. de Callières' *Du Bon et Mauvais Usage dans les manières de s'exprimer. Des façons de parler bourgeoises. Et en quoy elles sont différentes de celles de la Cour*, published in 1693, reveals the same attitude. At around this time, the *bourgeois* join the *peuple* in the list of inadequate speakers: Hindret (1687) attributes stigmatised forms to *la petite bourgeoisie de Paris* and Buffier (1709) to the *bourgeois de Paris,* though the degree of pejoration varies with the observer's social affiliations.

The reign of Louis XV (1715–74) was politically and militarily less successful than that of his illustrious predecessor. The development of capitalism, long-distance trade and colonial empires created a widening gulf between the conservative world-view of aristocrats with their fortune in land and the new realities in the minds of 'City' financiers. The absence of the King and the Court in Versailles accentuated the alienation of the city patricians, who became increasingly envious of the status enjoyed by their counterparts in London and gradually more receptive to the ideas of the 'Enlightenment', fed by writers of the stature of Montesquieu, Diderot, Rousseau and Voltaire. As the century wore on, the balance of power shifted from *la Cour* to *la Ville* and the status of the monarchy declined. In tandem with this the models for 'the best French' shift from Versailles to the *salons* of the high bourgeoisie in Paris. This is neatly symbolised by the variable realisation of the [OI] diphthong in such words as *roi, moi* which at this time became a shibboleth. Where the Court clung to the traditional pronunciation [we], the Paris bourgeoisie adopted the variant [wa], and, by the middle of the eighteenth century, this had become the high-prestige form (see Chaurand 1999: 277–80).

What both parts of the elite shared, however, was a desire to maintain distance between themselves and the people below them, a movement manifested in the gravitation of the rich towards the west of the city and the concentration of the poor in the medieval centre and in the east (see above, §6.1.3). On the sociolinguistic level this meant a rigorous pursuit by the elites of grammatical elegance and 'distinction'. *Bon usage* gave way to *bel usage*. The work of codifying linguistic norms proceeded with great intensity, and prescriptive attitudes, embodied most conspicuously in the grammar of de Wailly (1754), became ever more rigid. These attitudes were endorsed by even the most 'enlightened' figures of the age, like Voltaire, in the name of rationality and civilisation.

In the first part of the seventeenth century the reference-point for 'the best French' had been an empirical and provisional one: 'la plus saine partie de la Cour'. By the eighteenth century, the need was felt to anchor high-status norms less to the speech-forms of a particular social group (which were susceptible to changes in fashion) than to the universal principles of reason and logic. The adoption of French by the aristocracies of Europe as a cosmopolitan class-dialect encouraged the belief in the 'universality' of the language. Deviation from high-status speech-norms was now construed not simply as the failure to consort with the right sort of people, but as an inability to think clearly and logically. At the same time, higher levels of literacy (see above, §6.1.5) led to increased reverence for the written language, and to a desire to anchor linguistic norms in the permanence of writing rather than in the transience of speech. All the tenets of 'standard ideology' were fully elaborated in the eighteenth century, and with them came an ever more profound disparagement of the vernacular, not just on social grounds, but on grounds of rationality too (see above, §1.1.3).

Le Peuple

The prototype of the Urban Peasant lives on in eighteenth-century Paris, and the vernacular attributed to him gradually acquires a label. In the previous century no consensus had emerged about what to call low-class Parisian speech. Grammarians refer simply to the speech of *le (petit/bas) peuple* or *la lie du peuple*. A designation for 'ordinary Parisians' which found some favour was *badaut*:

Les badaux de Paris disent . . . *aider* en trois syllabes. (Ménage 1672)

Il n'y a que les badaux de Paris qui parlent de la sorte. (Ménage 1672)

Ne prononcez pas comme quantité de badauds qui disent . . . (Hindret 1687)

This term originally designated people who gawp stupidly at incidents in the street (see Rozan 1856: 73–7; Deloffre 1999: 48), and we commonly find it used, along with its derivative *badaudois*, to refer disparagingly to low-class Parisian speech:

Et *Erondelle* est du franc Badaudois, qui change tousiours l'*a* en *e*, *merry* pour *marry*, comme il l'observe fort bien *Mademe* pour *Madame*. (La Mothe le Vayer 1647)

Ce seroit parler en badaut que de dire *bonur*, comme quantité de gens disent à Paris. (Hindret 1687)

However, while this term was frequently used, it never achieved the fixity of labels like 'Cockney' and 'Chtimi'. In the eighteenth century, another label emerges to designate this stigmatised variety, and this one – *poissard* – becomes established more firmly.

In the second quarter of the eighteenth century, certain Paris intellectuals began expressing their impatience with the oppressive social norms of the time by using low-status speech-forms in their writing, deliberately flouting the rules of stylistic congruity laid down by rhetorical tradition. The 1730s see the creation of mock-academies like the *Académie du Bout du Banc*, parodying the language and behaviour of respectable society (see Valli 1984). A significant figure here is the playwright Marivaux, who incorporated numerous low-class forms into his *Télémaque travesti* (1736) and *La Vie de Marianne* (1741). In the subsequent decades, the cultivation of low-class speech becomes a high-class literary fashion in texts like the *Parades* of Beaumarchais, and in a whole genre referred to as *poissard* (see Moore 1935). The term *poissard* is first attested in Dubois (1531), for whom it meant 'thief'. It appears to be derived from the word *poisse* ('slime left on the hands and clothes of people who handle fish'). *Poissarde* was a synonym for *harengère* (see above, p. 156), referring primarily to the foul-mouthed Parisian fish-wives in the Halles and later to the vulgar speech associated with them. We have no evidence to suggest that this label was used by speakers of *poissard* to refer to their own way of speaking. It seems to have originated among literary people who had their own motives for being attracted to the dialect.

In the middle of the eighteenth century the *poissard* label was applied to a literary style, exemplified most conspicuously by J.-J. Vadé (1719–57), and by other authors like T. G. Taconet (1730–74) and A. C. Cailleau (1732–98). Novels, plays and poems written in this style came to enjoy great popularity and continued to do so until well into the nineteenth century. *Poissard* texts deal with the everyday lives of 'ordinary Parisians', and their depised language, suitably refined, is placed centre-stage. Here is a specimen:

Maneselle,
C'est pour vous r'marcier d' la magnere qu'vote mere a été r'bouissée par la soutenance d' vote farmeté à mon sujet; & c'est fort mal à elle d'avoir dit ça, si je n'avons pas des richesses, j'ons un savoir faire. Qu'alle ne fasse pas tant la Bourgeoise; si alle a d'la valeur c'est qu'alle a fait une brave & genti fille comme vous, sans ça j' n'en donnerois pas la moiquié de rien . . .[5] (*Lettres de la Grenouillère, Oeuvres de J.-J. Vadé*, IV, 27)

Poissard style is characterised by the presence of a large number of lexical colloquialisms and a rather restricted set of stereotypical low-status phonetic and morphological features, for example, [er] → [ar] (e.g. *marci*), [o] → [jo] (e.g. *siau d'* → *iau*) and forms like *j'avons*. Texts such as these were not written by or even for the proletariat, and it does not look as though the authors were using the language of the 'people' to maximise realism and authenticity. They view the urban populace in a way similar to that in which the pre-Romantics

---

[5] 'Mademoiselle, C'est pour vous remercier de la manière que votre mère a été rabaissée par le maintien de votre fermeté à mon égard; et elle a eu tort de le dire, [car] si nous n'avons pas de richesse, nous avons [néanmoins] un savoir-faire. Qu'elle ne fasse pas tant la bourgeoise; si elle a de la valeur, c'est qu'elle a fait une brave et gentille fille comme vous. Sans cela je n'en donnerais pas la moitié de rien . . .'

of the time were viewing the innocent exoticism of rural life, that is, as an anti-dote to the strait-jacketed urbanity of the dominant cultural tradition (see Milliot 1995: 306). Roche (1981a: 44–6) writes quite appropriately of 'le mythe pois-sard'. They are sociolinguistically interesting because they show the continued vitality of the Urban Peasant prototype in social consciousness.

Other eighteenth-century authors activated the prototype in a less innocu-ous way – to satirise, like their predecessors a century earlier, the political abuses of the time. The most significant of these are Nicolas Jouin's *Sarce-lades* (1730–48) and U. Coustelier's *Lettres de Montmartre* (1750). Between 1730 and 1748 Nicolas Jouin published a series of 'harangues' related to the Jansenist–Jesuit religious controversy (see above, §6.1.4). In the tradition of the *Mazarinades*, the author adopts the voice of the Common Man to excori-ate the abuses of the régime. The *Sarcelades* (1730–48) purport to report the views of peasants living in the village of Sarcelles (situated 10 km north of the city centre), and the author puts into their mouths the most strongly stig-matised Parisian speech-forms of the day (see Randell 1998). See Appendix, Text 5.

A similarly interesting text published in 1750 is the *Lettres de Montmartre* of U. Coustelier. The satire here is directed not only against abuses perpe-trated by members of the political and religious establishment, but also against uncultivated linguistic behaviour. This text represents perhaps the most devel-oped eighteenth-century expression of the prototype of the *Paysan de Ville*. See Appendix, Text 7. Within it we find an accumulation of all the cultural and linguistic features considered to be the antithesis of those used by the *Honnête Homme*. These embrace not only surface features of pronunciation and mor-phology, but also syntax, discourse structure and politeness strategies. The fact that the author has adopted an epistolary form not only reflects the contempo-rary taste for this genre, but it also allows him to caricature those members of society who had not yet fully acceded to literacy (see Lodge 1995b).

In the middle of the eighteenth century, the polarity between Good and Bad speech still dominates social attitudes to language. The Urban Peasant seems now, however, to have had his teeth drawn. He had been tamed and was being absorbed by the homogenising forces at work in the city. Use of stigmatised Parisianisms as a satirical voice of protest recurs at the time of the 1789 Rev-olution. However, it is striking that on that occasion use of vernacular forms in political pamphlets was adopted preferentially by royalist elements oppos-ing the Revolution (cf. Appendix, Text 6), and was largely rejected by the forces which overthrew the Ancien Régime. Indeed, the leaders of the Revolu-tion quickly reasserted the Ancien Régime's monoglot linguistic attitudes and policies in the service of democracy and reason (see below, §11.1.2).

Do we have empirical data which might give us slightly more direct access to everyday Parisian speech in the middle of the eighteenth century?

8.2.2   *Empirical data*

As far as people at the top of society are concerned, the norms of the high-prestige standard, which were being refined and promoted so vigorously over this period, remained an abstract ideal rather than a real-life language variety. The extent to which speakers' everyday speech approximated to these norms is something we can never know for certain, but evidence suggests that even the most well-bred speakers complied with them a good deal less than the written texts of the period imply. Contemporary observers routinely point out that vernacular forms were available to everyone, and that 'les mots proscrits de la langue sont positivement dans toutes les bouches, depuis les princes jusqu'aux crocheteurs' (L.-S. Mercier, quoted by Sainéan 1912: c.15). A remarkable specimen of vulgar, not to say obscene, speech on the Parisian stage in 1730 is to be found in Hausmann (1980), and it would be unreasonable to suppose that such plays were not patronised by the more cultivated members of society. Louis XVI's propensity to swearing and bad language is well known to historians.

The linguistic niceties cultivated by the elites in the literary *salons* hardly impinged upon the lives of the bulk of the Paris population. However, the proletariat was not left untouched by standardising influences, which became stronger as the century wore on, principally through the spread of literacy (see above, §6.1.5). Lohisse (1981) estimates that the level of literacy in France as a whole moved from 20 per cent in the late seventeenth century to 37 per cent a century later. Such low figures are to be expected in an overwhelmingly rural society. However, in Paris literacy rates were much higher. Roche (1981b: 201–41) notes that at the end of the seventeenth century 80 per cent of men and 60 per cent of women had been capable of signing their will, whereas a century later these figures had risen to 90 per cent and 85 per cent respectively. The ability to sign a will does not necessarily mean that they were, in a meaningful sense, literate, but it suggests at the very least that all social classes were participating to some extent in the move from an oral to an essentially written culture. Education was surprisingly widely available in the city (see above, §6.1.5), and, while it is easy to exaggerate its influence, it is most likely that schooling was a significant factor in the downward diffusion of standard language forms.

From the middle of the century we find an increasing number of personal documents (letters and diaries) produced by inexperienced writers, some of whom are women. Two examples worth quoting are written by the wives of famous writers. The first is from a woman from the higher class, wife of Denis Diderot:

Mademoiselle, je finie vostre lestre en vous priant de ne me point oublier pour du marte et si il est à bon conte vous pouriez en nanvoier à votre maman en nous moveant le prix juste elle y gagneroit quelque chose, mais si il est cher ne man navoiez que pour faire la bordure d'une plice. Nous faisons ce que nous pouvons pour consoler vostre chere

mère qui est fort changée. Songée à vous conserver pour elle et a lui écrire le plutaux qu'il vous cera possible. Adieu je vous anbrace et suis vostre tres humble servante
ce 21 aoust 1765   femme Diderot
(quoted by Seguin 1972: 25)

The second is from a woman of much lower condition. Thérèse Levasseur, wife of Jean-Jacques Rousseau, had started out as a laundry-woman:

Ce Merquedies a quateur du matin ceu
ventrois guin, mileu cen soisante e deu

Mon cher ami, quele goies que ge euues deu reuceuvoier deu voes cher nouvele. Geu vous asurre que mon ques pries neu tesnés plues a rien deu douleur deu neu paes vous voir e deu nous Ceuparés Çan pouvoir vous dire tous mes santiman, que mon quer a tousgour etés pour vous e quies ne changeraes gamès tan que dieu vous doneuraes des gour e a moi osies. Qule Çatfasion pour mois deu nous regondre tous les deus e deu pacés tous no douleur ançable. Geu n'atan que leu moman pour vous reu goidre e vous sanbracés du fon deu mon quer. Vous Çavés bien mon qure pour vous e que geu vous l'é tousgour dies, quleque par ou vous fusiés que geu vouslés vous alés goidre fut i les maire a pacés e les prescipiceu pour vous alés trouver, c'on n'avés qu'a meu dire que geu partirés bien vite, mes on n'a paes gugés a propoes deu meu leu dire. Geu n'e paes reusites a leu Çavoire e piceu que neu vouslés paes meu leu dire, geu vous asure que g'aves peur qu'i neu vous fut arivés quele que choseu, e que l'on meu leu cachés. Mo povre epries n'i atés plues ne la te[te]. Vous meu l'avés remies, Mon ché amies, deu tous au tous.

Mes i ceuraes ancor mieu remies quan geu ceurés oprés deu vous, e deu vous temoés tous la goies e la tandres deu mon quer que vous conescés que g'e tougour euus pour vous e qui neu finiraes qu'o toboes. C'es mon quere qui vous paleu, c'est paes mes levre. G'apîre le moman pour vous reugoidre. Geu neu tien plues a rien queu pour vous, Mon cher amies.

Ge sui avès tous l'amitiés e la reuconesçaceu
Posible e l'atacheman, Mon cher bonn amies
Votreu euble e bon amies
Theress Le Vasseur
(ed. Leigh 1970: 139–42)

The eccentricities present in these spellings are more explicable in terms of the misapplication of the rules of conventional spelling than through interference from non-standard pronunciation (see Branca-Rosoff and Schneider 1994). However, some texts occasionally shed light on social differences in speech, and this is particularly the case with the personal memoirs of the eighteenth-century Paris glazier J.-L. Menétra (1738–c.1803).

Menétra's memoirs (see Roche 1982) provide a vivid account of everyday happenings in the life of a working man in the second half of the eighteenth century, and they hold an obvious interest for social historians. On one occasion, for instance, Menétra met the philosopher Rousseau, and he had this to say about his wife whom we have just quoted: 'la maitresse dela maison me dit que cest mr rouseau et que cette grande breanne quil appelle Therese et son epousse' (256).

The almost complete absence of punctuation in the manuscript, and Menétra's capricious word-divisions induced Daniel Roche, in the only printed edition of the text (1982), to modernise and standardise the language in a way which makes it completely unusable by linguists. We have used the original manuscript, which is housed in the Bibliothèque Historique de la Ville de Paris, ms.678. It presents the following appearance:

comme cela mavoit. degarnis ma bourse je cherchoit a gagner chemin Lorqua la premiere couché je me trouvoit a table dhote ou je depensoit plus qua mon ordinaire mais comme jaloit me levez pour partir la fille de lauberge quy etoit une grosse grivoise et de bonne apetit me demanda si cettoit moy quy letoit venue apellée comme elle tenoit une chandelle alamain jeleteignis et profitois de cette circonstance lon lapelloit mes nous avions bien autre chosse a repondre elle me soitit un bon voyage et moy beaucoups de progeniture et ariva a montreaux et navoit La bourse bien sec.[6] (p. 106)

The text contains nuggets of sociolinguistic information, like references to the literacy of actors:

sefut la derniere foys que je bus avec luy etant mort quelque jours apres cettoit un Tres bon arlequyn malgrée quil ne savoit ny Lire ny ecrire il avoit beaucoup de memoire sa femme luy aprenant sest role.[7] (217)

Menétra refers to his own use of Paris *argot* for reasons of secrecy:

Latemps sepasse la porte est fermée il dise que cela leur ay deja arivée desetre Trouvée atardé et quil ont couché chez une blanchiseuse rue de loursine chenier me dit en argot quil faut les conduire chez luy il ne peuve plus marché il sont hort de rayson nous prenont un fiacre.[8] (191)

On his travels around the country, it transpires that Menétra did not have a noticeable Parisian accent:

---

[6] 'Comme cela m'avait dégarni ma bourse je cherchai à gagner chemin lorsqu'à la première couchée je me trouvai à la table d'hôte où je dépensai plus qu'à mon ordinaire [mais] comme j'allais me lever pour partir la fille de l'auberge qui était une grosse grivoise et de bon appétit me demanda si c'était moi qui étais venu l'appeler. Comme elle tenait une chandelle à la main je l'éteignis et profitai de cette circonstance. On l'appelait mais nous avions bien autre chose à répondre. Elle me souhaita un bon voyage et moi beaucoup de progéniture et (j') arrivai à Montereau et j'avais la bourse bien sèche' (Roche 1982: 107).

[7] 'Ce fut la dernière fois que je bus avec lui étant mort quelques jours après. C'était un très bon arlequin malgré qu'il ne savait ni lire ni écrire. Il avait beaucoup de mémoire, sa femme lui apprenant ses rôles' (Roche 1982: 197).

[8] 'Le temps se passe, la porte est fermée. Elles disent que cela leur est déjà arrivé de s'être trouvées attardées et qu'elles ont couché chez une blanchisseuse rue de Lourcine. Chénier me dit en argot qu'il faut les conduire chez lui. Elles ne peuvent plus marcher elles sont hors de raison. Nous prenons un fiacre' (Roche 1982: 177).

cette homme sinforme de quel pais je suis je repond que je suis de paris il me dit que
jenen et nulement Lacent je Luy dit que jay fait mon tour de france et que je suis revenue
par lions.[9] (249)

The spellings of the manuscript echo a number of stigmatised phonetic features (the figures refer to the pagination of the manuscript):

[ar] ~ [er], e.g. *airiere* 22, *boulevert* 294, *repere* 92, *farme* 27,
prarie 52, *ormoire* 27; compare also *atte* (= *était*) 89 and *allissé*
(= *Elysées*) 250.

[o] ~ [jo], e.g. *moigneau* 25, 74, 111, *scieau d'eau* 233.

[y] ~ [oe], e.g. *eurtansile* 195, *Eursule* 156, *eusage* 254; compare
also *calfutrée* 221.

Elision of unstressed vowels, e.g. *a quiser* (= *acquiescer*) 324, *depser*
(= *dépecer*) 153, *netoiroit* (= *netoyerais*) 82, *pairay* (= *payerait*)
167, 233, *paray* (= *paierai*) 294, *plotée* (= *pelotter*) 265, 267, 278,
ta (= *tu as*) 86.

[nj] ~ [n], e.g. *bourguinon* 81, 122, 133, *gasconne* (= *Gascogne*) 66,
128, *manifique* 267, *resiner* 299, *sinifia* 20, 47, 144, etc. Compare
also *magnable* 293, *magner* 87, 138.

[j] ~ [lj], e.g. *abilier* 29, 39, 53, etc., *ailant* (= *ayant*) 220, *biliars* 265,
bouilion 240, *broulier* 253, *chamailier* 43, *Chantilie* 186, *chatil-
ions* 167, *coulionons* 197, *depouilier* 45, *desabilier* 39, *etrilier* 57,
144, 257, *filiansaile* 236, *fouliere* 80, *moulier* 80, *pavilion* 49, 200,
300, *vielle rue* 260, *quincalerie* 66, *quincalier* 151, *gentilome* 61,
broulois 54.

Elision of post-consonantal [l/r] before final schwa, e.g. *ete* (= *être*)
136, *inombrabe* 266, *rende* 286, *traite* 294, *vende* 204, 285, *vive*
213.

Medial [r] ~ [z], e.g. *marchand foisin* (= *forain*) 126, *eriste*
(= *hésite*) 209, (cf. *esiste* 223, 240), *rispisoit* (= *respirait*) 89.

Elision of post-vocalic [r], e.g. *contois* (= *comptoir*) 141, 205, 206,
etc., *ereux* (= *erreur*) 259.

Voicing of medial [ʃ], e.g. *ajetter* 109, 132, 157, etc.

Reduction of consonant clusters, e.g. *lorque* (passim), *St epris*
(= *Saint Esprit*) 99, *bes* (= *beaux*) 65, *esplique* 214, 277, *pretexe*
43, 112, 175, *protitition* 298, *subtituer* 243, *abtenir* 189, *obtinoit*
143, 220, *astblenoit* (= *abstenoit*) 126, *insuter* 114, 129, *facutee*
290, *scupteur* 9, 138, *tulmute* 101, *infrutueuse* 271, *exatement* 247.

---

[9] 'Cet homme s'informe de quel pays je suis. Je réponds que je suis de Paris. Il me dit que je n'en
ai nullement l'accent. Je lui dis que j'ai fait mon tour de France et que je suis revenu par Lyon'
(Roche 1982: 218–19).

Treatment of learned words, e.g. *enfumee* (= *inhumer*) 261, *vilolons* 104, *procureul fiscal* 124, *interluctions* 193, *absurbe* 168, *serpetaire* 249, *subsiter* 302, *discestion* (= *discrétion*) 186, *sustilite* 296, *hispocrite* 10, 230, 290, *supertion* 10, 12, 89, etc. cf. *supertision* 90.

Menétra's sentence structures have been analysed in detail by Seguin (1992 and 1993), but a number of other non-standard morpho-syntactic features are worthy of note:

Analogical remodellings of the present, e.g. *Je vas* 92, 125, 132, etc., *ouvrit* (= *ouvre*) 138.

Past historics in -i, e.g. *defire* (= *défièrent*) 55, *obitime* (= *habituâmes*) 246, *habilire* (= *habillèrent*) 165, *prevoiris* 263, *retombit* 58, *seignit* 73, *soitit* (= *souhaita*) 106.

Past historics in -a, e.g. 3rd person endings *ouvra* 62, 296, *paroisa* 63, *parta* 164, *perda* 310. To these we could add a 1st person ending in *-ai* (*repondai je* 168), and others in *-a* (*acepta* 146, *demanda* 71, *entra* 121, *trouva* 73, 136, 322).

Compound past conjugated with *avoir*: *sortir* 121, *entrer* 204, *tomber* 289, occasionally involving non-standard past participles: *eveu* (= *eu*) 60, 94, 111, etc. and *finitte* (= *finie*) 294.

Relatives: *la somme/ce que javoit besoin* 80, 264, *un carreaux debois qu'il se serve* 83.

Reflexive pronouns: omission in structures such as *nous (nous) remetons* 96, 110, 127, 131.

Negation: omission of *ne* 92, 158, 160, 170, 193, 231, 240; double negatives, *ne pas les pas oublier* 104, *ne pas jamais eu envie* 199.

Unconstrained as it is by the conventional writing system of the day (in the author's earlier years particularly), Menétra's diary does not offer a phonetic transcription of his speech, but it provides precious echoes of the Paris vernacular before literacy and standardised orthography banished it almost completely from the written record.

8.3 Summary

It is well known that between the sixteenth and the eighteenth centuries there crystallised among the Parisian elites a set of high-status speech-norms, diametrically opposed to those of ancestral vernacular speech. What is less well known is that, judging from contemporary metalinguistic comment, there persisted in the city at the other end of the scale, a set of low-status, vernacular speech-norms, related to the speech of Paris's rural hinterland. Insufficient evidence survives to tell us the extent to which speakers at the bottom of the social pile, and indeed those at the top, approximated to these norms in their actual speech. We might suppose that the whole population was subject to differential pressure from the competing social and community norms, and that these influenced individual linguistic behaviour in varying degrees, depending on the speaker's social characteristics and on the communicative situation in hand.

Contemporary observers saw language in Paris as a polarity between High and Low, between Good and Bad. Such representations are 'folk theory' and offer an over-simplified view of sociolinguistic structure. In a population approaching half a million speakers, there could have been no pure sociolinguistic types. However, it is unwise to assume that the subjective responses of contemporaries have little or nothing to tell us. Evaluative attitudes to language are remarkably uniform across the community, so these representations are unlikely to have been solely the product of the elites' view of the world. The picture which emerges then is of the gradual embedding into the collective psychology of the city of the antithetical cultural prototypes which we have labelled the *Honnête Homme* and the *Paysan de Ville*. Reallocation of variant linguistic forms over this period did not occur haphazardly, but was guided, we suspect, by the 'Invisible Hand' evoked by Keller (1994), and was conditioned by the place occupied by the variants in question within each of these prototypes. Details of this process will provide the focus of Chapter 9.

9   Salience and reallocation

In cities in the modern world we can observe the process of reallocation in authentic linguistic data collected from representative samples of speakers and speech situations. In early modern Paris, since the quantity of empirical data giving access to the vernacular is minimal, we are left with the indirect, fragmentary and uncontrollable evidence provided by literary texts and metalinguistic works of various kinds. The effects of refraction inherent in contemporary representations of past sociolinguistic states are severe, so what can material like this tell us? Firstly, it provides information about the existence of sociolinguistic variants at that time, which otherwise would have been irretrievably lost to us. The range of forms which grammarians and literary authors represent is selective, what they say about their frequency and distribution is not entirely trustworthy, but the forms they attest almost invariably prove to be authentic. Secondly, material like this provides useful insights into the social value of the variants in question. When it was believed that what was relevant to change was the linguistic function of a structural unit, social information of this kind was irrelevant. It is now clear, however, that reallocation of the community's linguistic resources takes place less on the basis of linguistic function than on that of the symbolic value conventionally attached to particular variants. In this chapter we will bring together the information provided by metalinguistic works and literary authors on those morphological and phonological variables that were sociolinguistically sensitive during the proto-industrial period. Most of these have been introduced individually in earlier chapters.

9.1   Salience and imitation

Of critical importance in determining the fate of particular variables is the level of social awareness associated with them: in contact with speakers of other language varieties, speakers tend to modify those aspects of their own variety of which they are most aware, that is, the most 'salient' ones (see above §6.2.2 and Hickey 2000). A high level of salience associated with a particular variable may lead to the elimination of one of the variants or to its reallocation as a socio-stylistic marker, or as a social-class indicator. This means that if we can plot the changing levels of salience of particular variants across time, we may gain insights into the process of reallocation. Some of the sociolinguistic data surviving in proto-industrial Paris are highly amenable to analysis from this perspective: one measure of the salience of a particular variable is to be found in its capacity to engender metalinguistic comment and another lies in the extent to which it is selected for purposes of imitation, either in real-life conversation or in literature.

Proto-industrial Paris saw the production not only of a large number of grammars, dictionaries and commentaries on usage, but also of a quantity of literary or semi-literary attempts to mimic non-standard dialect. The quantity and importance of the metalinguistic evidence available on Parisian speech over this period should not be underestimated. Grammarians and lexicographers generated an output which is not rivalled in any other European city of the time (see above, §6.2.1). They were above all concerned with proscribing not describing vernacular usage, so the way they present non-standard forms does not allow us to reconstitute vernacular speech in a systematic way. However, they have at least the virtue of providing detailed, authentic information about what the main non-standard forms were.

We saw earlier (above, §7.3.1) that literary texts began to incorporate humorous imitations of low-class speech in Paris in the fifteenth century. These became very frequent in the seventeenth and eighteenth centuries, and they were still being produced in the early nineteenth century (see Bork 1978). For earlier, more positivist, generations of linguists these texts presented little or no interest:

Le langage des personnages qu'on met en scène manque totalement d'authenticité. C'est de l'article de Paris, fabriqué de toutes pièces avec des éléments toujours pareils, des *j'ons*, des *j'avions*, et quelques mots assez peu variés. (Brunot (1966: X.1, 269))

If we come to literary imitations of low-class speech expecting them to yield the same sort of information as samples of authentic language, we are bound to be disappointed. However, now that the role of subjective social evaluations in the development of language change is better understood, these representations of low-class speech call for closer attention. Trudgill has shown that one of the ways of accurately identifying what speakers perceive as the most salient characteristics of other people's dialects is imitation:

the most salient features of American English pronunciation, for English people, are precisely those which are reproduced during *imitation*. Most speakers of English English do not of course spend much of their lives imitating American English, but there are a number of speech events where this does happen, such as the telling of jokes involving Americans, and the playing of American roles by English actors. (Trudgill 1986: 12)

The texts imitating low-class Parisian speech are of varying length and present varying levels of linguistic detail. A number of them were published by Nisard (1872) and by Rosset (1911). We have assembled an electronic corpus of them which is deposited at the Oxford Text Archive (see Lodge 2000), extracts from which may be found in the Appendix (pp. 251–66):

1. **1550** *Epistre du biau fys de Pazy*, attributed to Jean Marot (ed. A. Grenier, *Œuvres complètes de Clément Marot*, I, Paris: Nizet, 1977).

2. **1644** *Nouveaux Complimens de la place Maubert, des Halles, Cimetière S.-Jean, Marché Neuf, et autres places publiques. Ensemble la résjouissance des harengères et poissonnières faite ces jours passés au gasteau de leurs Reines*, Paris (ed. E. Fournier, *Variétés historiques et littéraires*, Paris: Jannet, 1859: 229–39).

3. **1649–51** *Agréables Conférences de deux paysans de Saint-Ouen et de Montmorency sur les affaires du temps (1649–1651)* (ed. F. Deloffre, Paris: Les Belles Lettres/Annales de l'Université de Lyon, 1999).

4. **1649** *La Gazette des Halles touchant les affaires du temps*, Paris (Bibliothèque Mazarine, ms. 10482/ms. 12965).

5. **1649** *La Gazette de la Place Maubert. ou suitte de la Gazette des Halles touchant les affaires du temps Seconde nouvelle*, chez Michel Mettayer, Imprimeur ordinaire du Roy, demeurant en l'Isle Nostre-Dame sur le Pont Marie, au Cigne (Bibliothèque Mazarine, ms. 12965/ms. 21013).

6. **1649** *Suitte de la Gazette de la Place Maubert Par l'Autheur de la DE LA GAZETTE DE HALLES; touchant les affaires du temps*, chez Michel Mettayer, Imprimeur ordinaire du Roy, demeurant en l'Isle Nostre-Dame sur le Pont Marie, au Cigne (Bibliothèque Mazarine, ms. 12965).

7. **1649** *Le Caquet des marchandes poissonnieres et harengeres des Halles, sur la maladie du duc de Beaufort, soupsonné de poison, et leur voyage au palais de ce Prince*, Paris (Bibliothèque Mazarine, ms. 12607).

8. **1652** *La Conference de deux habitans de Saint Germain, Simon et Colin. sur les affaires de ce Temps*, Paris (Bibliothèque Mazarine, ms. 12036).

9. **1654** *Le Pédant joué*, Cyrano de Bergerac (ed. J. Prévot, *Cyrano de Bergerac. Oeuvres complètes*, Paris: Belin, 1977: 161–239).

10. **1660** *La Conference de Janot et Piarot Doucet de Villenoce, & de Jaco Paquet de Pantin, sur les merveilles qu'il a veu dans l'entrée de la reyne, ensemble comme Janoy luy raconte ce qu'il a veu au Te Deum et au feu d'Artifice*, Paris (ed. T. Rosset, Paris: Colin 1911: Appendice, pp. 60–71).

11. **1665** *Dom Juan*, Molière (ed. R. Jouanny, *Oeuvres complètes de Molière*, Paris: Garnier, 1962: III, 707–76).

12. **1666** *La Nopce de village*, Brécourt, Paris, chez Jean Guignard, dans la grand' Salle du Palais, a l'image Saint Jean.

13. **1730–48** *Le Vrai Recueil de Sarcelles*, N. Jouin, Amsterdam, 1764.

14. 1744 *Discours prononce au roy, par un paysan de Chaillot* (Bibliothèque Mazarine, ms. 103555).

15. 1750 *Lettres de Montmartre*, A.-U. Coustelier, alias 'Jeannot Georgin', published 'à Londres'.

16. 1790 *Premier dialogue entre une poissarde et un fort de la halle sur les affaires presentes* (Bibliothèque Historique de la Ville de Paris, ms. 12301).

This corpus is not exhaustive, and can easily be supplemented, for instance, with literary pieces belonging to the eighteenth-century *poissard* tradition studied by Moore (1935) and Franz (1983), and with passages drawn from writers like Marivaux and Rétif de la Bretonne.

How is the language of these texts to be interpreted? The authors, like all Parisians of their day, were evidently familiar with low-class speech, but they were not typical vernacular speakers. Their stylistic range went very high up the standardisation scale. As far as we can tell, they were all highly educated and in some cases literary men (see Carrier 1982). So what impelled them to write using this particular 'voice'? One might think that their prime object was to ridicule those uneducated persons in society whose speech was situated outside the norm, for this seems to have been the case with the *Epistre du biau fys de Pazy* (see above, §7.3.2). However, it is clear that, in the seventeenth and eighteenth centuries at least, this was not the motive, not even among the theatrical authors like Cyrano de Bergerac and Molière. In fact, the reverse is nearer the truth: in most, if not all, of these texts low-class speakers, although comic, are treated with a good deal of respect, their words seeming to incarnate the voice of the Common Man, railing against the follies of the high-ups in society. The despised language of *le Peuple* figures not as an object of mockery, but as the expression of popular dissent, potentially subversive of the established order (see Jouhaud 1985).

It is evident that the variants which figure in these texts are none of them fictitious. Caricatures give only a sketchy and unsystematic view of linguistic structure and place excessive emphasis on shibboleths and social markers. Most of the variants involved are 'strongly stratified and recognised sociolinguistic variables' (that is, 'stereotypes' in Labov's taxonomy). They occur here in concentrations not found in real life, and some may have been already archaic. However, all of them are attested elsewhere, in metalinguistic works of the time and/or in modern dialect surveys of the Paris region. The individual sociolinguistic variables used in these portrayals of *mauvais usage*, like those of *bon usage*, are in all cases authentic, and are attributed by contemporaries to low-class Parisian speech. We can suppose that if they were not, the comedy would fail.

Since we are dealing with social stereotypes, these parodic texts have strong affinities with one another. Their defining characteristic is the authors' use of non-conventional spellings to replicate stigmatised *pronunciations*. All contain large numbers of low-value *lexical items*. All reproduce a set of stigmatised *grammatical forms*. Some attempt to replicate the *syntax* of the spoken language. This similarity has tempted observers to see these texts simply as specimens of a literary genre feeding on itself. While the effects of intertextuality should not be underestimated, the pervasiveness of the variables involved in a wide range of texts (metalinguistic as well as literary), written over several centuries, suggests something situated deeper in the collective psyche (see §6.2).

No two realisations of the stereotype are, in fact, the same. The subtlety of the imitation varies from author to author: some imitate only a small number of stigmatised forms, which they repeat rather monotonously; others inject into their imitation a large number of features, of various levels of salience. Among the variables involved there exists a considerable degree of implicational scaling. Moreover, the selection and frequency of particular variants change across time: some variants are consistently present across the centuries, some see their frequency rise and others see it fall. Taken in sequence, different parodies give us an on-going, long-term picture of the fluctuating salience of particular stigmatised forms. They offer a barometer of the reallocation process at work across three centuries, and as such merit a controlled, quantified comparison (see Lodge 1996).

To gain an overview spanning the sixteenth, seventeenth and eighteenth centuries, we first examined the sole text dating from the middle of the sixteenth century (the *Epistre du biau fys de Pazy* (c.1550), see §7.3.2). We then took three texts each from the middle of the seventeenth and eighteenth centuries. These were contextually related, that is, they all performed roughly the same communicative function – satirical polemic. To represent the situation in the mid seventeenth century, we selected three political pamphlets produced at the time of the Fronde (texts 2, 3 and 4 in the above list). For the middle years of the eighteenth century we took polemical texts composed during the *Unigenitus* controversy (texts 13, 14 and 15). In order to make quantified comparisons between them, 1,000-word extracts were then taken at random from each of the texts. Manageable sections of these seven extracts are to be found in the Appendix, now re-numbered 1–7. In our chronological comparison, we took no account of variation in syntax or in the lexicon, and concentrated on morphological and phonological variables.

9.2   Morphological variation and change

Close studies on the morphology found in the seventeenth-century texts of this type have been produced by Rosset (1911: 381–94) and by Deloffre (1999: 157–77). Our object here will not be to provide a systematic morphological description, but merely to highlight the most salient variants found in our six texts from the mid seventeenth century and the mid eighteenth century, which may be compared with what we found in the *Epistre du biau fys de Pazy*. Five morphological features receive particular prominence, most of which were already highly salient in the sixteenth century (see §7.3.2).

(i) *je* + *-ons*. In all of our texts the construction of the clitic *je* with a verb in the 1st person plural and with the sense of 'we' enjoys very high salience and is more or less categorical. Cotgrave (1611) had attributed this form to 'vulgar Parisians'. This construction normally has plural reference, though quite commonly we are dealing with a royal plural.

Text 2:   Et nennin, *je ne somme pas* si babillarde; *je n'avon pas* le loisi d'allé pardre note argent pour donné des morciaux friands a monsieur a nos despens.[1]

Text 3:   Mai say tu ban que *je revinme* jesque dan nout vilage: bon jou bon soir, je ne sçay san que tu devins, je m'en alli sous l'orme, où je trouvi nout vilage amassé qui m'attendien pour var le zerticle de la Paix.[2]

Text 4:   Comere enfin parguieu je pense
L'on monstré à son Eminence
Comme sa hautez nous deplais,
L'en on dit deux mots au palais
parguié *j'en sommes* deveuglée
J'en voulons faire une vallée.[3]

Text 5:   Gn'a pas mal de tems, Nossigneurs, que *j'ons aieu* l'honneur de vous faire present d'une magnière de petit Sarmon que *j'avions affuté* pour Monsigneur l'Archeveque à la Coque.[4]

Text 6:   Sire, excusez la libarté,
De Chaillot je sis député,
Pour vous faire la révérence
Sur vote bon retour en France.
Vous vous portez mieux, Guieu-marci:
Je nous portons fort bian aussi.
Jesus! Que *j'avons eu* d'allarmes,
Et que *j'avons varsé* de larmes,
Quand la gazette nous apprit
Que vous étiais malade au lit.[5]

---

[1] 'Ah no, we are not such gossips; we aren't in a position to go squandering our money giving gents tasty morsels at our own expense.'

[2] 'But you know we came right back to our village: hello, good evening, I don't know what happened to you, I went off to the elm tree, where I found our village assembled and waiting for me to see the conditions of the Peace [treaty].'

[3] 'Good wife, by God, I think that at last we've shown his Eminence how his high-handedness displeases us. Words have been spoken about it at the Palais [de Justice]. By God, we've had our eyes opened. We want to make an inroad into this.'

[4] 'Not long ago, my lords, we had the honour to present you with a sort of little sermon which we had composed for my lord Archbishop Coque.'

[5] 'Sire, excuse the liberty I am taking, I am the deputy for Chaillot, paying you respects on your safe return to France. Your health is better now, thank God: we are keeping pretty well too. Jesus, what alarms we have had, and how many tears we have shed, when the gazette announced that you were ill in your bed.'

Text 7:   *Je vous on promis*, Monssieu mon parrain, de vous dire par paroles griffonées
sur Lettres queuques choses de mon voyage, *j'allons* vous les conter tout fin
dres comme *je les on* vûes; *j'ons* pris la voiture de l'iau: morguié que ceu
terrain est traite![6]

(ii) Simple past endings in *-i*. All of our texts give very high salience to
variation in the distribution of simple past endings in *-a*, *-i* and in *-u*.

Text 2:   Darnièrement, quand il estet yvre, il se *laissit* tombé du haut en bas, et si cela
ne l'y *coustit* rien.[7]

Text 3:   Je m'en *alli* sous l'orme, où je *trouvi* nout vilage amassé qui m'attendien pour
var le zerticle de la Paix.[8]

Text 4:   Comme a ce porteur d'iau, las qu'il la *manqui* belle,
Il doit fondre ses siaux pour faire une chandelle
Et l'aller presenté au sainct qu'il se *vouy*.[9]

Text 5:   Voyant donc qu'il avoit compté sans son hôte, & que queuques-uns de vous
autres avient damé le pion comme il faut, & pis craignant, voyez-vous, que
toute la bande des Mitriers n'*allit* li char sur le dos, dame! il s'est avisé de
faire semblant de se dédire.[10]

Text 6:   Las! quand notre Pasteur au Prône
Recommandit vote Parsonne,
Tout aussi tôt chacun de nous
Se *prosternit* à deux genoux . . .[11]

Text 7:   Car voyés vous bian mon parrain, quand je sommes partis du pied du Pont
Royal, j'allions ç'atoit eune marveille, le plus biau tems nous *accompagnit*
jusques aux îles, an les nomme comme ça les îles maquerelles.[12]

(iii) 6th person imperfect/conditional endings in *-aint/-ient/-iont*. We saw
earlier (see above, §4.1.2) that the traditional HDP forms for the 6th person
imperfect were normally in *-aint*, and that the standard forms in *-oient > -aient*
probably originated in the west. The rural forms in *-aint/-ient* occur quite
frequently in our sample of texts.

---

[6] 'We (= I) have promised you, dear godfather, that I would tell you in words scrawled on to
letters various things about my trip, we (= I) will tell you them exactly as we saw them; we
took the water bus: by God how that terrain is treacherous!'

[7] 'Recently, when he was drunk, he fell all the way down, but that didn't cost him a thing.'

[8] 'I went off to the elm tree, where I found our village assembled and waiting for me to see the
conditions of the Peace [treaty].'

[9] 'Like that water-carrier, what a lucky escape he had. He ought to melt down his buckets to make
a candle and offer it to the saint he vowed himself to.'

[10] 'Seeing that he had left his guest out of account and that some of you had checkmated him as
you had to, and then, fearing, you see, that the whole band of Bishops might come down on his
back, Goodness me, he decided to pretend to retract what he had said.'

[11] 'Alas! When our pastor prayed for you in his sermon, straightaway every one of us got down
on bended knee . . .'

[12] 'But you see, godfather, when we left the foot of the Pont Royal, off we went, it was miraculous,
the finest weather accompanied us to the Isles, they're called the Mackerel Isles'.

Text 2:   No examples.

Text 3:   La dessu je me resouveni que lé depité du Parleman y *avient* eté en coche.[13]

Text 4:   C'est un lieu haut & bien utille
Pour tous les gens de sa façon,
Qui caressent plus un garçon
Qu'ils ne *ferient* de belles filles.[14]

Text 5:   Voyant donc qu'il avoit compté sans son hôte, & que queuques-uns de vous autres *aviont* damé le pion comme il faut, & pis . . .[15]

Elsewhere in this text we find forms like *voudrint* (= *voudraient*).

Text 6:   Une bande de biaux espris,
Vous *aviant* rompu les oreilles
De mille fadaises pareilles:
Et qu'ils s'*étions* donné le mot
A qui paroîtroit le plus sot.[16]

Text 7:   Oh! pour ça il *étions* bian le fils de Moussieu son pere . . .; je sis fâché morguié qu'an mangiant comme nous autes aveuc les dents & la bouche, ils n'*avalions* que de l'iau; je n'aimons pas leur magniere de bere; je sis pour stila leur sarviteur; je la laissons aux granouilles, & pis s'ils m'*aviaint* parlé de vote parsonne, je vous l'envoirions par acriture.[17]

(iv) 4th person present subjunctive, imperfect indicative endings in -*iens*. We saw earlier (see above, §4.1.2) that the traditional HDP forms for the 4th person present subjunctive/imperfect indicative were normally in -*iens*, and that the standard forms in -*ions* probably originated in the west. The rural forms in -*iens* occur quite frequently in our sample of texts.

Text 2:   Pence-vous que je *soyen* icy pour vos biaux rieux?[18]

Text 3:   No examples in our extract, but forms like *allien* (= *allions*) and *venien* (= *venions*) are frequent in the text as a whole.

Text 4:   Si je *tenien* ses triquebilles,
Je les *doriens* a nos matous.
J'*espargneriens* autant de mous.[19]

---

[13] 'Whereupon I remembered that the deputies of the Parliament had been there by coach.'

[14] 'It's a high and very useful place for everyone like him, who caress a lad more readily than they would beautiful girls.'

[15] 'Seeing that he had left his guest out of account and that some of you had checkmated him as you had to, and then . . .'

[16] 'A group of wits had stuffed your ears with a thousand pieces of this sort of nonsense: and they had put their heads together to show which of them would look the most foolish.'

[17] 'O! on that score he was indeed the son of his respected father . . . ; damn it, I'm cross that, by eating like the rest of us with their teeth and mouth, they were swallowing nothing but water; I don't like the way they drink; for that, they can keep it; we leave that to the frogs, and then, if they had spoken to me about you, I would have sent it you in writing.'

[18] 'Do you think we are here for the sake of your pretty face?'

[19] 'If we had hold of his balls we would give them to our cats, we would save that amount of soft meat.'

Text 5: No examples in our extract, but conditional forms like *alliemes, feriemmes, seriemmes* are attested elsewhere.

Text 6: No examples.

Text 7: No examples in our extract, but conditional forms like *auriains* are attested elsewhere.

(v) 6th person present indicative endings. The traditional dialects in north Gallo-Romance are divided in their treatment of the ending of the 6th person: we find variants where stress falls on the ending (those in *-ont, -ant*) and others, notably in the west, where the ending is unstressed (those in *-ent*). See above, §4.1.2. Some of our texts highlight forms stressed on the ending:

Text 2: No examples.

Text 3: No examples in our extract, but Deloffre (1999: 170) points to the frequency of forms like *bouton* (= *ils boutent*) and *frappan* (= *ils frappent*) in the text as a whole.

Text 4: No examples.

Text 5: Il est bian vrai que gn'en a biaucoup de vous autres, Mossigneurs, qui n'*avont* guère fait mieux; d'autres qu'*avont* core fait pire; & pis d'autres qui n'*avont* rian fait du tout.[20]

Text 6: No examples.

Text 7: No examples in our extract, but forms like *voyaint* (= *voient*), *croyaint* (= *croient*) and *vivaint* (= *vivent*) are frequent in the text as a whole.

If we compare the morphology of these texts with what we found in Paris in the middle years of the sixteenth century (see above, §7.3.2), we are left with a rather slow-moving picture of vernacular speech in Paris, at least until the middle of the eighteenth century: the first three variables remained highly salient from the sixteenth to the eighteenth centuries. The latter two (*-iens* and *-ont*), which were already lower in salience in Parisian speech, declined significantly between the seventeenth and the eighteenth century, evidently through the generalisation of the standard forms (*-ions* and *-ent*).

9.3   Phonological variation and change

The central feature shared by all of these texts is the use of non-conventional spellings to denote stigmatised pronunciations. These spellings are not 'phonetic' transcriptions. Indeed, some of them seem to be 'for the eye only', signifying simply 'adopt a low-class accent when reading this'. The texts were written to be read aloud, and the performer was expected to supply additional low-class features not specified in the script, according to his individual histrionic abilities. In the introduction to his *Le Waux-hall populaire ou Les Fêtes de la Guinguette* (1769) Cailleau recommended that

---

[20] 'It is certainly true that there are a lot of you bishops who did scarcely any better; others who did even worse; and then others who did nothing at all.'

Tout ce qui est marqué par des guillemets à la tête de chaque vers, doit être prononcé d'un ton enroué, à l'imitation des gens de la Halle et des Ports: c'est en contrefaisant la voix et les gestes de ce peuple grossier, qu'on peut trouver quelqu'agrément à la lecture de ces sortes d'ouvrage, qui veulent être lus avec cette grâce originale et plaisante, qu'on a souvent de la peine à attraper. Le lecteur observera encore qu'il faut lire les vers poissards avec les abbréviations telles qu'elles sont marquées.

Vadé makes similar recommendations in the preface to his play *La Pipe cassée* (1758) (see Milliot 1995: 306). For all their vagueness and conventionality, these spellings nevertheless allow us to identify in a general way the stigmatised pronunciation being targeted. The most important are set out in Table 15 below. The majority of these low-status variants were the object of extensive metalinguistic comment from contemporaries. Here are examples of what the orthoepists had to say. The numbering follows that adopted in Table 15, the gap in the sequence (14–20) corresponding to variants about which no precise contemporary comment has yet been found.

Vowels

(1) [ɛr] ~ [ar], e.g. Estienne (1582): 'Plebs . . . praesertim Parisina hanc literam *a* pro *e* in multis vocibus pronuntiat, dicens *Pierre . . . guarre . . .* at vero aulici . . . *caterrhe* pronuntiant.' See Thurot 1881: I, 18–19; Brunot 1966: X.1, 94–5; Joseph 1987: 135 and 148–9; Ayres-Bennett 1990b: 154–5.

(2) **Distribution of** [e], [wɛ], [wa], e.g. Bèze (1584): 'pour *voirre ou*, comme d'autres l'écrivent, *verre*, on prononce vulgairement à Paris et on écrit très mal *voarre*'. See Thurot 1881: I, 356–9, 362, 375, 394, 411–13 Brunot 1966: X.1, 95–6; Joseph 1987: 136–7, 150–1, Ayres-Bennett 1990b: 155–6.

(3) [o] ~ [jo], e.g. Peletier (1549): 'les Parisiens . . . au lieu d'un *séau d'éau* diset *un sio d'io*'. See Thurot 1881: I, 439–40.

(4) [jɛ̃] ~ [jã], e.g. Tabourot (1588): 'les Parisiens prononcent . . . un *a* au lieu d'une *e*, surtout quand il suit un *i*'; '*ient* est de molle prononciation . . .' See Thurot 1883: II, 438 and 462.

(5) [ĩ)] ~ [ɛ̃], e.g. Tabourot (1588): 'le Parisien prononce tous les mots terminez en *in* en *ain*'; 'Autres y a qui prononcent à la parisienne *in* comme *ain*. Exemple, *i'ay beu de bon vain a la pomme de pain*, pour dire *i'ay beu de bon vin a la pomme de pin*.' See Thurot 1883: II, 483 and 485.

(6) **'Ouisme' – distribution of** [o], [u], e.g. Dumas (1733): 'on trouve des Parisiens qui disent *norir* pour *nourir*'. See Thurot 1881: I, 254; Joseph 1987: 135–6, 149; Ayres-Bennett 1990b: 154.

(7) [ɔ] ~ [œ] **in initial syllables**, e.g. Vaugelas (1647: 425): 'plusieurs Parisiens doivent prendre garde à une mauvaise prononciation de ce verbe, que j'ay remarquée mesme en des personnes celebres à la chaire et au

barreau . . . ils prononcent *commencer* tout de mesme que si l'on escrivoit *quemencer*'. See Thurot 1881: I, 268; Brunot 1966: X.1, 90–1.

(8) [ɛ] ∼ [i], e.g. Ménage (1672): 'Le peuple de Paris dit *arignée*. Il faut dire *araignée*.' See Thurot 1881: I, 17 350.

(9) [jɛ̃] ∼ [ɛ̃], e.g. Dumas (1733): 'quoique le peuple dise *ren* ou *rain* pour *rien*, il y a bien des gens letrés et au dessus du peuple qui disent *bèn ou bain* pour *bien. Si* l'usage seul parmi les honetes gens de la cour et de la vile confirme la bonne prononciation, celle de *ben* pour *bien* doit ètre reçue.' See Thurot 1881: I, 484.

(10) **Opening of word-final [e] in 5th person conditional**, e.g. Meigret (1550): 'l'offènce que vous fèt en l'oie la prononciation du menu peuple de Paris de *l'è* ouvert pour *l'e* clous: dizans *vous diries, fraperiês, doneries*, pour *diriez*, etc.' See Thurot 1881: I, 471–2.

(11) **Lowering of [ɛ̃] ∼ [ã]**, e.g. Dubois (1531): '*chi ens* non *ce ans* cum Parrhisiensium insignibus'. See Thurot 1883: II, 431.

(12) **Alternation [y] ∼ [oe]**, e.g. Richelet (1680): 'le petit peuple de Paris dit *abruver*, mais les gens du beau monde prononcent et écrivent *abreuver*'. See Thurot 1881: I, 453, 515 and 1883: II, 547; Ayres-Bennett 1990b: 156.

(13) **Maintenance of hiatus**, e.g. Vaugelas (1647: 322): 'ceux qui prononcent *a-oust*, comme fait le peuple de Paris, en deux syllabbes, font la mesme faute que ceux qui prononcent *ayder* en trois syllabes, *a-y-der*, quoy qu'il ne soit que deux'. See Thurot 1881: I, 315, 505 and 519.

Consonants

(21) [nj] ∼ [ɲ], e.g. Hindret (1687): 'quelques uns peuvent prononcer notre *gna, gne, gno, gnu*, et disent *nia, nie, nio*'. Conversely, he criticises 'la petite bourgeoisie de Paris' for pronouncing *un pagné, un jardign*, instead of *un panier, un jardinier*. See Thurot 1883: II, 310, 321, 347.

(22) [ʎ] ∼ [j], e.g. Hindret (1687): in 'la petite bourgeoisie de Paris', he finds 'beaucoup de gens . . . qui pour dire *bataillon, postillon, bouteille, bouillon* et autres mots où il entre des *i* accompagné de deux *ll* mouillées, disent *batayon, postiyon, boutaiye, bouyon*'. See Thurot 1883: II, 267, 298, 299; Brunot 1966: X.1, 97; Ayres-Bennett 1990b: 157. Hypercorrection seems to have occurred too, e.g. Hindret (1687), criticises 'la petite bourgeoisie de Paris' for saying '*il est meilieur*, instead of *il est meilleur*'. See Thurot 1883: II, 300.

(23) **Treatment of preconsonantal [l]**, e.g. Richelet (1680): '(*kécun* et *kéque*) tous les Parisiens qui parlent bien les prononcent en faisant sentir la lettre *l*'.

(24) **Elision of post-consonantal [l]/[r] before final schwa**, e.g. Richelet (1680): 'le petit peuple de Paris dit *marbe*, mais toute la cour et tous

ceux qui parlent bien disent et écrivent *marbre*'. See Thurot 1883: II, 281–2; Brunot 1966: X.1, 99.

(25) **Assibilation of medial [r]** ~ **[z]**, e.g. Erasmus (1528): 'Idem faciunt hodie mulierculae Parisinae, pro *Maria* sonantes *Masia*, pro *ma mere, ma mese*.' See Thurot 1883: II, 270–4; Joseph 1987: 155–6; Ayres-Bennett 1990b: 157.

(26) **Elision of [r] before [l]**, e.g. Bovelles (1533): 'Parrhisii hoc vitio laborant, ut quotiens *r* in media vulgari dictione praeit *l*, conflent duplicem *ll*, ut in *Charles . . . Challes*'; 'Infantes et Parrhisii . . . *vallet*, pro *varlet, paller* pro *parler*.' See Thurot 1883: II, 289.

(27) **Elision of post-vocalic [r]**, e.g. Duez (1669): 'le petit peuple de Paris prononce *cueillié* . . . Les honnestes bourgeois y disent *cueillère* . . . Nous disons *cueillèr* en Anjou: et cette prononciation est la véritable.' See Thurot 1881: I, 198, 270; 1883: II, 5, 150, 171; Ayres-Bennett 1990b: 156–7; but see also Andry (1689): 'le peuple de Paris est . . . fort accoûtumé à prononcer les *r* à la fin des infinitifs, comme *aller, venir*, etc. mais tres-mal et fort rudement'. See Thurot 1883: II, 154, 162.

(28) **Voicing of medial [ʃ]**, e.g. Chiflet (1659): 'ne prononcez jamais *ajetter*, comme fait le peuple de Paris'. See Thurot 1883: II, 228.

(29) **Elision of final [f]**, e.g. Estienne (1582): 'ceux qui suppriment l'*f* dans *clef* ne la suppriment point, comme le fait le peuple, dans *cerf*'. See Thurot 1883: II, 138–9.

(30) **Reduction of consonantal clusters**, e.g. Richelet (1680): 'le peuple de Paris dit *ostination*, mais les honnêtes gens disent et écrivent *obstination* et il n'y a point à balancer là-dessus, il faut parler comme les honnêtes gens, il faut dire *obstiner*'. See Thurot 1883: II, 369; Brunot 1966: X.1, 98.

(31) **ique > icle**, e.g. Tabourot (1588): 'les Parisiens prononcent les noms terminés en *ique* par *icle:* comme pour *boutique* ils dient *bouticle*, pour *musique, musicle*'. See Thurot 1883: II, 268.

(32) **Effacement of aspirate [h]**, e.g. Académie (1673): 'Dans tous les autres mots qui ne viennent point du latin, l'h aspire fort, quoyque le mauvais usage introduit par les gens de province d'outre Loire et mesme par le peuple de Paris s'efforce de l'abolir tout à fait.' See Thurot 1883: II, 396; Joseph 1987: 154–5.

(33) and (34) **Velarisation of [dj] and [tj]**: this development is not picked up by any of the orthoepists analysed by Thurot, but it is widely attested in the HDP (see *ALF* 403, 404, 846).

The non-conventional spellings used in our corpus of texts to represent these thirty-four pronunciation variables have to be interpreted with care. Firstly, they do not come near the rigour and systematicity of the experimental orthographies proposed by orthoepists like Meigret and Peletier du Mans in the sixteenth century, and Vaudelin in the early eighteenth (see Martinet 1969: 155–67). The texts had, after all, to be easily comprehended by readers trained in conventional orthography. Secondly, at a time when spelling was still not fully standardised, it is not always certain what the 'normal' spelling would have been, though in most cases, a modern reader familiar with written texts from this period can make a fairly accurate guess. Thirdly, very occasionally we find non-conventional spellings designed 'for the eye only', which serve merely to accentuate the non-conventional 'look' of the piece. It is usually safe to assume, however, that when an author deviates from 'normal' spelling, it is to highlight some low-status pronunciation variant.

Table 15 presents a list of the principal non-standard spellings found in these texts, with an indication of the non-standard pronunciation they were intended to prompt.

Armed with this list of variables, we can now calculate the incidence of the vernacular variants in each 1,000-word text in our corpus (see §9.1). This will permit us to rank the variants in order of frequency, helping us identify in an approximate way the most high-consciousness variants among them (stereotypes in the Labovian sense) at particular times. It should be noted, however, that no allowance is made here for lexical frequency.

9.3.1   The most salient variants, c. 1650

The three texts selected to represent the mid seventeenth century were Texts 2, 3 and 4 in the Appendix, pp. 251–60. Texts 2 and 4 purport to represent the speech of low-status inhabitants of the city itself, whereas Text 3 represents the speech of rustics from the Paris suburbs. Table 16 indicates the number of tokens of each stigmatised variant found in randomly selected passages of 1,000 words in each text. The variables (numbered as in Table 15) have been arranged in order of frequency, classified according to whether they are found in all three texts, in two out of the three, one out of the three, or in none. This table shows a good deal of consensus about what the most salient (i.e. the most stereotypical) vernacular variants were (Group I). At the same time, the table shows that the authors' representations of low-class speech were not rigidly bound by a set of pre-established conventions: the sets of variants found in Groups II and III indicate that each author had his own representation of low-class speech. Indeed, the variables found in Group IV, which are featured in the work of other contemporary parodists, are not found in any of our three texts.

It is possible to see differences in the portayal of low-class speech between Text 3 (the *Agréables Conférences*) and Texts 2 and 4 (the *Nouveaux Complimens* and the *Gazette des Halles*). Text 3 has a denser accumulation of stigmatised features, both in terms of the number of types and of the number

Table 15. *The main non-standard spelling variables, 1550–1750*

	Standard	Non-standard	Example	Thurot (1881, 1883)
Vowels				
(1)	'er'	'ar'	*tarre*	I, 18–19
(2)	'oi'	'oa', 'ai', 'a'	*voarre*	I, 356–9
(3)	'eau'	'iau'	*siau*	I, 439–40
(4)	'ien'	'ian'	*bian*	II, 438, 462
(5)	'in'	'ain'	*vain (= vin)*	II, 483, 485
(6)	'o'	'ou'	*estoumac*	I, 254
(7)	'com'	'quem'	*quemencer*	I, 268
(8)	'aign'	'ign'	*arignée*	I, 17, 350
(9)	'ien'	'en'	*ben*	I, 484
(10)	'iez'	'iais'	*donneriais*	I, 471–2
(11)	'en'	'an'	*prandre*	II, 431
(12)	'un'	'eun'	*preune*	I, 453, 515
(13)	'eu'	'aïëu'	*aïëu*	I, 315, 505
(14)	'cette'	'ste'	*ste*	–
(15)	'voilà'	'vla'	*vla*	–
(16)	'ai'	'a'	*vrament*	–
(17)	'e'	'eu'	*cheux*	–
(18)	'ui'	'i'	*pis*	–
(19)	'o'	'au'	*haume*	–
(20)	'un'	'in'	*in*	–
Consonants				
(21)	'nié'	'gné'	*pagné*	II, 310, 321
(22)	'ill'	'y'	*batayon*	II, 267, 298
(23)	'el'	'eu'	*queuque*	–
(24)	'ble', etc.	'be', etc.	*raisonnabe*	II, 281–2
(25)	'r'	'z'/'s'	*Masia*	II, 270–4
(26)	'rl'	'll'	*paller*	II, 289
(27)	'r' final	elided	*cuillié*	I, 198, 270, etc.
(28)	'ch'	'j'	*ajetter*	II, 228
(29)	'f' final	elided	*cer*	II, 138–9
(30)	Reduction of clusters		*ostination*	II, 369
(31)	'ique'	'icle'	*musicle*	II, 268
(32)	Elision of aspirate 'h'		*l'aut*	II, 396
(33)	'di'	'gui'	*Guieu*	–
(34)	'ti'	'qui'	*méquier*	–

of tokens. The rustics of Text 3 were clearly seen as having a broader accent than the town-dwellers of Texts 2 and 4. This was a perception widespread at the time. In his *Discours sur l'utilité des Lettres et des sciences par rapport au bien de l'Etat*, published in Amsterdam in 1715, Barbeyrac declares that:

Le menu peuple des villes ne parle pas si mal que les paysans et les villageois. (quoted in Milliot 1995: 287)

Table 16. *The most salient variants, c. 1650*

Variable	Standard	Non-standard	Text 2	Text 3	Text 4
Group I (variants attested in all three texts)					
(27)	'r' final	elided	25	41	13
(2)	'oi'	'oa', 'ai', 'a'	12	50	3
(25)	'r'	'z'/'s'	2	34	10
(11)	'en'	'an'	10	17	13
(1)	'er'	'ar'	13	14	7
(6)	'o'	'ou'	1	29	1
(3)	'eau'	'iau'	8	8	6
(5)	'in'	'ain'	4	12	6
(33)	'di'	'gui'	8	5	7
(34)	'ti'	'qui'	4	3	1
(30)	Consonant clusters		2	2	1
(21)	'nié'	'gné'	1	1	1
Group II (variants attested in two texts out of three)					
(24)	'ble', etc.	'be', etc.	15	18	–
(18)	'ui'	'i'	2	19	–
(15)	'voilà'	'vla'	8	7	–
(17)	'e'	'eu'	3	4	–
(22)	'ill'	'y'	–	5	1
(31)	'ique'	'icle'	1	5	–
(14)	'cette'	'ste'	4	–	1
(16)	'ai'	'a'	2	–	2
(23)	'el'	'eu'	1	–	1
Group III (variants attested in one text out of three)					
(13)	'eu'	'aiëu'	–	17	–
(9)	'ien'	'en'	–	15	–
(7)	'com'	'quem'	–	12	–
(32)	Elision of aspirate 'h'		1	–	–
(4)	'ien'	'ian'	–	3	–
(29)	'f' final	elided	–	1	–
(28)	'ch'	'j'	–	–	1
Group IV (variants not attested)					
(8)	'aign'	'ign'	–	–	–
(10)	'iez'	'iais'	–	–	–
(12)	'un'	'eun'	–	–	–
(19)	'o'	'au'	–	–	–
(20)	'un'	'in'	–	–	–
(26)	'rl'	'll'	–	–	–

What is striking, however, is the similarity of the accents: there are relatively few phonological features used by the town-dwellers which are not also used by the rustics. We should not make too much of this, of course, for the authors probably grouped together all non-standard variants (urban and rural) rather indiscriminately.

9.3.2   *The most salient variants, c. 1750*

To represent the situation in the mid eighteenth century we selected Texts 5, 6 and 7 in the Appendix (pp. 261–6). These three texts purport to represent the speech of the immediate suburbs of the city (Table 17). The first (Sarcelles) is drawn from a long series of *harangues* in prose and verse related to the Jansenist controversy. The second (Chaillot) is a short royalist tract in verse, and the third (Montmartre) a prose text (see Lodge 1995b). The portrayal of low-class pronunciation found here is less detailed than the one found in the seventeenth-century texts – there are twice as many variants which are not attested in any of the three texts (Group IV). The royalist tract (Text 6) is particularly perfunctory, and it looks as though the author was using, rather half-heartedly, a ready-made stock of vernacularisms in a crude attempt to fight the anti-establishment pamphleteers with their own weapon. The reduction in the number of phonetic variants found in these eighteenth-century texts may then indicate a conventionalisation of the genre, though it must be pointed out that there was little continuity in print between the seventeenth- and the eighteenth-century creations. It may also be that, during this period, dialect-levelling was taking place, that the most stigmatised rustic variants were disappearing as the proportion of non-natives in the Paris population diminished.

9.3.3   *Synthesis*

If we bring together the pictures of the most salient variables in the seventeenth and eighteenth centuries and compare them with the picture that emerged in the sixteenth century in Chapter 7, we have a sort of barometer of salience across the proto-industrial period, as set out in Fig. 3. The most striking observation to be made here concerns long-term changes in the salience of the eight variables highlighted in the sixteenth-century text (variables 27, 25, 2, 3, 1, 5, 31 and 6). Between the mid sixteenth century and the mid seventeenth very few changes are to be seen, but between the mid seventeenth and the mid eighteenth centuries the pattern is radically transformed.

Of the eight variables which were strongly salient in the sixteenth century only three remained so in the eighteenth century:

(1) [ɛr] ∼ [ar]
(3) [o] ∼ [jo]
(27) Elision of post-vocalic [r]

The fact that variables as salient as these should have coexisted in the community as long as they did suggests that they were each reallocated as social-class indicators.

Two of the original variables survived at a lower level of salience:

(2) Distribution of [ɛ], [wɛ], [wa]
(5) Lowering of [ĩ] → [ɛ̃]

Table 17. *The most salient variants, c. 1750*

Variable	Standard	Non-standard	Text 5	Text 6	Text 7
Group I					
(1)	'er'	'ar'	13	30	19
(3)	'eau'	'iau'	13	16	17
(4)	'ien'	'ian'	20	6	10
(33)	'di'	'gui'	13	6	15
(27)	'r' final	elided	1	4	22
(18)	'ui'	'i'	10	6	10
(23)	'el'	'eu'	3	2	8
(12)	'un'	'eun'	1	4	2
(21)	'nié'	'gné'	2	2	2
(22)	'ill'	'y'	1	2	1
Group II					
(24)	'ble', etc.	'be', etc.	–	20	7
(2)	'oi'	'oa', 'ai', 'a'	12	–	11
(14)	'cette'	'ste'	2	–	7
(10)	'iez'	'iais'	2	8	–
(34)	'ti'	'qui'	3	–	5
(17)	'e'	'eu'	2	–	6
(11)	'en'	'an'	2	–	4
(15)	'voilà'	'vla'	4	–	1
(5)	'in'	'ain'	4	–	1
Group III					
(8)	'aign'	'ign'	12	–	–
(30)	Reduction of clusters		–	4	–
(13)	'eu'	'aiëu'	–	–	1
Group IV					
(6)	'o'	'ou'	–	–	–
(7)	'com'	'quem'	–	–	–
(9)	'ien'	'en'	–	–	–
(16)	'ai'	'a'	–	–	–
(19)	'o'	'au'	–	–	–
(20)	'un'	'in'	–	–	–
(25)	'r'	'z'/'s'	–	–	–
(26)	'rl'	'll'	–	–	–
(28)	'ch'	'j'	–	–	–
(29)	'f' final	elided	–	–	–
(31)	'ique'	'icle'	–	–	–
(32)	Elision of aspirate 'h'		–	–	–

We might infer that these were changes in progress between the sixteenth and eighteenth centuries. For almost two centuries (sixteenth to eighteenth centuries) the realisation of the [OI] diphthong in Paris was something of a shibboleth, with [wɛ] being adhered to *broadly speaking* by the aristocracy and [wa] by the merchant class. Through a complex process of lexical and

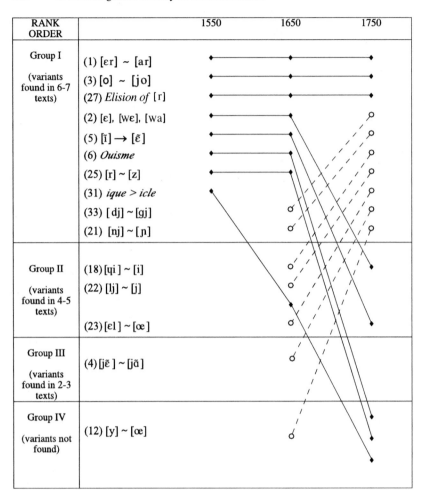

RANK ORDER		1550	1650	1750
Group I (variants found in 6-7 texts)	(1) [ɛr] ~ [ar] (3) [o] ~ [jo] (27) *Elision of* [r] (2) [ɛ], [wɛ], [wa] (5) [ĩ] → [ɛ̃] (6) *Ouisme* (25) [r] ~ [z] (31) *ique > icle* (33) [dj] ~ [gj] (21) [nj] ~ [ɲ]			
Group II (variants found in 4-5 texts)	(18) [ɥi] ~ [i] (22) [lj] ~ [j] (23) [ɛl] ~ [œ]			
Group III (variants found in 2-3 texts)	(4) [jɛ̃] ~ [jɑ̃]			
Group IV (variants not found)	(12) [y] ~ [œ]			

Note: While respecting the overall frequency ranking of the groups of variables (I-IV), we have occasionally modified the rank-order of the individual variables within each group to make the figure legible.

Fig. 3. Changes in salience 1550–1750

social diffusion, the three variants were eventually allocated their own part of the lexicon (see Reighard 1980), with variation becoming reduced by the middle years of the eighteenth century. Variable (5) [ĩ] → [ɛ̃] consistently lost salience over this period, and it is noteworthy that (11) [ɛ̃] → [ɑ̃] followed suit, with a time-lag, perhaps implying a push-chain lowering of [ĩ] → [ɛ̃] → [ɑ̃] (see Hansen 1998: 78–87). Variable (4) [jɛ̃] → [jɑ̃], on the other hand, sees its salience rise between the two centuries. Could it be that, coming at the end of the chain, this variable achieved salience as a change in progress after the lowering of the other nasals?

Three variables lose all salience between the seventeenth and eighteenth centuries:

(6) Ouisme – distribution of [o], [u]

(25) Assibilation of medial [r] ∼ [z]

(31) *ique > icle*

Over the period sound changes (6) and (25) moved to completion, either through the allocation of each to different parts of the lexicon or through one of the variants disappearing altogether. Lexical reallocation of [o] and [u] sounds, for example *pourceau ∼ portrait, couleur ∼ colonne*, was under way in the sixteenth century (see Pope 1952: §282; Brunot 1883: II, 251–4), as was that between medial [r] and [z], for example *chaire ∼ chaise, nariller ∼ nasiller* (see Pope 1952: §399). Once the question of the assibilation of [r] was resolved, the various realisations of this phoneme continued to have social significance into the nineteenth century. The uvular trill [R], referred to prescriptively as the '*r* grasseyé', developed initially in seventeenth-century Paris (Thurot 1883: 270). Opinions are divided about whether this variant first emerged in lower- or upper-class speech. Passy (1917: 98–9) and Straka (1979: 466–8) give it an upper-class origin, and indeed, it is hard to find it as a stigmatised variant in our corpus of texts (though this may result from the difficulty of representing in spelling the difference between the various allophonic realisations of /r/). The label 'grasseyé' is always negative, however, and upper-class variants are rarely stigmatised in metalinguistic texts of this period. In Molière's *Le Bourgeois Gentilhomme* (Act II, scene 4) apical [r] is firmly recommended by the elocution master to the upward-climbing *bourgeois*.

Not all changes between the seventeenth and eighteenth centuries involved loss of salience. Beside the three stigmatised variants which were consistently salient across the three centuries (variables 1, 3 and 27), certain others which were highly salient in the seventeenth century remained so in the eighteenth:

(33) and (34) Velarisation of [dj] and [tj]

(21) [nj] + vowel → [ɲ]

Several other variables gained salience in the eighteenth century:

(18) Reduction of [ɥi] → [i]

(22) Reduction of [ʎ] → [j]

(23) Treatment of preconsonantal [l]

(30) Reduction of consonantal clusters

(12) [y] ∼ [oe]

What is striking about these gains in salience is that they mainly involve features of register rather than dialect, that is, they are general features of rapid Parisian speech.

The picture that emerges from these data is one of slow phonological and morphological change between the sixteenth and seventeenth centuries and rapid change between the seventeenth and eighteenth. Perhaps this reflects, as we noted above (§9.2), a tendency to increased levelling of dialect-differences within the city between the seventeenth and eighteenth centuries. We noted earlier (§6.1.1) the decline in the proportion of non-natives in the eighteenth-century population.

9.4   Summary

The pervasive nature of the variables depicted in the texts we have looked at here, spread as they are across three centuries and corroborated by numerous contemporary observers, suggests that we are dealing with something more deeply embedded in the collective psyche than a mere literary stereotype. The inhabitants of a metropolis may not be united by their speech habits, which are remarkably variable, but they are by their linguistic attitudes and prejudices, which are remarkably consistent and slow to change. It is the sort of social evaluation we see here which, we believe, guided the process of reallocation of variants between standard and vernacular during the proto-industrial period.

Comic imitations of low-class Parisian speech shed light principally on changing social attitudes to particular parts of the language. They offer only the most simplified picture of the city's real-life sociolinguistic structure, blurring important dichotomies such as written/spoken, formal/informal and urban/rural in a rather disturbing way. However, it is hard to see them working as comedy unless they were based on a sociolinguistic reality which the audience could recognise. Taken with information available in other sources (notably the comments of contemporary lexicographers and grammarians), these data allow us to discern at the bottom of society, albeit vaguely and incompletely, a set of vernacular speech-norms that showed continued links with the hinterland dialect and that were distinct from those of the standard language being elaborated at the top, which was gradually diffusing downwards. Rosset (1911: 363) was probably right when he declared that:

il existait, au milieu du XVIIe siècle, à Paris et dans la banlieue parisienne, une prononciation populaire opposée à la prononciation que les grammairiens mettaient en règle et qui devenait peu à peu le bel usage.

The rustic links of this basilectal variety look to have remained solid between the sixteenth and seventeenth centuries, though by the middle of the eighteenth, they seem to have been attenuated as the proportion of native Parisians increased. We can have no precise idea about the socio-stylistic distribution of these vernacular forms in proto-industrial Paris, but it is safe to assume that most of them were present.

Part 4

The industrial city

10   Industrial growth, 1750–1950

The onset of industrialisation in the late eighteenth century introduced changes to the urban landscape of Europe which were unprecedented in scale, and less reversible than all previous ones had been. In those industrial cities that mushroomed out of small townships, like Manchester, Saint Etienne, Dortmund, new urban varieties arose as modified forms of their hinterland dialect, with the standard language being 'parachuted in' from outside. In long-established metropolises like London and Paris, urban dialect and standard language already coexisted within the community, so the effect of industrial growth was to realign the varieties in circulation, through an extension in the distribution and functional range of the standard language, and a radical modification of vernacular speech through dialect-levelling. We might expect the effect of standardisation and levelling to be to reduce dialect differences. However, when we look at Parisian speech at the beginning of the twentieth century, it is clear that industrialisation did not produce linguistic homogeneity. Urban speech varieties, as they evolve in the course of time, do not show a noticeable tendency to converge. Changes take place, but not such as to eliminate the differences (see Halliday 1978: 158).

In Part 4 we will begin by looking at the socio-demographic development of the industrial city up to the middle of the twentieth century (Chapter 10). Following Hohenberg and Lees (1985), we will end our story in 1950, not because that was the end of history, but because subsequent developments in communication and inter-continental migration have transformed Paris in ways that transcend those of the industrial period, and to examine these would impossibly extend the scope of this book. In Chapter 11 we will consider the possible effects of standardisation and dialect-levelling in nineteenth-century Paris. We will conclude in Chapter 12 with a historical survey of lexical variation in Parisian speech: standardisation and dialect-levelling may have had the effect of reducing social-dialect differences in the city, notably in grammar and pronunciation, but, as if to compensate, lexical variation appears to have increased its role at this time as a marker of socio-stylistic difference.

The transformations which separate the industrial city from its proto-industrial predecessor cannot be reduced to a single underlying principle: they are inter-related and affect simultaneously many levels of activity (economic, demographic, social, cultural). From an economic standpoint, the most basic changes arise from the principle of economy of scale. Enhanced organisational efficiency and technological advance led to cheaper production and increased consumption. Increased consumption called for increased production, and so on. Once launched, the process became self-sustaining. The transition from proto-industrial to industrial modes of production involves the concentration of workers in workshops and factories: efficiencies of size imply concentrations of people, that is, urbanisation. Whereas the European population in the late eighteenth century was still overwhelmingly rural, during the nineteenth century its urban population multiplied sixfold. Economies of agglomeration meant that this movement too became self-sustaining, cities providing fertile environments for small firms and large numbers of consumers. This caused the biggest cities (metropolises) to grow the fastest. Indeed, it was the combination of political, service and industrial activities that produced Europe's metropolises. In this short chapter, let us look first at demographic growth in industrial Paris, and then at the social and cultural effects of mass urbanisation, for they were to have major sociolinguistic consequences.

10.1   Demographic change

During the nineteenth century, Paris, in common with many other European cities, underwent an increase in population which was quite out of proportion to what had previously happened. Its population rose from 500,000 in 1800 to 2,500,000 a century later. The unprecedented scale of this increase relative to the city's growth over the previous seven centuries can be seen in Fig. 4.

Hohenberg and Lees (1985: 184) point out that 'cities that combined major central place functions with an expanding role in manufacturing and trading networks grew particularly rapidly. In fact, national capitals and major ports, where economic influence kept pace with political dominance, consolidated their position as primate cities.' This captures the Parisian developments perfectly. Within France, Parisian growth was quite exceptional. The large provincial towns of nineteenth-century France failed to participate fully in the movement of mass urbanisation observable elsewhere in north-western Europe, and this reinforced the demographic preponderance of the capital. At the beginning of the twentieth century Paris had more inhabitants than the combined population of all the other French towns with more than 50,000 inhabitants.

Parisian growth across the industrial period between 1801 and 1951 was not uniform, however (see Fig. 5.) Three phases can be distinguished. In the fifty years before 1851 the city doubled its population along a gently rising curve. Economic historians see this time as a prolongation of the proto-industrial period, with production surpluses generated more by increased organisational

thousands

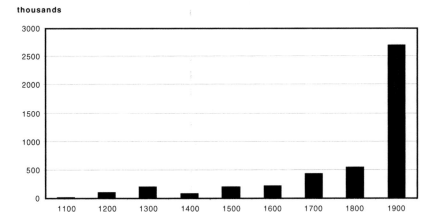

Fig. 4. Population of Paris, 1100–1900
Source: Compiled from data published in Dupâquier 1988 and the various
volumes of the *Nouvelle Histoire de Paris* (see p. 25).

thousands

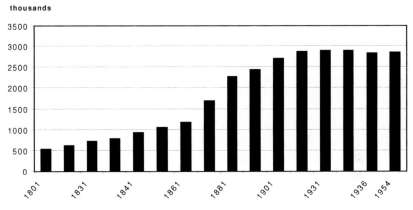

Fig. 5. Population of Paris 1801–1954
Source: Fierro 1996: 279

efficiency than by mechanisation. In the second half of the century the population doubled again, during what economic historians see as a 'second industrial
revolution', which took off as the impact of railways and mechanisation began
to be felt. From the beginning of the twentieth century until after the Second
World War the city's population stabilised at around 3,000,000.

These figures tell only part of the story, for, as space within the city became saturated, the new population gravitated to new industrial and residential
suburbs on the periphery (Map 19). Between 1820 and 1890 over half of Parisian

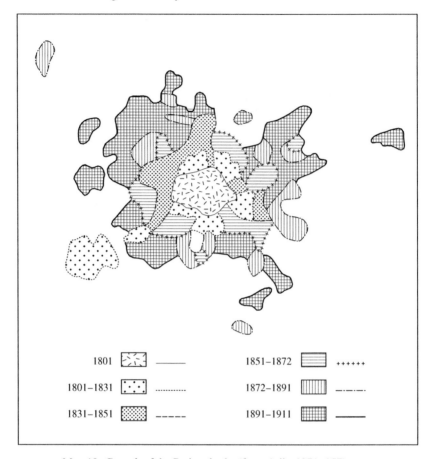

Map 19. Growth of the Paris suburbs (from Ariès 1971: 157)

growth came as a result of in-migration, and we can see the origins of the new-comers changing in step with the three phases of demographic increase we have just encountered (see Chevalier 1950). In the first half of the century they came, as in centuries past, from quite close at hand, the three greatest contributors being the Ile-de-France and Picardy (40 per cent), Normandy and Burgundy (each 13 per cent). In the second half of the century, the balance tipped towards migration over longer distances, stimulated no doubt by the development of the railways. The three greatest contributors were: Brittany, south-central France and the Massif Central. It is worth pointing out that the linguistic origins of the later migrants were more remote from the speech of Paris than those of the earlier ones. Similar in-migratory patterns were reproduced in the twentieth century, with the addition of sizeable numbers of foreigners, notably Belgians,

Germans, Italians and Swiss. To these we should add immigration from eastern Europe, notably Poland and Russia (after the Revolution of 1917). It is only after the Second World War that immigration from Africa and Asia became a significant contributor.

The three-phase process visible in demographic growth and in patterns of in-migration is replicated in changes in the social geography of the city. These have been plotted in an interesting way by Philippe Ariès (1979: 119–98). Like other demographic and social historians, he sees a decisive turning-point in the middle of the nineteenth century.

Les vieux Paris, qui se sont succédé depuis le moyen âge, ont disparu, abandonnant seulement quelques témoins de leur passé, enchâssés, comme des reliques, dans la marée de constructions nouvelles qui, à partir du milieu du XIXe siècle, a recouvert les anciens quartiers et débordé très loin vers la périphérie. (Ariès 1979: 119)

The maps indicate the relative density of the population of the different parts of the city at particular points in the period from 1800 to 1931 (Map 20). Ariès observes that in the first half of the nineteenth century the old city centre continued to absorb the general increase in the population, as it had done in the proto-industrial period, though signs of saturation and decantation towards the periphery begin to appear in the 1840s. In the second half of the nineteenth century the demographic centre of gravity abruptly shifted away from the medieval centre towards the north (Rochechouart) and north-east (Belleville and Ménilmontant). This reflects a major social transformation, as the rich continued to gravitate towards the west of the city and the poor towards the east. In the twentieth century the abandonment of the centre by the poor continued, with the development of the so-called 'Ceinture Rouge' in the north and east.

The decisive turning-point in the middle decades of the nineteenth century was the one in which the authorities, not surprisingly, were compelled to intervene to reduce overcrowding in the city centre. It is precisely this period which sees Haussmann's redesign of central Paris, the break-up of the traditional, tightly networked communities of the city centre and the constitution of huge new working-class districts on the outskirts (see Hohenberg and Lees 1985: 326–9). Distinct residential zones now divided the city by class, by wealth and by life-style, typified by the contrast between the *faubourg* Saint Germain and the 16th *arrondissement* on the one side, and the *faubourg* Saint Antoine and Belleville on the other.

10.2   Social change

The nineteenth century was for Europe a time of intense change, and by the middle of the century class structures that had been evolving slowly for a thousand years had been abruptly realigned. We can sum up the important social

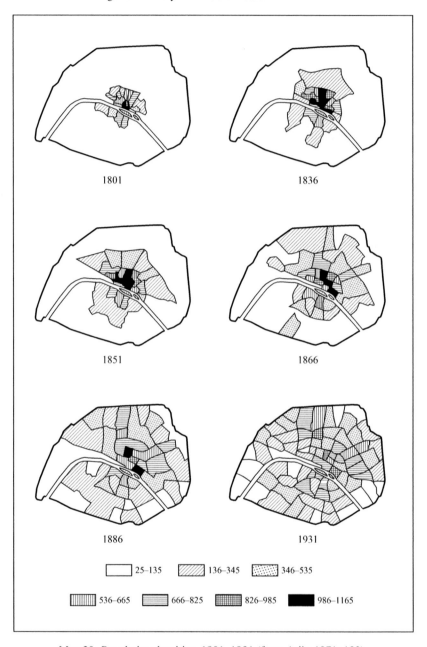

Map 20. Population densities, 1801–1931 (from Ariès 1971: 122)

effects of industrial urbanisation in Paris under the headings of liberalisation, proletarianisation and bureaucratisation.

The liberalising effects of the 1789 Revolution on the French capital were very considerable: the power of the aristocracy and the Catholic Church were damaged irreparably, and the city was endowed with an entirely new and more rational set of administrative structures. The psychological impact of the democratic Revolution was, of course, incalculable, and expectations were raised not just in France but across the continent. However, in France, as elsewhere, power remained vested in the hands of a tiny elite, estimated at around 4 per cent of the population, now composed principally of capitalists and financiers. They were no more enthusiastic about sharing power than their aristocratic predecessors had been. Political participation and the right to vote in France took many decades to be established, and only after more violent conflict.

Cities at the top of the urban hierarchy are particularly important sites for mass movements. The sheer size of Paris, coupled with strong class divisions and the presence of the national government, was conducive to political mobilisation, and the results were frequently explosive: after the traumas of the first Revolution and its imperial aftermath, the nineteenth-century city was wracked by three bouts of social conflict which grew progressively more violent: the July Revolution of 1830, the February Revolution of 1848 and the Commune in 1871. To begin with, political conflict occurred primarily between the new capitalist order and vestiges of the Ancien Régime. Later on it developed into a much more far-reaching class-struggle between the bourgeoisie and the proletariat, perceived by the rulers as *les classes dangereuses* (see Chevalier 1958). The Third Republic (1870–1940) initially saw the triumph of the bourgeoisie, but the trauma of the First World War, the *Front populaire* (1936) and the internecine strife under the Occupation led eventually to the dismantling of the old class structures.

The poor had always formed the overwhelming majority of the Paris population, but we might recall that in the proto-industrial city, through the system of trades and guilds, 'workers' generally retained a sense of 'belonging' to the system. Rich and poor in proto-industrial Paris were often bound together by multiplex network ties: an apprentice probably had the same person as employer, landlord and master of the craft-guild. In the nineteenth century, industrial specialisation caused these multiplex network ties to become uniplex ones. The industrial worker now had a series of different individuals fulfilling these various roles, and, importantly, he no longer owned the tools of his trade. Market capitalism turned human labour into a free-floating commodity, the development of wage-labour separating the worker from the employer-controlled means of production. The working population now became a proletariat, more or less alienated from the 'system', and gradually it developed a political consciousness, which played an increasingly important part in the life of the city as time went on. That said, it would be a mistake to regard the huge working-class population of nineteenth-century Paris as a monolith. It constituted a vast mosaic of sub-cultures, and political allegiance was not the only integrating force available to it.

The impact of technological change and the shift towards production for the market swelled the ranks not only of the proletariat but also of a middle class of owners, managers and professionals. This bourgeoisie expanded, drawing a greater proportion of the population into moderate affluence than ever in Western history. Moreover, it was joined by elements from a new breed of public servant. The nineteenth century saw a spectacular growth in administrative institutions and in the numbers of bureaucrats who spent their lives counting, taxing, permitting and inspecting. The informal, almost personal structures of the past were replaced one by one by official bureaucracies. Industrialisation and the development of the nation-state led to the progressive bureaucratisation of society.

The overall effect of industrial urbanisation was to create a society which was more fragmented, more mobile and, on the face of it, more anonymous than the one that preceded it. Industrial Paris has often been described as a melting-pot. However, it might be more accurate to describe it as an assemblage of nested communities, a mosaic of disparate groups struggling to maintain their identity. Cities contain both large-scale and small-scale environments. In public places – shops, offices, streets and large institutions – contacts are relatively brief and anonymous, and social networking is loose and uniplex; but in private social life – family, *quartier*, club, ethnic community – social identities are personalised and longer lasting, and social networking is dense and multiplex. The family meant an extended family, with kin acting as welfare agencies. Local communities grew up around the factory or in particular *quartiers* around particular bistrots (see Bourdieu 1983). Members of particular ethnic groups gravitated towards particular localities; for instance, migrants from the Massif Central tended to congregate in the neighbourhood of the Halles and the Hôtel de Ville. Initially at least, the different contingents of long-distance migrants tended to cling together in language-based colonies located, very often, near the railway station of their arrival (see Chevalier 1985). Despite high rates of geographic mobility, small communities and their mosaic of sub-cultures still managed to thrive in industrial Paris.

10.3   Cultural change

The proto-industrial period had introduced the divorce between high culture and popular culture (see §6.1.5), and in the period after 1800 this divide deepened, most conspicuously in the great national capitals of Paris and London. Elites distinguished themselves from the masses by residence, dress, leisure activities and general life-style, as well as by wealth and 'accent'.

For centuries past, the great concentration of wealth in Paris had attracted and maintained a remarkable number of writers, artists and musicians, who kept alive and renewed the cultural forms of the dominant tradition. This continued in spectacular fashion throughout the industrial period and down to our own day, and is thoroughly documented. The difference now, however, was that the number of 'consumers' of these art-forms was greatly increased through the expansion of the bourgeoisie: the newly affluent enthusiastically sought to join or at least to imitate the traditional elites. To a degree even greater than other nineteenth-century cities, Paris nurtured an active middle-class culture, as theatres, opera-houses, libraries, museums and botanical gardens multiplied. The poor were not formally excluded from these places, but in practice the cost and behavioural standards required excluded most of the urban population.

While elite culture showed strong continuity with the past, popular culture was completely transformed during this period. The transformation was gradual. During the first half of the nineteenth century many aspects of proto-industrial culture survived. European cities continued to have their own 'little tradition' of urban folklore, drawing vitality from many sources: surviving communal festivals like May Day, local fairs, the routines of work and the newly invented rituals of the Revolution and early trade unionism. In Catholic countries religious-based festivals continued strongly, with local saints' days and parish feasts complementing the annual cycle of pre-Lentan carnivals, Easter, Ascension, the Assumption, Christmas and the Epiphany. However, the boisterousness accompanying many of these celebrations roused the hostility of political authorities and middle-class citizens. What was harmless enough in a small village became a potential insurrection in a great metropolis. Informal popular festivals were gradually suppressed, a movement hastened by the demise of the traditional crafts and rhythms of work.

The second half of the nineteenth century and the early twentieth century in France saw the introduction of politically approved celebrations like the Quatorze Juillet and, later on, the Tour de France cycle race. As older forms of popular culture were discarded or even repressed, newer ones took their place, catering for specific interests rather than for the general collectivity. Outdoor recreation was transformed by the spread of bicycles, by easy access to the countryside through railway excursions, and by the development of public parks. Sports and musical clubs proliferated alongside cheap theatres, music-halls and, eventually, cinemas. Above all, a mass press developed, fostered by increasing literacy. The spread of education at this time changed irrevocably not only the nature of popular culture, but also the distribution, functional range and even the structural bases of the standard language (see Joseph 1987: 43–4).

The development of literacy in France has been minutely analysed by Furet and Ozouf (1977), who highlight the link between the universalisation of literacy and the growth of the market economy. We saw earlier that in the eighteenth century rates of literacy in Paris had been surprisingly high (see §8.2.2).

Napoleon I had been concerned with the higher levels of education – with the *Université*, the *Grandes Ecoles* and the *lycées* – and for him, elementary education and the education of the masses had not been matters of high priority. Private schooling had always been available for the well-to-do, while religious organisations provided a piecemeal system of elementary education for the children of the poor. However, during the subsequent decades of the nineteenth century, the demands of the market economy, coupled with high levels of migration into Paris of often illiterate country-dwellers, gave the problems of education for the poor a new urgency.

The state was first impelled to act after the July Revolution of 1830. The 'Guizot Law', passed in 1833, obliged all local councils to set up elementary schools in their *municipalité*, primarily for the children of the poor. The education budget of Paris rose from 320,000 francs in 1829 to 1,820,000 francs in 1848. However, this preliminary step in state education was applied with different degrees of effectiveness by different local authorities. Moreover, the education provided, although free, was not compulsory, and the educational levels reached by pupils were, apparently, much lower than those achieved in the private schools frequented by the rich. A spelling test administered in 1835 showed private-school pupils with an average error-score of 83 as against state-school children with a score of 138 (see Fierro 1996: 412). The February Revolution of 1848 led to an expansion of state provision. The 'Falloux Law', passed in 1850, brought education boards under the control of the local *préfet*, and by 1860 90 per cent of Parisian children were attending school in one way or another. The traumas provoked by the Franco-Prussian War (1870) and the Commune insurrection (1871) spurred on the politicians of the Third Republic to invest heavily in education to ensure the full mobilisation of the country's human resources. The 'Ferry Laws' (1881) made state primary education for all non-fee-paying, non-religious and compulsory. Although this legislation signalled very clearly the unitarist intentions of the Third Republic, Furet and Ozouf (1977: I, 175) indicate that in practical terms it came at the end of a process and not at the beginning, serving essentially to plug the remaining gaps in the school system. The development of the school system did not give everyone equal access to written culture, but it undoubtedly accelerated the spread of literacy and exposed the population to the ideology of language standardisation to a degree never previously imaginable.

10.4   Data-sources

It might be thought that in the modern period sources of historical data become less of a problem. This is not the case. It is true that in the twentieth century universal literacy and electronic recording have ensured the survival of a much more detailed historical record. However, for the nineteenth century we are still dependent on the same sorts of data as in the proto-industrial period (see François 1985). In the nineteenth century literary representations of the speech of 'ordinary Parisians' become more frequent. Interest was fuelled by Romanticism: the cult of Nature encouraged an interest in the speech of a naïve, spontaneous populace, as distinct from the contrived artifice of educated language; the spirit of nationalism and democracy promoted an interest in indigenous, popular culture, as opposed to the imported civilisation of Classical Antiquity. However, while the rural *patois* were sometimes viewed with affection, the linguistic ways of the urban proletariat elicited reactions mingling fascination with apprehension. They were seen on the one hand as a rich source for the exotic and bizarre, and on the other as the deviant, even degenerate expression of a rebellious and dangerous population. Caution about the evidential value of literary portrayals of 'popular' speech is expressed by Wolf (1990) and Gaitet (1992), who highlight the tendency to objectify and diminish the speech of the lower orders, as a means of domination and social control.

During the first half of the nineteenth century prescriptive attitudes to language reached a sort of paroxysm. Large numbers of works were published excoriating 'bad grammar' among the Parisian populace. These contain valuable material, but they cannot be used indiscriminately (see Saint-Gérand 1992). In the second half of the century a more 'scientific' approach to everyday speech becomes visible with the emergence of linguistics as an autonomous discipline (see Branca 1983; Chervel 1983). Gadet (1992: 8) points to a gradual shift in labelling from *le bas langage* to *le français populaire*. Scholarly detachment took some time to develop, however. Charles Nisard's *Etude sur le langage populaire ou patois de Paris et de sa banlieue*, published in 1872, broke new ground, but it was not characterised by scholarly rigour. Indeed, throughout its pages the author displays a dislike, not to say hatred, of the people whose speech he was describing.

Le patois parisien dénature les mots français plus brutalement et à la manière des voleurs. La cause en est à la disposition de l'organe vocal du peuple de Paris . . . , à son affectation évidente à forcer la prononciation régulière. (Nisard 1872: 128)

Charles Nisard was only an 'amateur' linguist with his own personal reasons for disliking lower-class Parisians – they were responsible for burning down the Paris Hôtel de Ville in May 1871, and he reports that this caused the destruction of records of years of his philological research (see Nisard 1876: i).

Nisard was followed by more reliable observers of the Parisian linguistic scene, notably Eduard Koschwitz (1895), Paul Passy (see Arickx 1971), and in their footsteps we find Henri Bauche (1920). As Bauche was a writer of popular plays and not a trained linguist, his work on proletarian speech focuses more on grammar and vocabulary than pronunciation, but his observations are sympathetic and inspire confidence. Like Passy before him, Bauche maintains, contrary to contemporary orthodoxy, that it is the standard which is derived from the vernacular, and not the other way round:

Le peuple de France a créé le français; il l'a fait, il a enfanté en ce qu'il a de véritablement français; il l'a mené jusqu'à nos jours au point où nous l'entendons aujourd'hui; et les écrivains et les savants, malgré une très grande influence dans la fabrication des mots nouveaux, n'ont fait que marcher à la suite. En réalité, le vrai français, c'est le français populaire. Et le français littéraire ne serait plus aujourd'hui, à ce point de vue, qu'une langue artificielle, une langue de mandarins – une sorte d'argot. (Bauche 1920: 30–1)

Bauche's work set the agenda for studies of colloquial French for much of the twentieth century.

Perhaps the great innovation of the twentieth century, as far as students of Parisian speech are concerned, was the development of sound recording equipment making phonetic records available for instrumental measurement. The first recordings in F. Brunot's 'Archives de la parole' date from 1912 and 1913 and are conserved in the Phonotèque nationale (see François in Antoine and Martin 1985: 298). Surviving from the early part of the century are recordings of popular songs (first in line are the songs of Aristide Bruant), and in the 1930s the soundtrack of films depicting lower-class Parisian characters (see Bernet 1995). The work of modern linguists, notably those following in the footsteps of Martinet (1945), now permits 'real time' analyses of the changes which have intervened in the past half-century in colloquial Parisian usage.

10.5   Summary

In this chapter we have highlighted the demographic, social and cultural developments in industrial Paris which are of the greatest relevance to dialect-development in the city up to the middle of the twentieth century. The industrial, demographic and social structures which we have described survived more or less intact until the Second World War. Thereafter, de-colonisation, massive in-migration from outside Europe and major changes in communications and mobility caused those structures to crumble, and new hierarchies to develop. It is easy to speculate about the sociolinguistic effects of industrialisation – homogenisation of Parisian speech at one level through standardisation and dialect-levelling, and at another level the emergence of new class-based stratification. However, finding hard evidence to demonstrate empirically that these processes were in fact occurring is by no means easy, even in the modern period.

11   Standardisation and dialect-levelling

The effects of industrialisation on the language of a city are contradictory: some are conducive to a reduction in variation, while others lead to an increase. In large-scale environments linguistic homogeneity is promoted by downward diffusion of the standard language and by dialect-levelling, but in smaller-scale environments speakers are forever anxious to preserve their class- and ethnic identities and to use language to this end. In the last two chapters we will see to what extent these patterns were followed in nineteenth- and early twentieth-century Paris.

'Dialect-levelling' is an umbrella term under which different authors subsume a variety of linguistic processes. Hinskens (1992: 11) defines it in the following way:

a process which reduces the number of features separating a dialect from other varieties, including the socially more prestigious standard language.

Armstrong (2001: 4) likewise sees the pressure for dialect-levelling coming from two directions: horizontally, from an increase in contacts between speakers of different dialects of roughly equal status, entailing a proportionate increase in individual acts of accommodation, and vertically from the downward pressure exerted by the standard language, particularly as a result of education and literacy programmes.

Trudgill (1986: 98) considers that the linguistic effects of dialect-levelling involve 'the reduction or attrition of marked variants' in contact situations. The notion of markedness is, of course, a relative one, implying the presence of forms that are unusual in some way (cf. 'salience', §6.2.2). But unusual to whom? In the case of horizontal contact between dialects of roughly equal (normally low) status, 'marked' refers to salient local or regional features, either in the dialect of incomers as viewed by Parisians, or in the dialect of Parisians as viewed by incomers. In the context of a downward movement of standardisation, 'marked' refers to stigmatised forms, which, presumably, only become 'marked' in the minds of their users once these people have acquired a strong awareness of the standard.

Trudgill associates dialect-levelling proper with another process, that of 'simplification'. Use of this term is also risky, for it can all too easily be construed prescriptively as denoting the product of inferior or lazy minds. Trudgill is at pains to make clear that there is no such ideological intention in his use of the term. Like that of markedness, the concept of 'simplification' is a relative one, involving (a) increases in morpho-phonemic regularity, and (b) the development of 'regular correspondence between content and expression'. Trudgill observes, for instance, that in phonetic simplification, mergers typically win out over distinctions. Andersen (1988) uses the term in a similar way when he suggests that 'open' dialects undergo rapid change and embody simpler phonological and morphological systems, while 'closed' dialects are conservative and possess rather complex phonological and morphological systems (see §2.3.1).

In this chapter, for the sake of clarity, we will investigate the question of dialect-levelling through standardisation separately from 'dialect-levelling proper'. We will look first of all at the 'top-down' effects of standardisation on Parisian speech in the nineteenth century, then at the 'horizontal' pressures of dialect-contact which led to 'reduction' and 'simplification'.

11.1   Standardisation

The standard languages which crystallised in the sixteenth century remained for a long time the prerogative of *literati* and the cultivated elites. In a sense, this is why they were created in the first place. The expansion of the market economy in the late eighteenth century required wider participation in standard-language norms. The efficient functioning of a national market in goods and services called for standardisation not only in the coinage, in weights and measures and in legal practices, but also, more fundamentally, in language. At precisely this time, the development of the nation-state led typically to language's being invoked as one of the most potent symbols of national identity. Social advancement, economic progress and patriotic sentiment all combined, therefore, in nineteenth-century Paris to give the ideology of standardisation greatly increased power over the minds of speakers.

11.1.1   Factors promoting standardisation

It is widely believed that the pivotal turning-point in the development of standardisation in France is to be found in the great Revolution of 1789. Brunot devotes two long volumes of his history of the French language to the turbulent twenty-five-year period of the Revolution and Empire (*HLF* IX and X). It is true that, on the lexical level, the whole terminology of political debate and national administration were transformed during this time (see Frey 1925). It is also true that this period saw the first attempt in modern times at a general mobilisation of the population, inducing a significant extension of Parisian speech-norms into the provinces. Increased mobility in and out of the capital in time of war must have weakened the long-established social network structures in the city itself, with predictable consequences for existing vernacular speech-patterns. Nevertheless, the most powerful sociolinguistic effects of the Revolution and Empire in Paris were more ideological than real. It is probable that the substantive extension of the standard within the capital, as in the rest of France, came later in the nineteenth century, in the wake of the unprecedented demographic and social changes which were transforming western Europe at the time of industrialisation (see above, §10.1–2).

We should not, of course, minimise the significance of the ideological changes of the Revolution. When it comes to linguistic norms, what takes place in the minds of speakers is of central importance. Diffusion of the standard language throughout the community in the nineteenth century involved not just a change of linguistic habits, but also the spread of a whole set of beliefs about language, which we referred to earlier as standard ideology (§1.1.2), namely: (1) the ideal state of a language is one of uniformity, (2) the most valid form of the language is to be found in writing, (3) the standard variety is inherently better (i.e. more elegant, clearer, more logical, etc.) than other varieties. The Ancien Régime had not felt the need to propagate the standard very far beyond the ruling elite. However, with the abolition of the monarchy in 1792, the French language was promoted to being the prime element binding the French people together. It became the central criterion of 'Frenchness', the badge of French nationhood, the symbol of rationality and patriotic values, to which the whole population was now expected to subscribe.

But what was understood by 'the French language' in this context? The revolutionary leaders and their successors conceived of their language in the same synecdochic way as their aristocratic predecessors had done: the label *le français* was reserved exclusively for the standard variety (on the role of synecdoche ('part for the whole') see Joseph 1987: 2). For all the egalitarian claims of the Revolution, prestigious linguistic models continued to be provided by powerful groups located at the top of society. The language of Reason and Progress was that of the educated elite, not that of the Paris mob. Many observers have highlighted the linguistic decorum observed in formal political debate during the revolutionary period (see Seguin 1972: 247). The new leaders of society were as hostile to proletarian speech in the capital as they were to *patois* speech in the provinces.

Although politically progressive, the Revolution was linguistically conservative, and the new elites maintained these attitudes throughout the nineteenth century and beyond. Indeed, the first half of the nineteenth century saw a distinct hardening of prescriptive attitudes in the French capital. Possession of the standard acquired not just a political but also a moral, even a religious, value.

The Bescherelle brothers introduce their 1836 Grammar with the following words:

... la grammaire n'est plus seulement un exercice de collège sur lequel s'assoupit la mémoire; c'est l'histoire de la pensée elle-même, étudiée dans son mécanisme intérieur; *c'est le développement du caractère national dans ses intérêts politiques et ses senti-ments religieux*, analysé ou plutôt raconté par la nation elle-même, par les interprètes les plus éloquents de cette nation ... (quoted by J.-P. Saint-Gérand in Chaurand 1999: 419; my italics)

Declarations of this type are not isolated or exceptional at this time. Such ideas were implicit in all the programmes of education developed across the century and effectively modified attitudes to language in great swathes of the population previously untouched by standard ideology.

Important as this ideological shift was, the extension of the standard language in nineteenth-century Paris would probably not have progressed without the momentous social and demographic changes which engulfed the city at this time. The swelling of the ranks of the bourgeoisie was critical here, for it greatly increased the proportion of Parisians needing to push their speech closer to the norms of the standard. Dittmar, Schlobinski and Wachs (1988) have shown how language can be seen as a form of social and cultural capital that is convertible (in varying degrees) into economic capital. All upwardly mobile citizens in the new industrial city came under strong pressure to 'improve' their speech, principally by imitating the prestigious models presented by groups higher up.

The Revolution broke the dominance of the traditional aristocracy, but new elites promptly emerged to replace it, associated notably with the world of finance. As early as the 1790s select groups at the top of society are to be found using language in overt ways to set themselves apart from the rest. The most famous of these were perhaps the 'Incroyables'. This set of 'trendy young things' were so called because of their frequent use of this particular word, which they pronounced 'incoyable' with the deletion of [r]. The group's predilection for r-deletion, perhaps associated with the spread of uvular [R], attracted widespread comment and caricature. A contemporary journalist has this to say about them:

Rien de moins intelligible que les entretiens des malades. Les mots seuls qu'on distingue dans cette série de voyelles sont ceux de ma *paole supême*, d'*incoyable*, d'*hoible*, et d'autres mots ainsi défigurés. (quoted in Brunot, *HLF* X, 101–2)

Similar leaders of linguistic fashion succeeded each other relentlessly through-out the nineteenth century, down to the *demi-monde*, the *cocottes* and the *horizontales* of the *Belle Epoque*.

Around 1820, elite society in Paris came to be referred to as *le Tout-Paris*. It numbered, apparently, some two to three thousand individuals, resident prin-cipally in the west end of town. Its component clans eyed each other jealously. The novelist Stendhal observes in 1823:

En y regardant bien, l'on pourrait découvrir jusqu'à trois ou quatre langues différentes dans Paris. Ce qui est grossier rue Saint-Dominique n'est que naturel au faubourg Saint-Honoré, et court le risque de paraître recherché rue du Mont-Blanc. (quoted in Brunot, *HLF* XII, 18)

The Rue Saint Dominique is situated in the old aristocratic *quartier* Saint Germain; the Rue du Mont-Blanc (now the Chaussée d'Antin) was the preferred residence of the city's merchant bankers; the faubourg Saint Honoré was peopled essentially by diplomats and top civil servants. As the *salon* declined as a focal point for such groups, its place was taken by the café, a tradition which went back to the eighteenth century but which now came into its own. However, other public events provided the setting for high-society networking and for reinforcing the norms of high-status speech: the theatre, the opera, horse-racing at Longchamp, receptions in the *Académie*.

While the existence of elite groups such as these gave the expanding bourgeoisie real-life models of good usage to imitate, another factor promoting the extension of the standard language in nineteenth-century Paris was, of course, public education (see above, §10.3). The essentially conservative speech-norms of the educated elite were used to inform the language-teaching programmes designed for the mass of the population. The great campaigns of literacy stimulated the production of large numbers of grammars, dictionaries and catalogues of common errors in speech. For an exhaustive year-on-year bibliography in the first half of the century, see Saint-Gérand (2000). Here are some of the most widely used (the place of publication is in all cases Paris):

1808 D'Hautel, *Dictionnaire du bas-langage ou des manières de parler usitées par le peuple.*

1821 J. C. L. P. Desgranges, *Le Petit Dictionnaire du peuple*

1823 J.-N. Blondin, *Manuel de la pureté du langage*

1826 A. Caillot, *Nouveau Dictionnaire proverbial, satirique et burlesque*

1829 J. E. J. F. Bainvilliers, *Petit Vocabulaire comparatif du bon et du mauvais langage*

1832 B. Le Goarant, *Nouvelle Orthologie française*

1833 C. A. Delvart, *Le Réformateur du mauvais langage*

1835 L. Platt, *Dictionnaire critique et raisonné du langage vicieux*

1840 C. Martin, *Le Glaneur grammatical*

1842 D. E. Lévi-Alvarès, *Les Omnibus du langage*

1843 T. Soulice and A. L. Sardou, *Petit Dictionnaire raisonné des difficultés et des exceptions*

1849 E. Eliçagaray, *Le Mauvais Langage corrigé*

The emphasis placed on the written word and the central importance accorded to orthographic accuracy increased the influence of spelling on pronunciation. With increased literacy, writing does not remain a mere record, but comes to embody a code of its own, capable of influencing the community of speech. Straka (1981: 222–45) has studied this question in precise detail, showing the braking effects of spelling on pronunciation in nineteenth-century Paris. The most spectacular of his examples illustrate the maintenance of vowel length through the presence of circumflex accents, in words like *tâche* and *pâte*, and the sounding of consonants originally inserted for purely etymological reasons only for the eye, in words like *dompter, promptement, cep*.

More generally, the broadening of educational opportunity raised very significantly the numbers of people exposed to the norms of the standard language and lowered the levels of tolerance of the vernacular in all its forms. In the provinces this meant getting rid of the *patois*. In the capital it meant eliminating the traditional dialect of the city inherited from the proto-industrial period.

11.1.2   Demise of the proto-industrial dialect

In Part 3 we saw an awareness in the population of proto-industrial Paris of a set of vernacular speech-norms at the bottom of society which were diametrically opposed to those of the standard language and were closely associated with the speech of the city's semi-rural hinterland. During the first half of the nineteenth century, which, as we have seen, was in some ways a prolongation of the proto-industrial period, we find evidence of the continued existence of many of these features in the linguistic consciousness of the city, though rather less evidence in specimens of naturally occurring language. Three sets of data might give us clues about the persistence of these forms: (a) the writings of inexperienced writers, (b) literary and semi-literary texts, (c) observations by prescriptive grammarians and lexicographers.

(a)   Relatively direct data

When it comes to charting the demise of the old Parisian dialect in actual usage (as opposed to perceived usage) relatively direct evidence is very elusive. The very process of learning to write filters out all traces of non-standard speech-forms. During the revolutionary and Napoleonic period large numbers of inexperienced writers were promoted to official positions and their writings were preserved. Letters to the new administrative bodies (see *HLF* X, 438–43), letters from soldiers away on campaign, the minutes of the proceedings of revolutionary tribunals (see Branca-Rosoff and Schneider 1994), all afford us some insights into the nature of everyday speech at the time. A certain amount of information is available here about the syntax of the spoken language, but these documents reveal little about non-standard pronunciation. The non-standard features we find here often result from incorrect application of written-language rules rather than from the interference of colloquial speech.

Occasionally we find direct notation, *sur le vif*, of specimens of everyday speech. Here is a short extract from the sales patter of a quack doctor operating on the quais de la Seine in the 1830s:

'Avec toutes ces qualités, la ppoudre ppersannne coûtera donc bien cher? Non, Messieurs, nous l'avons mise à la portée de toutes les bourses. Il y a des boâtes de 1 fr. 50 ou 30 sous [*pause*]. Il y a des boâtes de 1 fr. ou 20 sous qui sont les deux-tiers des boâtes de trente [*pause*]. Il y a des boâtes de 75 centimes ou des boâtes de 30 [*pause*]. Il y a des boâtes de cinquante centimes ou dix sous, qui sont les deux-tiers des boâtes de quinze, la moitié des boâtes de vingt, et le tiers de boâtes de trente [*longue pause*] . . . Enfin, Messieurs, il y a des boâtes, dites boâtes d'essai ou d'épreuve, et que je ne vends que pour dix centimes ou deux sous. Messieurs, si la ppoudre ppersannne, n'a pas rendu blanches en deux minutes, montre en main, les dents les plus noires, si elle n'a point arrêté la carie . . . si elle n'a point enlevé le tartre et le tuf . . . si elle n'a point corrigé la mauvaise haleine, toutefois pourtant que la mauvaise haleine ne provient pas de la putréfaction de l'estomac . . . si elle n'a point raffermi les dents dans leurs alvéoles, rendu leur couleur naturelle aux gencives . . . si elle n'a point calmé en un clin d'oeil la douleur de dents la plus vive, entrez dans ce cercle, démentez-moi, traitez-moi de fourbe et d'imposteur, prenez mon ordonnance, déchirez-la et jetez m'en les morceaux à la figure . . . Au cas contraire, dites-le à vos amis et connaissances, et rendez-moi justice . . .'
     P. S. Les jours où il vendait peu, Miette cherchait à humilier les pratiques qui n'achetaient que des boâtes de deux sous, en appuyant sur les mots: 'une boâte de ddeux sous à Moissieu', au lieu de se servir du terme poli de boâte d'essai qu'il n'employait que dans les occasions de forte vente. (ed. Saint-Gérand 1999)

There is little evidence here, however, attesting the persistence of old dialectal forms. As in previous centuries, we are reliant above all on more indirect evidence.

(b)   Literary and semi-literary texts

There survives well into the nineteenth century a large amount of literary and semi-literary evidence incorporating features drawn from the old Parisian dialect. For all the reasons we considered earlier, evidence drawn from such sources is fraught with difficulty, given the conventional nature of many literary or semi-literary representations of non-standard speech. Nevertheless, pamphlets, poems and plays written in the *poissard* style continued to enjoy favour with a Parisian readership, and their success depended to an extent on the audience recognising the stigmatised forms involved.

At the time of the French Revolution, as under the Ancien Régime, low-class forms were frequently used in political pamphlets to express the voice of the Common Man. The most celebrated example is probably the series of pamphlets issued under the title *Le Père Duchêne* (see Guilhaumou 1986). These texts were analysed by Brunot (see *HLF* X.1, 167–237), who shows that the technique involved above all the use of elisions characteristic of rapid speech, and of stigmatised lexical items and taboo words in an inappropriate context (that of political debate):

Quand je suis sur le Port Sain-Paul, *foutre*, v'la-t-y pas la mere . . . l'aze me *foute*, si je me rapelle son *bougre* de nom, la mere je t'en *fous*, qu'importe, c'est celle-là qui porte le café au lait aux blanchisseuses, qui me dit comm'ça: Ah ben! V'la que t'arrives . . .[1] (quoted in Brunot, *HLF* X.1, 181)

Other pamphlets (see in particular Cook 1994) adopt a rather wider range of stigmatised features and belong more obviously in the tradition of the *Sarcelades* and *poissard* literature we looked at earlier (see pp. 163–4). Here is an example:

FORT DES HALLES Eh ben, Mariejeanne, quoiqu' c'est qu' tu nous apprendras d'nouveau?

POISSARDE Pas grand'chose d'bon. J'avons payé ce matin l'pain d'trois lives & demie 15 sous; encore avons je eu ben d'la peine d'en avoir.

FORT DES HALLES Pargui ca n'est pas etonnant. Tant qu' j'arons a nourrir aveuc du pain mollet eun tas d'chiens d'nobles, j'sommes ben surs d'mourir d'faim. Et encore l'pis d'ca, c'est qu' el' cachont l'bled dans leux greniers & dans les carrieres.

POISSARDE Oh, ignia pas qu'eux qui amenont la famine. Et tous ces Calottins, ces Sancho-Panca d'moines, qui avont trognes si remplies & si marveyes, n'crais-tu pas qu'el n'avont pas fait des magasins, d'peur d'manquer?[2]

(*Premier Dialogue entre une poissarde et un fort de la halle sur les affaires présentes* c.1790, Bibliothèque Historique de la Ville de Paris, ms. 12031)

Texts like this were examined in some detail by Brunot (*HLF* X, 259–70), who was scathing about them, evidently disappointed that they are not authentic vernacular documents, emanating from genuine vernacular speakers. It is not without interest that this particular style should have been adopted most frequently by royalist pamphleteers, opposed to the now triumphant Revolution, and seeing power slipping away from them. As the Revolution unfolded, the tables were turned and the new 'establishment' evidently came to feel that the traditional voice of the Common Man was no longer appropriate for them.

The same archaic stigmatised features continue to surface in popular songs and in the theatre until the middle of the nineteenth century. Here is an example composed by one Marc-Antoine-Madeleine Désaugiers (1772–1827):

[1] 'When I'm down on the Port Saint-Paul, damn it, here's this mother, damn me if I can remember her bloody name, the mother damn it, what does it matter, it's the woman who brings milky coffee to the laundry-women, and she says to me: Well now, there you are at last . . .'

[2] 'MEAT PORTER: Well now, Mariejeanne, what news have you got for us ?

POISSARDE: None of it much good. This morning we paid three and half *livres* fifteen *sous* for our bread; and even then we had a lot of trouble getting any at all.

MEAT PORTER: Damn it, that's not surprising. So long as we are having to feed a great pile of these noble dogs with soft bread, it's a dead cert that we'll die of hunger. And then, the worst thing is that they hide the corn in their barns and quarries.

POISSARDE: O they are not the only ones bringing on famine. There are all those priests, those Sancho-Panza monks with their marvellously well-filled faces, don't you think that they haven't made stashes, for fear of going without?'

V'la qu' tout à coup la nuit tombe . . .
Et, pour divartir
J' vois comm' qui dirait d'un' tombe
D' s esquelett' s sortir:
A leurs airs secs et minables,
On s' disait comm' ça:
C'est-el d' s artist' s véritables
Qui jou'nt ces rol' s là?
Mais avant qu'un chacun sorte
(Et c'est là l' chiendent!)
V' la l' Fanfan qui nous apporte
Deux torches d' rev' nant
Morgué! que l' bon dieu t' bénisse,
Suppôt d' Lucifer!
J' croyions que j'avions la jaunisse,
Tant j'avions l'teint vert.
Bref, c' t Olivier z' est capable,
Dans l' méquier qu' i fait,
D'escamoter jusqu'au diable,
Si l' diable l' tentait:
Par ainsi, sans épigramme,
Crainte d'accident,
Faut toujours, messieurs et dames,
S' tâter z' en sortant.[3]

(*Le menuisier Simon ou la rage de sortir
le dimanche*, ed. Saint Gérand 2000)

[3] Then, all of a sudden night falls . . .
And, by way of entertainment
I see skeletons emerging
From what looks like a tomb;
Seeing their desiccated and wretched appearance,
This is what people were saying:
Are they real *artistes*
Playing these roles?
But before we all get up and go
(And there's the rub!)
The m.c. comes on with two ghostly torches
Damn it! God bless you,
Hounds of Hell!
We thought we'd caught jaundice,
Our faces had got that green,
In short, this chap Olivier,
Given the business he's in,
Is capable of nicking the devil himself,
If the devil tempted him:
In this way, dispensing with an epigram,
To avoid accidents,
Ladies and gentlemen,
You must always feel your pockets as you go out.

Moore 1935 and Franz 1983 provide numerous examples of texts written in this style in the first half of the century. The final disappearance from printed texts of the most stigmatised of these forms in the middle years of the nineteenth century may well post-date their disappearance from everyday speech, but at least it gives us a good idea about how long the old Parisian dialect continued to impinge on the collective consciousness. It is too easy to dismiss these texts as a mere literary exercise in intertextuality (see above, §6.2.3).

(c)   Linguistic commentators

Other indications of the slow demise of the proto-industrial dialect are to be found in metalinguistic works of the period, normally designed to 'improve' the speech of the lower classes. The best known of these are probably d'Hautel's *Dictionnaire du bas-langage* (1808) and J. C. L. P. Desgranges' *Le Petit Dictionnaire du peuple* (1821). The interests of the authors of these texts are mainly lexical, but they give plenty of information about old morpho-phonemic features which were evidently still widespread in the first half of the century. Here is a list of some of the stigmatised phonetic features found in Desgranges (1821), with cross-references to d'Hautel where appropriate. The figures in brackets refer to pagination in the 1821 edition.

Vowels

(1) **[ɛr]** ~ **[ar]**: *révarbère/réverbère* (77), *argot/ergot* (15), *ormoire* (65) (see d'Hautel 1808: 358–9). *Boulevere* (21), *chercutier/sertutier/charcutier* (25), *clerinette* (26), *clerté* (26), *dertre/dartre* (34), *eriere* (40), *erres/arrhes* (41), *kertron/quarteron* (56), *perdonner* (68), *pernace* (65), *serdine* (82), *verlope* (91), *yerd/yard/liard* (92) (see also Straka 1981: 220–1). *Abouler/ébouler* (9), *aculer/éculer* (10), *agriotte/aigriotte* (11), *cramaillère/crémaillère* (30) (see d'Hautel 1808: 335).

(2) **[o]** ~ **[jo]**: *assiau/asseau* (16) 'outil de couvreur et de tonnelier', *copiau/coipiau/coupeau/copeau* (28) 'les trois premiers mots sont des expressions de campagnards', *gaviau* (47), *mogno/moineau* (61), *muzio* (62), *naziau* (63) 'faute de rustaud', *piau* (69) 'c'est un mot digne du plus bas peuple', *ratiau* (77) 'prononciation villageoise', *roussiau/rousseau/ruisseau* (80) 'Dans la province, les petites gens disent un *roussiau*, les bourgeois mieux appris, un *rousseau*, et les français un *ruisseau*.' *Sauteriau/sauterelle* (82) 'mot de paysan', *siau/seau* (83) 'prononciation basse', *Viautrer/vautrer* (84) 'faute des plus grossières' (see d'Hautel 1808: 15, 336).

(3) **Distribution of [ɛ], [wɛ], [wa]**: *aveine/avoine* (18) 'affecté', *coreyeur/corroyeur* (28), *neyer/noyer* (63) 'prononciation défectueuse adoptée par quelques-uns de nos modernes puristes', *couane* (29) (see Straka 1981: 185–7).

(4) **[ɔ] ∼ [œ] in initial syllables**: *kmodités/commodités* (56), *Kmencer/ commencer* (56). Cf. *vapereux* (90) (see also Straka 1981: 189).

(5) **Alternation [y] ∼ [œ]**: *fumelle/femelle* (46); *pleume/plume* (71), *eune/une* (43) (see d'Hautel 1808: 379).

(6) **[jɛ̃)] ∼ [ɛ)]**: *Conbin gn'en a-t-il?* Demandent les gens du peuple (27).

(7) **'Ouisme' – distribution of [o], [u]**: *aujordui/aujourd'hui* (17).

(8) **Maintenance of hiatus**: *ehu/eu* (37).

Consonants

(9) **Medial [ʎ] ∼ [j]**: *escaye* (41), *gayote* (47), *meyeu/milieu* (60), *souye* (84), *yard/liard* (92) (see Straka 1981: 192–3). Cases of hypercorrection (?): *Biliet/billet* (20), *boulant/bouillant* (20–1), *calie/cahier* (24), *caliou* (24), *clincalier* (26), *culiere* (32), *faliance* (44), *jalir* (55), *juliette/juillet* (55), *maliet* (60), *orille/oreiller* (65), *papilion* (66), *papiliote* (66), *pavilion* (67), *ralier* (76), *talieur* (85), *valant* (90) (see Straka 1981: 174–7).

(10) **Elision of post-vocalic [r]**: *blanchisseux* (20), *boueux* (21), *passeux* (67), *ramoneux* (76), *tiroi* (87), *toujou* (87) (see d'Hautel 1808: 95, 330, 378).

(11) **Elision of post-consonantal [l]/[r] before final schwa**: *artique* (16), *buffe* (22), *diabe* (35), *miraque* (61), *onque* (64), *oraque* (65), *tringue* (88); *cadabe/cadavre* (23), *coconbe* (26), *coite/cloitre* (26), *lade* (57), *semece* (82), *sylvese* (83), *suc* (84) (see Straka 1981: 191–2).

(12) **Velarisation of [dj] and [tj]**: *guernaguié/grenadier* (50), *morqué/mortier* (62) (see also d'Hautel 1808: 207, 149, and Straka 1981: 180–1). Desgranges also notes the inverse development: *'Je loge au cintième. C'est ainsi que s'expriment les enfants de Paris; mais le seul mot admissible est cinquième'* (26).

(13) **[nj] + vowel ∼ [ɲ]**: *Conbin gn'en a-t-il?* Demandent les gens du peuple (27) (see also d'Hautel 1808: 326–7, and Straka 1981: 177–80).

(14) **Elision of pre-consonantal [l]**: *kequ'un/quelqu'un* (56) (see also Straka 1981: 192).

(15) **Voicing of medial [ʃ]**: *ageter/acheter* (11, 76) (see Bauche 1920: 131).

(16) **Deletion of aspirate [h]**: Desgranges 1821: 51–2; see also Straka 1981: 197–8.

A fuller analysis of Desgranges is to be found in Gougenheim (1929).

An uncritical reading of Desgranges must be avoided: like all lexicographers he was influenced by his predecessors, and many of the high-consciousness variables he picks up may have already fallen into disuse. He tends to blur urban/rural distinctions. However, complete scepticism about its value as a source for Paris vernacular speech is misplaced: the *Dictionnaire* is unlikely to have sold had it been a work of pure fiction. Gougenheim (1929) observes:

Il [Desgranges] est le premier témoin d'un bon nombre de faits de vocabulaire et ses indications sociales sont précieuses et intéressantes. Il rejoint d'autre part les textes de patois parisien au XVIIe s. et le poissard au XVIIIe s. et nous fait voir la continuité d'existence à Paris même, d'une façon en quelque sorte sous-jacente, d'un parler beaucoup plus archaïque que la langue littéraire.

Not all the lower-class features picked up by Desgranges were, in fact, destined to disappear. Some survive in modern colloquial French and some were absorbed into the standard language. Desgranges protests, for instance, about what was probably the uvular pronunciation of [R], referred to by prescriptive grammarians since the seventeenth century as the '*r* grasseyé': 'On croit que le gosier du grasseyeur veut imiter le bruit d'une lime qui râcle rudement les dents d'une scie' (p. 29). The presence in lower-class Parisian speech of uvular [R] alongside the traditional apical [r] had been commented on (adversely) since Cotgrave (1611) (see above, §9.3.3). It appears not to have been a particularly salient variable, and it was fully accepted into the standard during the nineteenth century, though traditionalists in the Conservatoire were still recommending apical [r] as late as 1913.

Although some of the variants picked up by Desgranges persisted longer as part of the lower-class Parisian accent *le parigot* (see Straka 1981: 174–203), most of them lost currency during the first half of the nineteenth century, at about the time when the old *poissard* literature finally loses its appeal. From the middle of the nineteenth century Parisian observers indicate that only faint traces of the traditional dialect were still to be found:

Il faut d'abord être et demeurer bien persuadé que ce patois n'existe plus. Paris l'a complètement oublié, et le peu d'endroits de cette ville où il a tenu le plus longtemps, comme les halles, les marchés, les ports et peut-être un ou deux faubourgs, en ont à peine conservé quelques formes. Si la banlieue en a gardé davantage, c'est si peu de chose qu'il n'y a pas là de quoi suffire à une restitution, même partielle, de ce bizarre langage. (Nisard 1872: 123)

Some of its forms lived on, however, in a new, class-based urban dialect which has come to be referred to prescriptively as *le français populaire*.

11.2   Dialect-levelling

Under this heading we will discuss the possible effects of contacts between native Parisians and incomers from distant provinces, which expanded considerably in the middle of the nineteenth century (see §10.1). If 'standardisation' reduced the distance between vernacular and standard, 'dialect-levelling proper', induced by everyday contact with speakers of external dialects, tended to increase it: certain features evolve more quickly in everyday speech than in the conservative standard, leading to sharper socio-stylistic differentiation.

Andersen (1988) drew attention to differences in the way dialects develop in central, focal areas (as in great metropolises) and the way they develop on the periphery (see above, §2.3.1). He sees dialect openness, characteristic of metropolitan speech, impinging directly on internal linguistic structure: on the whole, open dialects undergo rapid change and embody simpler phonological and morphological systems than closed dialects, subject to less external contact. The development of colloquial Parisian French in the industrial period may provide a useful illustration of these principles. The reductions and simplifications which characterise certain aspects of *le français populaire* are traditionally explained as the result of slovenly lower-class speakers corrupting the standard language. It is more realistic to suppose that they came about through the operation of normal dialect-contact phenomena, with upper-class speakers actively maintaining archaic distinctions for purposes of social distinctiveness.

As always, we can expect serious data problems when investigating the process of simplification in everyday speech, even in these relatively recent times. Little direct evidence survives, the first electric recordings of Parisian speech not being made before the first decade of the twentieth century. We have plenty of literary representations of low-class speech in novels and plays, notably those by E. Sue and H. Monnier. However, these rely heavily on lexical variables and limit their representation of popular pronunciation to a conventional use of apostrophes to indicate (rather perfunctorily) schwa-deletion. Some of the *chansonniers* from the end of the nineteenth century, such as Aristide Bruant, are more helpful, as we shall see later. Researchers in this field (see, for example, Straka 1981 and Morin 1989) have extensively used the work of contemporary lexicographers and early phoneticians, even though reliable systems of phonetic notation do not come into use until the last quarter of the century. Some of our best sources come from observers like Henri Bauche working early in the twentieth century. In much of what follows, we will be using the method of back-projection, with all the risks that this entails.

11.2.1   Phonological 'simplification'

Beside the elimination of highly salient low-class variants which we described in the previous section (§11.1.2), nineteenth-century Paris saw more gradual, longer-term modifications to its pronunciation, which attracted less overt comment. The changes in question all involve a reduction in the complexity of the phonological system, typical of what we find in 'open dialects'.

Vowel-length
A first change concerns vowel-length. In eighteenth-century Parisian speech, vowel-length was, according to Martinet, 'le trait fondamental du vocalisme'

(writing in Antoine and Martin 1985: 25). Notably in stressed syllables, each of the Parisian vowels had long and short versions with phonemic value. However, differences of length had probably always been accompanied by slight differences of vowel quality, and, progressively, the quantitative/quantitative balance shifted in favour of qualitative distinctions (see Morin 1989). By the middle of the twentieth century the quantitative system had been almost entirely replaced by a qualitative one in Parisian speech.

The *Dictionnaire phonétique* of Michaelis and Passy (1897) provides a useful snapshot of upper-class Parisian usage at the end of the century. Here we find that vowel length remains phonemic in certain positions, and not in others. In stressed open syllables (e.g. *chat* ~ *chats, joli* ~ *jolie*), the old quantitative distinction has been largely neutralised. Quantitative distinctions before final [s] had, in fact, been abandoned decades earlier, but some observers see them persisting before final [e] among older speakers at the end of the century (see Straka 1981: 194–7; Bauche 1920: 39–40). In stressed closed syllables, maintenance of the quantitative opposition varied with the height of the vowel. With the high vowels [i], [u] and [y] (e.g. *cime* [i] ~ *abîme* [i:], *tulle* [y] ~ *brûle* [y:], *dégoutte* [u] ~ *dégoûte* [u:]), a vowel-length distinction was apparently maintained, though it seldom played an important role. With the mid-vowels the situation was mixed. In the case of [ɛ], a phonemic opposition was maintained (e.g. *mettre* [ɛ] ~ *maître* [ɛ:]). In the cases of [oe] and [o], it was maintained concomitantly with a qualitative distinction (e.g. *jeune* [Ø] ~ *jeûne* [œ:], *pomme* [ɔ] ~ *paume* [o:]). With low vowels it had been replaced by a qualitative distinction (e.g. *tache* [a] ~ *tâche* [ɑ]).

Perhaps because the phonic distinctions involved here are more subtle than those listed earlier (see §11.1.2), vowel-length was not a high-salience variable in nineteenth-century Parisian speech, and we find little contemporary awareness of social-class stratification. It is reported that certain quantitative distinctions were maintained rather anachronistically in the musical style of the Paris *Conservatoire* until 1914, and we know that such vestiges of the old quantitative system as still survive in Parisian speech today do so only in the most careful styles among the most educated speakers. This suggests that neutralisation of these distinctions was initiated in everyday speech lower down in society, though it does not provide conclusive proof.

Lois de position

A second important phonological reduction in progress throughout the industrial period concerns the so-called '*lois de position*'. This involves the loss of phonemic opposition between the open and closed versions of the mid-vowels [ɛ], [ɔ] and to a reduced extent [œ]. The term 'law' is too strong. What we have is a 'tendency' for final closed syllables to attract the open vowels [ɛ] and [ɔ], and for final open syllables to attract the closed vowels [e] and [o],

Table 18. *The so-called 'loi de position'*

Phonemes	Example	*Loi de position*
Final closed syllables		
[e] ~ [ɛ]	*père ~ paire*	opening of [e] → [ɛ]
Outcome c. 1950	phonemic reduction	
Social variation	Sporadic retention of [e] in cultivated usage (Straka 1981: 204)	
[o] ~ [ɔ]	*saute ~ sotte*	opening of [o] → [ɔ]
Outcome c. 1950	Maintenance of two lexical sets: [ɔ] *alors*, [o] *rose*	
Social variation	Not strongly marked in Parisian speech, but opening of [o] is a salient regionalism.	
Final open syllables		
[ɛ] ~ [e]	*prêt ~ pré*	tensing of [ɛ] → [e]
Outcome c. 1950	Maintenance of two lexical sets: [e] *-ai, -et, -é* etc., [ɛ] *-ais, -êt, -ès* etc.	
Social variation	Vernacular tensing of [ɛ] – *chantai ~ chantais* (Bauche 1929: 39–40)	
[ɔ] ~ [o]	*turbot ~ turbots, sot ~ saut*	tensing of [ɔ] → [o]
Outcome c. 1950	Phonemic reduction	
Social variation	Not strongly marked in Parisian speech, but the process of lexical diffusion has been observed (Morin 1989)	
Non-final syllables		
[ɛ] ~ [e]	*raisonner ~ résonner*	tensing of [ɛ] → [e]
Outcome c. 1950	Maintenance of two lexical sets: [e] *pécher* [ɛ] *pêcher.*	
Social variation	Vernacular tensing of [ɛ] - *plaisir, aimer, les* etc. (Straka 1981: 213)	
[o] ~ [ɔ]	*hôtel ~ joli*	opening of [o] → [ɔ]
Outcome c. 1950	Maintenance of two lexical sets: [o] *-ô, -au*, [ɔ] *-o*	
Social variation	Not strongly marked in Parisian speech, except where [ɔ] → [œ]	

with non-final syllables admitting only [ɛ] and [ɔ] respectively (see Table 18 and Straka 1981: 203–21). The change is long-term and still continues, with the unrounded vowels being further along this path than the rounded ones. The locus of the shift towards a purely positional determination of the quality of mid-vowels in Parisian French looks to be vernacular speech.

Phonological mergers

Further reduction in the Paris vowel system occurred in the merging of the nasals [œ̃] and [ɛ̃] and of the low unrounded [a] and [ɑ].

The merging of [œ̃] ~ [ɛ̃] as in *brun* ~ *brin* through the loss of [œ̃] is noted as early as the seventeenth century, most prominently with the indefinite article *un*. This variable is picked up by Desgranges (1821), but it achieves high salience only in the second half of the century, by which time the merging of the two vowels seems to have become widespread in lower-class speech, though not in upper-class usage (see Straka 1981: 182–3). By the middle of the twentieth century, however, the merger had spread to most Parisian speakers (see Martinet 1969: 188; Hansen 1998: 79–142).

The merging of [a] ~ [ɑ] in Parisian speech is a long-term process. In the seventeenth century the distribution of the two vowels was largely governed by etymology, but during the late eighteenth and nineteenth centuries the front [a] diffused through much of the lexicon at the expense of [ɑ] (see Straka 1981: 214–15). At the end of the century there still survived residual cases where the distinction between the two /A/s was phonemic, for example *tache* ~ *tâche*, *rat* ~ *ras*. In lower-class speech, the distance between the two vowels was often increased through rounding of the back [ɑ] → [ɔ], for example, *gare*, [gɑr] → [gɔr]. In his *Le Père Goriot* (1835) Balzac had noted *ormoires* (= *armoires*), 'il prononçait ce mot à la manière du menu peuple' (see above, p. 214). This apparently induced upper-class speakers to defend their sociolinguistic distinctiveness by pushing their back [ɑ] closer to the front [a], encouraging thereby the spread of the merger. According to Martinet (1969: 185) a majority of Parisians kept the two a-sounds distinct in such pairs as these up to the middle of the twentieth century, but thereafter the distinction fell into steep decline.

Phonological mergers are also to be found in the consonant system, the most noteworthy being that of [nj] and [ɲ] as in *ma nièce* ~ *Agnès*. The reduction of [nj] in low-class Parisian speech had become salient in the seventeenth century (see Thurot 1883: II, 310, 321, 347) and it continued to be castigated in the nineteenth century (see Desgranges 1821, quoted above, p. 215). Michaelis and Passy (1897) indicate that the distinction was still maintained in upper-class usage, though it has subsequently been neutralised even there. A parallel reduction affected the laterals [lj] and [ʎ], as in *million* and *papillon*. The reduction of [lj] to [j] was widespread in lower-class Parisian speech in the seventeenth century (see Thurot 1883: II, 267, 298, 299), and seems to have spread to all classes by the beginning of the nineteenth century. Thereafter, the positions adopted by prescriptive grammarians were contradictory. Some, like Desgranges quoted above (p. 215), condemn the [lj] variant in *Biliet/billet* (20), *caliou* (24), *clincalier* (26), etc., while others, like Jullien (1875: 30–1), recommend it. All agreed, however, that the lower-class reduction of [lj] → [j] in words like *escalier*, was unacceptable.

To the variables involving segmental features we have outlined here must be added variation affecting features like liaison and intonation, which were, if anything, more salient. Conservative speech was marked by high levels of liaison. These were significantly reduced in lower-class speech (see Bauche 1920: 55–7). For example, in standard French a sentence like *Les̲ Anglais sont arrivés ici* contained three cases of liaison (underlined). Only the first of these would normally survive in colloquial speech. Moreover, 'false liaisons' were commonly introduced as plural markers, for example *vin z om* (= *vingt hommes*), *quat z officiers* (= *quatre officiers*). The most salient intonational variable involved the shifting of falling intonation from the final syllable of an utterance to the penultimate syllable, immortalised in the 1930s film *Hôtel du Nord* by the actress Arletty's famous '*Atmosphère*' (see Abécassis 2000).

The net effect of the phonetic simplifications we have discussed was the production of a working-class Paris accent which was quite distinct from the conservative standard (see Fouché 1936: 206–10). It is likely that the latter was held in check by normative pressures, notably those of literacy and the writing system (see above, §11.1.1), but Kroch (1978: 30) goes further, arguing that 'prestige dialects resist phonetically motivated change and inherent variation because prestige speakers seek to mark themselves off as distinct from the common people and because inhibiting phonetic processes is an obvious way to do this'.

11.2.2   Morpho-syntactic 'simplification'

Trudgill (1986: 103) applies the term 'simplification' to certain processes which commonly occur in dialect-contact situations, namely, increases (a) in morphophonemic regularity and (b) in the 'regular correspondence between content and expression'. Examples of these processes abound in the morpho-syntax of colloquial Parisian French in the late nineteenth and early twentieth centuries. However, by no means all of them can be pinned down precisely to Paris in the industrial period. Many are colloquial characteristics widely occurring in Romance: Berruto (1983) identifies a large number of similar developments in *italiano populare*. Moreover, while some vernacular changes are of recent date, others have been on-going in French for centuries and merely speeded up in the nineteenth century. For some years in the 1970s and 1980s German scholars held an interesting debate concerning the extent to which the characteristic features of colloquial Parisian speech were conservative or progressive in comparison with the standard language (see Bork 1975; Hunnius 1975; Hausmann 1979).

Increases in morpho-phonemic regularity

Despite the best efforts of standardisers to maintain the etymological *status quo*, regularisation of assymetrical paradigms by analogy continued unabated in colloquial Parisian speech (see Frei 1929). Apophonous verb-paradigms (verbs with alternating stems like *tu bois* ~ *vous buvez*) were commonly remodelled on the basis of the regular patterns of the first and second conjugations. Thus, *vous buvez* → *vous boivez, je sache* → *je save, il puisse* → *il peuve, cuire* → *cuiser, mouvoir* → *mouver*. Past tenses formed with the auxiliary *être* are formed with the more usual *avoir*, e.g. *il a tombé, il s'a trompé*. Likewise, nouns showing suppletion (the use of two or more historical, distinct stems to provide the inflected forms of a single lexical item) occasionally became invariable, e.g. *cheval/chevaux* → *chevals, mal/maux* → *mals*, while invariable adjectives join the dominant subtractive category (most adjectives in French distinguish gender by 'subtracting' the final consonant from the feminine form to give the masculine, e.g. [p'tit] (f.) → [p'ti] (m.)), e.g. *avare* (f.) → *avarde*, *pécuniaire* (m.) → *pécunier*.

Polyvalent *que*: the numerous markers of subordination like *parce que, pour que, lorsque* tend to be reduced to the single form *que*. To this might be added the *que* to be found in what look like relative clauses of the type *Le mec qu'est venu*. While the *qui* ~ *que* distinction in the relative pronouns remains solid with verbs other than *être*, the forms *dont* and *lequel* are generally rejected in favour of *que*, e.g. *Un copain que j'ai passé mon enfance avec lui*.

Simplified negation: the reduction of the double negative *ne . . . pas/rien/ jamais* to its second element. Bauche (1920: 139) declares 'On supprime presque toujours "ne" en langage populaire et souvent en français familier.' This is rare in Parisian speech before the nineteenth century, but evidently made great progress during that century (see Martineau and Mougeon 2003).

Increases in the regular correspondence between content and expression

A feature widely attested in cases of dialect-contact is the development of analicity and the elimination of synthetic forms. Synthetic languages accumulate a relatively large number of morphemes in each word, while analytical ones 'unpack' the morphemes and express them, often, as separate words. In French, this represents a profound, long-term typological change affecting the whole of the language and indeed the other Romance languages too. However, colloquial Parisian speech, since the seventeenth century at least, seems to have been in the vanguard of these changes towards analicity. A familiar example can be found in the gradual disappearance of the simple past (*il chanta*) in favour of the compound past (*il a chanté*), and in the preference for the periphrastic future (e.g. *je vais venir*) over the synthetic form (e.g. *je viendrai*). These changes appear to have occurred first in the capital, before diffusing out to more peripheral areas.

The tendency towards analicity can also be seen in the development of aspect-markers, preposed grammatical markers and invariable phrase-heads.

(i) Present continuous may be expressed by the prepositions *à* or *après*, or by the present participle (e.g. *il est à/après travailler, j'étais partant*). The aspect of imminence may be expressed by the preposition *pour* (e.g. *j'étais pour partir*).

(ii) Just as preposed determiners have been generalised as number markers in the noun phrase, so preposed subject clitics have been generalised to mark the person of verbs which, in speech, have become largely invariable (e.g. *Je chante, tu chantes, il chante*, etc.). In colloquial French the subject clitic commonly occurs even where a noun subject is present (e.g. *Mon père, il travaille pas*).

(iii) The use of *on* to replace the 4th person clitic *nous* can be seen as part of this process, though here it is worth noting that use of *je* as in *j'allons* (= *nous allons*) had been widespread in this context in colloquial speech, not just in the metropolis, but also in the provinces (see Hausmann 1979; Hull 1988).

Another typological change commonly observed in dialect- and language-contact is the typological shift towards a fundamental SVO structure (subject-verb-object). Codified forms of French retain a large number of VS sequences inherited from earlier periods, notably in interrogatives (e.g. *Viens-tu?*) and in sentences introduced by a closed set of adverbials (e.g. *aussi, peut-être*). In colloquial usage these have been eliminated:

(i) Sentences introduced by adverbials like *peut-être* traditionally invert subject and verb to give *Peut-être viendra-t-il*. Colloquial speech, however, retains SV order and inserts a preposed *que*, e.g. *Peut-être qu'il viendra*.

(ii) The canonical interrogative form in colloquial French is now SV plus rising intonation, e.g. *Tu viens?*, with the inversion present in the interrogative morpheme *est-ce que* being replaced by SV order, e.g. *Où c'est que tu vas?*

It is not possible to ascribe all of these cases of morpho-syntactic simplification to the mixing of dialects which occurred in the linguistic melting-pot of nineteenth- and twentieth-century Paris. Some pre-date this period. Many are features which occur widely in colloquial speech everywhere. It is reasonable to assume, however, that these tendencies were accentuated in everyday speech in the capital at this time. Many of the low-class features present survive in modern colloquial French, but a good number of them disappeared in the decades following the Second World War. Recent treatments of *le français populaire* (for example Guiraud 1965; Gadet 1992; Ball 2000) present succinct descriptions of these features, without always indicating how archaic many of them are today.

11.3   Aristide Bruant

By the end of the nineteenth century social awareness of a low-class urban dialect with discernible characteristics was sufficiently high for it to acquire a name: the label *parigot* is first attested in 1886. The popular song-writer Aristide Bruant celebrated the *parigot* speech-forms of the Paris working class in a series of songs which survive in electric recordings. These embody many of the low-status features we have described in this chapter. Here is a sample:

	Les Vrais <u>Dos</u>	souteneurs
	Ça, s'appell' des genss' à son aise,	
	Mais c'est pas eux qu'est les malins;	
	Si c'est toujour' eux qu'a la <u>braise</u>,	argent
4	C'est toujour' eux qui s'ra les <u>daims</u>.	dupes
	I's sont <u>frusqués</u> avec des p'lures	habillés
	Qu'on leur-z-y fait esprès pour eux,	
	L'hiver i's s' coll'nt dans des fourrures . . .	
8	Dame! Ya pas qu' nous qu'est des frileux.	
	Quand ça jou', qu' ça gagne ou qu' ça perde,	
	Ça s'en fout . . . et ça fait un <u>foin</u>! . . .	bruit
	Leux <u>gonzess's</u> aussi fait sa merde,	femmes
12	Ah! Si j'en t'nais eun' dan' un coin! . . .	
	Ma gosse, à moi, c'est eun' <u>gironde</u>,	fille bien faite
	Mais a' <u>cran'</u> pas comm' ces femm's-là	être orgueilleux
	D'ailleurs faut qu'a parle à tout l' monde	
16	Pisque c'est l' métier qui veut ça.	
	Quand on n'est pas <u>braiseux</u> d' naissance,	riche
	Pour viv' faut ben <u>truquer</u> un peu . . .	faire la prostituée
	Ces <u>gonc's</u>-là, c'en a t'i' d' la chance	hommes
20	Ça mange et ça boit quand ça veut.	
	Et pis ça nous appell' les <u>dos</u> . . .	souteneurs
	Ah! Nom de Dieu! J' suis pas bégueule!	
	Mais si 'y avait pas tant d' <u>sergots</u>	sergents de ville
24	Minc'! que j' leur-z-y cass'rais la gueule![4]	

(Bruant 1889–95: I, 117–19)

[4] **The Real Pimps**
They're called the well-off people,
But they aren't the bright ones;
If it's always them that have the money,
It's always them that'll be the suckers.

They're all got up in furs
Made up specially for them,
In winter they wrap themselves up in fur coats . . .
Hell! We're not the only ones to feel the cold.

When they bet on cards, whether they win or lose,
They don't care . . . and that gets talked about! . . .
Their women get up to filthy tricks too,
Ah! If I had one of them in a corner . . .

My own kid is a lovely looking girl,
But she isn't haughty like those women.
Besides, she has to speak to everybody
Since it goes with the job.

What are the vernacular features highlighted here?

Phonetic simplification:

(i) Schwa-deletion signalled by an apostrophe (e.g. *appell'* (1, 21), *s'ra* (4), *p'lures* (5), *s'coll'nt* (7), *qu'* (3, 9), *jou'* (9), *gonzess's* (11), *t'nais* (12), *eun'* (12, 13), *cran'* (14), *comm'* (14), *femm's* (14), *l'* (15), *d'* (17, 19, 23), *viv'* (18), *gonc's* (19), *j'* (22, 24), *minc'* (24), *cass'rais* (24)). This feature is in fact present in all varieties of spoken (as opposed to written) French. However, traditional versification conventions would have maintained these schwas in a verse text such as this.

(ii) Absence of liaison, signalled by an apostrophe (e.g. *toujour'* (4), *dan'* (12)).

(iii) 'False liaison' in *leur-z-y* (6, 24).

(iv) Reduction of consonant clusters (e.g. *esprès* (6), *viv'* (18)).

(v) Reduction of diphthongs (e.g. *pisque* (16), *pis* (21), *ben* (18)).

(vi) Elision of post-vocalic [r] (e.g. *braiseux* (17)).

(vii) Lowering of [y] → [eu] (e.g. *eun'* (12, 13)).

Morpho-syntactic simplification:

(i) Simple negation (without *ne*) (e.g. lines 2, 22).

(ii) Polyvalent *que* (e.g. verses 1, 2).

(iii) Invariable copula in relative clauses (e.g. verses 1, 2).

(iv) Use of the feminine subject clitic *a* < *alle* (lines 15, 19).

(v) Non-use of impersonal *il* (e.g. verse 4).

(vi) Use of the neuter *ça* to designate humans (e.g. verses 1, 3, 5).

Bruant's own electric recording of this song made in 1909 allows us to match spelling and phonetic realisation in a way not possible previously. No one informant can represent the speech of the community as a whole, but it gives us some idea of what late nineteenth-century vernacular Parisian speech sounded like. The most salient of all the vernacular features to be found in this song are, of course, the lexical variants which Bruant introduces in such great numbers. These will be the subject of our final chapter.

Paris vernacular speech between 1850 and 1950 is conventionally referred to as *le français populaire* (see above, §1.2.3). This label has always been

When you aren't born rich,
You have to be a bit of a whore . . .
Those blokes are dead lucky
They eat and they drink whenever they like.

Then they call us the pimps . . .
Ah! In God's name! I'm not daft!
If there weren't so many coppers around,
I'd bloody well smash their faces in.

problematic, not only because of its prescriptive connotations, but because of uncertainty over whether the variety designated is primarily a social dialect or a register (see Biber and Finegan 1994). Normally the two axes of variation operate conjointly, but it is legitimate to ask, at any particular historical moment, whether one axis is more basic than the other. It may be, in view of the relative rigidity of social stratification in late nineteenth-century Paris, that at that time it functioned more basically as a social dialect than as a register. However, since the middle of the twentieth century and the transformation of social structures in the 'post-industrial' era, it is preferable to see the sociolinguistic variables in question acting primarily as markers of register.

11.4   Summary

Shortage of suitable data means that even in the nineteenth century constructing a multidimensional picture of linguistic development has to be tentative. We can expect momentous demographic and social change in nineteenth-century Paris to have induced great changes to the sociolinguistic profile of the city. Standardisation pressures seem to have caused the most strongly marked phonetic and grammatical features of the traditional Parisian dialect to vanish by the middle of the century. Not all the old forms disappeared, however, for some clearly survived in the new urban dialect, born of industrialisation, which came to be referred to as *le francais populaire*. At the same time, high levels of in-migration from the provinces brought workers from villages in Brittany and the Limousin into closer proximity than ever before, with each other, with native Parisians and with official culture. Their engagement in inter-dialect communication almost certainly led to large-scale dialect-levelling, and this may explain the reductions and simplifications which were characteristic of colloquial Parisian speech at the end of the century.

The working out of the levelling process in nineteenth-century Paris cannot have been straightforward. On the one side, massive population increase fuelled by in-migration probably triggered a movement of dialect convergence: increased mobility causes a proliferation of weak ties which expose the population to standardising influences and facilitate the adoption of levelling changes, notably in the morpho-phonemic system. Large-scale modifications in social and demographic structure are commonly linked to a reduction of differences among the dialects of a language. On the other side, while industrialisation swept aside many of the hierarchies and networks inherited from the proto-industrial past, it also introduced new social groupings and new sources of conflict, which were likely to induce dialect divergence. As the speech of ever greater numbers of speakers was pulled in the direction of the standard language, the dominant social group kept its distance symbolically from the rest by not participating in the processes of 'reduction' and 'simplification' which characterised the development of colloquial speech. Moreover, as the century proceeded, it may be that a new and more salient role came to be played by variation in a different part of the language – the lexicon.

12   Lexical variation

In this final chapter let us explore the role of lexical variation in the sociolinguistic history of Paris. We have left this subject till last, not because it is the least important, but because the issues involved are recurrent and are best dealt with together rather than distributed piecemeal across the different periods. To many laypersons, what marks off Parisian speech from other dialects of French is not so much 'accent' or 'grammar' but its 'slang vocabulary'. Lexical differences between dialects are highly salient and are readily apparent to all speakers of the varieties concerned, without any linguistic training. Dialectologists and philologists have always been deeply interested in variation in the lexicon, and, in the case of French, they continue to produce exhaustive etymological descriptions of particular items (see von Wartburg 1923–) and impressive inventories of dialect-specific words (see, for example, Rézeau 2001). It is slightly anomalous, therefore, that sociolinguists, in the Labovian tradition at least, should have tended hitherto to keep lexical variation at arm's length.

The reasons for this are comprehensible enough. A variety's lexicon is less tightly structured than its phonetics and grammar: individual lexical items can be modified or exchanged with greater freedom than phonological and grammatical ones, and lexical choices, usually highly conscious, appear to be more random and short-lived. Whereas tokens of particular phonological and morphological variants can occur very frequently in short stretches of discourse, this is not the case with lexical variants, precluding classical Labovian exercises in quantification. Most importantly, lexical variants, unlike phonological and morphological ones, cannot as a rule be said to 'mean the same thing'. The fact remains, however, that variation in the lexicon plays a central role in the life of cities, and nowhere more so than in Paris. Far from being peripheral to sociolinguistic structure, 'words' approach the very core of the linguistic identity of the different social groups that make up any community.

Revealing insights into the problem of lexical variation in cities have been provided by the British linguist Michael Halliday (see in particular Halliday 1978). In a sense, Halliday starts where Labov leaves off, the quantitative approach giving way to a qualitative one. He takes as a basic premise that lexical variants – in contrast to Labov's sociolinguistic variables – are not semantically neutral, and that lexical differences between registers and between social dialects serve essentially to convey different meanings. The inhabitants of a city do not all talk to each other, they do not all speak alike, and, most significantly, they do not all *mean* alike (see Halliday 1978: 161). Different habits of meaning may not be amenable to the same type of empirical investigation as the formal aspects of speech (phonetic and morphological variables), but we must do what we can with them, if we are to have an all-round picture of the sociolinguistic development of Parisian speech. While lexical variation can be studied quantitatively up to a point, qualitative approaches cannot ultimately be avoided. It should be said that, working within the Labovian paradigm, Sankoff, Thibault and Bérubé (1978) attempted something along these lines with respect to the French of Montreal.

12.1   Lexical variation and social structure

Linguistic variants rarely remain value-free and the values that are assigned to them are social values, with variation serving as a symbolic expression of social structure. In all speech communities there exists a broad consensus regarding the social value of different parts of the lexicon: highly valued words are reserved for formal contexts, and are associated with people of higher status; lower-value words are reserved for informal situations and are associated with low-status speakers (see Fasold 1984: 53).

In the rhetorical tradition of Antiquity and the Middle Ages, the relationship between genre, vocabulary and social structure was a simple and direct one. We find this notion explicitly tabulated in 'Virgil's Wheel' (see Fig. 6). In medieval rhetoric the hierarchy of the 'three styles' correlated with a hierarchy of literary genres, the social rank of the protagonists, appropriate locations for action, etc.

In Old French literature, high-value words were conventionally attributed to the aristocratic characters who figured in dignified genres like lyric poetry and courtly romance. Low-value lexical items were attributed to the characters of lower social status, who figured in low-style literary genres like the comic *fabliaux* and late medieval farces (see above, §7.1). Built into the medieval code of courtliness, which dominated aristocratic aesthetics and social behaviour, were firm injunctions to nobles to practise *beau parler*, and to avoid the use of low-class words (*moz vilains*). The parodic *Roman de Renart* derived much of its effect from incongruities engineered between genre, style and social category (dignified human roles being filled by animals endowed with the power of speech). This same simple equation can be found in the stylistic rules governing French literature in the Classical period, and it is its presence in readers' minds that enabled the burlesque tradition to flourish parasitically alongside the established genres in the seventeenth century (see §8.1.1).

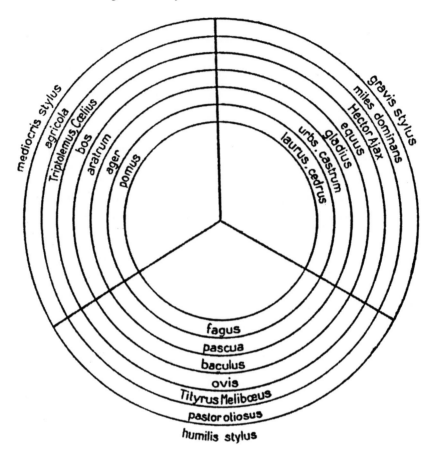

Fig. 6. Virgil's Wheel
Source: Faral 1924: 87.

However, one of the founding principles of sociolinguistics is that the relationship between particular linguistic items and particular social groups is not a simple and direct one, as rhetorical tradition and 'folk' linguistics would have it. 'Registers' (intra-speaker variation) and 'dialects' (inter-speaker variation) are interconnected, but the correlation between them is complex (see above, §1.2.1). The registers a person has access to may be a function of his place in the social structure, and a switch of register may entail a switch of dialect. At the same time, 'one person's dialect is another person's register: the items which one person uses under all circumstances, however informal, may be used by someone else only on the most formal occasions' (Hudson 1996: 470).

In what follows we will study changes in the social values attributed to different aspects of lexical variation in Parisian speech, and to do this we will draw extensively upon ideas developed by Halliday, notably his distinction between dialect and register (sub-categorised in terms of 'field', 'mode' and 'tenor', see §1.2.1) and his notion of 'antilanguage'. We will approach the question first from the perspective of register, then from that of dialect.

12.2   Register variation

At the beginnings of Parisian growth in the twelfth century the sociolinguistic state of the city was one of diglossia (see §1.2.3), with the L functions being naturally performed in French, while the H functions were conducted, as they had been since Roman times, in Latin. During the later Middle Ages and in the early part of the proto-industrial period, French increased its functional range at the expense of Latin, and the syntactic and lexical structures of the language were elaborated to keep pace. This involved, among other things, a widening of register variation within Parisian French. Insofar as registers are defined with respect to *uses* of language rather than *users*, one might expect correlations between register and social structure to be of minimal significance. This is not the case, however. The different registers of a language are accessed by speakers differentially, and inevitably attract different social values. Status hierarchies in the different areas of professional activity in the city led to a parallel hierarchisation of the lexical *fields* pertaining to them. The widening gulf between the written culture of the educated elite and the traditional oral culture of the masses, linked to the spread of literacy, prioritised the written *mode* over the spoken. The development of standard ideology (see §1.1.2) distinguished sharply between the formal *tenor* of discourse and the informal, with the former being associated more strongly with dominant social groups, and vernacular styles being consigned ever more dismissively to the 'people'. Let us take up these points one by one.

12.2.1   Field

Diversity in a city's vocabulary arises principally from the presence in the population of a multiplicity of different sub-groups, each one analysing the world in ways dictated by their diverse needs and preoccupations, and requiring specialised terminologies to express them. The bigger the community, the richer its sub-cultures. Traditional rural communities have elaborate taxonomies for particular agricultural activities, like ploughing and basket-making, which are not shared by the rest of the population. In large urban communities, the innumerable trades and professions each set up sophisticated lexical grids to handle their professional needs. Wright (1996) examined the extraordinarily rich vocabulary of boatmen working the Thames in medieval London. Pred's (1990) examination of the now lost vocabulary of nineteenth-century Stockholm could easily be replicated in other big cities of the same period. Just as the medieval French aristocracy had its rich vocabularies of courtliness, martial pursuits and hunting, so other groups in society, from lawyers and doctors to the whole polyphony of trades and professions exercised in Paris, each had their own technical terminologies. A valuable picture of the vocabularies of the different trades practised in medieval Paris is to be found in Estienne Boileau's *Livre des mestiers*. A great deal of space in Brunot's monumental history of French consists of lists of neologisms introduced at different times to cover developments in particular areas of activity (e.g. commerce, industry, finance). Lists of first attestations, classified primarily by field, are published regularly in B. Quémada's *Datations et documents lexicographiques* (1959–). Dauzat (1929) studied the specialised *argots* of various trades in early twentieth-century France. A whole social history of Paris could in fact be written on the basis of the different vocabularies used in the city. Georges Matoré saw lexicology as a branch of sociology (see Matoré 1953, 1985, 1988).

For all its interest, such a history cannot be undertaken here, and we must restrict our focus to the symbolical values carried by different parts of the lexicon. In the social psychology of the city the different lexical fields elaborated to facilitate different *uses* of the language could not remain dissociated from their primary *users*. The social pecking order of the different professions triggered a parallel hierarchisation of the words associated with them. In this way, to take an obvious example, *mots savants* (words coined from Latin and Greek by the educated professions) were always rated more highly than the *argots de métier* (the informal vocabularies pertaining to the various manual trades). Terminologies specific to particular social sub-groups easily became identity markers. In-groupers may deliberately use in-group terms to reinforce internal cohesion and exclusiveness. Gougenheim (1975: 151–6) provides interesting information about schoolboy *argot* in mid nineteenth-century Paris. At the same time, terms used innocently by in-groupers for referential precision may be perceived by out-groupers (with different needs and preoccupations) as being used for purposes of mystification and even furtiveness. What is 'terminology' for the in-grouper is 'jargon', even 'secret code' for the out-grouper. We will return to this.

The use of group-specific vocabularies commonly leads to resentment and hostile comment from outsiders. In the first half of the sixteenth century the latinate jargon of students on the Left Bank is ridiculed by Tory (*Aux Lecteurs* (1529), for example the use of *transfreter* for *traverser*, *deambuler* for *se promener*, *quadrivies* for *places publiques*), and the theme is taken up later by Rabelais in his famous passage featuring the *escolier limousin* (see Pfister 1993b). In the second half of the same century the Italianate speech of courtiers became the object of even more vigorous criticism (see Hope 1971: I, 228–48), culminating in H. Estienne's celebrated diatribes against italianisms published under the title of *Deux Dialogues du nouveau langage françois italianizé* (H. Estienne 1578). In the seventeenth century the contorted lexical constructions of *préciosité* were famously ridiculed by the playwright Molière. Similar examples can easily be found at all periods in the history of the city.

12.2.2   Mode

From the earliest times down to our own day (where the prestige of the written word is at last being challenged), writing was consistently seen as superior to speech, and the clerkly groups possessing literacy skills in medieval times were often viewed by the unlettered with superstitious awe. The development of vernacular (i.e. non-Latin) writing systems in the Middle Ages broke the monopoly of the latinate clerical elite, and the invention of printing at the time of the Renaissance made written texts available to an ever-widening public. The spread of literacy involved more than the dissemination of a different mode of communication, however: it brought about cultural changes involving further disparagement of the spoken word and vernacular styles.

It is impossible to dissociate 'mode' and 'tenor' very strictly, for vocabulary used more in spoken *mode* than in written is also, as a rule, more familiar in *tenor*. If there is an area where mode and tenor can be differentiated more clearly, it is that of the planned nature of writing versus the normally unplanned nature of speech. With the spread of written culture during the Renaissance, a premium came to be set on carefully elaborated originality of expression, in contrast to the spontaneously produced commonplaces and idiomatic expressions felt to typify speech. Whereas literate culture favours the making of deliberate and, as far as possible, original lexical choices, everyday speech often has recourse to banal, ready-made utterances and predictable lexical sequences. In seventeenth-century parlance colloquial expressions were all classified as *proverbes*, and in cultivated society they became the object of ridicule. Numerous collections of *proverbes* were published in Paris in the seventeenth and eighteenth centuries (see Kramer 2002). Here are some of the main ones:

1610   Beroalde de Verville, *Le Moyen de parvenir*
1633   Adrien de Montluc, *La Comédie des proverbes*
1640   Antoine Oudin, *Les Curiositez françoises*
1713   Philippe le Roux, *Le Dictionnaire comique*
1748   A.-J. Panckoucke, *Dictionnaire des proverbes français et des façons de parler comiques, burlesques et familières*

These publications embraced the more narrowly defined 'proverbs' which we recognise today (e.g. *contentement passe richesse, belle montre peu de rapport, on n'est pas d'abord vieux*), but they also included clichés and ready-made utterances (e.g. *jeaune comme un coin, doux comme un mouton, grande comme un four*). In medieval times the apposite use of proverbs had been seen as an embellishment, but the rhetoric of the seventeenth and eighteenth centuries rejected them as belonging to traditional, pre-rational culture (see Obelkevitch 1987: 58–60). *Maximes*, on the other hand, were cultivated assiduously in elite circles, as aphorisms containing universal truths conceived and expressed in an original, highly planned way.

With the spread of literacy in eighteenth-century Paris reinforcing that of standard ideology (see §8.3), the downgrading of the vernacular, and, along with it, all those members of society not participating fully in written culture, became systematic. This is plainly seen in the ridiculing of the speech of '*semi-lettrés*' in the *Lettres de Montmartre* (1750) (see Appendix, Text 7 and Lodge 1995b). Universal education in the industrial period made hostility to the vernacular in all its forms a concern of the state itself. Romantics like Victor Hugo objected to the by now well-established lexicographical tradition hierarchising the lexicon into H and L, and called for steps to democratise the dictionary:

> La langue était l'état avant quatre-vingt-neuf;
> Les mots, bien ou mal nés, vivaient parqués en castes;
> Les uns, nobles, hantent les Phèdres, les Jocastes,
> . . .
> Les autres, tas de gueux, drôles patibulaires,
> Habitent les patois; quelques-uns aux galères
> Dans l'argot; dévoués à tous les genres bas.
> . . .
> Je fis souffler un vent révolutionnaire.
> Je mis un bonnet rouge au vieux dictionnaire.
>   (V. Hugo, *Contemplations*, I, vii, ed. Garnier, Paris 1962)

However, while literary styles may have changed in the nineteenth century to give greater prominence to low-class forms, the normative tradition was too powerful for Hugo's pleas to have much impact on public attitudes.

12.2.3   Tenor

Halliday (1978: 33) sees 'tenor' as referring, at least in part, to variation in formality. Thanks to the large amount of dialect-contact in the city, colloquial Parisian French has always contained a bewildering array of near-synonymous words and expressions drawn from a multiplicity of sources, only some of which are identifiable. From the sixteenth century onwards lexicographers strove to control this diversity and codify the socio-stylistic value of particular items. As part of the general movement of reallocation, they were led to deny legitimacy to a proportion of colloquial words and to contain the rest within a hierarchy of style-categories geared, rather unsystematically, to levels of formality and to the supposed social origins of the words in question. A flavour of their approach is to be found in the following quotation from France's first great lexicographer, Robert Estienne:

Ce mot la sent sa boulie, ce mot la sent sa rave, ce mot la sent sa Place Maubert.[1]
(R. Estienne 1565: 32)

Over the following centuries Estienne's successors gradually evolved a conventional hierarchy of style-labels: *soutenu* → *littéraire* → *courant* → *familier* → *populaire* → *vulgaire* → *argotique* (see Maselaar 1988).

However, 'tenor' does not refer merely to variation in formality. It refers more fundamentally to the relationship between the participants as well as to such questions as the permanence or otherwise of the relationship and the degree of emotional charge in it. A characteristic of contemporary French is the existence of a very extensive 'parallel vocabulary', where low-value words duplicate socially approved terms and act as socio-stylistic markers, e.g. *fric* ~ *argent* ('money'), *bagnole* ~ *voiture* ('car'), *bouquin* ~ *livre* ('book'). The range of this vocabulary is much greater in French than in English, for example, which has relatively few comparable pairs (e.g. *chuck* ~ *throw*). Lexical variables like these behave quantitatively like other types of sociolinguistic variable (see Lodge 1989). However, the parallelism is not complete. 'Variation across registers involves different linguistic features, rather than semantically neutral variants of a single feature' (Biber and Finegan 1994: 6). Unlike phonetic and morphological variants, lexical variants are not 'different ways of saying the same thing'. While the denotations of *fric* ~ *argent* may well be the same (i.e. 'money'), the speaker's attitude and the likely pragmatic effects of each member of the pair are very different.

It is preferable, therefore, to try to understand the working of variation in tenor in pragmatic terms akin to those of positive and negative politeness (see above, §8.1.1):

Negative politeness	Positive politeness
Objective detachment	Subjective involvement
Universalistic	Context-bound
Distance	Proximity
Out-group	In-group
Social acquiescence	Social defiance

Politeness phenomena almost certainly provide more basic and more universal determinants of variation of tenor than the gradations of situations along a simple formality scale, and the social origins of speakers (see Lodge 1999b).

The parodies of low-class Parisian speech we examined in Chapter 9 incorporate a large amount of colloquial vocabulary. The principles by which words were allocated to low (rather than neutral or high) style are as a rule arbitrary

---

[1] 'This word reeks of boiled meat, this of turnips, this one of the Place Maubert.'

and opaque. Some had had higher social value in Old French and had simply fallen from fashion: *ainsin* (= thus), *illeques* (= there), *tout fin (clinquant) neuf* (= brand new), *trémousser* (= agitate). Others were evidently too undignified for formal contexts, for example *batifoler* (= frolic), *ébaubi* (= astonished), *enhazé* (= confused), *tarabuster* (= confuse), but we are unlikely ever to know why (see Clément 1899: 405–6). In other cases, however, interesting patterns emerge in the semantics of the words concerned: the allocation of many items to low style looks to be linked to the positive politeness features which they express.

Whereas negative politeness favours the objective communication of messages with high propositional content, colloquial speech typically betrays the subjective involvement of the speaker in what is being said (see Cheshire 1997). The texts considered in Chapter 9 contain a high proportion of interjections and exclamative expressions (e.g. *Aga, Samon, Nani* (or *nanin*), *Fi donc qu'alle est trigode!* and *Mon Guieu, qu'il y avoit des yeux qui . . .*). They avoid abstractions in favour of concrete metaphors, for example *bailler un chapiau* (= defraud), *maugré vos dents* (= despite your hostility), *graisser ses bottes* (= ingratiate oneself with someone). Whenever uneducated speakers are obliged to use 'learned' words, they automatically mispronounce them (e.g. *abolution = absolution, infection = affection*).

Whereas negative politeness culture seeks to emphasise the dignity of the participants, interposing distance between them, colloquial speech favours the reverse, seeking constantly to reduce the dignity of topics under discussion in the interests of social solidarity. In this way *garçon → drolle, activités → fredenes, écrire → grifonner, maison → taudis, parler → jaser, converser → parloter, imprimer → mouler, vomir → dégobiller, s'enivre → se guéder*.

Whereas negative politeness avoids direct evocation of issues pertaining to the intimacy of the participants, positive politeness seeks to promote in-group solidarity by doing the reverse and by frequent recourse to expressions relating to bodily functions and to taboo words, e.g. *Et me regardez l'oreille de ce poisson là: il est tout sanglant et en vie. Est-il dodu! et qui vaut bien mieux bouté là son argent qu'à ste voirie de raye puante qui sant le pissat à pleine gorge.*[2] These naturally include a large number of oaths and swear-words, e.g. *jarniguié, ma fique, morguié, palsanguié, tredame*. The higher the style-level, the more walls there are to protect the addressee against the encroachment that any communication makes on privacy (see Hudson 1996: 131).

Technically speaking, tenor and politeness strategies are features of *use* and situation, not of *user* and social stratification. Brown and Levinson indicate, however, that in complex societies dominated social groups tend to have

---

[2] 'Look at the gills on that fish for me: it's still alive and bleeding. Isn't it full of meat, and isn't it more worthwhile to spend your money on this rather than on that filthy, stinking skate [over there] which reeks of piss enough to turn your stomach over?'

positive-politeness cultures, while dominating social groups have negative-politeness cultures (1987: 246). Indeed, it is quite clear that since early modern times the urban elites have cultivated negative-politeness strategies in a most systematic way, vehemently rejecting the values implicit in positive politeness, which they attribute to the lower orders, in public at least (see above, §8.1.1).

12.3   Social dialect variation

If the different parameters of lexical variation which we considered under 'register' (variation according to use) become automatically charged with social meaning, this will be the case *a fortiori* with words associated with particular social 'dialects' (variation according to user). The use of vocabulary as an expression of group identity is well known, but we should not consider it to be necessarily superficial and skin-deep ('same underlying meaning, different surface forms'). Cities are pluralistic communities and much of the time variation in the lexicon reflects the coexistence of divergent attitudes towards society, divergent ways of apprehending the world, very different habits of meaning. It is in the biggest metropolises that we find the starkest contrasts, and, indeed, in Paris, as in London, Calcutta (studied by Halliday) and elsewhere, we find groups seeking to maximise their separateness from the rest of urban society, and expressing this through their vocabulary. We will devote the rest of this chapter to examining an extreme manifestation of this in Parisian speech: *argot*.

12.3.1   Parisian 'argot'

Parisian *argot* is impossible to pin down precisely, for not only is this part of linguistic reality fluid, but the labels used to designate it have not remained constant over the centuries. Chronologically, the French term *argot* denotes in the first instance the language of thieves and vagabonds, incomprehensible to the uninitiated, which flourished in proto-industrial Paris. Such closed, underclass 'languages' are to be found in a wide range of societies across the world, and an almost exact equivalent exists in the canting speech which developed in London at about the same time (see Gotti 1999). To say 'language' of thieves is too broad, however, for we are dealing here only with a special vocabulary, not with a special grammar or phonology. In Parisian *argot* the language was simply relexicalised, and, even then, not in all areas, only in those anti-social activities which were of particular concern to *argotiers*.

The first references in French to a secret vocabulary used by outlaws and marginals occur as early as the twelfth century (see the *Jeu de Saint Nicolas*, ed. A. Jeanroy 1982, ll. 701–4), and the label used to designate it at that time is not *argot* but *jargon* ('incomprehensible babbling'). The thirteenth-century romance of *Richart li biaus* narrates a concrete situation in which criminal *jargon* is used. Thanks to his familiarity with this *jargon*, a squire discovers the nefarious intent of a band of robbers, and is able to prompt the knightly hero of the romance into the appropriate punitive response:

> Richars un escuiier avoit
> Qui le *gargon* trestout savoit,
> En une estable va fain querre
> Et ot Milon qui se desserre;
> tous les larrons a appiellés:
> 'Oyés, signour, se le celés,
> en *gargon* dist, chil chevalier
> de lasus sont mi prisonnier;
> quant au mangier seront assis
> cascuns sera u mors u pris,
> lor avoir donrray a ma gent.'
> Quant li escuiiers ce entent
> Mout sagement arrier s'en vait,
> A Richart vient con par souhait.
> 'Sire, dist il, tout sons tray,
> car nous serons ja envay
> de nos ostez, fort larron sont,
> nostre avoir ja departi ont,
> et si nous doivent au souper
> a cascun la tieste coper,
> bien ay entendu lor *gargon*.'[3]
> (ed. A. Holden 1983; ll.3335–55)

Despite late-medieval challenges from labels like *le jobelin, le blesquin* and *le narquois*, *jargon* persisted as the prime designation of this vocabulary for many centuries. The works of the fifteenth-century poet François Villon, notably his *Ballades en jargon*, make ample use of words and expressions drawn from this source (see Sainéan 1912: 17–24; Guiraud 1968). Half a century later, Tory (1529: *Aux Lecteurs*) condemns this mode of speech in the following way:

---

[3] 'Richard had a squire who had a thorough knowledge of "jargon". He sent him into a stable to fetch some hay, and there he overheard Milon holding forth, addressing all the bandits in this way: "Listen, men, and keep it hidden – he says this in 'jargon' – those knights up there are my prisoners. When they sit down to eat, each one will be captured or killed, and I will give their possessions to my followers." When the squire hears this he goes back very discreetly and returns to Richard exactly on cue: "Sire", he says, "we are all betrayed, for today we will be attacked in our homes. The bandits are strong and they have already shared out our goods. And they are about to cut off all our heads as we sit at supper. I have understood their 'jargon' pretty well." '

Tout pareillement quant Jargonneurs tiennent leurs propos de leur malicieux Jargon & meschant langage, me semblent qu'ilz ne se monstrent seullement estre dediez au Gibet, mais qu'il seroit bon qu'ilz ne feussent oncques nez. Jaçoit que Maistre François Villon . . .[4]

The term *argot* began to replace *jargon* only in the seventeenth century, and an important vehicle for propagating this change was O. Chéreau's *Jargon de l'Argot réformé* (first published in 1628, and often re-issued right down to 1849). The new label *argot* looks to be a Parisian pronunciation of the word *ergot* (derived from *ergoter*, 'to haggle' or 'to hassle (clients)'), which had come to designate the collectivity of thieves and beggars in the city. References can be found to the *royaume de l'argot*. Subsequently the name for the group was transferred to their mode of speech. The old word *jargon* lost its special association with the criminal fraternity and came to be a general pejorative term applied by out-groupers to any specialised terminology which they feel is not their own.

The label *argot* has remained in place from that time on, apart from a brief challenge in the nineteenth century from the expression *la langue verte*. However, the reality behind the word has not been so stable, for the in-group vocabulary of thieves of earlier times has become in modern times, broadly speaking, a set of strongly marked lexical items deemed to be violently anti-social. The pivotal period in this change looks to have been the early nineteenth century, as the old proto-industrial structures broke down.

12.3.2   The proto-industrial phase

Like canting speech in London, Parisian *argot* (or *jargon*) was born of the particular social and demographic conditions which prevailed in the city in late medieval and early modern times. We have seen (above §6.1.1) how the demography of the proto-industrial city was characterised by the presence at the bottom of society of a large and shifting population (up to one third of the total, according to some estimates) made up of in-migrants who were poorly integrated into the social structures of the city. It is clear from Geremek's (1976) reconstruction of the life of marginal groups in late medieval Paris that many of these people survived by preying on the wealth of the established population through begging, prostitution or thieving. The impending arrival in town of bands of beggars and vagabonds was a recurrent source of alarm for the established residents who, not without reason, saw their property threatened.

---

[4] 'In the same way, when "jargon"-speakers express themselves in their malicious "jargon" and malevolent way of speaking, they seem to me to show themselves destined simply for the gibbet, and that it would be good if they had never been born. Despite the fact that Master François Villon . . .'

Vagrants were notoriously difficult to police and control, and posed a permanent threat to public order. Indeed, there were certain parts of Paris, especially cemeteries, where marginals and criminals congregated and which were no-go areas for the police (see above, §6.1.3). The most notorious was a location near the Rue Montorgueil with its *Cour des Miracles* (see Sauval 1724, quoted in Sainéan 1912: 311–24). Throughout the early modern period the municipal authorities were obliged to take ever more repressive measures to combat the threat they posed – with predictable lack of success.

As for the marginals themselves, it appears that, uprooted from their provincial origins, they felt and behaved like any group under pressure: they made common cause with each other and established within their ranks a set of power hierarchies of greater or lesser solidity. For a modern parallel we could note that the most fertile period for the production of *argot* in the first half of the twentieth century was probably the First World War, when French troops in the trenches were living under unbearable pressure (see Roques 1995). Contemporary information (heavily embellished no doubt) is to be had from a series of works published in the first part of the seventeenth century:

1596   Péchon de Ruby, *Vie généreuse des mercelots, gueuz et bohémiens* (reprinted 1612, 1627)

1600   *Cabale des filous*

1621   Daudiguier, *L'Antiquité des larrons*

1623   Le Père Garasse, *Doctrine curieuse des beaux esprits du temps*, pp. 68–70

1623   *Pasquil*

1628   O. Chéreau, *Jargon de l'Argot réformé* (reprinted 1632, 1634, 1660)

1630   R. Mollancheur, *Response* (or *Jargon* de Chéreau)

1630   *Complaincte au grand Coesre*   (Esnault 1965: v–xvi)

Although set up in opposition to 'straight' society, we are led to believe that the structures devised by thieves and vagabonds in late medieval Paris nevertheless replicated the hierarchies of the established social order. Marginals in Paris allegedly organised themselves into corporations calqued on the trade guilds upon which the economic structure of the city was based. The principal 'corporation' of thieves and beggars was known as the *Argot* (= the collectivity of beggars), and its head had as title the *Grand Coesre*. The principal criminal activities (begging, thieving, pimping) were each organised into elaborate hierarchies and the different specialities within each of them strictly delimited. The training of apprentices followed a similar pattern to that found in legitimate guilds: masters who instructed newcomers were *instituteurs* and their charges *mioches* (see Calvet 1994b: 25).

It is more than likely that authors of the works listed above, targeting a readership of established citizens, attributed a higher level of internal organisation and complicity to the community of vagabonds than existed in reality.

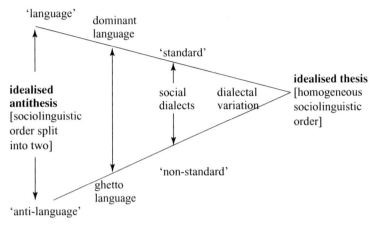

Fig. 7. Language and anti-language
Source: Halliday 1978: 179.

People living in fear invariably exaggerate the degree of conspiracy present in the groups ranged against them. However, this sort of organisation has been observed to happen in marginal groups across the world, and it is quite likely that the inadequacy of the authorities' grip on so vast an urban population in the early modern period did allow a vigorous counter-culture to flourish within the Paris underclass. That such a counter-culture should have developed some sort of specialised, even secret mode of speech is to be expected. To use Halliday's terminology, the unassimilated groups of people on the margins of society formed a sort of 'anti-society' within the city, and they expressed themselves through their own 'anti-language'.

Halliday (1978: 164–82) summarises his thinking on anti-language in a diagram (Fig. 7). Halliday sees language variation within a particular speech community as located at a particular point on a continuum between two idealised extremes of heterogeneity and homogeneity. In this analysis, 'anti-language' represents a polarised case with maximal distance between the legitimate 'language' and an alternative vision of society expressed through 'anti-language'. By definition, *argot*, though often normal, economical, logical and (linguistically) pure, can claim no more than a marginal existence within the standard (see Joseph 1987: 123). Although Halliday does not consider proto-industrial Parisian *argot* specifically, this variety contains so many similarities with London's canting speech, which he studies as an example of anti-language, that it is clear that it too belongs in this category.

Proto-industrial *argot* comprised first and foremost the technical vocabulary of a criminal sub-culture. As a special register of the language *argot* came about as a result of relexicalisation (i.e. new words for old). Hence we find alternative words for types of criminal act (e.g. *enturner, faire mousser la lourde, torchir les tenants, travailler à la bombe*), classes of criminal and victim (e.g. *crocheteurs, vendengeurs, beffleurs, envoyeurs, caves*), tools of the trade (e.g. *lingre, tranchant, doffe*), law-enforcement officers (e.g. *bavard, curieux, perdreau, poulet, rouan, roussin, bourrique, cogne*), punishments (e.g. *bascule*), prisons and so on (e.g. *trou, Biscaye, Pelago, Lontou, Toulabre, Lorcefée*). Penal life in the galleys was an important generator of *argot* at this time. However, if this vocabulary were just the result of relexicalisation, it would be no different from any other technical vocabulary, albeit of an anti-social group.

What makes Parisian *argot* into an anti-language is not the fact that it is *re*lexicalised (i.e. that it creates its own technical terms), but the fact that it is *over*-lexicalised. The accumulation of alternative synonyms found in *argot* is larger than life. It presents not just one alternative word for, say, 'police', but dozens (see Guiraud 1956: 61). Such lexical exuberance is normally explained by students of slang as the result of a never-ending search for originality, for the sake either of secrecy or of liveliness and humour. Halliday, however, sees more to it than this.

There is, of course, plenty of evidence pointing to the cryptic function of proto-industrial *argot* (see Guiraud 1956: 9–30, 54–76). The most authentic non-literary attestations of criminal slang in this period are to be found in judicial records. The first of these are the court proceedings of the trial of the 'Coquillards' in Dijon (1455–8). The Coquillards were a remnant of the bands of armed men who had used the anarchic situation prevailing during the Hundred Years' War to engage in freebooting acts of pillage and brigandage. The Dijon records contain a list of seventy or so more or less secret terms (here referred to as *le jobelin*) used by members of the band to disguise their criminal activities. These documents have been closely scrutinised (see Sainéan 1912: 15–17; Guiraud 1968: 274–83; Matoré 1985: 301–3). Similar cases of criminals 'turning King's evidence' and divulging the lexical secrets of their partners in crime occur sporadically until the middle of the nineteenth century. Nicolas Ragot's poem *Le Vice puni, ou Cartouche* published in 1725 incorporated a glossary of *argot*, apparently extracted from Cartouche shortly before his execution. The records of the trial of the 'Chauffeurs d'Orgères' in 1800 contain another list. Most celebrated of all were the memoirs, published in 1828, by the ex-convict turned police informer F.-E. Vidocq. These represent proto-industrial *argot* in its terminal stage, but they provide a large amount of lexical information even so.

We should also note that the *argot*-speaking community appears to have engaged from an early date in the development of linguistic codes like *largonji* (from *jargon*), *louchebem* (from *boucher*, i.e. a code used by the butchers of the Halles) and *verlan* (from *l'envers*, i.e. back-slang). Codes like this flourish in dominated social groups across the world, rough equivalents being found in London English in back-slang and rhyming slang (see Calvet 1994b: 54–70). Taken with the forensic evidence, all this suggests that *argot* was used to protect secrecy within the criminal fraternity. But was secrecy its prime function?

We need to bear in mind that most of the historical evidence about *argot* is filtered through the writings of members of established society, who, feeling threatened, may have exaggerated the importance of its cryptic dimension. Secrecy may have existed more in the minds of established citizens than in the minds of criminals themselves. H. Estienne (1578: 407) had already hinted at the tendency to mythologise the language of Parisian marginals. The meanings of any technical vocabulary are normally opaque to the uninitiated. Moreover, it is difficult to see the commercial printer who published Villon's *Ballades en jargon* in 1489 deliberately choosing to publish a set of poems which only initiates in the underclass would understand, and words drawn from *argot* were frequently used in literary texts throughout the sixteenth century (see Sainéan 1912: 24–44). *Argotiers* are reported by Berthaud (1650) to have operated quite openly on the Pont Neuf, and we saw earlier (p. 167) how Menétra, not a member of any criminal fraternity as far as we can tell, communicated with his associates in *argot*. While secrecy may be the motivation for the obscurity of certain words, Esnault (1965) argues persuasively that other factors related to the social isolation of marginal groups are more important.

The function of anti-language is not primarily to maintain secrecy, nor to provide its practitioners with a resource for verbal fun, though these may happen as a by-product, but to maintain the life of a group under pressure. The deviant norms of anti-language are more than just different ways of saying the same thing, and they are more than just technical terms of the trade reserved for the initiates. *Argot* embodies an alternative vision of the world and acts as a voice of rebellion against the whole value-system of established society. Le Page (1985) details the effects of outside threats on the focusing of linguistic norms within the group. Milroy (1992: 213) points to the presence of tightly networked groups, along with their powerful linguistic norms, both at the bottom and at the top of society. Just as members of the ruling elite under the Ancien Régime produced their own special language variety, reflecting their preoccupations (e.g. *la carte du tendre* and the terminology of aristocratic courtship) and protecting their identity and status from the encroachments of those beneath, so the underclass, feeling itself to be under permanent pressure from above, developed its own set of distinctive lexical norms. *Argots* develop on the margins of society to foster cohesion and solidarity within the group, and a sense of separateness from the hostile world outside.

Permanent renewal of *argot* vocabulary ('the never-ending search for originality') plays a crucial role in this, identifying those who are currently core members of the group, those who are falling by the wayside, and those who just do not belong at all (dismissed in Paris *argot* as *caves*, 'suckers'). A general characteristic of *argot* seems to be obliqueness of meaning and form: *argot* words are as a rule semantically and morphologically opaque. This springs less from a desire for secrecy than from a desire to mark off the in-grouper (who knows) from the out-grouper (who does not). The lexical exuberance of *argot* is not just an exotic and bizarre add-on. Its presence is essential if *argot* is to perform its central role in maintaining the life of the group and the status hierarchy within it.

12.3.3   The industrial phase

In the industrial period the specific social conditions which had given rise to criminal *argot* in Paris ceased to exist, and we find the medieval anti-language being brusquely transformed. It survived into the industrial period, but only 'with its teeth drawn' (see Halliday 1978: 177). The expansion of the city's population between 1800 and 1850 forced the municipal authorities to take effective measures to bring firmly under social control the lawless bands of criminals and marginals which had been such a feature of the proto-industrial city. Modern policing methods were introduced, along with the modern penal system. Over this period the disintegration of the tightly networked communities in the medieval city centre and the development of sprawling new working-class suburbs ensured that the old bonds of solidarity and cohesion among the poor, along with the old modes of criminality, were no longer sustainable. New forms of social deviance developed. What we now see is that, as traditional *argot* vocabulary ceased to be the prerogative of closed groups (insofar as it ever had been), it was adopted by the new industrial working class as a symbol of proletarian identity and, up to a point, as its voice of protest.

Once Parisian *argot* was disaffiliated from the specific social groups that originally created it, it becomes increasingly difficult to find objective ways of distinguishing it from colloquial vocabulary in general. A proportion of nineteenth- and twentieth-century *argot* words are classified as such simply because they appear on earlier lists of *argot* words. However, since an essential feature of *argot* is permanent renewal, as time goes on, the proportion of new, previously unattested *argot* words automatically increases. The difficulty this poses is that the neologising techniques employed to renew *argot* are indistinguishable from those used elsewhere in the language (see Gadet 1992: 102). A proportion of *argot* words can be seen to be borrowed from a range of regional dialects, reflecting the capital's function as demographic melting-pot, but dialect words enter mainstream Paris vocabulary as well. Many *argot* words are coined by truncation, or are derivatives formed with the help of (usually pejorative) suffixes like *-ard, -asse* and *-os*. However, these devices are available for lexical renewal in other registers too (see Delaplace 1998).

Some *argot* words are created by codes like *verlan* and *javanais* (inserting -*av*-
after an initial vowel, thus *beau* → *baveau*), but these codes are available to all
speakers of the language. Many *argot* words are 'normal' words which have
undergone sometimes dramatic semantic shifts through metonymy and, especially, metaphor. However, this means of neologising is hardly a prerogative of
slang.

If the category *argot* retains any validity, it cannot be in terms of morphology
but in terms of the particular meanings and pragmatic functions it expresses.
Argot words are characterised by obliqueness of meaning and form, their prime
function being to distinguish the in-grouper from the out-grouper. They express
in an extreme way the rejection of prevailing social norms. They do so either
by evoking anti-social behaviour and taboo subjects, or through implying ag-
gressive, pejorative or cynical attitudes. The preferred domains of *argot* are
deviant, anti-social behaviour and subjects considered taboo by polite society.
Argot words proliferate in the fields of criminality (e.g. 'to steal': *fourbir, laver,
nettoyer, blanchir, lessiver, éponger, essorer, rincer, repasser, polir*), prostitution (e.g. 'pimp': *proxo, maquereau, brochet, barbeau, barbillon, dos-bleu,
hareng*), and low life (e.g. 'sucker': *cave, pigeon, jobard, godiche*). Taboo subjects like sexuality, human bodily functions and money attract a large number
of terms: Calvet (1994b: 44) notes in one recent dictionary of *argot* seventy-one
words designating money, sixty-three designating coitus, thirteen designating
defecation, etc.

Guiraud (1956: 43–50) draws attention to the 'dégradation des valeurs' and
the 'sarcasme et l'ironie' which characterise the semantics of *argot*. He quotes
Jules Marouzeau on this topic:

Il (= *l'argot*) ne comporte guère de mots pour traduire l'attendrissement, la compassion,
l'humanité, la générosité, l'abnégation, l'altruisme, la tolérance et même l'élémentaire
bonté; toutes les nuances de l'amour, affection, attachement, inclination, sympathie,
tendresse aboutissent chez lui au désinvolte et inexpressif *béguin*.

Dignified roles in society are systematically mocked with such terms as
adjupète ('adjutant'), *singe* ('boss'), *épicemar* ('épicerie owner'), *probloque*
('landlord'). Even those entities which the *argotier* most loves and admires
(e.g. cars and sexually attractive women) all receive pejorative names (e.g.
cars: *tire, caisse*; women: *ménasse, gonzesse, julie, polka*).

Marina Yaguello (1978) draws attention to the large number of misogynistic
terms present in *argot*, and infers from this, wrongly in our view, that the French
language as a whole contains a built-in anti-feminist bias. A great deal of research has been devoted to understanding the workings of the sociolinguistic
gender pattern, whereby males show a greater unwillingness to comply with
high-status speech-norms than females. This has been attributed to the greater
importance for men of covert prestige and the increased pressures placed upon

them to demonstrate their freedom from social constraints. Whatever the motivations may be, the fact that males have greater recourse to *argot* than females is not disputed.

Insofar as *argot* vocabulary involves the rejection of established social values, it would be understandable if, in the second half of the nineteenth century, such words were widely adopted by the industrial proletariat in a society now dominated by the capitalist bourgeoisie. How far working-class speech differed lexically from bourgeois speech in real life is impossible to say. Even in our own day, the socio-stylistic distribution of lexical variables in actual usage has not given rise to systematic study. All we can say is that educated observers of the Parisian scene were struck by the extent of lexical differences between the classes. This is certainly the view of the situation presented by nineteenth-century literary authors. Partly as a result of the Romantic fascination with the Outsider, and partly, no doubt, as a result of middle-class fears of *les classes dangereuses*, the vocabulary of criminality became the object of great interest to the cultivated part of society. Vidocq's memoirs led to underworld slang being widely accepted in 'respectable' literature, with the novels of Victor Hugo, Honoré Balzac, Eugène Sue, followed by the works of Emile Zola, the Goncourt brothers and Jean Richepin. This established an enduring literary convention which made *argot* an indispensable component in any portrayal not only of the criminal fraternity, but of working-class males in general, right down to our own day. This convention has been extremely tenacious, in films (see Abécassis 2000) as well as in detective novels, most famously in those of 'San Antonio'. Gaitet (1992) cautions against a naïve reading of these literary representations of the speech of the Paris poor: the social stereotyping which is involved was not ideologically innocent and constituted a means of social control.

However, more 'scientific' observers were also struck by the salience of lexical variation at this time. The second half of the nineteenth century saw the publication of a large number of dictionaries and studies of low-class Parisian vocabulary. Here are some of the most important:

1856 F. Michel, *Etudes de philologie sur l'argot*   (Paris: Firmin Didot)
1866 A. Delvau, *Dictionnaire de la langue verte*   (Paris: Flammarion)
1872 L. Larchey, *Dictionnaire historique, etymologique et anecdotique de l'argot parisien*   (Paris: Dentu)
1876 C. Nisard, *De Quelques Parisianismes populaires et autres locutions*   (Paris: La Butte aux Cailles)
1889 M. Schwob, G. Guieysse, *Etude sur l'argot français*   (Paris: Emile Bouillon)
1889 A. Vitu, *Dictionnaire analytique du jargon*   (Paris: Ollendorff)
1894 C. Virmaître, *Dictionnaire d'argot fin de siècle*   (Paris: Flammarion)

1900   J. Lermina, H. Levêque, *Dictionnaire thématique français–argot*
                                                                            (Paris: Chacornac)
1901   A. Bruant, *L'Argot au XXe siècle*   (Paris: Flammarion)
1901   Rossignol, *Dictionnaire d'argot*   (Paris: Ollendorff)
1901   R. Yve-Plessis, *Bibliographie raisonnée de l'argot et de la langue verte en France du XVe au XXe siècle*   (Paris: Daragon)

The popularity of these works attests, at the very least, a rise in salience of lexical variation, perhaps as phonetic and grammatical differences between the sociolects were levelled (see above, §11.2.1–2). Bauche (1920) devoted a good third of his *Le Langage populaire* to vocabulary. As *argot* words became available to everyone, they became more a feature of register than of social dialect. Nevertheless, the need for access to an anti-language was not spread evenly across the social classes, sexes or even age-groups. It looks as though working-class identity at the end of the nineteenth century was signalled most conspicuously, not by accent, but by lexis. The label *parigot* is a blend of *Paris + argot*. It is possible to draw parallels between the proletarian vocabulary associated with *la gouaille parisienne* (Parisian banter) and the type of working-class humour described by Dittmar, Schlobinski and Wachs (1988) in Berlin.

The period since the Second World War has seen the the transformation of the old industries, large-scale in-migration from outside Europe and the break-up of the nineteenth-century class-structure. The connection between lexical variation and the traditionally recognised social classes has loosened. The label *argot* now seems to refer to two sets of lexical items, which we can designate as 'dead' *argot* and 'living' *argot*. Dead *argot* comprises a closed set of items located at the negative end of the social acceptability scale: they are felt to be close to taboo- and swear-words, and their use symbolises a rejection of the evaluative norms of respectable society. Such words may have originated in the anti-language of the criminal fraternity, but nowadays, though they are used above all by males, they are available (theoretically at least) to everyone. For instance, upper-class speakers may use them for purposes of *encanaillement* – claiming (fictitious) solidarity with subordinates. Living *argot*, by contrast, consists of an open set of items constantly being renewed within the multifarious social sub-groups which create them for purposes of internal cohesion and external distinction. Such items, by definition, are not widely available. It is probably true to say that, in French, lexical variation possesses greater importance in signalling socio-stylistic differences than most other European languages (see Lodge 1989). This is evident, for instance, in the present-day speech of adolescents, notably second-generation immigrants from North Africa, who in recent years have cultivated the use of *verlan* and traditional *argot* as an identity shield.

12.4   Summary

If we try now to pull together the various threads we have been spinning across Part 4 and summarise what look to have been the fundamental sociolinguistic developments in Paris over the industrial period, we could say that they show contradictory movements of convergence and divergence. Standardisation pressures and large-scale dialect-levelling in the nineteenth century tended towards the reduction of dialect differences. The presence of weak ties not only exposed the population to standardising influences, but also facilitated the adoption of many levelling changes, notably in the morpho-phonemic system. At the same time, while industrialisation swept aside hierarchies and networks inherited from the proto-industrial past, it also introduced new social groupings, new bonds of solidarity and new sources of conflict. By the mid nineteenth century, class had become an active moulder of urban society. Bourgeoisie and proletariat gravitated to different parts of the city, and the cultural gap between the classes was accentuated. The emergence of industrial-style stratification, starkly opposing capital and labour, pulled in the direction of dialect divergence and resistance to standard norms. The new class-allegiances were reflected, up to a point, in variation in the morpho-phonemic system. However, since much of this variability was being reduced through standardisation and levelling, its capacity to symbolise new identities was diminished. As the period proceeds, therefore, it looks as though a more salient role came to be played by variation in a different part of the language – the lexicon. The 'anti-language' of proto-industrial times was adopted as a badge of predominantly male, working-class identity. Even today, lexical variation continues to play a role in signalling socio-stylistic differences which is arguably greater in French than in most other European languages.

Things were to change again, however, after the Second World War: mass immigration from outside Europe and greatly increased mobility led to a break-up of the industrial class system and the *parigot* associated with it. If the label *le français populaire* designated some sort of social dialect in the first half of the century, during the second half it has come to designate only a style. The fifty years that have elapsed since the end-point examined in this book – 1950 – have shown the speech of the city responding to unprecedented social and demographic change in ways which it would have been impossible to predict (see Peretz 1977; Lennig 1978; Laks 1980). This, however, is a different story.

Conclusion

In this book we have attempted, perhaps rashly, to sketch in the broad outlines of a sociolinguistic history of a great city across eight centuries. At every stage we have been hamstrung by the shortage of relevant data, our difficulties mounting the further we move back from the present day. Sociolinguists tell us that the vernacular is the essence of language, and that urban dialects are invariably vernacular in form. However, by its nature the vernacular is evanescent. Even in the modern world, observing the genuine vernacular is rendered exceptionally difficult by the 'observer's paradox'. In bygone worlds these difficulties multiply exponentially. Like a shy nocturnal beast, the vernacular vanishes as we approach, leaving only the faintest traces of its passage. We can be sure that it has always been around, but we can know pitifully little about what it was like.

Historical sociolinguistics cannot reach levels of certainty achievable in contemporary sociolinguistics. It can never do more than extrapolate from the tiniest of clues, 'join up the dots', make the best of a very bad job. Relevant sociolinguistic data surviving in Paris from the three periods distinguished in this book may be richer than what is found in most European cities, yet, even here, they are nowhere near as conclusive as we would wish. Are they substantial enough to support the claims we have been making?

To help us to piece the fragments together we devised an analytical model which drew parallels between the three phases of industrialisation in Paris and the linguistic processes of koinéisation, reallocation and dialect-levelling. While this model has proved to be robust and helpful, historical model-building remains a dangerous business. There is always the danger of forcing sparse data in directions which they would not necessarily take left to themselves. There is always the danger of over-schematisation, in our case, of shackling too closely the 'phases' with the 'processes' just mentioned. We have indicated that the three dialect-mixing 'processes' we have focused on are in fact on-going ones which are constantly occurring in all speech communities. Our claim here is that they have proceeded at different rates of intensity at different times.

We need to be restrained in what this book can claim to have shown. In the medieval period, back-projecting modern dialect material and correlating

it with the writing system used in thirteenth-century Parisian documents provided fairly strong evidence of koinéisation. However, it did not allow us to
reconstruct the spoken language of the time in anything other than the most
general way, and it did not allow us to say much about sociolinguistic stratification of the city. In the proto-industrial period, the metalinguistic comments
of the grammarians and the literary imitations of low-class speech provide a
clear insight into the way 'good' and 'bad' forms were reallocated in the collective consciousness. However, there survives pitifully little evidence to indicate the socio-stylistic distribution of the variables concerned in actual usage.
Nineteenth-century industrialisation appears to have levelled out the traditional
basilectal dialect of Paris, and to have instituted a new, class-based stratification of language. However, the metalinguistic sources used to demonstrate this,
allied to back-projection of twentieth-century vernacular speech-patterns, do
not allow a very secure image of sociolinguistic variation in the nineteenth-
century city to emerge. Even in a well-documented city like Paris, an accurate multidimensional picture of past linguistic states remains impossible to
draw.

These fairly modest conclusions are not without value, however. Conventional histories of the French language are unidimensional and standard-
oriented, treating language change in a social and demographic vacuum, and as
a process in which 'ordinary speakers' do not participate. This book has shown,
if nothing else, how the speech of Paris has evolved hand in hand with demographic and socio-economic change, how social differences and dialect-mixing
have had a crucial role to play in language change, and how the development of
the standard language in the city can only be fully understood in the context of
the city's vernacular. Language-internal and endogenous explanations of language change may be effective in accounting for the development of 'closed'
dialects spoken in remote and isolated areas. They are quite inadequate when we
come to deal with the language of a great metropolis, where social factors and
dialect-contact assume critical importance. Perhaps the general framework we
have created may now stimulate smaller-scale, more focused studies on some of
the other historical sociolinguistic material in Paris which undoubtedly remains
to be exploited.

Appendix. Literary imitations of low-class speech

TEXT 1

Epistre du biau fys de Pazy par autre que Marot, 1550

(ed. A. Grenier, *Œuvres complètes de Clément Marot*, I, Paris: Nizet, 1977)

Madame, je vous raime tan,
Mais ne le dite pas pourtan;
Les musaille on derozeille.
4 Celui qui fit les gran merveille
Nous doin bien to couché ensemble,
Car je vous rayme, ce me semble,
Si fort que ne vous lore dize,
8 Et vous l'ay bien voulu escrize
Affin de paslé de plus loing.
Pensé que j'avoy bien beroing
De deveni si amouzeu!
12 O que je sesoy bien heuzeu,
Ha! Madame la renchesie,
Se n'est que vostre fachesie,
Non pa pou vou le reprochez,
16 May si to que je veu touchez
Vostre joly tetin molet,
Vou m'appellé peti folet,
En me diran: 'Laissé cela:
20 Vou n'avé rien caché yla;
Dieu, vous deviné mou privé!
Ou pensé vou estre arrivé?'
Et me faite laide grimasse;
24 Et tout ainsi qu'une limasse
Qui ses deu cornuchons retise,
Je me recully san mo dise,
Tou quinau et tout marmiteu.
28 Quan la dame a le cueur [sic] piteu,
C'est une si joyeure chore!
Et, dit le Norman de la Rore,
Si une fille est orgueilleure,

32 C'est une chore pezilleure
    Pour un biau virage
    Qui ne s'en voize egratigné.
    May encore, qu'arié vou gaigné
36 Si j'en mousoy, ou envizon?
    Ha! cœur plu dur qu'un potizon,
    Tant tu me donne de travau!
    Si tu sçaviez sen que je vau,
40 Tu feriez de moi plus gran feste.
    J'ay eu le pry de l'arbalestre:
    Je chante comme un pazoquet;
    Je ne voua jamais san bouquet;
44 J'ay plus de bonnets que de teste;
    J'ay mon biau pourpoint des gran feste,
    Des jour ouvrié et des dimanche;
    Tou les moy deu chemire blanche,
48 Pour estre ny salle ny ort;
    J'ay este jusques à Nyort
    Deja deu fois pour voys le monde.
    Il est vrai que voureste blonde
52 Et aussi blanche comme laict;
    Et aussi je ne suy pas laid,
    Car chacun me dit en maint lieu:
    'Adieu, haut le biau fy, adieu!
56 Adieu hau! respon, si tu veu,
    Le bieau fy au jaune cheveu!'
    Je croi que tresbien il entende,
    Car j'ai les cheveu qui me pende
60 Dessus la chemire froncée;
    La petite jambe toussée
    Pour dansez haye de Bretaigne
    Et les passepié d'Allemaigne.
64 Il est vray qu' à la basse dance
    Je n'y vien pa à la cadance;
    May le branle et puy la recouppe
    Des deu pié je les vou recouppe
68 Menu comme chair à pasté.
    Le fy de Guillaume Gasté
    Au pri de moi n'est qu'un canar.
    J'en veu bien croize Jan Benar
72 Ou Chanin, à qui Dieu pardoin.
    A propo, vou souvien ty poin
    Du jour de la Sin Nicoula,
    Que j'étien tou deux si tresla
76 D'avoir dancé? Vous commensite,
    Aussi trébien vou rachevite.
    C'est au jardin: mon pese entry,
    D'avantuze me recontry

80 Auprés de vous, et sy avoy
    Touriou l'yeu dessu vostre voy
    Laquelle me sembly depui
    Aussi claize que l'iau de puy.
84 May se Piar nos regardet,
    Qui de gran jalourie ardet;
    Et quan il m'eu bien espié,
    Vou me marchiste sur le pié
88 Si fort, en me sarran la main,
    Que j'en clochy le lendemain.
    Pour vous respondre, mon amy,
    J'ay veu vostre lettre à demy,
92 Car mon mazy lor arrivit,
    Qui en la lirant me trouvit,
    Et Dieu scet si je fu fachée.
    J'eusse voulu estre ecorchée,
96 Parmanda voize toute morte.
    May ce que plu me reconforte,
    C'est que mon mazy n'en vy rien,
    Et aussi que je sçay tro bien
100 Qui n'en eu pas esté conten.
    Notre aprenti vin ecoutan
    Pour ouy ce qui me diset.
    May mon pauvre cueur souspiset
104 De gran douleur et de tristesse.
    Si je n'eusse este la maistresse,
    Mon amy, j'estetz affolée.
    Votre lettre m'a consolée
108 Quan j'ai connu que m'aymer tan;
    Je ne le veux croize pourtan
    Car les homme son tou trompeu,
    Et les femmes on touriour peu
112 D'estre par leu dits aburée,
    J'enten qui ne son pas rurée.
    Et de moy, la mercy à Dieu,
    Je puy bien allez en tou lieu
116 Et frequentez parmy le monde.
    Vou me dites que je suis blonde,
    May je cray qui vous plait à dise;
    Aussi je ne m'en foua que rise;
120 Si sui je comm' une autre belle.
    Vous m'escrivé que suis rebelle:
    Et quan vou me voulé touchez,
    Que je ne vous laisse aprochez:
124 Il est bien vrai que je men fache,
    Car une belle dame cache
    Tou les jour et le plus souven
    Son biau tetin et son devan.

128   Par votre lettre vous vanté
       Que comme un oyreau vou chante:
       Je vous respon qu'en sui bien ayre;
       Car quan je sezets à mallaire
132   Vostre chan me resjouyset.
       Un jour mon mazy me diset
       Qui voudroit sçavoir le musicle,
       Pour la chanté en la bouticle.
136   Vou me mandé par vostre lettre
       Qu'avez le pri de l'abalestre,
       Et qu'este for propre et mignon,
       Touriour vestu comme un oignon,
140   Don en cela vou m'avé fait
       Un singulier plaisir parfait;
       Car c'est l'honneur d'un biau jeune homme
       d'avoir habillemen gran somme,
144   Et aussi que c'est la raison
       Qu'un biau fy de bonne maison
       Set touriour fort bien accoustré.
       De ma par, je vouray montré,
148   Si vouravé bonne memoise,
       Notre jeu de bille d'ivoize
       Et ma zobbe d'un fin dra noir.
       Vous varriez, si voulé veoir,
152   Tou mes manchesons de velour,
       Mes solié qui ne son pas lour
       Pour enjamber nostre ruissiau,
       Et ma cotte de dra de Siau
156   Bien teinte, que me la donna
       Le sise Jean, quan ordonna
       Et voulut par son testamen
       Que je l'eusse soudainemen.
160   Ha! si j'estien tou deu ensemble,
       Je vous contesoy, se me semble,
       Cen mille bon peti prepo.
       Toute nui je per le repo,
164   Tan et si fort en vou je pense;
       Je ne set quelle recompense
       Vous m'en fesez; si suis je seuse
       Que n'atten maintenant que l'heuse
168   Que vous revenez de Lyon.
       Vous me donrez un million
       De biau cordon de saye fine,
       Pour en donner en ma voisine,
172   Laquelle à vou se recommande.
       Autre chore ne vou demande
       Qu'autant en un mot comme en cent
       Qu'a vour aymé mon cœur consent,

176   Vou supplian, mon douramy,
       N'estre à me respondre endormy,
       Si ne vené bien to icy,
       Car je sesetz en gran souci,
180   Si je n'avetz de vo nouvelle.
       Je prie à Dieu qui seynt telle
       Que pour vrai je les vou desise,
       Et à tant fesay fin d'escrise.
184   C'est de Pazy ce jour et an
       Que je m'en ally droit a Lan.

TEXT 2

***Nouveaux Complimens de la place Maubert, des Halles, Cimetière S.-Jean,
Marché Neuf, et autres places publiques. Ensemble la résjouissance des
harengères et poissonnières faite ces jours passés au gasteau de leurs
Reines, Paris, 1644***

(ed. E. Fournier, *Variétés historiques et littéraires*, pp. 229–39. Paris: Jannet, 1859)

DES POISSONNIÈRES ET DES BOURGEOISES

LA BOURGEOISE *Parlez, ma grand'amie, vostre marée est-elle fraiche?*

LA POISSONNIÈRE Et nennin, nennin, laissez cela là, ne la patené pas tan;
       nos alauzes sont bonnes, mais note raye put; je panse qu'aussi bien fait
4   vote barbue.

LA BOURGEOISE *Je ne m'offense pas . . .*

LA POISSONNIÈRE Ouy, Madame a raison, le guieble a tort qu'il ne la prend;
       il est vray que j'avon le mot pour rire et vous le mot pour pleuré.

8 LA BOURGEOISE *Mamie, donnons trêve . . .*

LA POISSONNIÈRE Vois en poirez en un mot traize francs. Et me regardez
       l'oreille de ce poisson là: il est tout sanglant et en vie. Est-il dodu! et qui
       vaut bien mieux bouté là son argent qu'à ste voirie de raye puante qui sant
12   le pissat a pleine gorge.

LA BOURGEOISE *Je voy bien qu'il est excellent . . .*

LA POISSONNIÈRE Parle, hé! Parrette! N'as-tu pas veu madame Crotée,
       mademoiselle du Pont-Orson, la pucelle d'Orléans! Donnez-luy blancs
16   draps, a ste belle espousée de Massy, qui a les yeux de plastre! Ma foy!
       si ton fruict desire de notre poisson, tu te peux bien frotter au cul, car ton
       enfant n'en sera pas marqué!

UN POURVOYEUR *Ma bonne femme, n'avez-vous point là de bon saumon*
20   *frais?*

LA POISSONNIÈRE Samon framan! du saumon frais! en vous en va cueilly,
       Parrette! Ste viande-là est un peu trop rare. Ce ne sont point viande pour

nos oyseux: car j'iré bouté de seize à dix-huict francs à un meschant
24   saumon, et vous m'en offrirez des demy-pistoles. Et nennin, je ne somme
pas si babillarde; je n'avon pas le loisi d'allé pardre note argent pour donné
des morciaux friands a monsieur a nos despens. Si vous voulez voir un
sot mont, allez vous en sur la butte de Montmartre, note homme dit que
28   c'est un sot mon: car darnièrement, quand il estet yvre, il se laissit tombé
du haut en bas, et si cela ne l'y coustit rien.

LE POURVOYEUR *Vous vous raillez donc ainsi des* . . .

LA POISSONNIÈRE J'en ay une belle et une bonne; mais, par ma fiyguette!
32   je la garde pour note homme: c'est pour son petit ordinaire; il se rirole
comme t'y faut.

LE POURVOYEUR *Ce n'est pas cela que je* . . .

LA POISSONNIÈRE Un peu, si vous le trouvez bon! Je pance, marcy de ma
36   vie! que j'en pouvon bien avoir, y nous en couste bon et bel argent, bien
plaqué, bien escrit, marqué et compté en preuf à deux. Monsieur, vla l'vote
peti faict, comme dit l'autre, sans aler aux halles.

LE POURVOYEUR *Elle me semble bonne* . . .

40   LA POISSONNIÈRE Sans vous surfaire la marchandise d'un degné, elle vous
coutra, au dernié mot, trente sous, à la charge qu'elle est frache et bonne,
et me l'emportés.

LE POURVOYEUR *Quelle apparence y a-t-il que je paye* . . .

44   LA POISSONNIÈRE En despit soit fait du beau marchand de marde! Hé! je
pense qu'ou estes enguieblé! Allez, de par tout les guiébles! a vote joly
collet, porté vote argent au trippes! Vous ayrez du mou pour vote chat.
Pence-vous que je soyen icy pour vos biaux rieux? Aga! ce monsieu crotté,
48   ce guièble de frelempié, ce pauvre poissart, ce detarminé à la pierrette! Y
voudret bien porter des bottes à nos despans, ce biau monsieu de neige et de
bran! Parlé hau, monsieur de trique et nique, parlé! Parlé, parlé, monsieu
de Trelique-Belique! Aga ce monsieu faict à la haste, ce monsieu si tu
52   l'est, ce dégouté, ce jentre en goust! Parlé, Jean de qui tout se mesle et
rien ne vient à bout! Ce taste-poulle, le guièble scait le benais et le fret
au cu! Parlé, ho Dadouille! Helà! qui la chaut! y su, ma foi! Ira-ty, le
courtau? Parné-le. Parné-le, il a mangé la marde! Vien, vien, voicy une
56   raye derrière moy au service de ton nez! Allé! Marci, guiene, va cherché
une teste de mouton cornue qui pura comme vieille charogne, et de pances
et des caillettes plaine de gadou! Encore faura-ty qu'en ait la patience qui
ne scait point de jours maigres! Jésune, jésune, jusqu'à la coquefredouille,
60   pleure-pain, et ne t'attans pas de mangé de la marée ce carresme à nos
despens: car tu n'en airas pas, si je ne m'abuse bien, ny toy ny ès autres!
Nostre-dince, et qui m'a baillé st'alteré-là?

Vla qui me porte ben la mène d'un godenos. Tené, vla Pierre Dupuis,
64   vla laquet. Est-y creté! L'effronté! il est encore tout estourdy du batiau.

Hé! qu'est-ce? Je pence, ma foy, qu'i nous trouve belle? Y nous regarde
tant qu'i peu a tou ses deu rieux. Voyez st'écuyé de cuisaine à la douzaine,
le vla aussi estonné tout ainsi que s'il estet cheu des nues. Y! Allons!
68 lra-t-elle, la pauvre haridelle? Fricassé-luy quatre oeufs. Le vela arrivé!
Quand s'en retournera-t'y? Par la mercy de ma vie! ce tu ne t'oste de
devan moy, je t'iray la devisagé! Ne pense pas que je me mocque!

  LE POURVOYEUR *En vérité, je ne m'ébahis plus si le peuple commun vous*
72 *appelle . . .*

  UNE AUTRE POISSONNIÈRE Samon, ma foy! vela un homme bien vuide
pour tourner quatre broche! Vo nous en velé bien conté! Vote mère grand
est en fiancaille. N'a vou point veu Dadais, vendeur de fossets? Tené,
76 vla Guillemin croque-solle, carleux de sabots. Donnez ste marée pour la
moitié moins qu'elle nous couste! Vrament! c'est pour vote nez! Ma foy!
ce ne sert pas là le moyen de porté bague d'or aux doigts ny de donné
des riche mariage à nos filles. Aguieu, Jocrisse! Qu'on s'oste bien vite de
80 devant note marchandise, sur peine d'avoir du gratin!

   Vostre très-humble et affectionné serviteur.
   Le Boiteux,
   Dit le Beau Chanteur

TEXT 3

Agréables Conférences de deux paysans de Saint-Ouen et de Montmorency sur les affaires du temps, 1649–51

(ed. F. Deloffre, Paris: Les Belles Lettres/Annales de l'Université de Lyon, 1999)

CONFÉRENCE V − PIAROT

Hé ban n'importe cest une tache douile, ça sen va à la leuscivre. Mai say tu
ban que je revinme jesque dan nout vilage: bon jou bon soir, je ne sçay san
que tu devins, je m'en alli sous l'orme, où je trouvi nout vilage amassé qui
4 m'attendien pour var le zerticle de la Paix. Dé que je fu venu, nan lé baiy à
luise à Colin, qui lui queme un Ange, quer y chante l'Eupitre queme un enragé,
quan y leust luy tou depi un bou jesqu'a l'outre, vla tou le monde qui se boutte
a marmuze: voize diset lun, vla ban opezé, je some ban planté pour rvardi, nou
8 vla tretou oussi gras que de liau; queman sdiset loutre, ne vlati pas la taye à cu,
morgué je nan poigeron poen ce quarquié cy; ban entandu slidije, quer jay beu
l'argen de mon viau, je nan poigeray poen; ty es laisti chouar sdit le receveux,
stu nas poen doutre chifflet ton chian est pardu, nan ne tan rabattra pas une
12 oborle, lui ce placart tou ton sou, si tu li trouve je veux que nan me pele la
berbe. Enfen je feme luize é reluize, é à la parfen nan conclui qui nan jazet rian,
é qui diset an seuleman que le Rouay an fezait sn'infirmation pour y prouvoar

selon Guieu é rairon. Là dessu nan tin consey, é nan regoulu qui faillet éluize
16   deux depité pour aller faize leu harangle au Rouay, pour ly preché nout misere,
é ly demandé la remission de la taye pour la moiquié d'un an; là dessu y fu
quesquion de lé lomé é de choiri le pu caplabe, morgué je quemance a me cazé
a tou mon biau pourpoen vioulet, a rebroucher mon cappiau & ma moustache,
20   é bouté la main su lé roignon, güian nan de targi gueze à méluize aveu courain
Guillot, aveu qui jon eté Margouillé dan nout Parouesse, a fin de party é quan?
Le landemain drès le poitron jaquet, Dame tan que la ni fu longue, je ne cloi pas
lieu, je ne fesas que ruminé à par mouay la belle embleme que je devas faize
24   au Rouay; enfen dres que le jour luisi, je fi bouttre un biau bast tou clinquan
neu à nout juman, là dessu le guiebe me tenti de bouttre dé botte de couir une
foua en ma vie, nout Greffié men pretti de vieille boucanée é dure queme du fé,
guian y faillu ban dé machene pour en choussé une, enfen a li entri; mai quen
28   ce vin à la jambe gouche, ou j'ay evu grace à Guieu lé lous, je pensy regnié ma
vie, quer nan me declaqui la cheville du pié, é si je ne peume jamai en veni à
bou; la dessu nan voulut dechoussé l'outre, mai ce fu ban pi, nan me fit crié lé
hau cri, le couraen Guillot savisi de la couppé su le coudre du pié, mai en la
32   voulant fandre y me fi une grande balafre su la jambe: y faillu enfen la laissé, &
bouttre une gestre à loutre jambe; nou vla don monté à chevau su nout juman,
le courin Guillot se boutti su le bast, je me plaqui driere son cu; mai ce fut ban
pis, nout fieux Jaquet se bouti a braize queme un anragé qui vlet var le Rouai,
36   le Couraen ne le vlet pas, mai nout Parette fesi si ban qualle le fesi grimpé su
le crouppion de nout beste, nou vla don partis, montez queme dé sain Georges,
mai je neume pas fait ven pas que nout juman qui est un peu quenteuse, sentant
Jacquet qui li chatouillet le driere fi une cabriole é nou plaqui tout tras dans
40   une maze, morgué jetas pi qu'anragé de var mé biau zabi tout fangeux, y faillu
nou depouié nu queme la main pour sché no hardre; stanpandan je consultion
su qualle voatuze jyrion a sain Gearmain, Guillot vlet pranre sn'asne, mai nout
Greffié li di que nan se moquezait de li, é qu'nan le pranrait pour le depité de
44   Vaugirard; la dessu je me resouveni que lé depité du Parleman y avient eté en
coche. Je mavisi don datlé nout juman à la charrette à Georget, jy boutti une
belle couvartuze varte, é je monteme tou deux dedans, é nout fieux Jaquet su
la beste, guian y nous feset biau var allé queme en triomphle, nan nou conduisi
48   jesque au chemin de Suresne, é pi je feume à la grace de Guieu; quan je feume
à mi chemin je mavisi de demandé au couren Guillot san qui vlet dize au Rouai,
morgué sdity parle stu veux, guiebe emporte si je di un petit mo; parguiene sli
dije stu ne jaze je ne dizay rian; jarnigué sdity c'est tay qu'an a lomé le primié,
52   y fau que tu chante ton ramage, Dame sa me boutti ban an transe, quer je ne
mattendais pas de jazé tou seu; enfen pourtant je m'enhardissi, é je di en par
mouai: morgué Piarot de quay as tu peu, tas ban parle à dé Preridan, é ta peu
de parlé au Rouai, a ti pas dé zouseilles queme tai, oncor ne sont elles pas si
56   grandes, va di tou san que tas su le cœuz, tes pu sage que tu ne panse, pargué

je devin tout é cou regoulu queme Bertol: Mai pourtan afen de n'estre pas pris
sans var, je mavisi darté nout charette, je devali aveu nout fieux Jaquet, é jli
di: Jaquet pran que tu sas sas le Rouai, je men va te faire m'n'emblesme; y se
60 plaqui don su son cu, é mouai je man vins li faize le pié de viau, je me deffuli é
li ytou, é pi jli di: sans cezimounie, Monseu le Rouai, reboutton nout cappiau;
voise, sdit Guillot, Monseu le Rouai vla ban debuté.

. . .

TEXT 4

La Gazette des Halles touchant les affaires du temps, 1649

(Bibliothèque Mazarine, ms. 10482/ ms. 12965)

[p. 3] Comere enfin parguieu je pense
L'on monstré à son Eminence
Comme sa hautez nous deplais,
4   L'en on dit deux mots au palais
parguié j'en sommes deveuglée
J'en voulons faire une vallée
S'il aime tant d'estre Emenant,
8   A Mon-Faucon soit y pendant
Nen le verra de tou la ville
C'est un lieu haut & bien utille
Pour tous les gens de sa façon,
12 Qui caressent plus un garçon
Qu'ils ne ferient de belles filles,
Si je tenien ses triquebilles,
Je les doriens a nos matous.
16 J'espargneriens autant de mous,
Mais j'appercoy une marchande
Madame voyez ma limande
A vous besoin de macriaux,
20 J'en avons de frais & de biaux
Ma marchandise est toute en vie
[p.4] Le coust ly en fait perdre l'envie,
Revenons a nos partuisans
24 Qui voulien que nox preridens
N'eussions point de voix au chapitre
Je lieus avons rendu leur tiltre
Comme il avien par le passé
28 Sans qu'on lieux ait rien effacé
Et si j'obtiendron leu demande
Fut elle encor tra fois plus grande
Aga parguieu je le voulon
32 Et c'est ainsin que je parlon
Si je vendons de la morue
En son-je nous moins absolue

Tesmoin le curé que j'ons fait,
36 Voulez-vous voir un plus beau traict
    Nous avons demandé Brouselle
    On l'apporte sur notre selle
    L'en voulon a ce porteur d' iaus
40 Y fra bien de quitter ses fiaux
    Qu'il dise que je son des filles
    Si je ne tenons nos paroles
    Comme a ce petit meurtrier
44 Ce voisin de l'Isle Louvier
    Qui fuyoit de nostre colere,
    Ce petit venu de notaire
    Car Jour de Guieu je luy montrons
48 Que nos mary ne son poltrons
    Qu'ils ont bien autant de vaillance
    Que luy & tout son alliance
    [p. 5] Et si j'avon le petrina
52 Aussi prompt qu'à son arcena
    Que la peste soit la bougra[i]lle
    Ce ne sont ma foy rien qui vaille,
    Mais dison comme l'autre dit
56 Hors du peuple est de Dieu maudit
    Je menerien bien les affaires
    Si le bon Roy nous laissit faire,
    Car j'avons veu téz qu'on nous voit
60 Le troisiesme reigne de Roy,
    Helas tesmoin monsieu son pere
    C'estoit un homme sans colere,
    Un homme qui auroit eu de nou
64 usques à nos mouchois de cou,
    Quand je dirois nostre chemise
    En bonne foy je l'eussien mise,
    Dieu luy fasse paix et pardon
68 En fin pour vous faire cour don
    Il nous voulien mettre en brassiere
    Mais je ne nous en soucion guere.
    Arrive tout s'en qui pourra
72 S'il faut se battre il le faura
    Bon courage ma camarade
    Faison nou une barricade
    Alentour de nostre bacquet
76 De bons gros bros de vin clairet
    Pour toxin nous prendron le varre
    Et puis nous boiron, tant que tarre
    laison voir peté le rena
80 Et Guieu sur tou, dit l'armoina.
    FIN

TEXT 5

Sarcelades, 1764

(N. Jouin, *Le Vrai Recueil des Sarcelles, mémoires, notes et anecdotes*. 2 vols. Amsterdam)

A nossigneurs les mitriers ramassés à Paris cheux les Grands Augustins
Au mouas de Mai 1748.

Gn'a pas mal de tems, Nossigneurs, que j'ons aieu l'honneur de vous faire present d'une magnière de petit Sarmon que j'avions affuté pour Monsigneur l'Archeveque à la Coque. L'an nous a dit du depis que vous l'aviais quasiment louangé. Je n'en ons pas battu nos femmes pour ça, comme vous pensez. Parguié pis donc que vlà qu'est comme ça, j'ons rumainé à par nous & j'ons pensé que falloit core vous bailler sti-là que je venons de bredouiller à Monsigneur de Biaumont du Repaire, notre nouviau Minitrier.

Vous connoissez bian un çartain Pichon, Jésuite, qu'a fait moûler un Livre de son ingégnure, par lequeul il voudroit bian nous damner tretous, en nous faisant commégnier à bis & à blanc, & aveuc pas plus de çarimonies & de façons, que pour avaler une preune. Ce Pichon crayoit que tout le monde alloit bonnement bailler dans le panniau, & que j'allions tretous le suivre en enfar, en commegniant à sa mode; mais du guiantre si la plus moindre personne en a tant seulement aieu la pensée! Le Belïtre, tidié, a trouvé à qui parler! Voyant donc qu'il avoit compté sans son hôte, & que queuques-uns de vous autres aviont damé le pion comme il faut, & pis craignant, voyez-vous, que toute la bande des Mitriers n'allït li char le dos, dame! il s'est avisé de faire semblant de se dédire. Il a écrit une lettre à Monsigneur de Biaumont, comme par laqueulle il dit qu'il se dédit. Monsigneur de Biaumont qui, depuis que je l'avons, n'a pas tant seulement core dessarré les dents, pour nous dire un mot du bon Guieu, & qui nianmoins l'avoit si balle dans toute ste gabaire ici, pour nous bailler un plat de son méquier, s'est contenté de nous faire vendre bian char deux ou trois mots de lettre, moûlés cheux Simon son Mouleux, où il nous dit pour tout potage, que je devons tre bian éguifiés de vouar un Jésuite qui ne barguaine point à dire qu'il s'est trompé, & qui le dit core, Guieu fait comme & parce qu'il n'a pas pu faire autrement. Parguié vlà-t-il pas de quoi bian s'éguifier!

C'est donc sus ça que je li ons agencé notre Sarmon. Vous vouarrez-mon, Mossigneurs, si ça parle comme il faut. Il est bian vrai que gn'en a biaucoup de vous autres, Mossigneurs, qui n'avont guère fait mieux; d'autres qu'avont core fait pire; & pis d'autres qui n'avont rian fait du tout; & c'est justement & i a point de cause de a, que je venon vous bailler le Sarmon que je li lavons fait. Si vous vous connoissez bian vous-mêmes, si vous croyez un brin en Guieu, vous en ferez votre profit, tout comme s'il s'addressoit à vous, Vous déferez ce que vous avez fait, et vous ferez ce que vous n'avez pas fait. Je nous en tenons là, & je ne vous disons pas davantage.

Notre Sarmon, si vous le luisez, comme je crayons bian que oui, vous dira le reste.

Aguieu, Mossigneurs les Mitriers, je vous ferons tout ce que vous voudrez, quand vous ferez tout ce que vous devez être.

Harangue . . . . Prononcée le 5 Avril 1748.

> Parguié, Monsigneur de Biaumont,
> Je crairions vous faire un affront,
> Si j'étions venus à la Ville
> 4 Vouar Monsigneur de Ventremille,
> Quand il étoit où vous velà,
> Et que je vous laissassions là,
> Sans venir en carimonie
> 8 Vous dire que je sous en vie,
> Et vous ôter notre chapiau;
> Ça ne seroit ni bian, ni biau.
> Vous n'avez pas une bedaine,
> 12 Comme il avoit, mais votre maine,
> Comme une autre, vaut bian son prix;
> Et mêmement dans tout Paris
> Gn'en a guère de plus drolettes,
> 16 Mais vous êtes comme vous êtes,
> Ça n'y fait rian; gros ou menu,
> Grand, ou petit, drait ou tortu;
> Bonjour, Monseigneur Ventremille,
> 20 Je sommes venus a la ville
> Gaillards et dispos, Guieu marci.
> Vous vous portez fort bien aussi,
> Comme an voit a votre frimouze
> 24 Qu'an prendroit pour une talmouze.
> Ça nous fait un fort grand plaisir
> De vouar comme ça reussir
> Ceux qu'ont soin de vous faire vivre.
> 28 Que le bon Guieu donc les delivre
> De tout mal, de tout ennui,
> Car an en a bian aujourd'hui . . .
> Vous ne savez pas, palsanguiene
> 32 Monseigneur, ce qui nous amene?
> Je venons tretout en troupiau
> Pour vous oter notre chapiau,
> Et pour vous dire, ne vous deplaise,
> 36 Que vous nous avez fait bian aise
> En nous otant notre curé.

TEXT 6

Discours Prononcé au roy, par un paysan de Chaillot, 1744

(Bibliothèque Mazarine, ms. 103555)

Sire, excusez la libarté,
De Chaillot je sis député,
Pour vous faire la révérence
4   Sur vote bon retour en France.
Vous vous portez mieux, Guieu-marci:
Je nous portons fort bian aussi.
Jesus! Que j'avons eu d'allarmes,
8   Et que j'avons varsé de larmes,
Quand la gazette nous apprit
Que vous étiais malade au lit.
Las! quand notre Pasteur au Prône
12 Recommandit vote Parsonne,
Tout aussi tôt chacun de nous
Se prosternit à deux genoux,
Et dit d'une voix unanime,
16 Mon Guieu, de ce Roy Maggnianime,
Que j'aimons mieux qu'argent comptant,
Quoique l'aimions biaucoup pourtant,
Ne tarminez la destinée
20 Qu'au bout de la centiéme année;
Après cela qu'en Paradis,
Il s'en aille, j'en sons d'avis;
Mais présentement rian ne presse,
24 Que vote bonté nous le laisse,
Jusqu'à ce que sous j'en serons,
Long-tems encore je l'aurons.
Enfin grace à la sainte Viarge,
28 A qui j'avon brûlé maint ciarge,
Vous vela guari tout-à-fait,
Dont j'ons le cueur bian satisfait.
Si vous saviais la joie & l'aise
32 Que j'avons eu, par parentese,
Quand j'aprîmes que vous étiés
Guai, gaillard dessus vos deux piés. . . .
Mais jà vous le sçavez peut-être,
36 Chacun a mis sius sa fenêtre,
Des escargots de lampions:
On a chanté des Te dions:
Et pis j'avons à la taverne
40 Bû, non pas de l'iau de citerne,
Ni de l'iau de Seine non pus,

Mais du piot du pere Bacchus,
Criant cent fois à toute outrance,
44   Vive note bon Roy de France.
Nicolas note Magister
Fit sur un genti peti air,
Un Rondiau touchant vote gloire,
48   Avec un biau refrain à boire:
Jarnigois à vote santé
Je l'avons diablement chanté.
J'avons queuque légiere envie,
52   De vous en envoyer copie
Ecrite par eun Imprimeux,
Ou bian eun habile Graveux,
Mais note Réverend Vicaire
56   Nous conseillit de n'en rien faire,
En nous disant que de Paris
Une bande de biaux espris,
Vous aviant rompu les oreilles
60   De mille fadaises pareilles:
Et qu'ils s'étions donné le mot
A qui paroîtroit le plus sot.
La chose étant ainsi, je pense,
64   Que j'avons fait avec prudence,
De renguainer note Rondiau,
Dont le fredon est pourtant biau.
A pourpos, est-il bian vray, SIRE,
68   Ce que j'avons entendu dire?
On dit des marveilles de vous:
On dit que vous alliais aux coups,
Ni pus ni moins qu'un mousquetaire.
72   Par ma fi, c'est trop téméraire,
Et je prenons la libarté
D'en blâmer vote MAJESTE.
Saves-vous morgué que ces bales
76   Souventes fois sont des brutales;
Qui ne vous respecterions pas
Pus qu'un de vos moindres soldats?
Que seroit-ce si d'aventure,
80   Vous atrapiais queuque blessure,
Qui borgne ou boîteux vous rendît
Ou roide mort vous étendît?
Eh! Jerni par la sainte ampoule,
84   Jette-t-on les bons Rois au moule?
Hélas! Que ferions-nous sans vous?
Je serions au gobet des loups:
J'entens, de la Gendarmerie
88   De la Souveraine d'Hongrie,
Très-sainte Viarge, *Io benigna!*

Gardés-nous de ces ogres-là.
Et vous, note Auguste Monarque,
92 Comme le patron de la Barque,
Par charité consarvez-vous,
Sinon pour vous, au moins pour nous.
Quand retournerez en Campagne
96 (Où le bon Guieu vous accompagne,)
De vote Parsonne ayez soin,
Baïez l'ennemi de pus loin:
C'est la grace qu'on vous demande,
100 Et que l'on tiendra pour très-grande;
Car tant que vous serez vivant
Il n'opérera que du vent.
Adieu, SIRE, je me retire;
104 Ne sçachant pus trop que vous dire;
Sinon que je sis de bon coeur,
Vote Sujet & Sarviteur.

GUILLOT LE BEDAUT

TEXT 7

Lettres de Montmartre, 1750

(A. Coustelier, alias 'Jeannot Georgin', published 'à Londres')

LETTRE V – AU PROCUREU FISCAL

Je vous on promis, Monssieu mon parrain, de vous dire par paroles griffonées
sur Lettres queuques choses de mon voyage, j'allons vous les conter tout fin
dres comme je les on vûes; j'ons pris la voiture de l'iau: morguié que ceu
4 terrain est traite! Car voyés vous bian mon parrain, quand je sommes partis
du pied du Pont Royal, j'allions ç'atoit eune marveille, le plus biau tems nous
accompagnit jusques aux îles, an les nomme comme ça les îles maquerelles:
mais palsanguié je n'eumes pas sitôt passé en avant que velà que le Ciel se
8 boutit à nous aclairer comme si je n'eussions vû goute, & à gronder, je ne
sçavons contre qui. Je l'aurions morguié bian tanu quitte de son charivari, &
tous ceux-là qui voyagiant aveuc moi itou; je dansîmes comme les milles, j'en
avions stapendant si peu d'envie, que je nous recommandîmes tous à tous les
12 Saints du Paradis; tant y a, que la mer, n'est-ce pas, fait vomir? Ma fique alle se
fit tout le contraire: J'eumes tretous un trémoussement qui parfumit le baquiau
faut sçavoir; mais an ne sent rian quand an a peur de trépasser; je n'ons jamais
tant cru bere trop d'iau; & moi donc qui n'aimons pas à en bere de peur qu'alle
16 ne se sit faute aux moulins; j'allions stapendant comme le bon Guieu vouloit;
chacun & chacune itou marmotoit à par soi entre ses dents son En manu, quand

tout d'un coup je nous crûmes dedans: dame, chacun se boutit à crier Guieu sçait comme, & vomir itou, mais faut sçavoir comment da; j'arrivîmes stapendant
20 maugré les grondemens du Ciel à un Pont; je demandimes ce queu c'étoit, queu ça, un Moussieu qui étoit bian sçavant me répondit comme ça queu c'étoit le Pont de Savre; vous qui sçavés la Geografi, vous sçavés itou ceu Pont-là. Ah morguié! si j'y ratourne que l'an m'y fesse, comme dit le Provarbe, j'aimons
24 le planché des vaches; m'est avis que l'an est plus en cartitude de sa vie. Ah morguié! l'iau a des bargignages qui ne me plaisaint pas. Enfin tant y a qu'après biaucoup de peine, sans compter la peur j'arrivîmes à tarre. Chacun tirit de son côtié aveuc l'infaction de son vomissement; j'allîmes dret à Varsaies, mon
28 Guieu, queu Châtiau! j'ons resté troas jours à ste fin de le voar tout anquié, & si Guieu me le pardonne, je croians que je n'en ont pas vû le quart: queu de chambres, queu d'images, queu d'hommes, & des femmes de piarre, de marbre. J'ons cru voar le Paradis. Oh! pour stila si, comme dit Moussieu le
32 Curé, le Paradis est plus biau que ce qui est biau, il doit être bian biau. J'ons vû le Roy, je l'on d'abord reconnu; j'ons dit dret que je l'on vû, c'est ly morguié, & stapendant sa parsonne n'a jamais été apperçue à Montmaitre; il m'a regardé da, Moussieu mon parrain, mais morguié il ne m'a dit rian, je sis faché qu'il ne
36 m'ait pas au moins donné queuques paroles par-ci par-là; jarniguié que je les aurois consarvé, c'est queuque chose de biau que les paroles d'un Roy, n'est-ce pas, Moussieu mon parrain? Car ce qui est biau est rare: vous ne sçavés rian encore da; j'ons entendu la Messe, une grande bande de Moussieux & de
40 violloneux chantiaint comme ça, vous auroit ébaubi; que ste Messe doit faire plaisir au bon Guieu. J'ons vû la Roine, Madame la Dauphine & Monsigneur le Dauphin itou, queu biau Chrequien! Oh! pour ça il étions bian le fils de Moussieu son pere, & Madame la Dauphine qui est grosse itou d'un enfant qui
44 sara bian itou le fils de Monssieu son mari; je les on on vûs manger tretous; je sis fâché morguié qu'an mangiant comme nous autes aveuc les dents & la bouche, ils n'avalions que de l'iau; je n'aimons pas leur magniere de bere; je sis pour stila leur sarviteur; je la laissons aux granouilles, & pis s'ils m'aviaint
48 parlé de vote parsonne, je vous l'envoirions par acriture; mais motus de vous, de moi, de Moussieu mon pere itou. Par ainsi, je sis vote fillau,

JEANNOT GEORGIN

Bibliography

Abécassis, M. 2000. *The Representation of Parisian Speech in the Cinema of the 1930s*. Unpublished doctoral thesis, University of St Andrews.

Académie française. 1673. *Cahiers de remarques sur l'orthographe françoise*, ed. C. Marty-Laveaux, 1863. Paris: J. Gay.

Agnel, E. 1855. *Observations sur la prononciation et le langage rustiques des environs de Paris*. Paris: Schlesinger-Dumoulin.

—— 1870. *De l'Influence du langage populaire sur la forme de certains mots de la langue française*. Paris: Dumoulin.

ALF, see Gilliéron and Edmont (1901–10).

Ambrose, J. 1996. *Bibliographie des études sur le français parlé*. Paris: INaLF.

Andersen, H. 1988. Centre and periphery: adoption, diffusion and spread. In: J. Fisiak (ed.), *Historical Dialectology. Regional and Social*, pp. 39–83. Berlin, New York, Amsterdam: Mouton de Gruyter.

Anderson, L. and Trudgill, P. 1990. *Bad Language*. Oxford: Blackwell.

Antoine, G. and Martin, R. 1985. *Histoire de la langue française 1880–1914*. Paris: Editions du CNRS.

—— (eds) 1995. *Histoire de la langue française 1914–1945*. Paris: Editions du CNRS.

Arickx, I. 1971. En marge du dictionnaire phonétique de H. Michaelis et P. Passy, ou la prononciation d'un Parisien à la fin du siècle passé. *Travaux de linguistique* (Ghent) 2: 187–200.

Ariès, P. 1971. *Histoire des populations françaises*. Paris: Seuil.

Armstrong, N. 2001. *Social and Stylistic Variation in Spoken French*. Amsterdam, Philadelphia: Benjamins.

Autels, G. des 1551. *Replique de G. des Autelz aux furieuses defenses de Louis Meigret*. Lyon: Tournes et Gazeau.

Ayres-Bennett, W. 1987. *Vaugelas and the Development of the French Language*. London: MHRA.

—— 1990a. Women and grammar. *Seventeenth Century French Studies* 12: 5–25.

—— 1990b. Variation and change in the pronunciation of French in the seventeenth century. In: J. N. Green and W. Ayres-Bennett (eds), *Variation and Change in French*, pp. 151–79. London: Routledge.

—— 1996. *A History of the French Language through Texts*. London: Routledge.

—— 2000. Voices from the past. Sources of seventeenth-century spoken French. *Romanische Forschungen* 112: 323–48.

Babelon, J.-P. 1986. *Nouvelle Histoire de Paris: Paris au XVIe siècle*. Paris: Hachette.

Bacon, R. 1859. *Compendium studii philosophiae*, ed. J. S. Brewer. London: Rolls Series.

—— 1897. *The 'Opus Majus' of Roger Bacon*, ed. J. H. Bridges. Oxford University Press.

Bader, H. 1969. *Von der "Francia" zur "Ile-de-France"*. Zurich: Winterthur.

Bairoch, P., Batou, J. and Chèvre, P. 1988. *La Population des villes européennes. Banque de données et analyse sommaire des résultats. 800–1850*. Geneva: Droz.

Balibar, R. 1985. *L'Institution du français*. Paris: PUF.

Ball, R. 2000. *Colloquial French Grammar*. Oxford: Blackwell.

Bar, F. 1960. *Le Genre burlesque en France au XVIIe siècle*. Paris: D'Artrey.

Bauche, H. 1920. *Le Langage populaire*. Paris: Payot.

Beaulieux, C. 1927. *Histoire de l'orthographe française*. Paris: Champion.

Bec, P. 1971. *Manuel Pratique de Philologie romane*. 2 vols. Paris: Picard.

Béchade, H. D. 1981. *Les Romans comiques de Charles Sorel*. Geneva: Droz.

Bell, A. 1984. Language style as audience design. *Language in Society* 13: 313–48.

Bergounioux, G. 1989. Le francien (1815–1914): la linguistique au service de la patrie. *Mots/Les langages du politique* 19: 23–40.

Bernet, C. 1995. Le français familier et populaire à la radio et au cinéma. In: G. Antoine and R. Martin 1995: 191–206.

Beroalde de Verville, F. B. 1610. *Le Moyen de parvenir*. Paris: no publisher named.

Berruto, G. 1983. L'italiano populare e la sempleficazione linguistica. *Vox Romanica* 42: 38–79.

Berthaud, le Sieur 1650. *La Ville de Paris en vers burlesques*. Paris: Veufve G. Loison.

Bèze, T. de 1584. *De Francicae Linguae recta pronuntiatione tractatus*. Geneva: Slatkine Reprints, 1972.

Biber, D. and Finegan, E. (eds) 1994. *Sociolinguistic Perspectives on Register*. Oxford University Press.

Blanche-Benveniste, C. 1997. *Approches de la langue parlée*. Paris: Ophrys.

—— and Jeanjean, C. 1987. *Le Français parlé*. Paris: INaLF.

Bloch, M. 1913. *Les Régions de la France*, IX: *L'Ile de France*. Paris: Bibliothèque de synthèse historique.

Bloch, O. 1928. L'assibilation de *r* dans les patois gallo-romains. *Revue de linguistique romane* 3: 271–4.

Bork, H. D. 1975. 'Néo-français' = français avancé? Zur Sprache Raymond Queneaus. *Romanische Forschungen* 87: 32–5.

—— 1978. Aspects de la langue du paysan dans la littérature française. In: H. Baader (ed.), *Onze Etudes sur l'esprit de la satire*, pp. 179–96. Tübingen: Niemeyer.

Bortoni-Ricardo, S. M. 1985. *The Urbanisation of Rural Dialect Speakers: A Sociolinguistic Study in Brazil*. Cambridge University Press.

Bourcelot, H. 1966. *Atlas linguistique de la Champagne et de la Brie*. Paris: CNRS.

Bourdieu, P. 1983. Vous avez dit 'populaire'? *Actes de la recherche en sciences sociales* 46: 98–105.

Boussard, J. 1976. *Nouvelle Histoire de Paris. De la fin du siège de 885–6 à la mort de Philippe Auguste*. Paris: Hachette.

Bovelles, C. 1533. *Liber de Differentia vulgarum linguarum et Gallici sermonis varietate*. Paris: R. Estienne.

Branca, S. 1983. Les débats sur la variation au milieu du XIXe siècle. *Recherches sur le français parlé* 5: 263–90.

Branca-Rosoff, S. and Schneider, N. 1994. *L'Ecriture des citoyens*. Paris: INaLF (Klincksieck).

Brasseur, P. 1980. *Atlas linguistique de la Normandie*. Paris: CNRS.

Braudel, F. 1981. *Civilization and Capitalism, 15th–18th Century. The Structures of Everyday Life*, trans. S. Reynolds. London: Collins.

Braudel, F. 1986. *L'Identité de la France*. 3 vols. Paris: Arthaud-Flammarion.

Brereton, G. E. and Ferrier, J. M. 1981. *Le Ménagier de Paris*. Oxford University Press.

Brochon, P. 1954. *Le Livre de colportage en France depuis le XVIe siècle*. Paris: Gründ.

Brown, P. and Levinson, S. 1987. *Politeness: Some Universals in Language Usage*. Cambridge University Press.

Bruant, A. 1889–95. *Dans la rue. Chansons et monologues*. 2 vols. Paris: A. Bruant.

—— 1901. *L'Argot au XXe siècle*. Paris: Flammarion.

Brunot, F. 1905–72. *Histoire de la langue francaise*. 13 vols. Paris: A. Colin. Abbreviated to *HLF*.

Buffier, C. 1709. *Grammaire françoise sur un plan nouveau*. Paris: N. Le Clerc.

Burnley, D. 1989. *The Language of Chaucer*. London: Macmillan.

Bury, E. 1996. *Littérature et politesse: l'invention de l'honnête homme 1580–1750*. Paris: PUF.

Cailleau, A. C. 1769. *Le Waux-hall populaire ou Les Fêtes de la Guinguette*. Paris: Cailleau.

Callières, F. de 1693. *Du Bon et Mauvais Usage dans les manières de s'exprimer*. Paris: C. Barbin.

Calvet, L.-J. 1994a. *Les Voix de la ville. Introduction à la sociolinguistique urbaine*. Paris: Payot.

—— 1994b. *L'Argot*. Paris: PUF (Que Sais-Je?).

Caron, E. 1996. Les passions du bas moyen âge français, ou la prise en charge bourgeoise de l'imaginaire chrétien populaire. *Moyen Français* 38: 125–37.

Caron, P. (ed.) 1992. *Grammaire des fautes et français non conventionnel*. Paris: GEHLF, Presses de l'Ecole Normale Supérieure.

Carrier, H. 1982. *La Fronde. Contestation démocratique et misère paysanne. 52 mazarinades*. Paris: EDHIS.

Cauchie, A. 1570. *Grammatica gallica*. Antwerp: Buckwolden.

Cazelles, R. 1972. *Nouvelle Histoire de Paris: Paris de la fin du règne de Philippe-Auguste à la mort de Charles V, 1223–1380*. Paris: Hachette.

Cerquiglini, B. 1991. *La Naissance du francais*. Paris: PUF (Que Sais-Je?).

Chagniot, J. 1988. *Nouvelle Histoire de Paris: Paris au XVIIIe siècle*. Paris: Hachette.

Chambers, J. and Trudgill, P. 1998. *Dialectology*. 2nd edn. Cambridge University Press.

Chartier, R. 1981. La Ville dominante et soumise. In: G. Duby (ed.) 1981: III, 15–285.

Chaurand, J. 1983. Pour l'histoire du mot 'francien'. In: *Mélanges de dialectologie d'oil à la mémoire de R. Loriot*, pp. 91–9. Dijon: ABDO.

—— (ed.) 1999. *Nouvelle Histoire de la langue française*. Paris: Seuil.

Chauveau, J.-P. 1989. *Evolutions phonétiques en gallo*. Paris: CNRS.

Chaytor, J. 1945. *From Script to Print*. Cambridge University Press.

Chédeville, A. 1981. De la cité à la ville. In: G. Duby (ed.), II, 31–181.

Chereau, O. 1628. *Le Jargon ou langage de l'argot réformé.* Paris: Du Carroy.

Chervel, A. 1983. La 'langue parlée' au XIXe siècle. *Recherches sur le français parlé* 5: 163–75.

Cheshire, J. 1982. *Variation in an English Dialect.* Cambridge University Press.

—— 1997. Involvement in 'standard' and 'unstandard' English. In: J. Cheshire and D. Stein (eds), *Taming the Vernacular*, pp. 68–82. London: Longman.

Chevalier, L. 1950. *La Formation de la population parisienne au XIXe siècle.* Paris: INED.

—— 1958. *Classes laborieuses et classes dangereuses pendant la première moitié du XIXe siècle.* Paris: Plon.

—— 1985. *Les Parisiens.* 2nd edn. Paris: PUF.

Chiflet, L. 1668. *Essay d'une parfaite grammaire de la langue françoise.* Paris: Maugé.

Clément, L. 1899. *Henri Estienne et son oeuvre française.* Paris: Picard.

Cohen, G. 1949. *Recueil de farces françaises inédites du XVe siècle.* Cambridge, Mass.: Medieval Academy of America.

Cohen, M. 1987. *Histoire d'une langue: le français.* Paris: Messidor/Editions Sociales.

Colletet, F. 1666. *Les Tracas de Paris.* Paris: A. Rafflé.

Cook, M. 1994. *Dialogues révolutionnaires.* Exeter University Press.

Cotgrave, R. 1611. *A Dictionarie of the French and English Tongues.* London: Islip (reprinted Scolar Press, 1968).

Crowley, T. 1996. *Language in History.* London: Routledge.

Dauzat, A. 1922. *La Géographie linguistique.* Paris: Flammarion.

—— 1927. *Les Patois.* Paris: Delagrave.

—— 1929. *Les Argots.* Paris: Delagrave.

—— 1935. *Où en sont les études du français?* Paris: D'Artrey.

Dees, A. 1980. *Atlas des formes et constructions des chartes françaises du 13ᵉ siècle* (ZRP, Beiheft 178). Tübingen: Niemeyer.

—— 1985. Dialectes et scriptae à l'époque de l'ancien français. *Revue de linguistique romane* 49: 87–117.

—— 1987. *Atlas des formes linguistiques des textes littéraires de l'ancien français* (ZRP, Beiheft 212). Tübingen: Niemeyer.

—— 1988. Propositions for the study of Old French and its dialects. In: J. Fisiak (ed.), *Historical Dialectology* (*Trends in Linguistics*, Studies and Monographs 17), pp. 139–48.

—— 1989. La reconstruction de l'ancien français parlé. In: M. E. H. Schouten and P. T. van Reenen (eds), *New Methods in Dialectology*, pp. 125–33. Dordrecht: Foris.

Delaplace, D. 1998. *Apocope, argot et lexique.* Unpublished doctoral thesis, Université de Lille III.

Delbouille, M. 1962. La notion de 'bon usage' en ancien français. *Cahiers de l'Association Internationale des Etudes Françaises* 14: 10–24.

—— 1970. Comment naquit la langue française? In: *Mélanges offerts à M. Georges Straka*, I, pp. 187–99. Lyon/Strasbourg: Société de linguistique romane.

Deloffre, F. 1954. Notes sur les *Agréables Conférences* en patois parisien (1649–1651). In: *Mélanges offerts à M. Charles Bruneau*, pp. 133–45. Geneva: Droz.

—— (ed.) 1999. *Agréables Conférences de deux paysans de Saint-Ouen et de Montmorency sur les affaires du temps (1649–1651).* New edn with additional bibliography, 1961–98. Paris: Les Belles Lettres.

Delvau, A. 1866, *Dictionnaire de la langue verte*. Paris: Flammarion.

Demaizière, C. 1988. Deux aspects de l'idéal linguistique d'Henri Estienne: Hellénisme et Parisianisme. *Henri Estienne. Cahiers V.L. Saulnier* 5: 63–76.

Descimon, R. 1989. Paris on the eve of Saint Bartholomew: taxation, privilege, and social geography. In: P. Benedict (ed.), *Cities and Social Change in Early Modern France*, pp. 69–104. London: Unwin Hyman.

Desgranges, J. C. L. P. 1821. *Petit Dictionnaire du peuple*. Paris: no publisher named.

De Vries, J. 1984. *European Urbanization 1500–1800*. London: Methuen.

D'Hautel. 1808. *Dictionnaire du bas-langage*. 2 vols. Paris: L. Collin.

Dittmar, N., Schlobinski, P. and Wachs, I. 1988. The social significance of the Berlin urban vernacular. In: N. Dittmar and P. Schlobinski (eds), *The Sociolinguistics of Urban Vernaculars*, pp. 19–43. Berlin: De Gruyter.

Diverres, A. H. 1956. *Le Chronique métrique de Geofroi de Paris*. Paris: Les Belles Lettres.

Dubois, J. (Sylvius) 1531. *In Linguam gallicam isagoge, una cum eiusdem grammatica latino-gallice*. Paris: R. Estienne.

Duby, G. 1980–5. *Histoire de la France urbaine*. 5 vols. Paris: Seuil.

Duez, N. 1639. *Le Vray Guidon de la langue françoise*. Leiden: Elsevier (Geneva: Slatkine Reprints, 1973).

Dumas, L. 1733. *La Bibliothèque des enfants*. Paris: Simon.

Dupâquier, J. *et al.* 1988. *Histoire de la population française*, I: Des *Origines à la Renaissance*. Paris: Presses Universitaires de France.

Durand, M. 1936. *Le Genre grammatical en français parlé à Paris et dans la région parisienne*. Paris: D'Artrey.

Duval, P.-M. 1961. Lutèce gauloise et gallo-romaine. In: G. Michaud (ed.), *Paris. Croissance d'une capitale*, pp. 41–72. Paris: Hachette.

Eloy, J.-M. 1997. *La Constitution du picard: une approche de la notion de langue*. Louvain: Peeters.

Erasmus, D. 1528. *De Recta Latini Graecique Sermonis Pronunciatione*. In: M. Cytowska (ed.), *Opera Omnia Desiderii Erasmi Roterdami*, I.4, pp. 1–103. Amsterdam: North Holland Publ. Co., 1973.

Ernst, G. 1980. Prolegomena zu einer Geschichte des gesprochenen französisch. In: H. Stimm (ed.), *Zur Geschichte des gesprochenen Französisch* (*Zeitschrift für französische Sprache und Literatur*, Beiheft 6), pp. 1–14. Wiesbaden: Franz Steiner.

—— 1985. *Gesprochenes Französisch zu Beginn des 17. Jahrhunderts* (*ZRP*, Beiheft 204). Tübingen: Niemeyer.

—— 1996. Problèmes d'édition de textes à caractère privé des XVIIe et XVIIIe siècles. Unpublished paper read to the *Groupe d'études en Histoire de la Langue française*, Paris.

—— and Wolf, B. 2001. *Textes privés des XVIIe et XVIIIe siècles* (*ZRP*, Beiheft 310 (CD-ROM)). Tübingen: Niemeyer.

Esnault, G. 1965. *Dictionnaire historique des argots français*. Paris: Larousse.

Estienne, H. 1578. *Deux Dialogues du nouveau langage francois*, ed. P. M. Smith. Geneva: Slatkine, 1980.

—— 1582. *Hypomneses de Gallica lingua peregrinis eam discentibus necessariae*, ed. and trans. J. Chomarat. Paris: Champion, 1999.

Estienne, R. 1549. *Dictionnaire françois–latin*. Paris: H. Estienne.

—— 1557. *Traicté de la grammaire françoise*. Geneva: H. Estienne.

Faral, E. 1924. *Les Arts poétiques du XIIe et du XIIIe siècles*. Paris: Champion.

—— and Bastin, J. 1959. *Oeuvres complètes de Rutebeuf*. 2 vols. Paris: Picard.

Farge, A. 1979. *Vivre dans la rue au XVIIIe siècle*. Paris: Gallimard.

Fasold, R. 1984. *The Sociolinguistics of Society*. Oxford: Blackwell.

Favier, J. 1974. *Nouvelle Histoire de Paris: Paris au XVe siècle*. Paris: Hachette.

Fierro, A. 1996. *Histoire et dictionnaire de Paris*. Paris: Laffont.

Foisil, M. 1989. *Le Journal de Jean Héroard*. 2 vols. Paris: Fayard.

Fondet, C. 1980. *La Dialectologie de l'Essonne*. Paris: Champion.

—— 1995. Contribution à la question des origines du français: quelques aperçus à partir de la dialectologie de l'Essonne. In: M. Tamine (ed.), *Ces Mots qui sont nos mots. Mélanges d'histoire de la langue francaise, de dialectologie et d'onomastique offerts au professeur Jacques Chaurand*, pp. 189–206. Charleville-Mézières: Institut Charles Bruneau.

Fouché, P. 1934. L'évolution phonétique du français du XVIe siècle à nos jours. *Le Français Moderne* 2: 217–36.

—— 1936. Les diverses sortes de français au point de vue phonétique. *Le Français Moderne* 4: 199–216.

—— 1952. *Phonétique historique du français*. Paris: Klincksieck.

—— 1967. *Le Verbe français: étude morphologique*. Revised edn. Paris: Klincksieck.

Foulkes, P. and Docherty, G. (eds) 1999. *Urban Voices. Accent Studies in the British Isles*. London: Arnold.

Fourquin, G. 1956. La population de la région parisienne aux environs de 1328. *Le Moyen Age* 62: 63–92.

—— 1964. *Les Campagnes de la région parisienne à la fin du moyen âge*. Paris: PUF.

Francard, M. (ed.) 2001. *Le Français de référence: constructions et appropriations d'un concept: actes du Colloque de Louvain-la-Neuve, 3–5 novembre 1999*. Louvain-la-Neuve: Peeters (Institut de Linguistique).

François, A. 1959. *Histoire de la langue française cultivée*. 2 vols. Geneva: A. Jullien.

François, D. 1985. Le langage populaire. In: G. Antoine and R. Martin (eds), pp. 295–327.

Franklin, A. 1977. *Dictionnaire historique des arts, métiers et professions exercés dans Paris depuis le XIIIᵉ siècle*. Marseille: Laffitte Reprints.

—— 1984. *Les Rues et les cris de Paris au XIIIᵉ siècle*. Marseille: Laffitte Reprints.

Franz, P. 1983. Travestis poissards. *Revue des Sciences Humaines* 190: 7–20.

Frei, H. 1929. *La Grammaire des fautes*. Geneva: Slatkine.

Frey, M. 1925. *Les Transformations du vocabulaire français à l'époque de la Révolution (1789–1800)*. Paris: PUF.

Friedrichs, C. R. 1995. *The Early Modern City 1450–1750*. London: Longman.

Furet, F. 1961. Structures sociales parisiennes au XVIIIe siècle. *Annales E.S.C.* 16: 939–58.

—— and Ozouf, J. 1977. *Lire et écrire. L'alphabétisation des Français de Calvin à Jules Ferry*. Paris: Editions de Minuit.

Furetière, A. 1666. *Le Roman bourgeois*. Paris: T. Jolly.

Gadet, F. 1992. *Le Français populaire*. Paris: PUF (Que Sais-Je?).

Gaitet, P. 1992. *Political Stylistics: Popular Language as a Literary Artifact*. London: Routledge.

Garrioch, D. 1986. *Neighbourhood and Community in Paris, 1740–1790*. Cambridge University Press.

Gauthier, P. 1995. Traits linguistiques communs. In: P. Gauthier and T. Lavoie (eds), pp. 27–67.

—— and Lavoie, T. 1995. *Français de France et français du Canada*. Lyon: Université Lyon III.

Genin, F. 1841. *Lettres de Marguerite d'Angoulême*. Paris: Renouard.

Géraud, P. H. J. F. de 1837. *Paris sous Philippe-le-Bel, d'après des documents originaux, et notamment d'après un manuscrit contenant Le Rôle de la Taille . . . 1292*. Paris: Collection de Documents Inédits sur l'Histoire de France, sér. 1.

Geremek, B. 1976. *Les Marginaux parisiens au XIVᵉ siècle*. Paris: Flammarion.

Gilliéron, J. and Edmont, E. 1901–10. *Atlas linguistique de la France*. Paris: Champion. Abbreviated to *ALF*.

Giry, A. 1894. *Manuel de diplomatique*. Paris: Hachette.

Glatigny, M. 1992. Les fautes de français dans les *Hypomnèses* d'Henri Estienne. In: P. Caron (ed.), pp. 171–84.

Gondret, P. 1989. L'utilisation du patois parisien comme niveau de langue dans la littérature française au XVIIe siècle. *Cahiers de l'Association Internationale des Etudes Françaises* 41: 7–24.

Gorog, R. de 1989. Early seventeenth-century spoken French and Héroard's Journal. *Romance Philology* 43: 431–42.

Gossen, C.-T. 1962. Langues écrites du domaine d'oil. *Revue de linguistique romane* 26: 271–308.

—— 1967. *Französische Skriptastudien*. Vienna: Österreichische Akademie der Wissenschaften.

Gotti, M. 1999. *The Language of Thieves and Vagabonds*. Tübingen: Niemeyer.

Gougenheim, G. 1929. *Le Langage populaire dans le premier quart du XIXe siècle*. Paris: Les Belles Lettres.

—— 1931. L'observation du langage d'un enfant royal au XVIIe siècle d'après le Journal d'Héroard. *Revue de Philologie française* 45: 1–15.

—— 1966–75. *Les Mots français dans l'histoire et dans la vie*. 3 vols. Paris: Picard.

Gregersen, F. and Pedersen, I. L. (eds) 1991. *The Copenhagen Study in Urban Sociolinguistics*. Copenhagen: C. A. Reitzels.

Gueunier, N., Genouvrier, E. and Khomsi, A. 1983. Les Français devant la norme. In: E. Bédard and J. Maurais (eds), *La Norme linguistique*, pp. 763–87. Quebec: Le Robert.

Guilhaumou, J. 1986. Les mille langues du Père Duchêne: la parade de la culture populaire pendant la Révolution. *Dix-Huitième Siècle* 18: 143–54.

Guiraud, P. 1956. *L'Argot*. Paris: PUF (Que Sais-Je?).

—— 1965. *Le Français populaire*. Paris: PUF (Que Sais-Je?).

—— 1968. *Le Jargon de Villon ou le Gai Savoir de la Coquille*. Paris: Gallimard.

Gumperz, J. J. 1971. *Language in Social Groups*. Stanford University Press.

Halliday, M. A. K. 1978. *Language as Social Semiotic*. London: Arnold.

Hansen, A. B. 1998. *Les Voyelles nasales du français parisien moderne*. Copenhagen: Institut d'études romanes.

Harris, J. 1985. *Phonological Variation and Change*. Cambridge University Press.

Haudricourt, J. 1948. Problèmes de phonologie diachronique (français *EI* > *OI*). *Lingua* 1: 209–18.

Haugen, E. 1966. Dialect, language, nation. Repr. in: J. B. Pride and J. Holmes (eds), *Sociolinguistics*. Harmondsworth: Penguin, 1972.

Hausmann, F.-J. 1979. Wie alt ist das gesprochene Französisch? *Romanische Forschungen* 91: 431–44.

—— 1980. Zur Rekonstruktion des um 1730 gesprochene Französisch. In: H. Stimm (ed.), *Zur Geschichte des gesprochenen Französisch (Zeitschrift für französische Sprache und Literatur*, Beiheft 6), pp. 33–46. Wiesbaden: Franz Steiner.

Hautecoeur, L. 1961. L'urbanisme à Paris de la Renaissance à la monarchie de juillet. In: G. Michaud (ed.), *Paris. Croissance d'une capitale*, pp. 97–133. Paris: Hachette.

Hickey, R. 2000. Salience, stigma and standard. In: L. Wright (ed.), *The Development of Standard English 1300–1800*, pp. 57–72. Cambridge University Press.

Hilty, G. 1973. Les origines de la langue littéraire française. *Vox Romanica* 32: 254–71.

Hindret, J. 1687. *L'Art de bien prononcer et de bien parler la langue françoise*. Paris: D'Houry.

Hinskens, F. 1992. *Dialect Levelling in Limburg*. The Hague: CIP-DATA, Koninklijke Bibliotheek.

Hohenberg, P. M. and Lees, L. H. 1985. *The Making of Urban Europe 1000–1950*. Cambridge, Mass.: Harvard University Press.

—— 1996. Urban systems and economic growth: town populations in metropolitan hinterlands 1600–1850. In: P. Clark and B. Lepetit (eds), *Capital Cities and their Hinterlands in Early Modern Europe*, pp. 26–50. Aldershot: Scolar Press.

Holden, A. J. 1983. *Richars li biaus: roman du XIIIe siècle*. Paris: Champion.

Holtus, G., Metzeltin, M. and Schmitt, C. (eds) 1990. *Lexikon de Romanistischen Linguistik*, VI: *Französisch*. Tübingen: Niemeyer.

Hope, T. E. 1971. *Lexical Borrowing in the Romance Languages*. Oxford: Blackwell.

Hudson, R. A. 1996. *Sociolinguistics*. 2nd edn. Cambridge University Press.

Hull, A. 1988. The first person plural form: *Je parlons*. *French Review* 62: 242–7.

Hunnius, K. 1975. Archaische Züge des langage populaire. *Zeitschrift für französische Sprache und Literatur* 85: 145–61.

Jacob, P.-L. 1859. *Paris ridicule et burlesque au XVIIe siècle*. Paris: Delahaye.

Jacquart, J. 1996. Paris: first metropolis of the early modern period. In: P. Clark and B. Lepetit (eds), *Capital Cities and their Hinterlands in Early Modern Europe*, pp. 105–18. Aldershot: Scolar Press.

Jeanroy, A. 1982. *Le Jeu de Saint Nicolas*. Paris: Champion.

Jong, T. de 1992. Langue écrite et langue parlée à Paris aux 13e et 14e siècles. *Actes du congrès international de linguistique et philologie romanes*, pp. 73–83. Corunna: Fundacion Pedro Barrié de la Maza.

Jordan, A. 1989. Le langage des honnestes gens. *History of European Ideas* 11: 435–48.

Joseph, J. E. 1987. *Eloquence and Power. The Rise of Language Standards and Standard Languages*. London: Frances Pinter.

Jouhaud, C. 1985. *Mazarinades: la Fronde des mots*. Paris: Aubier.

Journal d'un bourgeois de Paris, 1405–49, ed. A. Tuetey. Paris: Société de l'Histoire de Paris et de l'Ile-de-France, 1881.

Jullien, B. 1875. *Les Eléments matériels du français*. Paris: Hachette.

Keene, D. 2000. Metropolitan values: migration, mobility and cultural norms, London 1100–1700. In: L. Wright (ed.) *The Development of Standard English 1300–1800*, pp. 93–114. Cambridge University Press.

Keller, R. 1992. *On Language Change*. London, New York: Routledge.

Kerswill, P. 2002. Koineization and accommodation. In: J. K. Chambers, P. Trudgill and N. Schilling-Estes (eds), *The Handbook of Language Variation and Change*, pp. 669–702. Oxford: Blackwell.

—— and Williams, A. 2002. 'Salience' as an explanatory factor in language change: evidence from dialect levelling in urban England. In: M. C. Jones (ed.), *Language Change*, pp. 81–110. Amsterdam: Rodopi.

Kibbee, D. A. 1990. Language variation and linguistic description in sixteenth-century France. *Historiographia Linguistica* 17: 49–65.

Koschwitz, E. 1895. *Les Parlers parisiens*. Paris: H. Welter.

Kramer, M. 2002. Sources littéraires des *Curiositez françoises* d'Antoine Oudin. *Revue de linguistique romane* 66: 131–57.

Kristol, A. M. 1989. Le début du rayonnement parisien et l'unité du français du moyen âge: le témoignage des manuels d'enseignement du français écrits en Angleterre entre le XIIIe et le début du XVe siècle. *Revue de linguistique romane* 53: 335–67.

Kroch, A. 1978. Towards a theory of social dialect variation. *Language in Society* 7: 17–36.

—— 1996. Dialect and style in the speech of upper class Philadelphia. In: G. Guy, C. Feagin, D. Schiffrin (eds), *Towards a Social Science of Language*, pp. 23–45. Amsterdam: John Benjamins.

Labov, W. 1966. *The Social Stratification of English in New York City*. Washington, D.C.: Center for Applied Linguistics.

—— 1972. The study of language in its social context. Repr. in: J. B. Pride and J. Holmes (eds), *Sociolinguistics*, pp. 180–202. Harmondsworth: Penguin.

—— 1973. *Sociolinguistic Patterns*. University of Pennsylvania Press.

—— 1975. On the use of the present to explain the past. In: L. Heilmann (ed.), *Proceedings of the 11th International Congress of Linguists*, pp. 825–51. Bologna: Il Mulino.

—— 1987. Exact description of the speech community: short *A* in Philadelphia. In: R. Fasold and D. Schiffrin (eds), *Language Change and Variation*, pp. 1–57. Washington: Georgetown University Press.

—— 1994, 2001. *Principles of Linguistic Change*, I: *Internal Factors*, II: *Social Factors*. Oxford: Blackwell.

Lagorgette, D. 2003. Insultes et sounding: du rituel à l'exclusion. In: S. Santi and J. Derive (eds), *La Communauté. Fondements psychologiques et idéologiques d'une représentation identitaire*, pp. 117–48. Grenoble: Maison des Sciences de l'Homme – Alpes.

Laks, B. 1980. *Différentiation linguistique et sociale: quelques problèmes de sociolinguistique française*. Thèse de 3e cycle, Université de Paris VIII.

La Mothe le Vayer, F. de 1647. *Considérations sur l'éloquence françoise de ce tems*. Paris: A. Courbé.

Larchey, L. 1872. *Dictionnaire historique, étymologique et anecdotique de l'argot parisien*. Paris: Dentu.

Lass, R. 1990. How to do things with junk: exaptation in language evolution. *Journal of Linguistics* 26: 79–102.

—— 1997. *Historical Linguistics and Language Change*. Cambridge University Press.

Lathuillère, R. 1984. Pour une étude de la langue populaire à l'époque classique. In: *Mélanges de langue et littérature médiévales offerts à Alice Planche*, pp. 278–86. Paris: Les Belles Lettres.

Lavedan, P. 1975. *Nouvelle Histoire de Paris: Histoire de l'urbanisme à Paris*. Paris: Hachette.

Lebsanft, F. 2000. Die eigene und die fremden Sprachen in romanischen Texten des Mittelalters und der frühen Neuzeit. In: W. Dahmen, G. Holtus, J. Kramer, M. Metzeltin, W. Scheickard, O. Winkelmann (eds), *Schreiben in einer anderen Sprache*, pp. 3–20. Tübingen: G. Narr.

Lefebvre, A. 1991. *Le Français de la région lilloise*. Paris: Sorbonne.

Le Goff, J. 1980. Contributions to G. Duby (ed.), II, pp. 9–25, 189–405.

Lehmann, P. 1959–62. *Erforschung des Mittelalters: ausgewählte Abhandlungen und Aufsätze*. Stuttgart: A. Hiersemann.

Leigh, R. A. 1970. *Correspondance complète de Rousseau*, XI. Geneva: Institut et Musée Voltaire.

Lennig, M. 1978. *The Modern Paris Vowel System*. PhD thesis, Pennsylvania State University.

Le Page, R. and Tabouret-Keller, A. 1985. *Acts of Identity*. Cambridge University Press.

Lepelley, R. 2001. Phonétique et romanisation du domaine gallo-roman. *Revue de linguistique romane* 65: 113–43.

Le Roux, P. J. 1718, 1735. *Dictionnaire comique*. Amsterdam: Michel le Cene.

Lespinasse. R. de and Bonnardot, F. 1879. *Histoire générale de Paris: les métiers et corporations de la ville de Paris*, XL. Paris: Imprimerie nationale.

Levine, M.V. 1990. *The Reconquest of Montreal: Language Policy and Social Change in a Bi-lingual City*. Philadelphia: Temple University Press.

Lewicka, H. 1960, 1968. *La Langue et le style du théâtre comique français des XVe et XVIe siècles*. 2 vols. Warsaw: Panstwowe Wydawnictwo Naukowe.

—— 1974. *Etudes sur l'Ancienne Farce francaise*. Paris: Klincksieck.

Lloyd, P. 1979. On the definition of Vulgar Latin. *Neuphilologische Mitteilungen* 80: 110–22.

Lodge, R. A. 1989. Speakers' perceptions of non-standard vocabulary in French. *Zeitschrift für Romanische Philologie* 92: 485–99.

—— 1995a. A comic papal legate and his language. *Neuphilologische Mitteilungen* 96: 211–21.

—— 1995b. *Les Lettres de Montmartre* et l'idéologie normative. *Revue de linguistique romane* 59: 439–65.

—— 1996. Stereotypes of vernacular pronunciation in 17th–18th century Paris. *Zeitschrift für Romanische Philologie* 112: 205–31.

—— 1998. Vers une histoire du dialecte urbain de Paris. *Revue de linguistique romane* 62: 95–128.

—— 1999a. Convergence and divergence in the development of the Paris urban vernacular. *Sociolinguistica* 13: 1000–17.

—— 1999b. Colloquial vocabulary and politeness in French. *Modern Language Review* 94: 355–65.

—— 2000. Paris speech in the past [electronic resource]. http//www.ota.ahds.ac.uk.

—— and Varty, K. 2001. *The Earliest Branches of the Roman de Renart*. Leuven, Paris: Peeters.

Lohisse, J. 1981. The silent revolution: the communication of the poor from the sixteenth to the eighteenth century. *Diogenes* 113–14: 70–90.

Lombard, M. 1957. L'évolution urbaine pendant le haut moyen âge. *Annales E. S. C.* 12: 7–28.

Loriot, R. 1984. *Les Parlers de l'Oise*. Dijon, Amiens: Association bourguignonne de dialectologie.

Lusignan, S. 1987. *Parler vulgairement*. Paris: Vrin.

—— 1996. L'enseignement des arts dans les collèges parisiens au Moyen Age. In: O. Weijers and L. Holtz (eds), *L'Enseignement des disciplines à la Faculté des arts*, pp. 43–53. Amsterdam: BREPOLS.

Lyons, J. 1981. *Language and Linguistics*. Cambridge University Press.

Magendie, M. 1970. *La Politesse mondaine et les théories de l'honnêteté en France au XVIIe siècle*. Geneva: Droz.

Manessy, G. 1994. Modes de structuration des parlers urbains. In: E. Elhousseine and N. Thiam (eds), *Des Langues et des villes*. pp. 7–27. Paris: Didier Erudition.

Marchello-Nizia, C. 1979. *Histoire de la langue française aux XIVe et XVe siècles*. Paris: Bordas.

Martin, H.-J. 1999. *Livre, pouvoir et société à Paris au XVIIIe siècle*. 2 vols. Geneva: Droz.

Martineau, F. and Mougeon, R. 2003. A sociolinguistic study on the origins of *ne* deletion in European and Quebec French. *Language* 79: 118–52.

Martinet, A. 1945. *La Prononciation du français contemporain*. Geneva: Droz.

—— 1955. *L'Economie des changements linguistiques*. Berne: Francke.

—— 1969. *Le Français sans fard*. Paris: PUF.

Maselaar, P. 1988. Les marques 'familier' et 'populaire' envisagées des points de vue lexicologique et lexicographique. *Cahiers de lexicologie* 53: 91–106.

Mathieu, A. 1559, 1560. *Devis de la langue françoyse*. Paris (Geneva: Slatkine Reprints, 1972).

Matoré, G. 1953. *La Méthode en lexicologie*. Paris: Didier.

—— 1985. *Le Vocabulaire et la société médiévale*. Paris: PUF.

—— 1988. *Le Vocabulaire et la société du XVIe siècle*. Paris: PUF.

Matzke, E. 1880, 1881. Der Dialekt von Ile-de-France im XIII und XIV Jahrhundert. *Archiv für das Studium der neuren Sprachen und Literaturen* 64: 385–412, 65: 57–96.

Meigret, L. 1550. *Le Tretté de la grammaire française*, ed. F. J. Hausmann. Tübingen: Gunter Narr, 1980.

Ménage, G. 1672. *Observations sur la langue françoise*. Paris: Barbin.

Mercier, L.-S. 1782. *Tableaux de Paris contenant des moeurs publiques et particulières*. 10 vols. Amsterdam: publisher not named.

Michaelis, H. and Passy, P. 1897. *Dictionnaire phonétique de la langue française*. Hanover, Berlin: C. Meyer.

Michaëlsson, K. 1927. *Etudes sur les noms de personne français d'après les rôles de Taille parisiens* (rôles de 1292, 1296–1300, 1313). Uppsala Universitets Arsskrift.

—— 1936. *Lexique raisonné des noms de baptême. A – B*. Uppsala Universitets Arsskrift.

—— 1947. Questions de méthode anthroponymique. *Onomastica* 1: 190–204.

—— 1954. L'anthroponymie et la statistique. In: J. Saahlgren, B. Hasselrot and L. Hellborg (eds), *Quatrième Congrès international de sciences onomastiques*, pp. 308–94. Lund: Blum.

—— 1958. *Le Livre de la Taille de Paris l'an 1296* (Acta Universitatis Gothoburgensis, 64). Goteborg: Almqvist & Wiksell.

—— 1959. Quelques variantes notées dans la prononciation parisienne au temps de Philippe le Bel. In: *VIII Congresso Internazionale di Studi Romanzi*, Part II.2, pp. 287–97. Florence: Sansoni.

—— 1961. *Le Livre de la Taille de Paris l'an de grâce 1313* (Acta Universitatis Gothoburgensis, 57). Goteborg: Almqvist & Wiksell.

—— 1962. *Le Livre de la Taille de Paris l'an 1297* (Acta Universitatis Gothoburgensis, 67). Goteborg: Almqvist & Wiksell.

Michel, F. 1856. *Etudes de philologie sur l'argot*. Paris: Firmin Didot.

Milliot, V. 1995. *Les Cris de Paris ou le peuple travesti. Les représentations des petits métiers parisiens (XVI⁰ – XVIII⁰ siècles)*. Paris: Publications de la Sorbonne.

Milroy, J. 1981. *Regional Accents of English: Belfast*. Belfast: Blackstaff Press.

—— 1984. Present-day evidence for historical change. In: N. F. Blake and C. Jones (eds), *Progress in English Historical Linguistics*. University of Sheffield Press.

—— 1992. *Linguistic Variation and Change*. Oxford: Blackwell.

—— and Milroy, L. 1985. Linguistic change, social network and speaker innovation. *Journal of Linguistics* 21: 339–84.

—— 1999. *Authority in Language*. 3rd edn. London: Routledge.

Milroy, L. 1987. *Language and Social Networks*. 2nd edn. Oxford: Blackwell.

Mistère du Viel Testament, ed. J. de Rothschild. 6 vols. Paris: Société des Anciens Textes Français, 1878–91.

Monfrin, J. 1968. Le mode de transmission des textes écrits et les études en dialectologie. *Revue de linguistique romane* 32: 17–47.

—— 1972. Les parlers de France. In: M. François (ed.), *La France et les Français* (Encyclopédie la Pléiade, 32), pp. 745–75. Paris: Gallimard.

Monjour, A. 1989. *Der Nordostfranzösische Dialektraum*. (Bonner romanistische Arbeiten, 32). Frankfurt: Peter Lang.

Montluc, A. de 1633. *Comédie des proverbes*. Paris: F. Targa.

Moore, A. P. 1935. *The 'Genre Poissard' and the French Stage in the Eighteenth Century*. New York: Publications of the Institute of French Studies, Columbia University.

Morin, C.-Y. 1989. Changes in the French vocalic system in the 19th century. In: M. E. H. Schouten and P. T. van Reenen (eds), *New Methods in Dialectology*, pp. 185–97. Dordrecht: Foris.

—— 1994. Les sources historiques de la prononciation du français au Québec. In: R. Mougeon and E. Béniak (eds), pp. 199–236.

—— 2000. Le français de référence et les normes de prononciation. In: M. Francard (ed.) *Le Français de référence: constructions et appropriations d'un concept. Actes du Colloque de Louvain-la-Neuve, 3–5 novembre 1999*, I, pp. 91–135. Louvain-la-Neuve: Peeters (Institut de Linguistique).

Mougeon, R. and Béniak, E. 1995. *Les Origines du français québecois*. Sainte Foy: Les Presses de l'Université Laval.

Mousnier, R. 1975. *La Stratification sociale à Paris aux XVIIe et XVIIIe siècles*. Paris: A. Pedone.

Mugglestone, L. 1995. *Talking Proper*. Oxford University Press.

Muscatine, C. 1981. Courtly literature and vulgar language. In: G. S. Burgess and A. D. Deyermond (eds), *Court and Poet*, pp. 1–19. Liverpool: Francis Cairns.

Nisard, C. 1872. *Etude sur le langage populaire ou patois de Paris et de sa banlieue*. Paris: Franck.

—— 1876. *De Quelques Parisianismes populaires et autres locutions*. Paris: Maisonneuve (reprint: La Butte aux Cailles, 1980).

Obelkevitch, J. 1987. Proverbs and social history. In: P. Burke and R. Porter (eds), *The Social History of Language*, pp. 43–72. Cambridge University Press.

Oudin, A. 1640. *Curiositez françoises pour supplément aux dictionnaires*. Paris: no publisher named.

Palsgrave, J. 1530. *L'Esclarcissement de la langue françoyse*. References to the 1969 facsimile edition published by Scolar Press, Menston.

Panckoucke, A.-J. 1748. *Dictionnaire des proverbes français et des façons de parler comiques, burlesques et familières*. Paris: Savoie.

Paris, G. and Robert, U. 1876–93. *Miracles de Nostre Dame*. 8 vols. Paris: Société des Anciens Textes Français.

—— 1888. Les parlers de France. *Revue des patois gallo-romans* 2: 161–75.

—— 1889. Les parlers de France. *Romania* 17: 475–89.

Passy, P. 1891. Le patois de Sainte-Jamme (Seine-et-Oise). *Revue des patois gallo-romans* 4 (13): 7–16.

—— 1917. *Les Sons du français*. Paris: Didier.

Patrick, P. L. 2002. The speech community. In: J. K. Chambers, P. Trudgill and N. Schilling Estes (eds), *The Handbook of Language Variation and Change*, pp. 573–97. Oxford: Blackwell.

Peletier du Mans, J. 1550. *Dialogue de l'ortografe et prononciation françoese*. Poitiers: Marnef (Geneva: Slatkine Reprints, 1964).

Penny, R. 2000. *Variation and Change in Spanish*. Cambridge University Press.

Peretz, C. 1977. Aspects sociolinguistiques du parler parisien contemporain. In: H. Walter, *Phonologie et société*, (Studia Phonetica, 13), pp. 65–77. Paris: Didier.

Pernoud, R. 1966. *La Formation de la France*. Paris: PUF (Que Sais-Je?).

Petit-Dutaillis, C. 1950. *La Monarchie féodale en France et en Angleterre. X^e – XIIIe siècle*. Paris: Albin Michel.

Petyt, K. M. 1980. *The Study of Dialect: An Introduction to Dialectology*. London: Deutsch.

Pfister, M. 1973a. Die sprachliche Bedeutung von Paris und der Ile-de-France vor dem 13. Jh. *Vox Romanica* 32: 217–53.

—— 1973b. Parodie der französischen Gelehrtensprache bei Geoffroy Tory und François Rabelais. In: K. Heitmann and E. Schroeder (eds), *Renatae Litterae. Studien zum Nachleben der Antike und zur europäischen Renaissance. August Buck zum 60. Geburtstag am 3. 12. 1971 dargebracht von Freunden und Schülern*, pp. 193–205. Frankfurt: Athenaeum-Verlag.

—— 1993. Scripta et koiné en ancien français aux XIIe et XIIIe siècles. In: *Ecritures, langues communes et normes: formation spontanée de koinés et standardisation dans la Gallo-Romania et son voisinage*, pp. 17–41. Neuchâtel, Geneva: Université de Neuchâtel/Droz.

Picoche, J. and Marchello-Nizia, C. 1994. *Histoire de la langue française*. 4th edn. Paris: Nathan.

Picot, E. and Nyrop, C. 1968. *Nouveau Recueil de farces françaises des XVe et XVIe siècles*. Geneva: Slatkine Reprints.

Pillot, J. 1550. *Gallicae Linguae Institutio*. Paris: Grouleau (Geneva: Slatkine Reprints, 1972).

Pirenne, H. 1939. Les villes du moyen âge. In: H. Pirenne, *Les Villes et les institutions urbaines*, pp. 304–431. Paris, Brussels: Nouvelle Société d'Editions.

Planhol, X. de 1994. *An Historical Geography of France*, trans. J. Lloyd. Cambridge University Press.

Ploog, K. forthcoming. Interférences et restructurations entre le bien et le mal (parler). In: P. Viaut (ed.), *Contact de langues, frontières, législation européenne*. Bordeaux: Maison des Sciences de l'Homme d'Aquitaine.

Poerck, G. de 1963. Les plus anciens textes de la langue française comme témoins d'époque. *Revue de linguistique romane* 27: 217–53.

Pooley, T. 1996. *Chtimi: The Urban Vernaculars of Northern France*. Clevedon: Multilingual Matters.

Pope, M. K. 1952. *From Latin to Modern French*. Manchester University Press.

Posner, R. 1997. *Linguistic Change in French*. Cambridge University Press.

Pred, A. 1990. *Lost Words and Lost Worlds: Modernity and the Language of Everyday Life in Late Nineteenth-Century Stockholm*. Cambridge University Press.

Quémada, B. 1959. *Datations et documents lexicographiques: matériaux pour l'histoire du vocabulaire français*. Paris: Klincksieck/CNRS.

Radtke, E. 1994. *Gesprochenes Französisch und Sprachgeschichte* (*ZRP*, Beiheft 255). Tübingen: Niemeyer.

Ramée, P. de la (Ramus) 1572. *Grammaire de P. de la Ramée*. Paris: A. Wechel (Geneva: Slatkine Reprints, 1972).

Randell, E. 1998. *The 'Sarcelades' of Nicolas Jouin*. Newcastle University: unpublished MLitt. thesis.

Rauhut, F. 1963. Warum wurde Paris die Haupstadt Frankreichs? In: H. Bihler and A. Noyer-Weidner (eds), *Medium Aevum Romanicum. Festschrift für E. Reinfelder*, pp. 267–87. Munich: Huber.

Reenen, P. van 1991. Comment distinguer les espaces dialectaux? *Revue de linguistique romane* 55: 479–86.

Reenen, P. van and Reenen-Stein, K. van (eds) 1988. *Distributions spatiales et temporelles, constellations de manuscrits*. Amsterdam: John Benjamins.

Reighard, J. 1980. The transition problem: lexical diffusion vs. variable rules. In: E. C. Traugott, R. Labrum and S. Shepherd (eds), Papers from the 4th International Conference on Historical Linguistics. *Current Issues in Linguistic Theory* 14 (Amsterdam Studies in the Theory and History of Linguistic Science), pp. 349–54.

Remacle, L. 1948. *Le Problème de l'ancien wallon*. Liège: Bibliothèque de la Faculté de Philosophie et Lettres.

Rézeau, P. (ed.) 2001. *Dictionnaire des régionalismes de France: géographie et histoire d'un patrimoine linguistique*. Brussels: De Boeck/Duculot.

Richelet, P. 1680. *Dictionnaire des rimes*. Paris: Florentin.

Rickard, P. 1968. *La Langue française au 16e siècle*. Cambridge University Press.

—— 1976. *Chrestomathie de la langue française au XVe siècle*. Cambridge University Press.

—— 1989. *A History of the French Language*. 2nd edn. London: Hutchinson.

Rickford, J. R. 2002. Implicational scales. In: J. K. Chambers, P. Trudgill and N. Schilling Estes (eds), *The Handbook of Language Variation and Change*, pp. 142–67. Oxford Blackwell.

Robson, C. A. 1955. Literary language, spoken dialect, and the phonological problem in Old French. *Transactions of the Philological Society*: 117–80.

Roch, J.-L. 1992. Les dénominations du faux mendiant de 1350 à 1630. In: P. Caron (ed.), pp. 85–94.

Roche, D. 1981a. *Le Peuple de Paris*. Paris: Aubier Montagne.

—— 1981b. La culture populaire à Paris au XVIIIe siècle: les façons de lire. In: Casa de Velàsquez, *Livre et Lecture en Espagne et en France sous l'Ancien Régime*, pp. 159–65. Paris: ADPF.

—— 1982. *Journal de ma vie. Jacques-Louis Menétra. Compagnon vitrier au 18e siècle*. Paris: Montalba.

Romaine, S. 1982. *Socio-Historical Linguistics. Its Status and Methodology*. Cambridge University Press.

Roques, G. 1995. Les argots entre les deux guerres. In: G. Antoine and R. Martin (eds), pp. 153–68.

Rosset, T. 1911. *Les Origines de la prononciation moderne étudiées au XVIIe siècle*. Paris: Colin.

Rozan, C. 1856. *Petites Ignorances de la conversation*. Paris: Hetzel.

Sainéan, L. 1907. *Les Sources de l'argot ancien*. Paris: Champion.

—— 1912. *Le Langage parisien au XIXe siècle*. Paris: Boccard.

Saint-Gérand, J.-P. 1992. L'étamine des idéologies. In: P. Caron (ed.), pp. 153–70.

—— 1999. La langue française au XIXe siècle. In: J. Chaurand (ed.), pp. 379–504.

—— 2000. Repères bibliographiques pour une histoire de la langue française au XIXe siècle. http:// www.chass.utoronto.ca/ epc/ langueXIX/.

Salmon, G. L. (ed.) 1991. *Variétés et variantes du français des villes états de l'est de la France*. Paris: Champion.

Sankoff, D., Thibault, P. and Bérubé, H. 1978. Semantic field variability. In: D. Sankoff (ed.), *Linguistic Variation. Models and Methods*, pp. 23–43. New York: Harcourt.

Saussure, F. de 1971. *Cours de linguistique générale*. Paris: Payot.

Saville-Troike, M. 1989. *The Ethnography of Communication*. 2nd edn. Oxford: Blackwell.

Scarron, P. 1643. *La Foire Sainct Germain*. Paris: J. Bréquigny.

Schildt, J. and Schildt, H. 1986. *Berlinisch. Geschichtliche Einführung in die Sprache einer Stadt*. Berlin: Akademie Verlag.

Schneider, E. W. 2002. Investigating variation and change in written documents. In: J. K. Chambers, P. Trudgill and N. Schilling-Estes (eds), *The Handbook of Language Variation and Change*, pp. 67–96. Oxford: Blackwell.

Seguin, J.-P. 1972. *La Langue française au XVIIIe siècle*. Paris: Bordas.

—— 1992. L'ordre de mots dans le *Journal* de J.-L. Menétra. In: P. Caron (ed.), pp. 29–37.

—— 1993. *L'Invention de la phrase au XVIIIe siècle*. Louvain, Paris: Peeters.

—— 1999. La langue française aux XVIIe et XVIIIe siècles. In: J. Chaurand (ed.), pp. 227–344.

Siegel, J. 1985. Koines and koinéization. *Language in Society* 14: 357–78.

Simoni-Aurembou, M.-R. 1973a. *Atlas linguistique et ethnographique de l'Ile-de-France et de l'Orléanais*. Paris: CNRS.

—— 1973b. Aspects phonétiques de l'atlas de l'Ile-de-France et de l'Orléanais: unité ou diversité? In: *Les Dialectes romans à la lumière des atlas régionaux*, pp. 378–96. Paris: CNRS.

—— 1995. L'aire linguistique centrale. In: P. Gauthier and T. Lavoie (eds), pp. 251–306.

—— 1999. Aperçus sur la langue de l'Ile-de-France. In: J. Chaurand (ed.), pp. 564–72.

Sivertsen, E. 1960. *Cockney Phonology* (Oslo Studies in English 8). Oslo University Press.

Smith, P. M. 1966. *The Anti-Courtier Trend in Sixteenth-Century French Literature.* Geneva: Droz.

Solnon, G.-L. 1987. *La Cour de France.* Paris: Fayard.

Stein, G. 1997. *John Palsgrave as Renaissance Linguist.* Oxford: Clarendon Press.

Stein, P. 1987. Kreolsprache als Quelle für das gesprochene Französisch des 17. und 18. Jh. *Archiv für das Studium der Neueren Sprachen und Literaturen* 224: 52–66.

Stimm, H. 1980. *Zur Geschichte des gesprochenen Französisch (Zeitschrift für französische Sprache und Literatur,* Beiheft 6). Wiesbaden: Franz Steiner.

Straka, G. 1952. La prononciation parisienne. Ses différents aspects. *Bulletin de la Faculté des Lettres de Strasbourg* 30: 212–25.

—— 1979. *Les Sons et les mots.* Paris: Klincksieck.

—— 1981. Sur la formation de la prononciation française d'aujourd'hui. *Travaux de linguistique et de littérature* 19: 6–248.

Suchier, H. 1888. Die französische und provenzalische Sprache und ihre Mundarten. In: G. Groeber (ed.), *Grundriss der Romanischen Philologie,* I, pp. 561–688. Strasbourg: Trübner.

Tabourot, E. 1588. *Les Bigarrures du Seigneur des Accords,* ed. F. Goyet. Geneva: Droz, 1986.

Thurot, C. 1881, 1883. *De la Prononciation française depuis le commencement du XVIe siècle.* 2 vols. Paris: Imprimerie nationale.

Tory, G. 1529. *Champ Fleury.* The Hague: Mouton (Johnson Reprint Corporation). 1970.

Trask, R. L. 1997. *A Student's Dictionary of Language and Linguistics.* London: Arnold.

Trudeau, D. 1992. *Les Inventeurs du bon usage (1529–1647).* Paris: Editions de Minuit.

Trudgill, P. 1974. *The Social Differentiation of English in Norwich.* Cambridge University Press.

—— 1986. *Dialects in Contact.* Oxford: Blackwell.

Vadé, J.-J. 1758. *Oeuvres.* 4 vols. Paris: Duchesne.

Valdman, A. 1982. Français standard et français populaire: sociolectes ou fictions. *French Review* 56: 218–27.

Valli, A. 1984. Changements de norme, décalages grammaticaux et représentations du français parlé: l'exemple du *Télémaque travesti* de Marivaux. *Recherches sur le français parlé* 6: 7–21.

Vaugelas, C. V. de 1647. *Remarques sur la langue française,* ed. J. Streicher. Geneva: Slatkine Reprints, 1970.

Villon, F. 1923. *Oeuvres,* ed. L. Thuasne. 3 vols. Paris: Picart.

Vitu, A. 1889. *Dictionnaire analytique du jargon.* Paris: Ollendorff.

Wacker, G. 1916. *Ueber das Verhältnis von Dialekt und Schriftsprache.* Halle: Niemeyer.

Wailly, F. de 1754. *Grammaire françoise.* Paris: Dubure l'aîné.

Walter, H. 1977. *Phonologie et société.* Paris: Didier.

—— 1988. *Le Français dans tous les sens.* Paris: Laffont.

Wardhaugh, R. 2002. *An Introduction to Sociolinguistics.* 4th edn. Oxford: Blackwell.

Wartburg, W. von 1923–83. *Französisches etymologisches Wörterbuch.* 24 vols. Bonn: Klopp.

—— 1962. *Evolution et structure de la langue française*. Berne: Francke.

Weinreich, U. 1953. *Languages in Contact*. The Hague: Mouton.

—— Labov, W. and Herzog, M. I. 1968. Empirical foundations for a theory of language change. In: W. P. Lehmann and Y. Malkiel (eds), *Directions for Historical Linguistics*, pp. 95–195. Austin: University of Texas Press.

Williams, R. 1976. *Keywords: A Vocabulary of Culture and Society*. London: Croom Helm.

Wittmann, H. 1995. Grammaire comparée des variétés coloniales du français populaire de Paris du 17e siècle et origines du français québecois. *Revue québecoise de linguistique théorique et appliquée* 12: 281–334.

Wolf, L. 1984. Le français de Paris dans les remarques de Vaugelas. *Cahiers de l'Institut de Linguistique de l'Université de Louvain* 10: 357–66.

Wolf, N. 1990. *Le Peuple dans le roman français de Zola à Céline*. Paris: PUF.

Wood, M. (ed.) 1923. *Foreign Correspondence with Marie de Lorraine, Queen of Scotland, 1537–1548*. Edinburgh: Scottish History Society. Third Series, vol. IV.

Wright, L. 1996. *The Sources of London English: Medieval Thames Vocabulary*. Oxford: Clarendon Press.

Wüest, J. 1979a. Sprachgrenzen im Poitou. *Vox Romanica* 29: 14–58.

—— 1979b. *La Dialectalisation de la Gallo-Romania*. Berne: Francke.

—— 1985. Le patois de Paris et l'histoire du français. *Vox Romanica* 44: 234–58.

Wyld, H. C. 1921. *A History of Modern Colloquial English*. London: Fisher Unwin.

Yaguello, M. 1978. *Les Mots et les femmes*. Paris: Payot.

Index